Christina Newman

October 1976.

THE FAR SIDE OF THE STREET

THE FAR SIDE OF THE STREET

BRUCE HUTCHISON

Macmillan of Canada   Toronto

Canadian Cataloguing in Publication Data
Hutchison, Bruce, 1901-
The far side of the street
Includes index.
ISBN 0-7705-1431-6
1. Hutchison, Bruce, 1901- 2. Journalists—Canada—Correspondence, reminiscences, etc.
I. Title.
PN4913.H88A3 070.9'2'4 C76-017114-9

Printed in Canada for
The Macmillan Company of Canada
70 Bond Street
Toronto, M5B 1X3

For my wife and our children

Contents

List of Illustrations

Preface

The reader of this book deserves a cautionary word in advance to prevent misunderstanding. It is not a book of history, politics, economics, science, or any serious subject. Some historians, politicians, economists, scientists, and even philosophers and other persons of substance, are included here, but quite incidentally. No attempt is made to study the public business as I watched it in the course of a long lifetime, to argue any social doctrine, or to reach any final conclusions, since I have none. The book, in short, is only the rambling personal record of an old newspaperman whose friends persuaded him to write it when he should have known better. To those friends I am indebted for their faith and affection, but they are not responsible for the facts, opinions, errors, or mere fantasies included here. The company of men and women, living and dead, who have borne a friend's infirmities and urged me to set down the record in the wistful hope that it might tell something about Canadians in the twentieth century is too numerous to mention. Two men, however, command my special thanks. John Gray and Hugh Kane, publishers rightly admired for their experience and judgment, encouraged me to write as I pleased, reckless of the outcome. From their hands the manuscript was passed to the able professionals in Macmillan's Editorial and Production departments, to whom I am very grateful. I alone am to blame for any flaws still remaining. The human friends, the friends of another sort, and the fair land of Canada, which gave me so much happiness, all have my gratitude at the end.

1

The Burning Umbrella

My father, who was rich in affection and in nothing else, used to set out every morning for the office he hated and the minor civil service job he despised with ten cents in his pocket for car fare and twenty cents for lunch, a stout cane in his hand, and a glowing pipe in his mouth.

On wet days he carried an umbrella instead of a cane but in all weather the pipe glowed fiercely. On three famous occasions its sparks ignited the umbrella, which burned in splendid conflagration to the delight of the neighborhood. My father only muttered his private curse, "Judas Iscariot, priest!" (its meaning known to him alone), and continued his march without a moment's pause, the umbrella's red-hot, naked skeleton held aloft like some standard in a hopeless battle, an oriflamme, a fiery cross from the Scottish highlands of his ancestors.

Doubtless these were absurd fancies in my boy's mind as I watched him from the far side of the street and yet fancies that still haunt a mind now aged, cranky, and forgetful, remembering best the least important events. Absurd but all too authentic. For around that gallant little figure striding down a mean street in Victoria, British Columbia, could be seen the true allegory and paradigm of my own long life, though I lacked the wit to see it then. Always, in affairs great or petty, in Canada or in distant lands, among unlikely persons, I would watch from the far side of the street, the safe side, as spectator merely, while other men fought the fire.

More than umbrellas were consumed across the street. Empires, nations, governments, and treasures incalculable burned in my time, leaving humanity to march on with numberless steel skeletons in hand until new umbrellas could be invented to burn farther down the street.

It would be pleasant, near my street's end, to say that much have I travelled in the realms of gold and many goodly states and kingdoms seen. Actually, my travels for the most part were confined to the realms of dross, with sorties now and then beyond the sidewalks into dark wilderness, or up high mountains where brief fragments of reality may be glimpsed in cleanly air and sidereal space. Sometimes, not often, I approached that untravelled world whose margin faded forever and forever as I moved. But I knew it was there, my eyes too dim to see it; seen by none, perhaps, except children, dogs, saints, and old folks with eyes unclouded by learning. Between these alternative views of life as all physical or half invisible, every man must make his choice. After long perplexity I made mine.

Concerning what little I have seen from the far side of the street and from the mountain top, why write a last book or testament when the testimony is so dubious? Why this tale without a moral, this argument without an answer, this play without a plot, this miniature stage overcrowded by a cast of heroes, villains, and buffoons, of statesmen at the summit and criminals in the gutter, of big men disappointingly small at close range and small men surprisingly large, each playing his separate part in tragedy, comedy, or more often farce, myself as audience, critic, and laborious note-taker? Why put down here these disordered memories, and in the first person singular, that nakedness which I have so long tried to avoid in print? Why write at all when you don't have to?

In the first place, sheer ego, of course, since no man writes professionally if he lacks it. Secondly, because, in Dr. Johnson's adage, only a blockhead writes except for money and I never wrote for anything else. Thirdly, after almost sixty years of it, writing becomes as automatic as eating or sleeping, the journalist a Pavlovian dog that reacts to every passing stimulus.

Finally, because this record, however trivial, may indicate the changing nature of a Canadian folk widely renowned for their weak sense of humor, the stranger failing to understand our family joke; best of all, the joke of a nation long identified beyond any possible error but searching high and low for its identity, like a man searching for a hat already on his head.

Apart from my own mild adventures, I write because, in a lifetime of at least two thousand years, as time should be reckoned, I may have learned something about the world and, within it, a Canada now gone and quite unbelievable to most of its contemporary inhabitants, together with certain men who made and unmade it, their consequences, good and bad, still unknown today. Two thousand years, yes. In my generation more has happened than in all the preceding centuries oddly known as the Christian era. A thing worth thinking on but strictly preface. For soon, when the next generation inherits our opulent, mismanaged estate, it will inherit also a dilemma possibly fatal, certainly with no precedent in all recorded time.

To me that discovery came very late to dissolve, overnight, a vast hoard of false premises and all the smug, encrusted fallacies called the conventional wisdom. The discovery came too late for my generation and now, as I shall try to state it here, must seem a rather shocking heresy to my companions on the march. They helped and loved but never knew me, save one who has departed, taking with her the music, laughter, and courage that she alone could give me.

A single lifetime but long enough to let me live in the frontier Canadian society of log cabin, stable, wood fire, and well water, of dusty, muddy towns, of real cowboys before Hollywood debased their kind and Indians as yet hardly touched by the blessings of the white man's superior civilization.

After that, the innocent, boyish, gee-whiz society of commerce chambers, service clubs, and boosters, of Henry Ford's Model T in every garage and Herbert Hoover's two chickens in every pot, with bourgeois progress perpetual ordained by God for a Canada which still worshipped Him on Sunday and was justly entitled to His favors through the rest of the week.

Then the manic society of war, depression, and revolution; the permissive society of leering hedonism, oldest wine in newest bottle, now called consumerism, and bound, not far ahead, to consume our midget world; the society of agnosticism, atheism, and humanism drained of humanity; the Good Society, the Great Society, the Affluent Society, the Just Society, all in death throes, their successor in agony of birth; always the society of mass much worse than the individuals who compose it and cannot shake off their home-made Frankenstein.

Most of my generation paid no heed to these flimsy catchwords and could not understand even the actual society changing around it from day to day. We lived in revolution, wrangled about it, gave it pompous names, and solemnly prophesied its hideous climax, but we never believed in it for ourselves, the bell tolling only for others. Revolution had become the norm of life everywhere. Disregarding it we lived, as our heirs will hardly believe, in a contentment denied to them. We enjoyed our lives and, as Canadians, were undoubtedly the luckiest people on earth.

All this bounded by one lifetime. As in the *Tale of Two Cities*, we have seen the best of times, the worst of times, the typical recurring times of human experience in cycle turning endlessly to which men give dates, definitions, and neat, senseless categories. Thus, in my own narrow experience, Capitalism, Communism, Fascism, Liberalism, Conservatism, Socialism, Internationalism, Nationalism, and, most cherished of all, Education, that universal solvent and panacea with teeming variants thereof inspired nightly in conventicles of Tooley Street's three illustrious tailors.

Ideologies, philosophies, and dialectics they are termed in these days of the higher verbal mystification — words, words, words, uttered at three-hour luncheons by men of wealth who deplore the idleness of the workers and, most pathetic of all current notions, await the return of normality, since no ruling class can ever willingly admit the arrival of another; by labor leaders of the new class who demand equal rewards for everyone but themselves; by Socialists who expect to transform the cosmos and sweep back the Atlantic of uncontrollable events with the whisk broom of some magical statute; by politicians who have no time to think but must please an imaginary public consensus to avoid electoral defeat; by journalists like me who explain without knowing and shout the day's news, as old as history, until the Tower of Babel seems, by contrast, a monument to clarity and coherence. Words and labels, full of sound and fury, signifying little or nothing understandable to me.

Yet one fact became slowly undeniable, though almost invariably rejected. No matter what the methods used, societies, ideologies, and theories everywhere threaten to destroy the individual human creature. No doubt they must when loss of liberty is the price of technology and the machine controls the driver. Driverless, the collective social machine will lurch into the abyss. Driven, it crushes the pedestrian. Driverless or driven, the technical juggernaut is the blood enemy of its inventor, the man.

Here again re-emerges, in its latest and most terrifying version, the oldest human riddle, the Jeffersonian paradox of government too weak to preserve freedom or too strong to let it live at all. Therefore look not in statistical blue books and official documents for the symbol of our age. Look to the swarming superhighway where men move on wheels, seldom knowing why or whither, careless of destination so long as they move. Look there for the true omen and augury. Look homeward, poor lost angel — but where, nowadays, is home?

Through this reeling spectacle, observed from the safe side of the street, drifts, wraithlike, my father's dauntless little figure, umbrella burning like society, and with him many men more eminent, to the world more successful, to me less.

In the procession march six Canadian prime ministers with whom my relations were curious, sometimes preposterous, outrageous even; several foreigners whom history celebrates as great; a mixed bag of politicians, professors, scientists, economists, bankers, actors, artists, writers, ranchers, woodsmen, camp followers of all sorts, and fascinating madmen saner as a rule than the certifiably sane—a few big names to be dropped, the rest obscure droplets on a misted windowpane but all, in reality, quite different from their popular images. Wraiths now, skeletons of memory like my father's umbrella.

The wonder to me in my old age is how little I have seen. And toward the end I understand, as no young man does, the bitter substance of Dan Chaucer's farewell: "The lyf so short, the craft so long to lerne." I haven't learned it yet.

If there was not an original idea in my armory of pop guns and pea shooters, how many such ideas have ever appeared in the world? Perhaps half a dozen in a score of past centuries and, in my craftsman's habitat of politics, none that I could detect. Politics, however, was not my real habitat. It was a livelihood, no more, where I lived on the avails of the democratic process, never joining the toilers in the vineyard but profiting by a rare facility in the theft of other men's thought and, for most of a century, accepting without question a set of Self-Evident Truths simply untrue. And yet, even among close friends, I have somehow been known as a political reporter. As a disguise, this suited me well enough, hiding my sole interest and possible usefulness.

The avails were sufficient for my needs and no crime, according to law, as they are in another trade, but no reason for pride either, of which I also had a sufficiency. My essential nourishment was found elsewhere in a patch of woods and garden—at first the carefree playground of youth, then a hunger almost physical, and ultimately, a consolation and a meaning. Deeper than that, a parable and a verity gleaming through all the workaday fraud. One moment there could give the man who listened more than years of toiling reason. Besides, I was a clumsy hand at reasoning anyhow and always distrusted it.

Toil of a different sort brought larger profits, non-taxable. In the garden I reaped fifty annual crops. In the forest I worked with native materials to build my wooden houses, sheds, wharves, and privies, none of which were likely to last long. But my walls of stone look permanent enough to convince the archaeologists of a later civilization that some almost human hand, maybe some primeval religious cult, had once erected here the altars of its savage deities.

Still better, the lonely campfire over the hills and far away, the thrice-boiled, smoky tea more potent than alcohol, the silent mountain men who, wordless, had so much to tell of unconventional wisdom and a world unseen by urban eye. At the end of many trails, on horse or foot, I warmed my hands beside those fires, ready to depart, and meanwhile led my double life, never doubting which side my happiness was buttered on.

Unfortunately, politics furnished my daily rations since it was the only subject half mastered in my trade with less than half my mind. Unlike most reporters who regard cynicism as necessary equipment, I speak of Canadian politicians with respect, knowing them, as a species, to be more honest on average, and usually more intelligent, than the men of the professions and business. Swimming in an illuminated aquarium like captive fish and shiny electric eels, they have to be.

Their trade, the manipulation of power, is among all trades the most difficult, demanding the highest skill. The businessman works with calculable profits and losses, the engineer with fixed arithmetic, the lawyer with known laws, the chemist with unchanging elements. The politician can never reckon profits or losses in advance. He works without arithmetic or fixed laws. The elements in his chemical retort change their combinations from day to day, always at the risk of lethal explosion.

But whatever the risks he must seek and seem to control power. It is the fuel of his being, the tool of his trade, the justification of his skill — and very dangerous. For power frequently becomes an occupational disease like the related disease of money, the two commonly infecting the same organs, beyond cure. I have seen, close up, enough heart-breaking cases to realize that more men have been destroyed by this double malady than by all the wine, women, and song in the world. On some well-known Canadian tombs, and others yet unoccupied, let us reverently engrave Acton's warning or Ozymandias' advice to the mighty.

The money disease did not infect me dangerously because I earned all that any sensible man requires. Power I did not seek (unless I needed a crumb of it, once in a while, for intramural purposes to protect my job or comfort). At every chance to enter politics I retreated in disorder, not for reasons of courage or morality but the opposite. Since youth I have felt a horror of crowds, of argument, of making decisions, while criticizing the men who had to make them. Instead of responsible power (assuming that I could have gained it) I sought irresponsible privacy, the one thing worth buying and now outside the reach of anybody but a millionaire, who generally doesn't want, deserve, or appreciate it. The game of power was for tough players, not for fellows like me whose ambition was made of flabbier stuff.

Even from the sidelines I began to see, early on, that the true focus of power in a nation, a town, or a newspaper seldom occupies its official residence or front office. More often it will be found in a back office, on a back street. Or it may have no address known to the postman on any street. If you are searching for the men of greatest power search not in parliaments, cabinet chambers, board rooms, or labor halls; search in some foul tenement, a remote laboratory, a Himalayan cave, or a tropic jungle, where an idea, perhaps a cockatrice, is hatching, just as the unwitting trinity of Darwin, Marx, and Freud repealed the basic creeds of all previous ages, the results mostly disastrous.

Such noxious eggs of the past and future need not concern the ordinary man. He can get through life in reasonable comfort without asking awkward questions. He can live well, and most of us do, on a diet of inherited prejudices, acquired illusions, and genial fallacies. Polished, reasserted, and even believed, they will carry you safely along your chosen rut, provided you don't look over the edges. They carried me, anyhow, until I looked and shed all my lifelong opinions. After that, the rut no longer served.

If the grand conundrums of our time are unanswered (though our leaders must pretend to answer them), we have begun, quite recently, to ask the right questions and to get some rough, tentative answers. Anticipating the few simple questions that will recur in different guises throughout this book, and putting the cart a good country mile ahead of the horse, what are we to say about the prospects of our common creaturehood?

Can we expect that our dust speck and satellite of an inferior sun, with a frail, poisoned atmospheric envelope around us, will permanently support the human race in its present numbers, habits, and appetites, not to count its exponential, rabbit-like proliferation? The answer, accepted by the educated and ignorant alike in the abstract, but rarely faced in the concrete, is an obvious No.

Short of that certainty, must the various systems of soft living in the so-called Western world yield in the end to peoples harder, leaner, hungrier, and more numerous? If these systems do not change their ways the answer, as I have come to believe, assuredly is Yes.

Lastly, can the human freedom won by so much blood and battle, with its protective apparatus called democracy, survive an inevitable fall of living standards (as they are falsely reckoned), and a rise in the power of society's quarrelsome giants as they divide a shrinking affluence? The answer, at least for me, is a stuttered Perhaps.

These vagrant opinions, or lack of them, are a misleading and discouraging introduction to a book on things of a contrary and happier sort. I mention them out of sequence at the beginning to clear the deck for sham battle. It is more than possible, of course, indeed it is highly probable, that my book and I are still wrong in a new fashion. As happens to old men who reject their previous beliefs, I have become a swirling weather vane, a box of rattling contradictions, a walking question mark myself. But so is the universe, in our purblind vision, a larger box holding the same general contents. Only clearer eyes, denied to most men, can see that the contradictions are in truth complementary.

Though such things are outside my optical range, I can claim an elephant's memory for trivia, a mental attic stuffed with worthless and yet precious odds and ends, the broken shards of Canada when it was young, the wealth of a poor boy dreaming his unreal dreams in a real attic beside the St. Lawrence, or in a squalid shack beyond the Rockies two thousand years ago.

What, then, is left of that youthful baggage? Not much, except the immortal wisdom of Dickens' Police Inspector Bucket who, in his search for criminals, judged that any move was a probable move so long as it was in the wrong direction. Even wiser, it seemed to me at the time, was a nameless man in a British Columbia town who, on the day of the Munich deal, cabled Prime Minister Neville Chamberlain an inspiring message of three words: "Events will follow." They did, too, while the author, having smashed some shop windows to emphasize his point, was confined to a psychopathic ward, and the great contemporary lunatics were left to cry havoc in the street.

So followed events, so flowed the dark currents like the noble rivers of Canada to the sea, so marched the procession, so spun the globe in endless convolution, until today's movie has a familiar backward look, an air of *déjà vu* and sickly-sweet nostalgia. When I was young the look, naturally, was forward and laden with fair promises as I started out on my first serious reporter's assignment in Ottawa among men whom my father, the conservative of old fashion and unfashionable honor, called "those damned Liberal swine". But if his only living son worked for a Liberal newspaper and might even become a Liberal himself, a shame hardly to be borne, my father bore it valiantly, with his flaming umbrella. In front of that bumptious youth stretched a long, twisted road, leading to a strange destination, behind him a boyhood also strange and, in modern Canada, impossible for any boy to duplicate.

2

The Stone House

The fifth day of June 1901 was little noted or long remembered except by the inhabitants of an old stone house at the corner of Dibble and Edward streets in Prescott, Ontario, who on that date registered an addition to their numbers in the family Bible. According to information from sources usually reliable, I was born in the same room and bed where my mother had been born some thirty years earlier.

That birthplace was chosen not for sentimental but for practical reasons. My mother had returned to her parents' home from Cranbrook, British Columbia, to obtain the skill of the doctor who had brought her and all her siblings into the world. The loss of my mother's first infant son for lack of medical facilities in a primitive western hamlet was not to be repeated.

Apparently all went well this time. It is further recorded, though not in writing, that my Catholic grandmother, a personal friend of the Pope, rushed into the bedroom ahead of anyone else and drew a hasty cross on my forehead with her finger to claim me for her Church. But my Protestant grandmother soon reversed my religious life by arranging an immediate baptism in the Church of England.

A vital question decided, and my grandmothers reconciled, I was taken at the age of six weeks to Cranbrook. Given the very narrow time margin, I could, and generally do, consider myself a native British Columbian. Yet my first memories are of the stone house in Prescott and of my mother, Constance, who was pretty then, her hair falling in a golden cascade down to her waist or fluffed in massive plumage on her head. She visited the old home frequently to show me off, I suppose, before a numerous and peculiar household.

My widowed Granny Leslie, a formidable woman of finely chiselled face and billowing white hair, handsome in her age and supreme in her authority, presided over five daughters and two sons. Now married and living in distant places, they arrived and departed with their husbands, wives, and children at irregular intervals, bringing gifts or seeking loans. How Granny managed, on my grandfather's estate, to maintain such a large house, two servants, a gardener, a pair of horses, and a carriage, when his salary had been fifty dollars a month as local agent of the Grand Trunk Railway, was never explained. This sum of arithmetic still baffles me.

Husband and wife had been brought up in Dublin but, as the Leslie name indicated, were of Scottish descent, with a slight mixture of Irish, and clearly they had practised thrift. They emigrated to Prescott in the time of Ireland's troubles, around 1840, he a poor, scholarly man, she a bride of striking beauty in her girlish portrait. Edward Leslie had died years before my arrival, much respected in the town, they say. He was a faithful worshipper at the Church of England, a dedicated follower of John A. Macdonald, a local organizer of the Conservative Party and the owner of some valuable property in other St. Lawrence towns — all this, and private schooling for his daughters, on a monthly income that such a man could earn in a day or less now.

His letters disclose a studious mind stocked with wide reading, a rather pathetic Victorian consciousness of his gentility, a deep religious faith, and a Christian tolerance. Despite his rigid code, he seems to have possessed a sense of humor. The faded program of an amateur concert, dated 1852, bills Edward Leslie, Esq., as soloist in a comic song. He needed all those qualities to survive a hard double test.

Into his devoutly Protestant home he had welcomed my father's mother, a widow, half French, who had learned her Catholicism at headquarters in Rome and had watched the Pope christen her son. No doubt she regarded the Leslies as heretics to be saved from sin, if possible, but these delicate issues of theology were not discussed. Granny Hutch, as we called her, had been given her own room, prayed at her own little shrine, attended her own church up the street, and contributed to the household what she could from the scant remains of a great English fortune. Enormously stout and always merry, she was beloved by everyone.

Two aged women of strong will and opposite religions in the same house in an age when religion, like partisan loyalty, still counted must have been a strain on Grandfather Edward, but it was minor compared to his real misfortune. His second daughter had married a wealthy young Scotsman, my Uncle Sam, who, sensible most of the time and especially kind to me, would go violently insane now and then, rage through the house, threaten the whole family with his gun, and disappear for a week or two, no one knew where. Once he shot a bullet into the bed of a visiting nephew from Boston, who was luckily absent at the moment. Luckily, too, his marriage was childless. His wife was too proud to have him removed, insanity being a disgrace, not a disease, in those days.

Besides its queer human contents the Prescott house held many wonders for a boy. Its walls were two feet thick, made of gray limestone by the Scottish masons who had built the Rideau Canal and needed other employment. Its rooms were crammed with ugly, expensive, mid-Victorian furniture from England, shining mahogany in the dining room and tinkling glass bric-a-brac everywhere. And over all the aroma of floor wax, brass polish, lavender sachet bags, rose-leaf potpourri in china bowls; and in the kitchen the oven-smell of mighty roasts, bread, and heavy puddings, the aunts and servants all abustle, each with her own handwritten cookbook and favorite recipe.

Then, in the cool cellar, the sweetish scent of apples, barrels of them, of piled firewood, salted beef, and hanging poultry, Ontario's indigenous perfume. Or in the attic, with its clean pine-board smell, a boy could find opulent treasures of discarded clothes, tail coats, top hats, crinolines, whalebone corsets, three ancient muskets, a brace of muzzle-loading pistols, and a rusty sword of unknown ownership—everything needed to dress up a company of boys and girls on a rainy day. But I did not find a key, mislaid with many others, which would open, long afterward, a different treasure then lying forgotten in a damp London vault. Nor did I notice a plaster bust of John A. Macdonald, though it also had an odd future in a wooden house across the continent.

The Prescott garden was spacious, overtopped by elms, and its unripe plums, cherries, and grapes gave me some memorable cramps treated with the usual castor oil. At the back door stood a dilapidated sentry box, the theme of much boasting to my playmates because it had been used in either the Fenian Raids or the War of 1812; the exact details were obscure. Near by rose the Windmill surrounded by a battlefield famous in Canadian history. We played on its grassy slope, ignorant of the tragedy enacted here by Von Schoultz and his mad American invaders.

Best of all were the days when Uncle Sam took me fishing down the river, or rowed over to Ogdensburg and bought my first ice cream. We even attended a dark theatre where pictures of cowboys and Indians moved, jerkily and unbelievably, on a screen. After that the old, familiar lantern slides that did not move held no interest for me.

Repaying my uncle's kindness, I experimented with matches and set the lace curtains of his bedroom on fire while the family was at church. The French-Canadian maid dragged me out, my clothes smouldering, locked the door, and did not think of calling the fire department, but the thick stone resisted the flames. On his return from church Sam was persuaded that one of his neglected tobacco pipes had caused the damage.

He continued to take me to Ogdensburg. The small American town looked like a metropolis, a very Baghdad on the St. Lawrence and a rich entrepôt of smuggled delights. By ferry in summer, or on winter ice, towing handy sleds behind them, my aunts shopped regularly in Ogdensburg and brought their contraband home in bags concealed under voluminous skirts. Or, if necessary, they wrapped bales of cloth around their bodies until they lurched up the Prescott street like overloaded galleons from the Spanish Main, the cargo always including a toy for me.

These Christian ladies, ardent supporters of the Conservative Party and its high Canadian tariffs, had never committed any other crime, but they saw nothing wrong in breaking the customs law and enforcing Liberal free trade for themselves. That was the immemorial custom along the river, the sacred riparian right of its dwellers, and the government inspector on the ferry wharf was fair and easy game, even on the rare occasions when he was sober.

Though I had been brought there earlier, my memories of Cranbrook came later. As I first remember him, my father, who seemed old, could not have been far into his thirties. He was a chunky, muscular man of middle height and weathered outdoor look, his face notably clean-cut and handsome, his speech still faintly tinged with an English accent, just as his life was tinged with an unusual origin.

Since he never wanted to talk much about the unhappy past, I learned it only in rough outline. His grandfather, Robert, had somehow accumulated or inherited riches in Edinburgh—a vain and hearty fellow, as it appears from his many expensive miniature portraits, most of them showing him in the kilt of the Stuart clan — and had moved to London with a wife painted just as often, and evidently pampered and adored all her life. There they set up housekeeping in grand style and sent their son, my grandfather, to Oxford for the proper education of a gentleman who would never have to work.

My father always suspected that these aristocratic pretensions were supported by a vulgar cooperage factory, but nothing as plebian as barrels was ever mentioned in the family circle. His father, William Corsten, whose portraits show a pale, austere, indoor face, did not turn out as expected, probably to his parents' disappointment. Instead of adorning London society, he tutored the son of Napoleon III in Paris and became a professor of Protestant theology. His rooms at Oxford, pictured in his neat, mechanical water colors, which now hang on my own wall, were lined with books and ponderous ornaments—the sanctum of a scholar, and also a born zealot.

When the Oxford Movement erupted in his Church of England he joined it eagerly, along with his friends John Henry Newman and Henry Edward Manning, who were to become Catholic cardinals. Already married to a second wife, the first having died after bearing a son, he could not enter the priesthood but chose the next best alternative. He gave most of his fortune to his adopted Church, moved his family to Rome, took a house beside the Vatican, and acted as some sort of chamberlain, lay servant, and pamphleteer to Pope Pius IX. In gratitude, when my father was born, the Pope personally baptized him with the shattering, myriad names of Giovanni, Marie, Pio, Benedictus, Francisco, Paulo. Evidently Pius, the great Ultramontanist, was not as stern a character as history has painted him. He kept candies in his desk and gave one every morning to the toddling child of his clerical assistant.

This story, told in fragments during my childhood, sounded improbable to me at the time. I could hardly believe it now if I did not possess photographs of my father, a sad-faced, pitiable urchin, dressed as a mascot in the uniform of the Swiss Papal Guard or, in ridiculous clerical robe, kneeling at prayer before some Vatican altar. The silk skullcap worn by the Pope at the baptism, and now in my house, confirms the unlikely record. At any rate, my father was dosed with too much theology too soon, and intended to escape it as soon as he could. But if he fled one church he was soon to embrace another, and he could never escape his religious feelings.

His father's health failing, the family moved back to England and set up housekeeping again in Hampstead. Enough of the original fortune was left to maintain a pretty sumptuous establishment where some interesting guests were welcomed, among them the novelist and artist George du Maurier, a red-headed Irishman (nicknamed "the privileged lunatic") who happened to be George Bernard Shaw, and others from the world of letters, the theatre, and politics. My grandfather, with all his religion and money, must have become a lonely, ambitious man in his last years and obviously a social lion hunter. But his second son (the first having entered a Benedictine monastery) was just the opposite. He found home life smug, absurdly genteel, and almost intolerable.

Young John, as he soon called himself, dropping all the other names for good, spoke only Italian when he reached England at the age of seven and a tutor was employed to teach him English. Then he was packed off to Downside, a Catholic school near Bath, for suitable education, with infrequent holidays at home in London and with austerity beyond belief in the meantime.

These bitter school days, and the future ahead of them, permanently separated John from his father. At sixteen, when he scraped through Downside, his education had been mainly derived from penny-dreadful books on the romance of the New World. He could stand no more of England and theology. He must go to Canada. His father agreed reluctantly, arranged for the erring son to study ranching somewhere, anywhere, on the Canadian Prairies, and wrote him off as a predestined failure, the family's first humiliation.

John's apprenticeship to a farmer outside Moosomin was hardly educational in classic terms, but it offered a rough slice of a Canadian life now forgotten. He paid the farmer twenty-five dollars a month for a room in the garret of a ramshackle house and for the privilege of working about sixteen hours a day in the fields and barns. At night, the farm wife being no needlewoman, he made underwear out of flour sacks for her children on a primitive sewing machine. In wintertime he harnessed a team of oxen to a sleigh and hauled poplar logs for fuel from a river bottom some twenty miles away. Once, caught in a blizzard, all direction lost, he burned the logs to keep himself and the oxen alive until morning — a narrow escape, the first of many.

After two years of a curriculum well designed for ambitious young Englishman, he was ready to buy his own ranch. His father provided the necessary funds, adding that they would be the last, and the ranch was bought, I do not know exactly where. A house was built of sods, because no lumber or logs were available. A herd of sheep was set to grazing the prairie grass and promptly died from some mysterious disease.

About the same time the father died, too, in London, having left the bulk of his fortune to the Church and very little to his widow. A rich family was now broke. And somewhere out on the Prairies an ambitious young Englishman had no ranch, no profession, no money, and no prospects. But he had something of superior value. He had a wife.

At some friendly home in Moosomin he met an attractive visitor from the east and within a week proposed marriage. The proposal seems to have been accepted with dubious approval in Prescott since the suitor had no known assets except his enduring devotion and charming manner when he visited the Leslie home. But John and Constance were married in Winnipeg in 1897.

Before the marriage, he had prepared a home for her and a new life for both of them. Seeking fortune a second time, he moved to British Columbia, left the train at Golden, bought an Indian cayuse for ten dollars, and rode southward to the village of Cranbrook, then only a sawmill and a cluster of shacks near old Fort Steele. How he managed there I don't know but with his unskilled hands he had soon built a bungalow, which still stands, and established himself in a real-estate business.

Those were happy years for my parents, the great happy time for the whole infant Canadian nation, never to be repeated in later times when happiness is measured by the Gross National Product. Of such quaint measurements the people in the far

West had yet to hear. All they knew was that a wheat boom had begun to transform the Prairies, just as a mineral and timber boom had begun to populate the lush valleys of British Columbia. Within the valleys a humble but unique civilization had taken root.

The inhabitants of a boom town like Cranbrook expected to be rich in a year or two. Surrounded by an empty wilderness and the Rockies' pinnacles, they had little money but they lived high, dined and danced in full evening dress, played tennis in white flannels, drank too much whisky at all-night stag poker games, rode their horses to picnics with lavish refreshments of food and wine, contrived amateur theatricals, and on any convenient excuse organized a parade down Baker Street.

In these festivities my father, known to everybody in Cranbrook as Hutch, appears to have been the moving spirit. With his booming vocal gifts and a megaphone, he was the mounted impresario and Almighty Voice of the parades, which I watched with fascination (as always, from the far side of the street). At some concert I can still see him, dressed up in a mock cowboy outfit, with false mustache and cardboard nose, delivering a monologue in a bizarre English accent, and on Sunday reading the lesson in the Church of England near our bungalow, far from Rome.

When a troop of strolling players arrived to produce a popular tear-jerking drama, "The Squaw Man", and the leading actor had occasion to drink himself insensible, Hutch replaced him, without rehearsal, his improvised lines being hilariously applauded.

Even better were the visiting circuses, the procession of solemn elephants, the mangy lions in cages, the spangled ladies on trick horses, the miracle of the big tent suddenly sprouting like a fungus at the edge of town; or the invariable Uncle Tom show, with real bloodhounds, giant Negroes, ice floes made of canvas, and little Eva (too old and somewhat blowzy) ascending to heaven on wires. Then the summers on Kootenay Lake, where the sleek white sternwheelers floated like swans, and I, drowning, was dragged from the water by a boy named Jack Wilson, whose future and mine were thenceforth bound together.

Despite all these jolly trappings of a Kootenay civilization authentically *sui generis*, Cranbrook and the towns like it were still on the outer fringe of Canada's happy time, remote from the nation and careless about the land east of the Rockies, or even in the next valley.

All the men wore identical Stetson hats, the badge of the true West, emblem of a separate western spirit which had not yet acquired its modern alias of separatism. Most of them avoided boots, preferring buckskin moccasins. My own were made by the wife of a work-shy Indian named Barnabas. He measured my foot with a piece of string and next week brought me the finely finished product of the squaw's needle.

While the boom towns grew fast, and were already obsessed with the ideal of growth for growth's sake, without seeing where that must lead, everything had gone wrong with our family in Cranbrook. Even now I cannot tell what happened. All I can remember from my fifth year is that my father was desperately poor again in a new house, half finished, like most of his work and, later, mine. His real-estate business had collapsed. He worked for a time as a reporter on the *Cranbrook Herald* under its gaudy publisher, an expatriate American who dyed his hair coal-black and at every banquet made the same speech, opening with "I care not where the man may come from, if he should spit upon the dear old Union Jack, then damn him straight to hell!"

After a brief stint of reporting my father started his own paper in the new smelter town of Marysville. Both town and paper quickly disappeared. Then he built a greenhouse and sold plants, discovering his real talent and lasting benediction in the earth. My mother, her long trials now only beginning, took in boarders and slaved for them in the kitchen, day and night. A second happy time would come but it was long ahead and the time of sorrows had come already. For reasons naturally hidden from a child my parents left Cranbrook, separately, but, as it would turn out, their union was unbreakable.

Where my father went in the next three or four years he never told me in more than passing hints, but he must have gone far. Reporter in Boston and Spokane; seller of law books all over the Southern States (knowing no law and picking up malaria on the way); author of whimsical and often excellent rhymes modelled on Kipling, his idol, and published in obscure magazines; actor in roving stock companies; manager of a third-rate opera (knowing no music); dabbler in mines and real estate, always at a loss—these poor scraps of unhappy recollection sifted down to me after a long silence and some half-remembered travels of my own.

From Cranbrook my mother took me back to Prescott and the old stone house, where Granny Hutch was still living with my last remaining aunts. Next, we were in Waltham, Massachusetts, in the house of my Uncle Herbert. A widower and naturalized American citizen notable for his generous heart and bubbling loquacity, he commuted by train to his well-paid executive job in Boston.

His household included a teen-age daughter, four sons, and an obese and beloved Negro cook named Kizzy, my protector against a tribe of untamed cousins who throve in joyous anarchy. My mother was expected to discipline these lawless waifs but, inevitably, she failed. They baited her, did as they pleased, and chose me for the butt of their inbred, unconscious Americanism. The skirmish at Lexington, a few miles away, had been fought many generations ago, but the cousins took delight in explaining, with rude crayon maps, that the British were defeated in every battle. This fierce national pride, in children only one generation removed from Loyalist Ontario, was a harmless but striking portent of Manifest Destiny in which at the time I saw only systematic torture. Some four decades were to pass before I would begin to understand that portent, and then in the presence of two native Americans named Roosevelt and Willkie.

Most of the time, however, the cousins, tired of baiting Canadians, treated me well in their fashion. They taught me to skate on neighboring ponds. I helped them, with a hose, to flood and freeze the full length of Greenwood Avenue so that only our toboggans, and no pedestrians, could move on it; the police failing to detect the malefactors. Spring came at last and we tapped maple trees, boiled gallons of sap over a fire in the woods, and produced minute quantities of syrup and sugar — an unrecognized but genuine taste of Canada. We caught pickerel on hook and string, the older boys shooting them with a .22 rifle, heedless of the game laws. To my horror, they also caught huge bullfrogs and cut the legs from the living bodies, an act that would send me running home in tears. We fought pitched battles with stones and sods against the Irish boys from an adjoining neighborhood, who were called "Muckers" and regarded as an inferior species — another unnoted portent.

For weeks in advance we saved our nickels and pennies to buy firecrackers, rockets, and deadly bombs. These were exploded, to the general alarm of the community, on Slam-Bang Night, the eve of July 4. I did not understand this tribute to the American Revolution but enjoyed the fun and proudly wore a ribbon bearing tawdry portraits of George Washington and Abraham Lincoln. Nor, of course, did I realize that I was seeing here, in a typical small town, a cross-section of American civilization before its age of innocence had passed.

A different and truly native slice of that civilization could be seen in the home of Ma Jones (the only name I ever knew her by), a towering, square-jawed woman, the very essence and distillation of New England with all its grim, kindly strength. She had a husband named Pa, who looked exactly like Santa Claus, white beard and all, slept in the basement, and never appeared to work. There were also four unmarried daughters of middle age who, long before women's liberation was even a word, held high professional posts in the Massachusetts government service.

Every Saturday night, on a clanking streetcar, my mother took me to the Jones household, its members being closer to her than any blood relatives. Now that they are gone I look back on Ma and her daughters as the finest product and enduring stuff of American life, the secret of its past, the hope of its future. But as a child I saw only some doting elderly ladies who plied me with sweets and let me crank up the latest prodigy of invention, a gramophone. Through its metal horn, to my amazement, came music and human voices from a wooden box where, I assumed, midget singers lived by means unknown.

Still more wonderful was the Joneses' summer home at Clifton Heights. There Pa taught me to fish off the rocks, and sometimes we caught a perch, a minor halibut, or a hideous eel, and once or twice a lobster in an illegal trap. Though unable to swim, I once stole a boat and rowed it to a sand bar a long way from shore. As the boat drifted away I would have drowned in the rising tide if some passing fisherman had not rescued me when the water was already up to my waist.

For a boy of five years my sample of American civilization, north and south, was pretty wide. As I could not imagine then, it would widen far beyond Prescott, Cranbrook, and New England. But nowhere in my travels would I find a duplicate of the Jones family. Doubtless millions of Americans still belong to the same invulnerable breed or the nation would have fallen apart before now. But my path lay in other directions. It lay, about the year 1908, on the opposite side of the continent.

3

The Wild West

The *Princess Royal* was a tiny and obsolete vessel but she looked huge and magnificent to me on my first ocean voyage. Her engines throbbing, her foresail billowing, her spars alive with seagulls, she swept grandly out of the Vancouver harbor and down Georgia Strait.

My mother and I had been expected by her sister, Emily, and brother-in-law, Archibald McVittie, in Victoria, but through some misunderstanding no one met us at the wharf. A cab, costing a dollar, was unthinkable. We walked to the Beacon Hill streetcar line and, for ten cents, were carried to South Turner Street.

There, in a house old even then, my Uncle Archie gave us a warm family welcome. He was a successful land surveyor of middle age, an inveterate speculator in worthless mines, and a good man, though his bristling black beard somewhat frightened me. Aunt Em, a tall, handsome woman of rare courage, which she would need in the bitter days ahead, showed me kindness beyond repayment. So, in the rough manner of children, did my cousin Archie junior, a gangling solemn boy one year older than I and much superior in virtue, and his younger sister, Margaret, whose flaming red hair was a landmark on South Turner Street.

We had come for a short visit. Thanks to the McVitties' generosity, it lasted for about two years. That was lucky, since we had nowhere else to go. Though it was never mentioned, and all three children were treated alike, even a small boy could not be unaware of this charity, and at times it hurt. But life on South Turner Street, before the pioneer James Bay district became a high-rise concrete jungle, was a pleasant surprise, and Victoria a town of enchantment. Its population was still small, its English character still authentic and not yet mere bait for tourists. No other Canadian or American town, then or afterward, begot that same style of living — and even Victoria could not keep it.

James Douglas's wooden fort beside the harbor had gone long ago, but the flavor, the privilege, and the absurd pomp of its frontier aristocracy lived on, later magnified and vulgarized by real wealth. In this social climate, and in a mild physical climate unknown in the rest of Canada, a distinct breed, almost a separate species, a queer little nation within the nation, had evolved — gardeners, cricketers, rugby players, horsemen, anglers, afternoon-tea drinkers, crumpet eaters, amateur musicians, and actors, outdoor people all, compact of earth, forest, and sea, passionately parochial, not especially intelligent but, in habits, gentle and civilized. That breed already was dying.

The stately rituals of the upper class of pioneer birth or sudden fortune were reported in the *Colonist* with reverence and a capital letter as Society, the remote offspring of England and equally Victorian in spirit. We, of course, observed our betters with awe and envy. The sprawling, timbered mansions on Rockland Avenue, the walled gardens of Government House, the profligate luxury of the new Empress Hotel, the feudal politics of the domed Parliament Buildings, the imagined wickedness of the glittering bars along Government Street (then deep in winter mud or summer dust), the first automobiles lately appearing, the black cabs with their shiny horses—all these were far beyond our reach. As sincere Christians, the upper classes shared with the lower a draughty wooden Church of England, called the Cathedral, but they sat apart in strictly reserved pews that were deeply padded with crimson pillows. Our religious education now began. Every week my cousins and I attended morning service, and then afternoon Sunday school in a decaying rookery back of the Cathedral.

If aristocracy awed and religion bored us, we and our playmates had the nearby splendors of Beacon Hill Park mostly to ourselves. On sunny days we ate our breakfast there — hard-boiled eggs and cold toast—before school opened in Miss Alice Carr's kindergarten.

This rustic academy of a single room and the old-fashioned family home beside it would be made famous by Alice's sister. I remember Emily Carr as a dowdy, dumpy woman with many pet animals, and a monkey riding on her shoulder. The world of art remembers her as Victoria's only true genius and perhaps the only painter of any nation who could understand and paint the Pacific rain forest.

Alice, a brisk, chirpy little spinster, enforced strict discipline, but allowed white doves to flutter about her schoolroom and ignored their deposits on all the desks. Amid these distractions she finally taught me to read and write, a considerable feat at my ripe age of eight. That she would also teach my daughter, in the same room, by the same methods, among descendants of the same doves, was not likely to cross the mind of a boy then concerned exclusively with boyhood's inscrutable affairs.

We lighted great fires of driftwood on the sea rocks below Dallas Road, baking potatoes in the red embers, boiling mussels in a tin can, and feasting on ambrosia that no grown man will ever taste. We played footfall and baseball above the cliffs. We skated on the tarns of the park when the thermometer sank under zero, to climate-proud Victoria's disgrace, and the water leaking through the roof of the South Turner house froze in a solid sheet across the kitchen floor. Kai, the cook, accepted it all quite calmly, but he was a Chinese and therefore a philosopher; he was also a lavish bringer of gifts from Chinatown—firecrackers and sticky sweets for the children, silks, carved boxes, or ivory figurines for the elders.

When we each had a nickel on Saturdays we walked downtown to the Grand Theatre and revelled in two full hours of short, blurred movies, accompanied by piano music, and interspersed with live performances on stage by acrobats, trained dogs, and conjurers. Very high-class stuff we thought it. After the show we waited patiently at the barroom doors up the street to ask the patrons for the golden bands off their cigars and collected these precious souvenirs in large quantities but could find no practical use for them.

Without warning, my father appeared on this cheerful scene at Christmas time. He had brought his wretched opera company to town for a much-advertised performance in the original Victoria Theatre on Douglas Street.

What correspondence had passed between my parents in these years I did not know, but they met in the antique lobby of the Balmoral Hotel, and I, watching them with sudden shyness, realized that their long separation was at an end. Mother's tears told me that much. In full evening dress, just before the night's show across the street, my father looked extremely rich, though his entire wealth at the moment amounted to about twenty dollars. In fact the opera company, like all his ventures, was now bankrupt. No matter, the family was reunited and that Christmas joyful.

What happened to the bankrupt opera company I did not hear or care. Enough that I had a father again and that he had privately requested me to call him Dad. In some inexplicable way I was now the equal of my cousins, the wound of inferiority healed. Dad was happy, too. He helped to trim the tree on South Turner Street, told us stories of the Wild West, gave his wonderful imitation of a tipsy Frenchman with a stutter reciting "The Charge of the Light Brigade", extracted innumerable paper balls from his Stetson hat, spent most of his money on presents, and, as I subsequently learned, left town next day with six dollars in his pocket.

Soon his letters, filled with optimistic news, were coming from Merritt, which I was able to locate on the map as a place south of Kamloops. He had established a real-estate business in a new town already growing fast and expected to prosper abundantly before long.

One chilly night in the autumn of 1910, Mother and I found ourselves on the platform of the Merritt railway station. Dad was nowhere in sight. But presently he came running and puffing out of the darkness and explained that the train had arrived ahead of schedule. We walked down a muddy lane to the Coldwater Hotel. Its blazing gas lights, the crowded barroom, the men in chaps and gaudy mackinaw coats, their saddle horses hitched outside, and on the street some ladies in splendid dresses and hats trimmed with luxuriant ostrich plumes — all this seemed to me a spectacle of astounding grandeur. Here, I thought, was the true Wild West. I had reached the land of the cowboys. It was just like the movies.

Next morning Dad showed us his office opposite the hotel. On the front window was painted in big gold letters the impressive legend "John Hutchison, Limited, Notary Public, Real Estate, Mines, Investment". The office, a dark room lighted by a hanging coal-oil lamp, had a counter and, behind it, two desks, one with a typewriter, the second heaped with books and papers. The walls were covered by maps and photographs of farm lands, forests, and mountains.

Such was the latest venture of John Hutchison, Limited, apparently limited to him, since no associate ever appeared in the office. But he assured Mother that his business was prospering. The town's population, almost eight hundred people, would shortly pass the thousand mark and rival Kamloops', because Merritt had been strategically located at the shipping point of a coal mine and the big Douglas Lake cattle ranch.

For the present Merritt consisted of two short business streets, lined by wooden stores with false fronts, some still unfinished, and beyond them little houses here and there on a flat plain, surrounded by dun-colored hills on the horizon.

What interested me most were the horses — everywhere horses — ridden by men in real cowboy outfits, broad-brimmed hats, buckskin jackets, chaps, high-heel boots, and jangling spurs (though the mounted Indians disappointed me because they dressed like the white men and wore no feathers). Nobody carried a revolver as in the movies and that was disappointing, too. Even stranger, some of the men who did not ride wore identical cloth caps, scarves around their necks, tweed jackets, and overalls. These, I learned, were the Scottish miners from the adjoining village of Middlesborough. They spoke in a peculiar accent, kept to themselves in the bars, were looked down upon by the community, and, being mostly natives of the county of Fife, were known with obvious condescension as Fifers.

Everyone greeted us warmly on the street that morning, called Dad by his familiar nickname of "Hutch", shook hands politely with Mother, and patted me on the head. Hutch, as always, was a popular man.

Among others, he introduced us to a very aged and sickly figure with a white beard whose name was Merritt, the founder of the town. A few months later the whole populace attended his funeral and I saw his coffin carried on a farm wagon and lowered on ropes into a grave blasted from the frozen winter earth. It was my first funeral but it failed to impress me. My attention was distracted by the long procession of sleighs and buggies, the Indians and their squaws on horseback, and, at a discreet distance, some ladies in a fine carriage, glossy fur coats, and beflowered hats. I did not yet understand their profession but they looked rich and beautiful.

Before then we had left the magnificence of the Coldwater Hotel for a rented house, really a shack, on the naked edge of town. It was about twenty feet square, or less, and contained a kitchen alcove, a living room where Dad slept on a cot, and a bedroom where Mother and I slept in a double bed. There was no plumbing, only a well in the back yard from which the water was hauled up in a coal-oil can, with a privy close by. When winter came, at a temperature of thirty or forty degrees below zero, and a trip to the privy was like a polar expedition, I realized that the Wild West had certain disadvantages. The well-plumbed homes of Prescott, Cranbrook, and Victoria began to take on a faintly nostalgic memory.

Our house, heated by a big coal stove in the alcove, was warm enough. But under the winter gales it shook and groaned as if it might blow away, and the inner walls of the bedroom glistened with hoar frost.

Still, we managed. Mother, the veteran of a Prescott kitchen, cooked meals fit for the best hotel and better than any available elsewhere in Merritt. She boiled the laundry in a tin tub (which also served for our weekly baths) and wrung out the clothes by hand until, after months of saving, she could buy a wringer at Menzies' store.

Most nights Dad would come home with a five-dollar bill, the fee charged for putting his notary's seal on some legal document, usually the naturalization papers of immigrants from Italy or eastern Europe—Wops, Bohunks, and Polacks, as everybody called them. On more profitable days he brought a couple of bottles of beer; the parents drank it at dinner as a kind of toast, I suppose, to the happier days ahead. Sometimes he brought several bills, and once or twice, in some business deal, he made as much as a hundred dollars. Then our accounts at the grocery and butcher stores would be paid off. As a boy could not understand, this inarticulate man was trying, bravely and desperately, to repay us for the years of separation, trying above all to make a friend of his son. In that, at least, he was succeeding better than either of us yet understood.

No guest ever visited us, nor did we see the inside of any other home. Even at Christmas we ate our turkey and plum pudding alone. But there was a bottle of wine that night and I had a sip of it, diluted with much water. In the nearest house along the road lived neighbors who seemed highly prosperous, but they were half-Indian and we had nothing to do with them. Gales, cold, and poverty could not break the law of caste ordained in Rome and Prescott.

To me, however, life in Merritt was idyllic. I had been sent to school, a long walk down the railway track, but learned nothing from the teacher, a Toronto dude who had just arrived in town, obviously hated it, rapped my knuckles with a copper-edged ruler, and constantly expectorated tobacco juice to sizzle, with pungent odor, on the stove. At noon the other pupils, boys and girls, ate sandwiches and cookies packed in old lard pails. I was given superior food, hot and greasy, at a restaurant on the main street conducted by a roly-poly little man named Lucky Frank. He evidently had some private financial arrangement with Dad, whose credit was still good.

But the school was a minor distraction. Most of the time I played hookey with two remarkable friends.

Harry Anderson, a precocious and overgrown youth of about sixteen, delivered bread, cake, and confectionery for a bake shop, and I was permitted to assist him. We travelled far across the countryside behind a piebald mare, her sleigh bells tinkling the old Canadian music. I enjoyed the tinkle and the exciting speed but Harry had business more important than the bakery in mind. By his spare-time studies and years of toil he would make himself the chief engineer of the British Columbia government.

On the fringe of town we served a cluster of dingy houses which, as he explained to me (with some shocking clinical information), was the red-light district. In fact, red lamps burned over every front door. The ladies of these establishments, whom I had already seen on the streets, gorgeously attired, now wore daytime kimonos and shawls, their hair unbrushed, their faces pale and surprisingly wrinkled, I thought. They greeted us kindly at the door, bought bread and cakes, but never asked us to come inside. They had their code. For my labors I was paid in candy at the bake shop where the aroma of hot bread gushed from a brick oven, nobler in my nostrils than all the perfumes of Arabia.

My second friend was known only as Texas or, more commonly, Tex. He must have been close to eighty years old — a stooped and shaky giant with a mane of white hair and a dangling beard of faintly yellow color. But Tex could still run a livery stable for some absentee owner. He lived alone in a small room next to his favourite horse, Bud. Whisky was his only other companion, and he smelled strongly of both.

At first Tex ignored me when I hung hopefully about the stable, gazing in wonder at the sleek horses in their stalls, but when I offered to help him shovel manure and push hay down from the loft he seemed to appreciate my possibilities. After that, I often worked with him and was even allowed to lead the horses to their drinking trough behind the stable—a great honor, as he assured me. One day, feeling especially weak and asthmatic, he let me take Bud to the blacksmith and I watched that skilful craftsman heat the steel shoes to cherry color, hammer them on the anvil, plunge them into steaming water, and nail them to the horse's hooves. In payment for these services Tex sometimes gave me a nickel or a dime, once a whole silver dollar.

His chronic asthma was treated regularly with the best medicine from the Coldwater bar and it revived him wonderfully. At such times, lying on his rumpled bed, medicine glass in hand, he became reminiscent and eloquent. I forget the details but it was well known to everyone that he had fought Indians all over the early West (a ragged arrow scar on his arm sufficient proof of one terrible encounter), had held up stagecoaches and trains before going straight and becoming a sheriff in Virginia City, and had nearly lost his life in a shoot-out with bank robbers (as the scar across his temple attested). I did not question these adventures, but gradually began to doubt them when Harry told me that Tex was a confirmed liar who probably had never fired a gun or broken a horse. Besides, I now had more important business of my own.

Recently I had peered through the window of a print shop. It amazed me. The three printers set type by hand, their fingers moving like some automatic machine, their faces jaundiced in the gas light, sweaty from the heat. The foreman (if I have not confused him with other foremen in a long experience with printers) was a squat and temperamental genius. He wore a tattered black wig, which he usually threw on his table or, in moments of anger, on the floor, uttering terrible threats against his crew and his Maker. "God Almighty," he would shriek, "get into the witness box! Now then, you son of a bitch, what have you got to say for yourself, eh?" No answer came to his inquiries, but despite the general ambience of dementia a weekly newspaper floated off the clanking flat-bed press. The smell of ink and hot metal filled me with a new excitement. Perhaps the future course of my life had been settled already by this first crude but magic glimpse of journalism.

Even the print shop, however, was still a comparatively small concern. Since our arrival in Merritt my overmastering ambition was to buy a horse. No ambition in later time could equal that poignant longing. Any horse would do but the price, at the lowest possible figure, was far beyond me.

By diligent research I learned that an Indian cayuse would cost about $20 or more, depending on its quality. Every cent I got from my parents and Tex, or earned by running occasional errands for a a grocery store, was hoarded in a tin box and counted every night. By mid-December I had accumulated the extraordinary sum of $15.75 and so reported to Dad. In a reckless gesture he promised to pay the balance of the cost as a Christmas present if I could find a horse at a maximum price of $25.

On Christmas Eve, as if by fate, an old Indian named Chief Blood rode into town from Lower Nicola, dragging an extra horse behind him. After he had become very drunk, from sources unknown and illegal, he stationed himself in front of Lucky Frank's café and, from the saddle, announced to the passers-by that he would sell the second horse, a bay, for thirty-five dollars.

No one was attracted by this offer because the second horse appeared to be the most pitiable living creature in Canada. Literally starved on the winter range, it could hardly move. Its bones were thrust almost through its hide. Its head hung down to touch the sidewalk.

Nevertheless, it was a horse. I ran to Dad's office and persuaded him to consider Chief Blood's proposition. With one glance at the horse, Dad, who understood horses, turned away in disgust. But when he saw the look on my face he came back and offered the Indian twenty dollars. As Blood hesitated between this bid and his own need of whisky, some joker in the sidewalk crowd shouted: "I'll give you twenty-five — cash!"

"Twenty-seven," said Dad in an oddly calm voice.

"Sold, by Jesus!" cried Blood.

His thirst had overcome his financial judgment and I owned a horse. What papers were signed and what arrangements made in the office I did not inquire. Chief Blood, his thirst quenched, rode out of town. I led my half-dead purchase to the livery stable where Tex, remarking that he had never seen so worthless a horse in all his life, allowed me to feed it hay and even a quart of oats. The next day, the three of us alone in our little house, was the happiest Christmas I had ever known.

I christened the horse Dock, the name of Mother's first pony in Cranbrook, kept it in a barn near the house, crammed it with hay and oats, curry-combed its matted coat until it shone, and watched it take on weight with astounding speed.

For lack of a saddle or bridle, I learned to tie an Indian hackamore and, with this rope halter, was soon ready for my first ride, bareback. A cheap boy's saddle and bridle were purchased by mail order from Eaton's in Toronto and from then on I spent most days riding, feeding, or combing Dock. His belly was now so fat that my short legs could hardly straddle him, but I seldom fell off.

With my latest friend, a dark, silent Indian boy named Jesus, who owned a lively buckskin, I rode across the frozen range and into the hills. Sometimes we galloped breakneck through the town, thinking ourselves desperadoes or United States cavalry. Or we would try to keep up with the stagecoach on its daily run to Princeton until its six horses quickly outstripped ours.

My parents supposed that I was at school. Perhaps they were too busy and too worried to watch my education, though my clinging redolence of horse, stable, and manure should have alerted them. The school teacher did not seem to notice my absence.

As spring came, the range turned green overnight and our horses eagerly nibbled the young bunch grass. We would tether them to a tree and fish in the Coldwater River, now and then catching a few trout, after we had hit on the secret of affixing a caddis worm to a Royal Coachman fly hook. Skewered on a willow twig and cooked over an open fire, the trout tasted fine. In one of these expeditions we observed from a hiding place in the woods the birth of a range colt. It emerged smoothly from the mare, and when she had licked it clean of the bloody placenta it stood up immediately on its long, quivering legs.

This was not the sort of thing that a boy could discuss with his mother. Anyhow, she was fully engaged in the extra chores of springtime. She housecleaned, hung the carpets on the line, beat them, and scrubbed the bare floor. Having somehow acquired a broody hen, she installed it in a barrel beside the house. Presently a dozen chicks hatched out. Then a sudden wind storm in the night rolled the barrel, chicks and all, down the road. We collected about half of them alive and noticed that one looked different from the others. It soon matured into a white duck, which waddled through the house as it pleased like a pet dog until it was decapitated, with its mates, by a mink. Mother wept next morning while I buried the bodies, weeping also.

The expected boom did not come with spring. Merritt was not growing as planned. A huge mineral treasure lay not far away in the hills but it was not to be found for half a century yet. My father's business, such as it was, had deteriorated. Though he had started to build a large new house across the river, he brought home less money and no more beer. But on the twenty-fourth of May, Queen Victoria's birthday, failing to arouse any civic enthusiasm, he borrowed a friend's rifle, walked to the rodeo field outside town at dawn, and there, all alone, fired into the air a royal salute of twenty-one shots, dislocating his right shoulder in the process. Dad would always be an Englishman at heart, without ever seeing England again.

Two important events briefly kindled the town's passions that year. The opening of a steam electrical plant, with toasts, speeches, and a splendid ball in the loft of Menzies' store, guaranteed Merritt's progress. The historic national election of 1911 split the community in sharp partisan cleavage.

Through the open windows of the Coldwater Hotel barroom I could hear the men arguing by the hour over their drinks about something called Reciprocity, which puzzled me and my friends. Dad took the Conservative line, of course, regarded Reciprocity as madness, or treason, and said that a man named Laurier was "disloyal" — why or to what he did not explain. But the words "Liberal swine" entered my vocabulary at an early age.

They, and Reciprocity, mattered little to me at that time. Mother and I spent the hot summer on Nicola Lake with my McVittie cousins, their father being engaged in land deals and making a vast fortune, on paper. In this summer of riding, fishing, camping, and brief affluence I could not suspect that my Wild West days were about to end. In the autumn they ended for good.

Broke once more, the new house half built and its mortgage

foreclosed, Dad gave up his business and, with a little Conservative Party pull, got himself a clerk's job in the provincial government service. We all moved back to Victoria, Dad into fifteen years of quiet misery, Mother into a kind of humble security, I into serious education at last.

4

The Fortress

The tiny bungalow on Wilmer Street, then at Victoria's outskirts, seemed luxurious after the shack in Merritt. It was covered all over with brown shingles and contained five rooms, a bathroom, a basement, and that novel gadget, a coal furnace. Two amateur contractors had just built the house, somewhat roughly, as a speculation. My parents bought it for the frightening sum of $4,500. How Mother had saved $500 for the down payment is a mystery that still puzzles me, but in her own small way she was a genius of finance.

On Dad's salary of $100, later $125, and finally a maximum of $135 a month, she served nothing but the best food, in unlimited quantity, cooked by the old Ontario recipes. At second-hand stores and auction sales she found some excellent furniture and added to it several fine old mahogany pieces from the home in Prescott. We were always well clothed and the house was well furnished and heated. Moreover, we were solvent, independent, and, for the first time, invulnerable, even a little proud of our estate. To us it was a fortress against the world entire.

Apart from the house mortgage we owed no debt. Never while we lived there was the monthly interest payment overdue, the capital amount sinking slowly, oh how slowly, year by year. On pay day at the government office Dad received his salary cheque, cashed it at the bank, took forty dollars to the mortgage company, and brought the rest home to Mother. She kept it in her bureau drawer and disbursed it, dollar by dollar, as if she were managing a national budget (and managing it more efficiently than any finance minister of my future acquaintance).

Dad got enough for carfare, his twenty-cent lunch in town, pipe tobacco, and clothes. He was always immaculately dressed, his suit pressed, his shoes shined, a flower in his lapel, a stout English cane in hand, or that umbrella which so often burned. I got twenty-five cents a week and thought it ample. Mother, I suppose, got the satisfaction of her independence, freedom from debt, and our unquestioned trust.

As the real head of the household she took the front bedroom for herself. Dad and I slept on cots in the back one, hoping that some day a third might be added, though this looked improbable. If the house must serve as it was, Dad had begun already to turn our narrow lot into a garden. It soon became the showpiece of the district and opened to a lonely man his escape from the suffocating routine of his job.

Most of the front yard was covered with bare rock, but he carried rich leaf mould in a box from the vacant land around us to make flower beds. They sprouted in vivid, exotic colors against the wild golden broom along empty Wilmer Street.

The back yard, free of rock, produced vegetables and berries, leaving room for a chicken house and a dozen or two Rhode Island Reds, their big brown eggs so plentiful that I peddled them throughout the neighborhood, collecting scraps of garbage from my customers to nourish the flock. With new chicks frequently hatching, there was some fat rooster or superannuated hen to be killed on most Saturdays for Sunday dinner. Dad hated that job, and performed it alone with an axe in the basement while Mother and I listened from above to the last horrifying screech of the victim. But those Sunday dinners could not be bought at any price, in any Canadian restaurant, nowadays.

Mother entertained no visitors and visited no other house. Her only extramural interest was the Christian Science Church, to which she had lately been converted. She attended twice a week and Dad and I accompanied her on Sundays, for reasons more of loyalty than religion. He had come a long way from the Vatican in Rome and I some distance from the Church of England in Prescott.

Looking back now, I see that beneath a refined Victorian gentility, almost too fastidious, Mother was the hub and governor of that little family, the central influence and anchor of my life until I met a woman equally strong who totally dominated me to the end. If Mother had more strength than I, or Dad, her charities always exceeded her stern economies. She gave what she could to her church, a dollar or two every month, smuggled food to poorer neighbors, and, in the last of her hundred years, still knitted innumerable quilts for refugee children in foreign lands that she had never seen and could not locate on the map. Altogether, an extraordinary woman of unshakable religious faith. I loved but did not fully value or understand her quality before I was old myself. That I was the centre, hope, and pride of her brave and lonely life occurred to me only when she was gone.

On Wilmer Street we were poor but comfortable, at times even festive, our glimpses of Victoria's fashionable society remote but sufficient, our single extravagance the flourishing legitimate stage of those days. Somehow Mother always found money to buy us gallery tickets for the latest travelling show at the palatial new Royal Victoria Theatre where some of the world's great artists performed. Or else we walked to the suburban Oak Bay Theatre and saw a movie for ten cents apiece, attended by our black Aberdeen terrier, Boda, who slept and snored politely under our seats. There we observed the first rude, flickering films of an unknown actor named Charlie Chaplin. He appeared to have a certain vulgar talent.

My interests, however, lay mainly outside the home. With only a smattering of education so far, and almost illiterate, I had entered the original Boys' Central School. Fortunately I found some excellent teachers in that old brick ruin. They must have been excellent since they compelled me, by regular use of their straps on hands or bottom, to learn something at last. I even liked to learn and apparently learned quite fast with much homework every night.

Those teachers crammed me so hard that I skipped three grades and had passed into high school, by a tough written examination, a few weeks after my thirteenth birthday. But there was plenty of time for the cadet corps, the indoor rifle-shooting team, the lacrosse team, which won the city championship in a famous overtime game, and the hockey team, which played in Lester Patrick's new arena at six o'clock Saturday mornings, when ice rent was only fifty cents for each player.

More important than all these winter sports were the summers at the McVitties' new place on Cowichan Lake. Though I could not understand it then, nothing had more effect on my disposition and future than the days in a wilderness as yet hardly touched by man. We did not know then that the McVittie cottage stood in the middle of Canada's most valuable forest, awaiting its sure destruction. At that time perhaps a hundred people altogether lived around the lake and, having no road, travelled in their boats. A general store, a summer hotel for trout fishermen at the head of the river, a small logging camp, a single farm, and half a dozen rustic homes were, unknowingly, the vanguard of a migration that was soon to strip the mountains clean, carve roads everywhere, and build three sawmill towns, one of them on the site of Uncle Archie's little house.

Ignorant of these prospects, Cousin Archie and I roamed the forest as we pleased. Its darkness on the brightest day, its dampness in the season of drought, its eerie silence or its moan and creak under storm, its brush so rank and clinging that no man could travel it until he had chopped out a trail, its air of stealth and menace like some animal in wait for prey — these things would penetrate and dye the whole web of my being, but not in boyhood. For a boy of thirteen years the forest was only a playground where we made some interesting discoveries.

On the bank of Sutton Creek we could touch, without moving, three cedars, the smallest twelve feet in diameter. Every week we scrambled up the stream with fishing rods and grasshoppers for bait and returned with twenty or thirty trout. Or we would row our clumsy boat, the two of us alone, to the mouths of more distant creeks, fish them, and camp for several days, nourished mainly by trout and well-boiled tea. Already we were expected to care for ourselves like men.

One day when the March brothers, from the nearby farm, followed their howling dogs, Archie and I went along too, until we found a cougar stretched on the branch of a maple tree. The immense tawny cat snarled and spat, its tail waving, as if it might leap down on us at any moment. With mature judgment for my age, I volunteered at once to get Jack March's gun from the farm, a mile away. I covered that distance in record time and, as we watched, Jack took aim. Blood spurting from its head, the cougar fell between us, writhed briefly, and lay still. The four of us carried the body home, suspended from a pole. Jack skinned it for a hearth rug and collected the government's bounty of forty dollars.

Archie and I each had a .22 rifle. We used them to shoot a few fool hens out of season, easy marks as they stared at us, fearless, from a branch. We even joined an unlawful pitlamping expedition one night in the Marches' hayfield, but when I saw the glazed, piteous eyes of a dying buck deer I gave up shooting, while continuing to kill fish without the least compunction.

All this time I was pursuing a more innocent hobby, which was to have useful results. After long, slow accumulation, I had paid the massive sum of twenty-five dollars to some correspondence school in Detroit and it taught me cartooning by mail. My career was thus settled in advance. I would become a professional cartoonist. So I did, with years of bungled effort — probably the worst cartoonist who ever sold his work to Canadian newspapers.

Still, it was a beginning, my drudgery not altogether wasted. But a boy hunched over a drawing board all day on a windy verandah while his companions played must have been a curious sight. And I was sitting there in furious concentration on the afternoon of August 4, 1914, when a launch wallowed up the lake from the hotel seven miles away to bring us the news of European war.

It did not impress me much at the time but it soon changed our comfortable life. The collapse of the land boom ruined Uncle Archie. Jack March immediately enlisted, fought through the whole war in Europe, unwounded, and on his return was killed by a falling tree near the farm. Without his help meanwhile his father could hardly keep the farm going at all.

Henry March was a tall, black-bearded man who moved slowly, spoke quietly, and achieved a solitary triumph. On balance, I would judge him the most successful man I ever met. From a good English private school he had come to the lake with a young bride, a few dollars, some farm tools, and a team of oxen. Here he settled, built a big log house and, inch by inch, hacked his first meadow out of the forest. No man who has not done it can imagine this brutal labor.

An even greater success was March's home. When I first saw the log house it was overtopped by the maples planted as seedlings in his young days. His wife, now middle-aged, her hair white, her English complexion still rosy, and her manners unchanged by all these years in the jungle, kept the house spotless, fragrant with blossom from her garden, and shiny from much polishing.

She canned venison, grouse, vegetables, and fruit. In the early, hardest days, she cured and smoked bacon, made soap from grease and lye, candles from mutton tallow. She milked a cow and churned butter which her husband took to the end of the lake in an Indian dug-out canoe, paddling fourteen miles there and back, before he could buy a launch. The butter and the odd chicken or pig were traded for necessities like flour, tea, and sugar.

Mrs. March, a gentle creature, a lady by any definition anywhere, was firm in her household rules. Before dinner every night the husband and two sons must bathe in water carried by bucket a quarter of a mile from the lake, must appear at table in clean clothes, and listen as she said grace. After dinner March would retreat into his books and newspapers, his wife to her endless darning, patching, and dressmaking. Somehow both sons were sent to an English-style private school in Duncan — Jack, the elder, to fight for his country and find his death at the hands of an older enemy, and Charles, the younger, to inherit the farm, prosper on it, and see the unwelcome advent of civilization.

In the first years of the war, I was seeing, but of course not recognizing, a humble epic such as few modern Canadians will ever see. The farm had been much improved by now, a mechanical pumping system installed, more land cleared, oxen replaced by horses, the Indian canoe by a sturdy launch. But the war had taken Jack and most young men overseas, no farm labor was to be found in this remote area, and to reap a crop Henry March depended on three boys.

Charlie was almost a man, and as good a one as I would ever know. Archie and I, though still in our early teens and unaccustomed to work, were eager for money. At wages of ten cents an hour (more than March could afford) we weeded and thinned his vegetable seedlings. When the mowing machine broke at the worst possible time, the four of us harvested about thirty acres of hay by hand. After several days of torture in the hot field, I learned to use a scythe, to cock hay and load it on the wagon. March said nothing, worked harder than any of us, never complained when I broke two expensive scythe blades on the colossal stumps, and no doubt wondered whether I would make a man of myself some day.

His own standards would always be outside my reach. As local justice of the peace, for example, he was expected by the government to keep his eye on a retired German army major and his wife who lived five miles down the lake and were classed as enemy aliens, perhaps dangerous (a quaint official notion in Ottawa). They had been ordered to report to March regularly but since they had no launch, no more money from home, and no assets except a few chickens and a milking goat, March interrupted his own work and visited them every week, taking food from the farm. Without his guarantee of their behavior, the Germans probably would have been interned; without his food, they might have starved. Such people as March and his wife are rare in this world. I never saw their like again.

The home on Wilmer Street was little affected by the war (though the rise in beef prices to the unbelievable peak of twenty-five cents a pound convinced Mother that the economic system was tottering). I had entered the grand new Victoria high school and now began, strangely enough, to relish education. At night, while Dad read his gardening books and Mother sewed, I spent two hours or more on homework. But over the week-ends I found time to raven through the works of Scott, Dickens, Thackeray, Maupassant, and Conrad, among others, the books purchased second-hand or borrowed from the public library. Persuaded that scholarship was my natural bent, I plunged enthusiastically into the school's debating society, delivered ponderous, well-rehearsed speeches on matters of which I knew nothing, and even debated in Vancouver with a team just as ignorant. Victory in that contest confirmed my singular gifts and exploding self-esteem. Obviously I must become a lawyer.

Then, acting Shylock in a school play, false-bearded, grease-painted, and sympathetically applauded in the *Colonist*, I realized that my future was on the stage. Fortunately, or unfortunately, at this point, I stumbled into print. My puerile stories and worse cartoons were published in the school paper and I became its editor. When the *Victoria Daily Times* let me write a column of school news for its Saturday edition the thing went to my head. I knew that I was cut out for journalism and itched for the chance, which seemed a long way off, to become a full-time newspaperman.

Concerned only with my own affairs, already an adolescent intellectual snob and, in retrospect, a rather nasty piece of work altogether, I paid scant attention to the war. Nor did my contemporaries and rivals in the fierce politics of our high school.

Older boys, some of them our friends, who had graduated ahead of us, were dying in the trenches of Europe. The *Colonist* printed the long casualty lists every morning and Dad read them by the kitchen stove before breakfast. Canada was being drained of its best blood, changed from a colony into a nation. But the anguish and the blood-letting hardly touched our life at school as we prepared for university. If we thought of it at all, the war seemed far away and bound to end soon in the triumph of Right over Wrong, the birth of an ever-peaceful world, safe for democracy, as President Woodrow Wilson had frequently promised. We sometimes read his speeches in the newspapers and agreed (though Dad was prejudiced against an American who had remained neutral for so long).

In the depth of a world calamity beyond our comprehension, we received, on Wilmer Street, a sudden break of luck. The estate of Granny Hutch, who had recently died, the last remnants of once great wealth, came to about a thousand dollars, more money, I dare say, than Dad had owned in cash since he left England and, by our standards, a fortune. Now he could add to the house a bedroom of his own and buy the two adjoining lots, which were soon ablaze with flowers. There was even a little money in the bank for the first time and a new watch on my wrist.

Still more amazing, Aunt Charlotte had sold the Prescott house and, among its forgotten oddments, had found a key labelled "Silver in London bank". What could it mean? Charlotte was about to throw key and label away with the other trash when it occurred to her that they might mean something. So she sent them to Dad. He had never seen these relics before but, with forlorn hope, sent them to the old family solicitor's firm in London.

Some six months later (and this in the middle of the German

submarine war) a large and heavy wooden crate arrived, via the Panama Canal, in Victoria. Dad and I opened the crate and inside it discovered an oaken chest, a craftsman's masterpiece, bound with hoops of rusty iron. And within the chest, layer on layer, was the family silver — candelabra, mugs, knives, forks, spoons, and filigreed ornaments, all blackened with age after lying, unnoticed, in some damp London vault for more than half a century.

Dad started at once to clean them. Every night in the kitchen, he brushed and rubbed them until they glowed. He traded two spoons for a big pendulum clock now ticking as steadily as ever on my mantel shelf. For Mother he bought the latest type of washing machine, with enormous wheels and gears, which, on Saturdays, I propelled by hand.

The oak chest, its bottom rotted out by the London damp, was stored away until, sixty years later, I cleaned and rebottomed it and, sanding off a black square of metal, exposed a shiny brass plate. On the plate were engraved the words "Robert Hutchison, Chest 2". Where Chest 1 had gone was never known but the second I gave to my son, who bore the name of his great-great-grandfather in Edinburgh. The Scottish breed, or myth, dies hard.

All these little family affairs were thrust from my mind on a decisive day in the spring of 1917. Benjamin Charles Nicholas, the immortal Benny, had agreed to coach our debating team. We called at a dingy home near the high school and were received by a man who looked very old to me, though actually he was in his mid-forties — a short man, bald as an egg, rumpled, and, as always, floating in a cloud of cigar smoke.

He coached us on the subject of debate, the railway problem in Canada, with impressive knowledge, but kept glancing at me out of the corner of his eye until, taking me aside, he asked if I would like to join his staff at the *Daily Times*. On the instant the deal was closed. After matriculating in June, at the age of sixteen, I would become a newspaperman.

All thought of university, the law, the stage, or any other occupation quite forgotten, I waited with unbearable impatience for my job. But something went wrong. For reasons of office finance, Benny could not take me on yet. I must wait until autumn.

In an agony of disappointment I found a summer job at a mine on Quatsino Sound where Archie was at work after his first year of university. Dad walked with me to the Victoria wharf and, carrying only a two-dollar bill in my pocket, I boarded the *Princess Mary* for a stormy, misty voyage up Vancouver Island's west coast, into the unknown.

Unknown indeed it was. The miners' camp stood halfway up a high mountain and the mine itself still higher. For two weeks, with old men and draft dodgers for companions, I swung a sledge hammer to break chunks of copper ore while the boss set off dynamite at random, launching frequent avalanches of rock down the mountainside. My special job was to pack dynamite caps over the trail (although I was terrified of explosion). I also learned to split shakes out of cranky hemlock, since no cedar was available. Never, not for a single day, did the rain stop falling, never was I dry except in my bunk, and never had I been so shocked as by the insanitary habits, stench, language, and carnal recollections of my fellows.

If the life of the world's workers was not what I had expected, I was ahead of the game, having cleared $30 net in a mere fortnight on the war-inflated wage of $2.75 a day. By then, however, the mine was going broke and the boss fired most of the crew. We were the lucky ones. The purser on the *Princess Maquinna* foolishly cashed our cheques for the voyage home. Archie and the men still at the mine found their cheques worthless.

Needing more than thirty dollars for the uncertain future, I rode to Cowichan Lake on my bicycle and was given a job at the comfortable home of the Stokers—he a gruff, kindly old doctor and colonel retired from the Indian army service, she a deaf, blunt, but wildly generous dowager who spent her time collecting native plants.

As I understood the arrangement, they wanted thirty cords of wood cut from the towering firs near their house and would pay me a dollar a cord, my board and lodging free. Dr. Stoker helped to fell the trees with a double-ended, seven-foot saw and left me alone to cut them into four-foot lengths, then split them with hammer and wedge.

For a youth who had never handled such tools the work was not easy. But after a few days I mastered that long, wavering saw blade, learned the fine art of splitting, piled up a daily cord, and fell into bed, exhausted. When he had measured thirteen cords Dr. Stoker said that was enough. I had misunderstood his commitment and was now unemployed again. The Marches came to my rescue. At their farm I spent the rest of the summer cutting more wood for my board, and even Henry was impressed by my sudden expertise.

In the autumn I returned to Victoria, still impatiently awaiting Benny's call. As no call came, I filled the time by taking, at the high school, a useless course then called senior matriculation, or first-year university. Not quite useless, however, since I learned typewriting and shorthand, both crafts handy in my intended trade. All through that boring, unhappy winter I heard nothing from Benny and was in despair. Would his call never come?

It came on the historic night of April 11, 1918. Early the next morning I mounted my bicycle, hardly able to ride it in my excitement, and before eight o'clock presented myself at the grimy, musty, magical office of the *Victoria Daily Times*.

5

The Eager Apprentice

To its editor, the *Daily Times* was not a newspaper. It was a beloved child and Benny Nicholas, a lifelong bachelor, its parent; a kingdom which he, as sovereign, ruled with the full consent of his subjects; a benign dictatorship of fantasy; an empire of innocent pandemonium, Victoria its capital, the rest of the nation its outer provinces and, still more remote, that world sure to be brave and new after the war. But for all his conceits and fictions, Benny was in truth the humblest of men; for all his howling furies the kindest; for all his railing impieties the most religious; for all his courtiers, friends, and sycophants the loneliest.

To a youth not yet seventeen years old these facts were not apparent. I saw only a fat, bald, and waxen little man who marched into his messy office at eight in the morning, threw off his coat, lighted a cheap cigar, and picked at his obsolete typewriter with two clumsy fingers. After an hour or so he dashed into the newsroom without a word to anyone and consigned a wad of copy to the air chute, which, if it happened to be working, carried his editorial up to the composing room.

If his morning mood was cheerful he would stop all the work of the office and deliver to his staff of eight men a political lecture, sometimes in gorgeous hyperbole and a deep musical voice, sometimes in leering vulgarity and wild, cackling derision. Or again, eyes distended, plump hands fluttering, he would seize on some astonished visitor, back him into a corner, dance around him, prod his belly, and shout imprecations or mad jokes into his face. Then, just as suddenly, he would retire to his own cubbyhole and not be seen until the next day.

Alternately encouraged and terrified by this frantic personage, I did not yet know that Benny was one of Canada's greatest newspapermen, who stayed in Victoria by choice alone, a writer of sparkling style, a public speaker of rare eloquence, and, within his violent Liberal Party prejudices, a keen student of politics. Later on, I came to appreciate these qualities—as usual, too late—and the solitude, heartache, and desperation behind them. I also learned that no man can keep other men in their true proportion, that every man has his heroes larger than life, his villains smaller, his universe bounded and shaped by frontiers of his own making. Thus to me Benny would remain a man far more important than the world judged him, a decisive influence on my future. As one of his friends said when Benny died, no one could feel mean in his presence. That said everything, and of few men could it be said.

At the beginning he gave me no instructions, only a broken desk in the darkest corner of the slovenly newsroom and a monstrous, long-discarded typewriter about the size of a threshing machine and just as noisy. Its keyboard was different from those I had learned to use but I could hardly complain about such a minor inconvenience when I now occupied the august position of sports editor. This actually meant that I must fill four columns of type a day, in a paper of some dozen pages and a circulation of ten thousand. I filled my space mostly with telegraph news while trying to write reports of local athletics in what I considered a brilliant, racy idiom of invented adjectives and tortured nouns.

Nobody seemed to care how or what I wrote since the paper was crammed with news of the European war and Benny was interested in nothing else. As I gradually mastered my threshing machine, though not my idiom, he pored over his wall maps of Europe, adjusted the battle lines every day with colored pins, and wrote, by the general opinion of his craft, the best editorials on the war then published in Canada.

For him the war was a clear test of morality, almost a religious experience. In its darkest, early days, he had told his cronies in the Pacific Club across the street that the conquering Germans would never take Paris. And when some doubter asked why he was so confident, Benny replied: "Because I believe in God." He did, too, in his own queer fashion.

For the sports editor the war was hardly more than a petty distraction from the vital job of filling space and writing, with secret rapture, perhaps the most bombastic and self-conscious jargon in print anywhere. On my first pay day I discovered that the wage for this labor was twelve dollars a week. It seemed generous and enabled me to pay my board at home.

Having scant interest in athletics, I soon became bored with the sports desk and had yet to hear that it was the traditional stepping stone to higher things. Nor did I realize that sports and politics were kindred professions, both essentially contests of skill, luck, and vanity.

My boredom was fortunately relieved after three months when Tom Merriman, a veteran of newspapers and war, limped into the office on crutches, a leg paralysed by the wounds of Vimy Ridge, and replaced me. On promotion to the police beat, I was instructed to forget my tawdry sporting style in favor of plain, factual English.

During the next year my experience of the Victoria underworld became intimate and friendly. Each morning, drunks, bootleggers, brothel keepers, prostitutes, pimps, Chinese opium smokers, drug peddlers, burglars, and occasionally a genuine murderer, paraded through the smelly little police court. In brief paragraphs, vexed by the need for dull accuracy, I recorded the sentences meted out by the magistrate. This sordid side of life in a town of smug outward respectability came as a brutal shock, but I soon got used to it and found crime as boring as sports.

My boredom was shattered by the assassination in Chinatown of the visiting prime minister of China. It happened on a Sunday evening, as if by special arrangement for my convenience. Detective Chief George Perdue and I, walking downtown after a Christian Science Church service, saw a young Chinese running toward us, gun in hand. At the corner of Pandora Avenue and Broad Street he paused to shoot himself through the head.

The deceased assassin, blood and brains around him on the sidewalk, was not a pleasant sight, but certainly a piece of world news, my chance to hit the big headlines. I proceeded to botch that opportunity in a flamboyant, grotesque report, which the city editor, with an even more grotesque misjudgment of news values, thrust into the back page of the *Times*. When the assassination was spread on front pages throughout the world, I felt at least partly vindicated.

That city editor, T. Harry Wilson, was himself a living grotesque, about whom gathered much vivid legendry. English, highly educated, of handsome face, clipped military mustache, and exquisite manners, Wilson had worked in many places and learned everything — except his own trade. In Victoria he worked about ten hours a day at his desk and for diversion in the evenings interviewed travellers at the Empress Hotel or on liners arriving from the Orient. Having informed himself on world affairs, he wrote reports grammatically correct but usually incomprehensible to the reader. These he clipped out of the paper and pasted in a scrapbook for posterity, though he was a bachelor and childless.

Now and then Benny threatened to fire him for some notable gaucherie. Whereupon, according to the office legend, Wilson would go home, turn on the gas stove, and prepare for a gentleman's necessary suicide, which was always interrupted at the last moment by Benny's arrival in a taxi. Then Wilson would be rehired to continue his literary carnage, as when, reporting a joint conference between two rival clubs of amateur rabbit fanciers, he wrote the precious headline: "Two Breeders Bodies

Meet." Benny was inflamed and delighted by the gem. He pinned it on his wall for public enlightenment and reminded the staff, in confidence, that Wilson should not be judged by normal standards, being widely suspected of virginity. But in the historic wreck of the *Princess Sophia* on the Alaskan coast, where the ship's company of some two hundred passengers all drowned, Wilson went too far.

Benny had been given a world scoop on that disaster through an unauthorized tip from a friendly wireless operator and, calling me to his telephone, waited while I took the message down in shorthand. Since I could not be trusted to write such a momentous story, for which the press of America was already panting, Dick Freeman, the experienced shipping editor, wrote it, in about five minutes, smack on afternoon deadline. Wilson carried the copy up to the composing room, persuaded the peevish old foreman to set it in type, and told Benny that it would reach the street immediately.

Of course, said Benny, the news would be splashed all over the front page. Why no, said Wilson, it had been placed where it properly belonged — in the marine column at the back of the paper, for obviously it was shipping news. But, he added proudly, it had been given the special distinction of a two-column headline.

With that, Benny exploded in a mighty oath, ordered the presses stopped, ran puffing and screaming up the stairs, watched the printers set a huge eight-column headline, and managed to get the story on the front page, an hour late but still a world scoop. Though Wilson's feelings were hurt, he merely complained, out of Benny's hearing, that it had been a mistake, a breach of journalistic rules, to move a shipwreck out of the marine department.

Poor man, kind-hearted, scrupulous, and overtrustful, he suffered Benny's vagrant moods and my effrontery with sublime patience until his premature death, never escaping from his imaginary scholar's world to see, much less to understand, the real world. Yet I doubt, in retrospect, that the rest of us understood it any better.

Wilson provided only one exhibit in Benny's museum of curios. Another was a companion of his youth, a lifelong criminal and a distinguished murderer who, after twenty years of imprisonment, appeared one morning to ask Benny's help. It was given automatically, as always. This man had brought with him a portfolio of dreadful pictures that he had painted in an American jail, and Benny insisted that his friends buy them. They did so until the painter, resuming his old profession, cracked rather too many safes in Victoria and disappeared.

Shortly afterward a wizened little waif with yellow hair falling to his shoulders called on Benny and announced that he was Jesus Christ returning to save the world. In proof of his identity he showed hideous scars on his hands, the nail marks from the cross. Benny said he did not doubt this information but, professing ignorance of theology, sent the visitor to the leading Christian minister of the town. Outraged by such sacrilege, the minister called Benny on the telephone in highest dudgeon.

"Mr. Nicholas," he protested, "you've sent me an imposter!"

"How would you know?" Benny replied. "The last time Jesus came you priests thought He was an imposter and crucified Him."

If Benny ran out of curios he invented them. One night, for example, the readers of the *Times* were puzzled by a short letter to the editor. It said merely that the writer, Mr. L. Puller, had identified a genuine Zipple in the woods outside Victoria. This, Mr. Puller added, was extraordinary since Zipples had never been seen before except in the Andes of South America.

Next day, letters poured in from entomologists, ornithologists, zoologists, biologists, botanists, and cranks, some accepting Mr. Puller's discovery, others declaring that the Zipple was an insect, bird, rodent, or plant which could not possibly live in Victoria's climate. The angry civic debate in the letter column, a welcome relief from war news, raged for a month, with occasional notes of injured innocence from Mr. Puller and solemn protests from his critics.

Benny told us that he had begun to suspect Mr. Puller's veracity. On the other hand, his discovery was too vital in a scientific sense to be ignored. Wilson agreed and spent all his spare time in the provincial library searching for some mention of the Zipple in the books of science. He failed, but insisted that Mr. Puller, by the authentic style of his letter, must be a man of integrity.

At length Wilson's trust was confirmed when he received in a cardboard box the skull of a Zipple, the ultimate proof. Hurrying from the office, he took the evidence to the provincial museum, where he was informed by experts that it was the skull of a cat with the teeth extracted and replaced upside down. Even that verdict did not quite convince Wilson. He still thought that some odious practical joker had tried to discredit Mr. Puller, a man of integrity.

Benny admitted that this might well be so, and most unfortunate from a scientific point of view. And yet, on mature reflection, he had suddenly realized that the initial L. in front of Mr. Puller's signature might stand for Leg. It was just possible that some wretch had indeed pulled Victoria's leg. In a dignified announcement the editor closed the Zipple correspondence.

These whimsies could not long distract Benny from the solitude of his life. He lived with his aged mother, whom he called Tiny, in a dismal apartment and, after office hours, in desperate idleness. Frequently he could be seen sitting on a bench outside the apartment house watching the traffic. Victoria's best-loved citizen, the sage whose advice cabinet ministers and troubled men of every sort were always consulting, knew a loneliness that no man knows until he encounters it himself.

If weather kept him indoors Benny would telephone a drug store and order up magazines, cigars, cigarettes, and chewing gum in wholesale quantities. He was appalled one night by the poverty of the messenger boy and ended by giving his family a little house and furnishing it. Often he would visit the house and play cards with the family, just as he sometimes visited the Lieutenant-Governor's residence, in full evening dress but conveyed by a broken-down Model T taxi, because the driver was an old friend.

Much better than official entertainment were the beach parties at the seaside summer camp of the talented Lugrin family where Benny and I and hordes of guests enjoyed hospitality, friendship, and music. Benny joined eagerly in the concerts around the nightly bonfire and his mellow tenor voice, unheard in his daytime speech, hushed us all as it soared in operatic arias. He also acted with gusto in the Lugrins' homemade theatricals, ad-libbing passionate lines of comedy or tragedy as the plot seemed to indicate. But all such momentary distractions could not assuage Benny's loneliness until instant death at his typewriter finally rescued him.

Through all these busy years he treated me almost as his son, and a second man was doing the same—a very different sort of man, perhaps a wiser but an equally lonesome man, whose imprint on my life, as on many others, would be indelible.

Arriving for the first time in the city police court, I found at the reporter's desk a square, stout, and florid person, the exact facsimile of John Bull in a cartoon, except for a baby's two incongruous dimples on a face of English oak. Percy Rawling was the only son of a prosperous London merchant and, like my father, had left England in his teens to farm on the Canadian Prairies. Then he sailed as a seaman on Pacific liners, worked in the mines of Colorado, became a reporter for the *Denver Post* in its wilder days, covered some historic murder trials in the labor wars, and made friends of some notable men like Clarence Darrow and Eugene Debs.

All this experience turned Percy into a voracious reader of books and a violent radical in politics. But after he had fought in the trenches of France, nearly died in the German gas at Ypres, and dynamited bridges for Lawrence in Arabia, he came back to

Canada a high Tory. Now, for the time being, he was reduced to my status as police-court reporter for the *Colonist*. Why he, a bachelor in his forties, and I, still in my teens, should have taken to each other on sight I cannot tell, but so our friendship began and lasted for three decades until Percy, like Benny, died at his typewriter.

During those years Percy trampled through the thickets of British Columbia journalism with the footsteps of a rogue elephant. His columns of satire and thunderous editorials in the Vancouver *Province* had a distinct craftsman's style of their own, richly flavored by the English classics. They infuriated provincial governments, often shocked the courts, and delighted the public. Percy's conversation, in gasps and gurgles from lungs ruined at Ypres, had the same pungency, a faint touch of Cockney accent, and a pagan's frequent quotes from the Bible. His political views held all reformers in laughing contempt.

"Your bloody Liberal politicians," he would say, as if I owned them personally, "keep on blatherin' about progress. Progress? Ha! Nothing but another indigestion cramp in some politician's gut. Economics? Just a lot of silly little men who don't even understand their silly little business."

After gasping and gurgling to catch his breath he would add, with dimpled solemnity, "Remember, my boy, everywhere and always the Liberals sold the pass. And they all claim a special and sublime virtue not because they've done anything useful, of course, but because, by God, their morals are better than ours. Their morals! Ha! Like a man who says he's moral because he never once murdered his poor old mother. And it would have been a good idea if he had, too, before she bred any more of those Liberal bastards."

Since the German gas had totally destroyed his sense of smell and left him with little sense of taste, he relished strong cheese, spicy viands, and neat rum. Best of all he liked to buy monstrous beefsteaks and "chump" chops from his personal butcher and wartime comrade, who, under his anxious scrutiny, cut them to precise dimensions for cooking over a beach fire by preference while Percy waited and drooled with anticipation.

Impatient and clumsy in everything, he drove his automobile at manic speed, often wrecking it, and for reasons unexplained chose me as his travelling companion, protégé, and confidant. Later, when I was married, my house was his refuge, my wife almost his daughter, my children his own. Visiting us, he always brought, in place of the conventional candy or flowers, a huge roast of beef or mutton and warned us, as we fell into endless argument: "If you don't treat me right, you young devils, I'm leavin', and don't think I won't take my roast with me, either." The argument was usually ferocious but he never left with his roast. And for all his profanity I never heard him utter an obscene word.

In public speeches, however, he could be brutal. Presiding at a banquet of his fellow war veterans, he introduced the city's chief magistrate, and leading undertaker, as "that natural-born, enthusiastic young body snatcher, His Worship the Mayor of Victoria" (who walked out of the meeting in a tantrum, just as Percy had intended).

His journalism, his friends, and his constant journeys could not assuage his loneliness. When he would never join our family for Christmas and, instead, boarded a train, dined alone at a Chinese joint in Kamloops, and took the next train back to Vancouver, it seemed to us that his life, like the universe, held a mystery, perhaps an irreparable grief.

These things did not cross my teen-age mind while we were on the police beat together. Besides, I was soon promoted to the City Hall, with the munificent wage of twenty dollars a week. There I became a close friend of Charles Shaw, nephew and main support of the Lugrin family, a tall, blond youth and my competitor from the *Colonist*, who had a bright future ahead of him. We contended mightily for civic scoops, wrote mischievous letters to the city council over false signatures, sponsored bogus plans for new industries in Victoria, and solemnly reported the Council's resulting hope and disappointment.

Though irresponsible and unscrupulous, Charlie and I worked hard, and both of us were earning much more than our weekly wage. Charlie had established a wide network of newspaper correspondence and mine was growing, too. My highly colored accounts of the Pacific Coast rum-running industry, then at its peak with frequent hijack battles and sometimes murder, found their way into various American newspapers, even the prestigious *New York World*, illustrated by rude pen-and-ink drawings. The years of toil to make myself a cartoonist had begun to pay off at last.

The pay was small, generally about five dollars at most for a feature piece, but working almost every night at home I wrote and drew enough to double my regular wage. At this time also I wrote my first brief news items for the *Christian Science Monitor,* becoming, later on, its national Canadian correspondent. My happy association with one of the world's greatest and kindliest papers was to last for the next fifty-four years.

Until the Armistice of November 11, 1918, I had expected, like other youths, to join the army on my eighteenth birthday in the following year. But having no appetite for heroism, then or ever, I was glad to escape that duty. All the current guarantees of enduring peace, prosperity, and Wilsonian democracy I swallowed, as most people did, without question. The Russian Revolution had not disturbed me either, since it was well known that there would be no revolution in America, that Communism never worked anywhere, and that the Bolsheviks were demented. It was also known, and widely noted in the press, that the Russians, by their hereditary nature, had no grasp of business, could not manage modern industry, nor operate any machine more complicated than a wheelbarrow; just as it was obvious that the even more backward Chinese could not fight with weapons more dangerous than firecrackers.

Thus began, in Victoria as elsewhere, the democratic world's twilight sleep between two wars, my own repose unbroken by any doubts. No man who did not live through the ensuing two decades can now understand how anyone then alive failed to see their sheer hallucination. But things appeared quite rational to us, and improving all the time.

From the pit of war the world climbed to the heights of the Bull Market, the silk-shirt era, the triumph of Capitalism, the boom eternal long planned by a wise Providence.

It is impossible now, when events move at the speed of sound, almost of light, to understand the leisurely time frame of the 1920s, a movie in slow motion. We did not hurry, since, in North America anyhow, we occupied the best of all possible worlds, constantly repaired its few lingering defects, and never for a moment suspected that revolution was already moving fast everywhere, obvious but invisible.

In such times the proper pursuit for any young man was to make money, better himself, and thus automatically better society at large. I welcomed that chance with unlimited expectations. The bruising poverty of my childhood, the remembered scars of humiliation, and the will to succeed must have given me a fierce energy which compensated, in part at least, for my lack of schooling. Ignorance, as I now see, was really a kind of asset. With a little more knowledge I would have realized that even my modest ambitions were impossible and not worth pursuing. Oblivious of my liabilities, I earned money wherever I could in a business scandalously underpaid.

At any rate, I was having fun and by the autumn of 1920 had miraculously saved five hundred dollars, had bought two expensive suits of clothes, at the price of thirty-five dollars each, and thus affluently outfitted, I made my first trip to the east since boyhood.

In Ottawa I inspected the new Centre Block without guessing that it would soon be my workshop. In Boston all my luggage and the second suit were stolen from a friend's automobile. In New York I had enough sense, or timidity, to refuse a job on the

World at the incredible wage of fifty dollars a week and that night, soaked with rain, watched in Times Square the bulletins announcing President Harding's election on a promise of "normalcy". In Washington I spent a day, and the rest of my money, seeing the sights from a rubberneck bus, awed by the stone façade of a capital never to be penetrated by the likes of me. Still, I must have learned something from my trip, and I arrived home broke but satisfied.

6

The Gothic Hill

Some funny things happened on my way to Mackenzie King's arcanum, to the journalism of politics, and to a series of unlikely accidents. The first accident, fortunate for me but not for him, was the late Kenneth Drury's illness while covering the British Columbia Legislature's annual session. Mumps, an odd arbiter of men's destinies, laid my colleague low and suddenly raised me up, far above my capacity and experience.

Obviously unfit for such an assignment at the age of twenty, I was dispatched as Ken's substitute to the legislative buildings in January 1921. There I would remain on and off for some twenty sessions — a dreary apprenticeship, but since I soon ceased to regard politics as more than a livelihood, that incarceration did not vex me. Besides, it was relieved by still more fortunate accidents in Ottawa.

Of British Columbia's public business in those days much was written, probably more by me than by my competitors because I worked intermittently for half a dozen papers. In later years, when the westernmost province had been accepted as a possibly significant though mysterious particle in the Canadian mosaic, many serious books were published to show why it became what it is or what it is usually, and often mistakenly, supposed to be. But the politicians described in these books are unrecognizable to a reporter who knew them as daily intimates.

Observed from the narrow roost of the press gallery, the lawmakers seemed very great men, at least to me. In the beginning I overrated, and after more intimacy underrated, them. I could not know until I had seen it for myself in wider arenas that politics, from the village council to the White House, the Mother of Parliaments, or the Kremlin, was the same struggle of ambitious men against one another and, generally in vain, against events beyond any man's control. The president, prime minister, or communist dictator is only the town alderman with some acquired skills, an extra gloss, and above all a bit of luck. And either man, at the bottom or at the summit, is equally frustrated by the nature of his trade, the cussedness of his clients, and the perversity of humankind.

My trade, too, is essentially the same in any place or time, be it in Egypt when hieroglyphics were used or at a present-day press conference on television. But the working habits have changed. When the Legislature was in session we worked from early morning to midnight, sometimes to dawn, pouring out interminable, dull reports on momentous issues like the scandals of the liquor business, the bankrupt Pacific Great Eastern Railway, and the never-ending feud between provincial and federal governments.

The modern Canadian who deplores the regionalism of his country cannot imagine how insular, prejudiced, and hermetic were Canada's regions half a century ago, or how their inhabitants enjoyed a life not yet informed, sophisticated, or improved, since they had tasted nothing better. We who reported it never doubted that society (a highbrow word seldom heard then) was steadily advancing, with progress ordained and inevitable.

That the reverse would happen, and only a few years hence, occurred to few men, assuredly not to me. So, full of faith and self-importance, I mass-produced the day's copy on my personal assembly line and, in addition, a signed column of supposedly acute analysis, wit, and color. For which I was paid a wage finally reaching the dizzy maximum of forty-two dollars a week.

In one all-night performance I wrote the reports for five separate papers when my senior colleagues had not yet recovered from a Conservative Party banquet. Surrounded by their sleeping bodies, I finished the job about eight o'clock in the morning, with the necessary false signatures to deceive the editors and the partisan slant required by each in his impartial news columns.

So far I had avoided drink altogether for reasons not of morality but of caution and had attracted some reproach, or sympathy, on that score. A teetotaller in journalism or politics was regarded with suspicion as a freak or a secret drunkard.

For similar reasons I also declined the funds freely distributed by the lobbyists of business. My attitude was considered unfair and uppity, if not subversive. Such rewards, nowadays unthinkable, were taken as a matter of course by honest men who were to be trusted absolutely in private affairs. One of them, in a later book of recollections, explained that I had refused to "participate" only because I earned so much money otherwise, not by talent but by toil. His interpretation, though hardly flattering, may be accurate.

By modern standards the lobbyists' fees were pathetically small. So were the returns on their investment. So, too, were the campaign funds, the graft and booty of politics before governments learned to bribe the voters with their own taxes on a scale that the frugal frontier politicians would envy. Anyhow, the newspaper proprietors had small right to complain when they paid starvation wages to reporters and much more to printers.

The contemporary proprietor of the *Times* once amazed us with a prodigal Christmas bonus of twenty-five dollars. A few days afterwards it was discovered that he, as a trusted accountant, had been systematically defrauding a department store to the total of about a million dollars. A minute fraction of this loot was generously shared with his employees. The store appropriated the *Times* and the embezzler went to jail, but none of us returned the stolen bonus. It was never repeated.

Poor as newspapermen were, they knew how to enjoy themselves. On one occasion, for example, we organized a splendid

Press Club ball in the Empress Hotel and hired a broken-down actor to disguise himself in rags and whiskers, make a revolutionary communist speech, and thus create a pleasant diversion.

The results surpassed our highest expectations — part of the crowd physically assaulting the revolutionist, part defending him, the ballroom turned to shambles, the ladies' dresses torn, gentlemen heaped and bleeding on the floor, police rushing in to stem the riot, Charlie Shaw and I, authors of this innocent merriment, watching it safely from the sidelines, unscathed, unsuspected, and well pleased with our devilish work.

An even more splendid occasion, indeed an event of international solemnity, was sponsored by the provincial government to mark the resumption of liquor sales in British Columbia after wartime Prohibition, and to entertain the still deprived legislators of Washington State.

The guests and their ladies arrived at the Union Club in full evening dress and with a prolonged thirst, soon quenched by the government's preliminary cocktails. No pain was visible as the eminent assemblage seated itself around a vast and glittering table in celebration of the ancient friendship between Canada and the United States. All the arrangements were perfect, the food delicious, the wines of finest vintage. Predictably, but, alas, unpredicted, the fraternal spirit could not be contained.

Senator J. W. de B. Farris, British Columbia's peerless orator, rising to deliver a message worthy of the continental brotherhood and howled down by rival orators; John Oliver, host and premier, who drank no alcohol, surveying the scene in unbelief and horror, his white beard twitching; a distinguished statesman from the northern hinterland bestriding the table to make his voice heard above the tumult, collapsing among the broken glasses, face and hands cut, his blood staining the white napery; carried insensible across the street to his room in the hotel where his jovial friends summoned an undertaker who removed the corpse, to wake with a scream next morning on a marble slab; the ladies in the club leaping up, one after the other, with squeaks of alarm as if mouse-bitten; an esteemed labor member of the Legislature found crawling under the table to pinch female legs and, forcibly ejected, sleeping peacefully in the gutter of Humboldt Street; Charlie and I, cold sober, viewing our betters in judicious neutrality and reporting their behavior with a decent minimum of truth — so ended a night of unrecorded North American history.

Five years of such diverse preparation convinced me that I was well equipped for higher tasks in Ottawa and a first close sight of the Prime Minister. In that January of 1925 William Lyon Mackenzie King had just passed his fiftieth birthday. He was in his physical and mental prime but, as yet unconsciously, was sliding toward ruin. At the age of twenty-four I was the youngest member of the Press Gallery, the hardest-working, and the luckiest. For within three months would come the greatest blessing of my life.

The diminutive figure behind the big desk in the Centre Block was not the Mackenzie King remembered by most living Canadians. Instead of the pale and shrivelled personage of his later years, I faced a brisk, cheerful, twinkling man who already, as he thought, had made the world of Canada his undisputed dominion.

He was short, corpulent, and bald, with a single wisp of damp hair plastered across his forehead. The face looked featureless, puddinglike, and weak. The back of the protuberant neck swelled above the stiff collar. But King's tailor had done his best with a difficult subject. The black suit, in the antique style which never changed, fitted perfectly. The long, starched cuffs almost covered the plump little hands, as delicate and soft as a woman's.

Oddly enough, it is those hands that I remember best from the first of our many meetings — hands so often clasped in prayer, hands of a physician, as King would assert in the time of Canada's future sickness, hands of a high destiny, the mundane tools of Providence, as he believed, or hands of a conjurer as his helpless enemies protested.

The voice, too, was memorable — so mild, low-pitched, and modest, as the smile was boyish, shy, deferential; the whole manner ingratiating and, in a fashion never observed by the public, quite charming. At least I was charmed and, of course, immensely flattered. For I had yet to learn that King, among his numerous arts, was a supreme artist of flattery, as he was also a subtle manipulator of other men's decisions (though seldom of their affections) and, if need be, a master of sudden butchery.

Even now the busy Prime Minister could take an hour to beguile an unknown young reporter, only because the remote *Victoria Daily Times* might come in useful some day. No stone of politics was too small for King to turn in an election year, no potential supporter too insignificant to be baited with favors and glued with birdlime.

Today he was laying on the birdlime with a trowel and his trick of apparent candor easily ensnared a new-hatched fledgling. To serve his immediate purpose, King talked at length, with frequent sighs, about the increasing difficulties of government, the nation's grave problems, so little understood, the Conservative Party's irresponsible criticism. Of that harangue, so long ago, I recall only one observation, much more revealing than I could then understand. It was a great mistake, King said, for a political party to define its policy in detail and "give the other fellows a target to shoot at". Even this brief lapse into practical politics was disguised with a kind of virtue, as if a surgeon might be forced to touch some corrupt organ before he could cure it. When Liberalism must sometimes stoop to conquer, then, I gathered, it stooped only for noble ends, the public good. Assuredly King had not committed, and would never commit, the mistake of clarity. If I had known it, as of course I did not, he was already blurring the too-detailed platform which his party had declared in choosing him (with serious misgivings) as its leader. And within the crafty blending apparatus of his mind, or intuition, he had begun to reverse Canadian Liberalism, to stand all its principles upside down — a process requiring some twenty years for completion and not to be understood by old-fashioned Liberals until long after that, too late for a second reversal.

In this first talk I could suspect none of these things but I would never change my original impression of King, even when the effects of his flattery had worn off. While most of the Press Gallery held him in contempt, expecting his early departure, I judged him a great Prime Minister, despite his cant and humbug, his subtlety, his womanish manners, and his flaccid look. So the future would prove (though it could never prove him a great human being).

For the Prime Minister it was a time of political pause and quiet reflection, almost somnolence, as he digested at leisure the remnants of the Progressive Party, the farmers' revolt against his Liberal Party in the West, and planned an easy autumn election sure to give his minority government the majority denied to him in 1921.

For me it was a hard and lonesome time but it would quickly end. I had certain plans, more reliable than King's, which contained the one vital element of any man's happiness beyond King's reach or desire, perhaps his comprehension.

Having come to Ottawa as the correspondent of the *Victoria Daily Times* and the *Vancouver Star*, at the enormous wage of seventy-five dollars a week, I found a cheap, dark, ghastly room on an alley near Bank Street in a resort infested mainly by vaudeville actors and their women, a single bathroom serving a score of denizens. My meals were also cheap, thanks to the Canadian taxpayer. For thirty-five cents I could buy an ample and nourishing, if somewhat revolting, meal well below its subsidized cost in the parliamentary cafeteria, known then as the Doggery. Once a week, on pay day, I might venture into the luxurious restaurant upstairs where Members of Parliament ate and schemed. But even with the taxpayer's unwitting contribution the restaurant price was a whole dollar, too much for me.

The Press Gallery was equally forbidding — a jealous fraternity of strict written rules and even stricter unwritten ones. This club, which claimed to be the most exclusive in Canada, regarded all newcomers with suspicion and me with a mixture of pity, astonishment, and contempt, no doubt well deserved. The workroom overlooking the frozen Ottawa River and the white Gatineau Hills would later become congested and desks would spill into the adjoining corridor, but in 1925 it housed only about twenty correspondents. Few of them seemed to do much work, the rest being engaged elsewhere in confidential conclave with the nation's rulers.

Alex Carisse, a dark little French Canadian, who was called the chief page but functioned as the high priest of the sanctuary, treated me with kindness. He provided a desk and explained that the times were more than usually dull, that nothing of importance would occur, and that little news need be written. He also assigned me a seat in the gallery of the Commons and, since I was an alleged Liberal, placed me directly above the Prime Minister.

From this vantage point I watched and reported day by day the ceaseless, savage duel between King and Arthur Meighen, which would spawn some of the gaudiest myths in Canadian history. Of course I did not then see, nor did anyone else, the meaning of the duel — the groping, inchoate social revolution foreseen by King before he was ready to proclaim or understand it; the counter-revolution and stubborn retreat personalized by Meighen, who knew exactly what he was trying to do but failed to see that he was already defeated—not by the fat little man across the aisle but by anonymous forces that neither yet understood.

The First World War had ended some six years before. The second was only fourteen years ahead. In the interval would come the Great Depression to shatter old fantasies and create new ones. Before the next twenty months had passed Canada would face two elections, the first apparently destroying King, the second finally destroying Meighen and raising constitutional issues still unsettled today. None of these events was visible, or imaginable, to either man, the Press Gallery, Parliament, or public. All we saw from the gallery was the lethal contest of two ambitious politicians, the Liberal with his spongy intuitions, the Conservative with his iron facts.

Meighen stood lean, haggard, motionless, a solitary eagle poised for the kill. His hands were locked together as if the prey were not worth any gesture. His voice was calm and metallic, his diction letter-perfect, his sentences sharpened to penetrate like talons, his arguments marshalled clause by clause in neat syllogism, his irony corrosive, his loathing of King naked, contemptuous, and self-destructive.

As Meighen spoke I could look straight down on King and watch a clear line of red ascend from the white collar to diffuse the bulging neck and spread slowly over the bald skull. The face was placid and expressionless but the tiny right hand tapped the stub of a pencil on the desk, an unmistakable symptom of inner fury. When the eagle had resumed his perch the Prime Minister would rise, fluttering and fussing like a sparrow, to deliver one of those ponderous, shapeless, labyrinthine speeches that had no beginning, no middle, almost no end. But King knew exactly what he was trying to do. He was buying time, waiting for the nation's politics to settle down, for the enemy to be consumed in his own flames. So, with King's inconceivable break of luck, the future would unfold, but not as either man expected.

Meanwhile, what were they debating? The old tariff, which never changed, except in minor detail; the old railway problem, which defied all satisfactory solution; a budget considered alarmingly high at about half a billion dollars; the grimy household minutiae of a nation that must soon face catastrophe, economic and military.

To the youngest reporter in the gallery the duel looked stupendous, the duellists like Titans bearing on shoulders immense the too vast orb of Canada's fate. Night after night, bearing my own load of notes and history, I hurried back to the press room and wrote dispatches as tangled and verbose as King's speeches. This sprawling copy seemed to suit my editors well enough. For in those days the newspapers reported Parliament seriously and at length, as the public demanded. They had yet to yield coverage of the Commons' long arguments to the slick, misleading capsules of television, while the decline of parliamentary institutions was regularly deplored on every editorial page.

My work was sloppy, weary, and lonely but I had nothing better to do. At eight o'clock in the morning, an hour before anyone else appeared, I would eat in the Doggery and begin a day that usually ended at midnight or later. Then, for air and exercise, I walked the empty streets alone until I seemed to recognize every building, store front, and tree in a capital not yet a city, little more than Colonel By's lumber village somewhat enlarged around the granite towers of Parliament.

Still, I was learning some things never recorded in *Hansard* or the official bluebooks. I was learning that much more than politics, personalities, or passing events colored and conditioned the ambience of Parliament Hill. Long as I would know this place I could not give a name to its peculiar emanation, a kind of flavor and seasoning almost palpable, with strange effects on all the inhabitants below the level of their conscious minds.

In part, I suppose, it was physical—the government buildings always warm, lighted, polished, and primped amid the bleak surrounding world of cold and dark, the odor of mellow oak and chaste stone, the feeling of comfort and security once you had passed through the bronze doors. In part it was mental — the sense of fellowship among a privileged élite, of isolation from the town and the harsh country beyond it, democracy present in speech and ritual, far off and harmless in fact.

Physically and mentally the Centre Block was a hothouse and nothing that grew there could escape its spell. The spell, of course, was synthetic and spurious but it penetrated everyone, just as hothouse flowers protected against the outside temperature grow rank and flabby on their artificial diet. So, too, must the Ottawa politician, unless he absents himself from Ottawa's felicity awhile to brave the real world and relearn the lessons of common humanity lost on his march up the Hill.

At this pinnacle, it is said, every motion of the public mind, every throb of the body politic, every passing mood of the nation will be registered by fine antennae—nowadays by opinion polls, computers, and that dubious something called "input". Then, automatically, the people's will must be served (as if the people themselves ever understood their own will, as if that will, when sometimes known, were always wise). But the democratic mechanism so elaborately contrived and generally feared seldom works that way. The barriers between governors and governed, though invisible and unadmitted, are as thick and muffled as the ramparts of the Hill. Or so it seems to me, and I never knew a man who lived for even a single parliamentary term behind those walls without a change in his disposition, for better or worse. The hothouse changes them all.

Despite my isolation among the isolated, I soon made two friendships to outlast this brief exile.

Grant Dexter had arrived a year earlier as correspondent of the *Winnipeg Free Press*, with Alice, his lovely young bride, and already had begun to alarm his competitors. A tall, rosy-faced, and outgoing youth of demonic energies, he had survived the European war, attracted the interest of the great editor John W. Dafoe, and was about to become the ablest political reporter that Ottawa had ever known and perhaps would ever know.

With his life, until its premature end, mine would be intimately fused. At first, however, he took little notice of me and regarded the Pacific Coast press as unworthy of any serious reader (which, at that time, may have been true). Only once was I in his home for dinner and then to meet another little-known man named J. S. Woodsworth, whose socialism was anathema to Grant, his character and lifelong affection very precious.

Arthur Irwin, also a veteran of the war and now correspondent of the Toronto *Globe*, a lean, silent, and superbly tailored fellow, was harder to know, his opinions sunk in a deep well to spill out, with sudden vehemence, at unexpected moments.

Though his desk stood next to mine, he gave me, every morning, no more than a passing nod. I thought him pompous and rather intimidating. But the real man soon emerged. Within a month we had struck up a friendship that continued for half a century while his extraordinary career of journalism and diplomacy was propelled by a rare analytical gift, a dry sense of humor, and a warmth of affection known only to his few intimates.

Charlie Bishop was then the gallery's acknowledged sachem, philosopher, and mayor of the palace. A short, swarthy man of genial deportment, soft speech, and flawless memory, he had reached a great age, more than forty years. Alone among the Anglos, he spoke perfect French and consorted with the Quebec correspondents, who remained at their own end of the room, polite but insulated—the fact of *deux nations* thus demonstrated in journalism as elsewhere and taken for granted on both sides. Serving a dozen papers from Halifax to Vancouver, Charlie seldom left his desk. Always in shirt sleeves, he scribbled with a pencil from morning to midnight and was said to earn almost twelve thousand dollars a year, though that figure seemed unbelievably high. At last Charlie's amazing energies ran out. Late in life, King recognized a true Liberal and appointed him to the Senate.

The same ultimate haven awaited Grattan O'Leary, whose energies were even greater, his writing more brilliant, and his mind already set in unshakable, and quite unattainable, Conservatism, as taught by his closest friend, Meighen. At least these two men knew the meaning of their ideology, as most of their contemporary successors do not. Grattan had left the gallery to edit the *Ottawa Journal* but he often visited his old haunt, rushing like a fireman on the way to a fire, emitting his own sparks of Irish wit, and naturally ignoring outlanders like Arthur and me, who had yet to earn his friendship or perceive the sweep of his romantic imagination.

Another occasional visitor to the gallery seemed far beyond my range and I did not venture to approach him. T. A. Crerar, a huge, muscular man with a shock of reddish hair and a sun-tanned prairie face, had led the Progressive Party in 1921 and abandoned politics for business permanently, as he believed. Neither of us then foresaw that we would be intimates in his final years, and mine. He soon entered King's government, as he had entered Robert Borden's during the first war, to represent the angry West, but the breach of disposition and principle between Crerar and his new leader could never be closed. I had yet to learn that cabinet solidarity, the core of the governing system, was in fact an endless civil war thinly disguised by official oaths of secrecy.

Three months thus passed in a blur of faces, speeches, gossip, and worthless copy from my typewriter. The humdrum was punctuated, once only, by that supreme annual rite, the Press Gallery dinner, of which I can still vividly recall the unreported spectacle of King and Meighen, suddenly relaxed, and standing on a desk, arm in arm, and singing "My Old Kentucky Home", not very well but in fair harmony.

To me these were three months of solitary waiting as the snow left the Gatineau Hills, the ice broke on the river, and Parliament's lawn turned green. Having already made the largest and wisest decision that any man can make, I awaited the second party to the contract.

7

The Land

My bride arrived in Ottawa from Vancouver on the early morning train. At noon, on April 12, 1925, we were married in the dark vestry of an Elgin Street church by a kindly, threadbare minister who finished the business in five minutes, wished us well, and gratefully accepted my extravagant honorarium of five dollars for his services. Only Arthur Irwin and an elderly widow, a friend of our family, attended as witnesses. The wedding, though legal, was not romantic but it united two peculiarly innocent youngsters beyond any chance of separation.

About things that concern him most, a man says the least. Here I say for the factual record that we were happy as only young lovers can be and so continued until our last years together. According to the Christian contract and, far beyond it, by our free choice, we forsook all others. Besides Dorothy Kidd McDiarmid there was no woman in my life, before or after our marriage, nor any man, except me, in hers.

Not alone in my retrospective judgment of more than fifty years, but in the common, unprejudiced opinion of our friends, Dot (no one ever called her anything else) was always superior to me in the decisive qualities of strength, generosity, and, above all, courage. Nothing frightened her when I was often afraid. No one disliked her when I was often disliked. With less worldly information and more wisdom, her perceptions were clearer than mine.

Things that I could not see Dot saw, or felt, at once, often before they happened. She had intuitions and psychic hunches lacking in my nature. Difficulties and embarrassments that I postponed or evaded she confronted directly and bluntly, unable to tell the whitest lie even if it would have been convenient and harmless. My charities, such as they were, leaned toward prudence, hers toward rashness. She commanded wider friendships and deeper affections than I could hope to earn because she gave more, to everybody. If the partnership was tilted in my favor, as our friends and children well knew, we depended absolutely on each other. Without Dot at its centre life could not mean much to me. That discovery was a long way off as we started on a honeymoon to Quebec and, returning to Ottawa, installed ourselves in a third-rate apartment on Charlotte Street. But our arrangements were not made lightly or ill-advisedly.

Two years had passed since our first meeting. I had undertaken the purchase of some ten acres of farm land in Saanich and the construction of a house; I had even fenced the property with my own hands and hired a man to plow a garden patch. At the time, these rather grandiose plans, far exceeding our visible means, were launched with little thought of consequences more enduring than our immediate debts. Unknowingly, we acted by guess and gamble, youth's special prerogative. Without facts or sufficient money Dot and I made the right decisions on the few things that really mattered. As against them all our countless mistakes counted for nothing.

She had been brought up in circumstances more fortunate than mine. Her people came from English stock on her mother's side and Scottish on her father's. The McDiarmids were an old Ontario family with many clergymen and much book learning on both sides. Dot's great-great-grandfather, John Decew, fought for his King in the American Revolution and, as a United Empire Loyalist, departed the new Republic. He built part of the original Welland Canal, the first flour mill on a tributary of the Niagara River, and, beside it, the massive stone house where Laura Secord brought the news of the American attack at Beaver Dams, on June 24, 1813. This ancestral history was a source of quiet pride in the family.

The McDiarmids were prosperous, too, as my family was not. Frederick Armand McDiarmid, a young lawyer out of Osgoode Hall, settled in Lindsay with his bride, Edith, whose maiden name had been Kidd and who was generally worshipped as Muzzie. Two sons, Neil and Harry, who would both fight as airmen in the First World War, and a daughter, who would be my wife, were born in Lindsay, Dot three months after my own birth not far away. Later the family moved to Victoria where F.A. (his invariable nickname) was the city solicitor and lived in high style, even owning a Cadillac of early vintage.

Such folk, though their home in Oak Bay stood only a mile or so from ours on Wilmer Street, were far outside my narrow circle. As a boy I sometimes saw Dot on the streetcar or in the skating rink but never met her until we were both twenty-three years old, and then by mere chance at the Victoria Tennis Club. We played badly but agreed to meet again. After that our future was set.

By now F.A. had moved his household to Vancouver and become a leading authority on municipal law, while Dot had spent a year with friends in China. He was a short, stocky man of square, determined jaw, deep erudition, and reckless liberality.

In features and temperament his daughter closely resembled him and he adored her. Of me he took a somewhat dim view when I first appeared at his camp on Shawnigan Lake, Vancouver Island. A cub reporter from the *Victoria Daily Times* was scarcely a fit husband for his darling. However, he soon adjusted himself to the inevitable, silently approved our engagement, and became my friend in the brief time left to him. That accommodation took Muzzie a little longer because, no doubt, her hopes were higher. But she also was reconciled and ended her widowed life, with everyone's devotion, in our home.

After the parliamentary session in Ottawa, Dot and I returned to Victoria for good. While I went back to my old job at the *Times*, we established ourselves in a wretched flat until we could build a house on our land in Saanich. As its site we had chosen a rocky slope clothed with oaks overlooking the blue line of the Sooke

Hills. But that house was never to be built. Except for the oaks, the thick moss, the wild lilies, and the spoor of wandering children, those rocks remain today exactly as the last ice age left them.

All our plans were changed when we realized that my parents needed us in their old age as, for the present, we needed them. By this time my father had escaped from the misery of the civil service and expanded his Wilmer Street garden into a plant nursery where gardeners of educated taste found exotic specimens from distant countries. He imported many rare seeds, sprouted them, talked to his plants, and was sure that they responded. Now he wanted more land for his business and we owned it.

Accordingly, our affairs were settled by a temporary arrangement. My parents' town house was sold for less than it had cost, a frightening mortgage of two thousand dollars negotiated, and a small bungalow planned for all of us in a grassy hollow between two miniature mountains sheltering it from the Pacific gales. A second house, for Dot and me, would be built when we could afford it, but the temporary arrangement proved to be permanent.

Two wonderful old Scottish carpenters undertook to build the bungalow at wages of seven dollars a day, with fifty cents for bus fare, and they saved that extra amount by riding four miles from town on bicycles. A still more wonderful workman whom we knew only as Dick the Digger, then past his eightieth year and barely five feet high, excavated the basement. All by himself, with shovel, pick, and wheelbarrow, he dug a hole ten feet deep while steadily chewing tobacco, swallowing the juice and fatally poisoning himself, but not until he had reached ninety. For the whole job he charged fifty dollars. On receipt of this fee he enjoyed his customary interlude of alcoholic recuperation.

My father, meanwhile, had established his new nursery on the old farm meadow and filled the crevices of the twin mountains with leaf mould and rock plants. Soon cascades of bloom were spilling down the rocks. Alpine gardening was too fancy for Dot and me. We planted vegetables and fruit trees in the black bottom land, with native Douglas firs on the boundary lines. Those seedlings are now three feet in diameter, first-class peeler logs, too valuable to be left much longer in peace. Some plywood factory doubtless will slice them up one of these days when the last remaining planter is gone.

By the autumn of 1926 Dot and I had used sledge hammer and cold chisel to break rocks and make a driveway from the twisting country lane. The bungalow was completed and we all moved in. Without Dot's calm authority this mixed household could not have survived, even as a temporary arrangement. Without her firm direction and laughing acceptance of their eccentricities my parents would have been quite lost. They gladly acknowledged her jurisdiction, their years of worry behind them. The only problem was to pay the bills.

We solved it by outdoor extravagance and indoor thrift. I was earning enough to cover our rising expenses and my father contributed his share from the thriving nursery. He had never been so prosperous and content. Against all his prejudices, we persuaded the old horseman to buy and drive a second-hand Model T Ford until it mounted the sidewalk on Douglas Street and moved, with slow dignity, through the plate-glass window of the Strathcona Hotel. After that he abandoned machinery and travelled to his club in town by bus.

Dot and I already had abandoned our plans for a separate house. When those two Scottish carpenters (now earning lavish wages of eight dollars a day) had added a new wing, a workroom for me, and a second storey, our joint house was almost complete. All it lacked was a third generation, which in due time began to arrive—Joan Edith, a boisterous daughter, and, two years afterward, Robert Bruce, a tranquil son. Throughout the long years ahead they never failed us, or their own children.

The six inhabitants of the house we had named Rockhome filled it with work, merriment, and friends. These were the best years of our lives and like Keats's autumnal bees we thought warm days would never cease. The Bull Market, near its peak in Wall Street, raised false hopes even in our remote neighborhood. The nursery was making good profits. The mortgage had been paid off. Every month Dot, as general manager, saved a hundred dollars for an insurance fund that would enable us to retire by middle age on a handsome monthly pension of thrice that amount. Inflation was then a foreign disease and North America immune to it.

Thus housed, landed, debt-free, and healthy, we flourished, the outside world well lost. But the world of urban sprawl was rapidly advancing upon us from Victoria and the distant world of nations had begun to disintegrate, all unnoticed by its governors.

Comfortable as it seemed, our snug establishment demanded much work. Before eight o'clock in the morning I was at my regular job in the *Times* and the job had doubled in scope. Besides Benny's paper I now represented the Vancouver *Province* at the legislative buildings. Its greatest editor, the legendary Roy Brown, a tall man of pink, boyish face and snow-white hair, had employed me with no instructions except his invariable maxim and working method. I should write, he said, "good newspaper stuff".

In hugger-mugger fashion I tried to satisfy him. Day after day the petty politics of British Columbia supplied all the news stories I could handle. Night after night I drew my crude political cartoons, most of them identified by a fictitious signature to avoid embarrassment when I met the libelled politicians, who never suspected my second incarnation as their libellers.

I often followed these men on election tours, seldom listening to their speeches because I knew the texts by heart. But when the federal Opposition leader, Mackenzie King, came to Victoria in 1926 after his ruinous Customs Scandal and fall from office, I listened to every word of his two-hour speech, took them all down in shorthand, and wrote until seven o'clock next morning.

His constitutional argument had cut little ice with the voters, so far as I could see. Nor could Meighen when he came to town.

The newly appointed and doomed Prime Minister was worn out by then. He had overslept in the Empress Hotel and, aroused late, appeared unshaven, haggard, and half awake on the steps of the legislative buildings to repeat before an expectant crowd the familiar ridicule of his last, disastrous campaign. Even in this state he was deadly. His description of King, who had clung to office until the eleventh hour, as "a lobster with lockjaw" and his dismissal of King's argument as "constitutional phlebitis" sounded great. With such eloquent acid he must surely win.

Or so he assumed, and so did I, with scant interest in the election, one way or the other. For less than half my mind and energy was now focused on politics and journalism, the larger part on our Saanich place and the McDiarmids' camp beside Shawnigan Lake. My two bosses, strictly urban creatures, supposed that my interest in the farmland and the forest was a week-end hobby, a whim soon to pass. I did not enlighten them. With practice and bland subterfuge I learned to combine my opposite pursuits in a rough but workable synthesis.

Benny having given me a column on his editorial page, I filled it most days with reports, sometimes faintly accurate, of events in the countryside and the lives of our defenceless neighbors. Conspicuous among them was a lady of stupendous girth, scarlet cheeks, magnificent headgear awash in fading silk roses, and a cockney accent almost intelligible, whom I met on the bus and christened Mrs. Alfred Noggins in print. Happily she never read the columns of political comment attributed to her when, too cowardly to express such outrageous opinions myself, I put them into her mouth and she became something of a celebrity. Then there was a person named Horace Snifkin whose erratic affairs and wild speculations so closely resembled mine that the most unsuspecting reader must have seen through this dual personality.

My worst mischief, however, was wreaked on my own children

by a kind of domestic parasitism, even literary cannibalism. But The Little Girl and Boy from Next Door (a weak disguise) were still illiterate and heard nothing of the speech and follies ascribed to them for public entertainment. These columns of gossamer and semi-truth, whipped up in half an hour, were, I think, the best stuff I ever produced and the least remembered.

Saanich was not my only source of fiction. Easier material was provided by our camp at Shawnigan Lake. In the beginning it comprised one narrow waterfront lot and a cottage so dark that coal-oil lamps were lighted on cloudy days before F.A. could read his ponderous law books. He had bought the property because his doctor recommended the curative mountain air and, lacking any carpenter's instincts, made no improvements. If he had books, tobacco, a canoe, and a fishing line, he asked nothing more. Muzzie, a woman of beaming good will for all mankind, was in a mood of bliss if she could fill multitudes of visitors with *cordon bleu* viands cooked on her rusty stove.

We lived like hardy pioneers. Water was carried from the lake in pails and later by a hand pump, usually out of order. All provisions were lugged on our backs over a half-mile path because we wanted no road to invade our privacy. Dot and I occupied a tent and rose at six in the morning to take a quick swim before I started for the *Times* office, a full hour's drive on a dusty gravel highway.

In the next quarter-century we acquired more land, remodelled the cottage, and with our unskilled hands built an extra cottage for our son, another for our guests, and a little office for me. If these clumsy structures did not quite make me a professional carpenter, stonemason, plumber, and house painter they were more satisfying than any work I did on the typewriter; also more durable.

It was difficult without a telephone to mix the crafts of journalism and physical labor but I managed it by the subtler craft of a chameleon. Once I had ceased to be a reporter and wrote only columns or editorials, my bosses could not be sure where I was or what I was doing. Patient men, they suffered my vagrancy so long as they received daily envelopes of copy and the occasional telephone call from a garage four miles up the road. Clearly, they supposed, I was working hard and I was, too—in the bush.

When I had become the so-called editor of the *Times*, visiting newspapermen were surprised to observe conferences on my homemade stone patio with colleagues who had travelled by canoe and, after strenuous paddling, required Dot's luscious food and stronger stimulants to promote deep editorial thought. Only invaders willing to brave a rugged trail could reach our hermitage by land, but many arrived despite this planned discouragement.

The diverse company, welcome and unwelcome, included youngsters in droves who joined ours and, in later time, brought youngsters of their own; politicians with confidential news to divulge or, more likely, with pleas for sympathy in the press; lawyers searching for Chief Justice J. O. Wilson, my fellow woodcutter and slave, who, in emergencies and overalls, would sometimes issue writs and injunctions from the patio while I waited impatiently for him to resume his higher duty on the cross-cut saw.

Even the great Yousuf Karsh appeared one day in the 1960s with his assistants, his cameras, and a wheelbarrow-load of electrical gadgetry. Assuming that Wilson was the hired camp roustabout, a natural mistake, Yousuf briskly ordered him to act as a stand-in for photographic composition and to hose down the arbutus trees and make them glisten for background effect. Wilson obeyed these commands without a word and not until the pictures were finished did I reveal his identity. Whereupon Yousuf, a gentleman of sensitive manners, could think of nothing to say and drowned his confusion by plunging, fully clothed, into the lake. The Chief Justice remarked only that he would take the Karsh and let the credit go.

Camp life, though known in foreign lands, takes on a redeeming madness peculiarly Canadian, a hunger for the old lost days of the *voyageurs* and *coureurs de bois*. Every urban man, if he has a lick of sense and manhood, considers himself a Radisson or Le Moyne at heart, temporarily in the fell clutch of circumstance, and some men, the better sort, actually break out of their luxurious prisons. By deliberate choice the wealthy tycoon and weekday executive makes himself a week-end mechanic, drudge, and peon. Whence cometh his salvation. A few hours of vigorous woodcutting will anoint the worst sinner with sweat and virtue. Where legislation fails, the camp remains the sure leveller, the clanking, grinding, unfailing engine of democracy, the safety valve of revolution.

But there are still larger contents in a woodland cabin. It holds secret memories, the echoes of voices no longer heard, and friendly phantoms, the freightage and ultimate treasure of a man's life as no city house is likely to hold them. The reason is simple enough. In the wilderness the human creature can be human, do as he pleases, and, with all the city disguises stripped off, reveal himself to himself and others. Here the truth, pleasant or unpleasant, emerges nakedly.

Here, too, he is surrounded by a society older and stronger than civilization, the integrated society of forest growth, animals, birds, and insects, citizens innumerable and nameless, all governed by the same harsh but just law. At the centre of this living organism stands the cabin, man's permitted sanctuary amid the invisible powers. To it he may flee in weak moments from the night, the cold, and the awful message of the stars.

In cabin and woods there is something else that, no matter how I tried, I could never put into written words, except as oblique, self-conscious question marks or obscure parentheses lost on the reader. Even now, when I have nothing more to hide and all the witnesses of my youth are gone, no words can fit the forest. Before its presence language has no meaning, calligraphy no use.

Yet only an eye sated with too much print or too many electronic images is blind to the forest's infinitely varied colors. Only the ear dulled by the city's rumble is deaf to the forest's distinct utterance—the sibilant breath of spring when wind is shredded through the infant foliage, the summer buzz of flies and crackle of dry twigs, the autumn hush and whisper of falling leaves, and then the tympanic boom of winter gale, music ever mixed and ever changing. Only the nose blunted by the city's fumes will not perceive the astringent whiff of conifer, the honeyed fragrance of blossom, the chaste scent of lichen and hot stone. Only the hand numbed by soft living can fail to distinguish, even in darkness, the separate touch of the cedar's smooth webbing, the rough texture of the fir, the soft female skin of arbutus, the crinkled sheath of alder, the cutting edge of sword fern.

It is not the palpable emanations alone that must alert the trespasser in the forest. Any man of average intelligence will see at once that forces are moving here beyond the reach of his five bodily senses, that the forest has a sixth sense of its own.

When countless billions of cells multiply above and below the ground by sure plan and long-tested architecture; when roots thinner than silk and strong as steel never cease their quest for moisture and hidden chemical; when pumps and capillary plumbing, which man has yet to invent or understand, carry the liquid upward to synthesize the tree's food by means unknown and exude the oxygen of all animal life; when trunk and limb swell and spread as if an engineer had designed them for stress and strain; when the forest, without eyes, unerringly finds the sun and burrows in the dark; when, mindless, it knows how to heal its wounds and rear its children; when, anchored to the earth, it marches generation by generation to recover its lost domain and expunge its human conqueror; when, outwardly helpless, it contains more power than all man's atomic bombs; when, indeed, the forest defies all laws and logic known to him, then, perhaps, man witnesses a kind of knowledge totally different from his own, a latent intelligence which, some day, he may learn to share. So far, he has only learned how to destroy it.

Such notions occurred to me, even in my youth, but I dismissed them as idle fancy, good for nothing more than newspaper columns. If my thoughts were ignorant and overlarded with grubby journalism, they lay too deep for tears, much too deep for print.

The real tears were not long in coming. My father, who had sensed these things, died too young, before I could appreciate the humble triumph of his life. But I knew him well enough to put his ashes in the rock garden where he had found his happiness. Dot's father had also died, still younger, and his widow, fortunately for all of us, moved into our household. Now three women of forceful character, a cranky breadwinner, and two obstreperous children occupied a single dwelling. No one except Dot could manage such an establishment. She coped so well, with blunt orders, soothing consolation, or saving laughter, as required, that our home in those years served us like a well-oiled machine. It was governed and illuminated by the finest human being that any of us would ever know. But we were now living, with complete ignorance, in a world about to be ruined overnight.

8

The Idiot's Tale

The Great Depression changed forever the society of all the Western nations, Canada among them. It brought suffering immeasurable, and largely ignored by others, to a minority of Canadians at home, and abroad led naturally to the Second World War. But to the majority in Canada, including my household, it seemed to make little real difference. If the Depression was indeed a tale told by economic idiots in high places, it was not, for most of us, the time of beggary, hunger, and shame which nowadays is pictured in the history books.

Our own case was typical. When the Vancouver *Province* cut my wages from fifty-five to fifty dollars a week for a full-time political reporting assignment in Victoria plus three cartoons a week, our standard of living actually rose because prices fell faster than wages. Since we had not yet learned enough about economics to reckon such matters statistically, we knew only that times, in general, were hard, but not for us. We always had a maid in the house, the best of food in our stomachs, two second-hand cars in the garage, and in our minds the smug, bogus security of the fortunate.

It never occurred to me that we were well off, that a revolution was silently under way on our doorstep, or that the patient misery of the poor was unnatural, unnecessary, and criminal. For a reporter, may God forgive him, the Depression, with a few decent lapses of sympathy, was just another news story. I covered it by day, drew my crude cartoons by night, and began to write cruder short stories for the magazines, selling them to the American slicks, and even one lurid script to Hollywood — a sloppy love story of the woods entitled "Park Avenue Logger"— for the unimaginable sum of two thousand dollars. With the money in my pocket, we went to Europe and thus did not have to see perhaps the worst movie ever put on the screen.

The conscience of America in those days, or at least my own, was well protected from the surrounding torment by an ugly mixture of ignorance, selfishness, and fear. In Canada, Disraeli's two nations may have existed from the beginning but now they appeared with a new and savage clarity, the employed and the unemployed, the comfortable and the destitute divided as by an international boundary. This, in retrospect, was the truly horrifying fact of the Depression, the gulf not merely of money but of mind or, more accurately, feeling between the nations, each foreign, remote, and almost incomprehensible to the other. Society was cracking but not many of us noticed it.

Now and then some flash of reality penetrated my private blackout as I watched the huddle of hopeless men, with their placards and listless chants, appealing for help outside the legislative buildings in Victoria, where a new Liberal government had promised but could not deliver the miracle of "Work and Wages"; or when, in Kamloops, I saw youngsters from the east clinging to the roofs of the freight cars. The local residents, all decent and kindly but bewildered and fearful, seemed to regard them as a kind of free public entertainment, a separate subspecies like caged animals to be hurried out of town before the next lot arrived. Occasionally I had just enough sense to feel a little sick, but not often. Where, I ask now, was my pity for these boys and the deepening agony of all humankind? The young are cruel and seldom unlearn their cruelty until they are too old to undo it.

Besides, young and old alike can insulate themselves, as if by suddenly growing an extra skin, from misery in the mass. We can take wholesale famine and flood in Africa or Asia as hardly more than a headline or a statistic, its human contents ignored, its results too big for understanding, its totality of suffering beyond imagination or the means of relief. But let a family down the street suffer any affliction and all the neighbors rush to its assistance. Let some child lack money for a surgical operation and contributions to its need pour in. Let a kitten be stranded on a telephone pole and the city fire department lays aside all other duties to rescue it.

By this automatic insulation from collective calamity, the nation of the fortunate simply could not visualize the nation of the hungry or admit to itself that such a nation really existed. Or if its existence could no longer be denied, then its misery must be thrust out of the comfortable mind (my own included) or blamed on someone else, usually the anonymous, callous state when, in truth, everyone was to blame.

Even more wonderful, and today unbelievable, was the dumb endurance of the hungry nation. Only a few minor riots flared up against a system which had no defence in morals and could not have been defended against general violence if the hungry had rebelled. Most amazing of all was the discipline, instinct, or mere habit that drove the hungry to live with hunger and cold when they could have been so easily fed, clothed, and housed. The human creature's survival quotient is higher than that of his intelligence, and it will have to be very high indeed to survive tomorrow's calamities probably much less soluble than the Depression. We can be sure at least of one thing — the hungry would never take another Depression as they took the last one, and no system, whatever its name and methods, could survive it.

Of all these truths, political, economic, and human, I remained ignorant when knowledge was most required. Still, I was learning some peripheral facts from improbable teachers; enough, anyhow, to realize dimly even then that the Depression was not just wicked but quite crazy. We must have been crazy to suppose that a continent full of food, productive machinery, and wealth without purchasing power to consume it should endure poverty and hunger because the infallible free market, the iron law of economics, and the will of God Himself had so ordered—all this in a society calling itself Christian, going to church on Sunday, and ignoring its own brutality for the rest of the week. Nothing but madness and terror, combined with an ignorance beyond belief, could explain such a monstrous spectacle.

I listened, without questioning their expert judgment, to some rich friends in Wall Street who solemnly warned me that the wild man then in the White House would inflate and bankrupt the sound American economy of idle workers, idle factories, and plentiful, unpurchased goods. Inflation at a time of surplus, deflation necessary to save a system already deflated into ruin—this was the prevailing wisdom in the high places of finance. With the same bewilderment, Roosevelt and his New Dealers were slaughtering hogs and curtailing food production to keep the price up when millions of Americans went to bed ill-nourished in cold houses and decayed slums.

It is simple, almost half a century later, to diagnose this madness, to wonder how it could have afflicted a civilized people on such a scale. But half a century from now our grandchildren, in their turn, will look back on today's equal though different madness with similar disbelief and wonderment. As ancestors we shall seem no more sane than our parents in the Depression. No generation can ever see the truly important events all around it. Only the next generation, with futile hindsight, sees them, and then proceeds to commit its own follies.

The follies of the 1930s struck me like a physical blow as I drove across the Prairies and saw the long cycle of drought added to the insanity of finance in double catastrophe—abandoned farms and empty houses, dust piled up to the top of the fence posts, the nation's heartland blowing away on the wind, the farmers who had plowed and worked this rich earth now fed, but not much, by the public treasury. Then, from my school days, I remembered Goldsmith's warning that "a proud peasantry, their country's pride, when once destroyed can never be supplied." And yet neither depression nor drought, nor even the loss of his home and meagre chattels, could destroy the Canadian farmer. When rain fell at last he came home and rebuilt his ruined estate.

In northern British Columbia, covering the provincial election of 1933, I saw another breed of men who could endure the world sickness because they endured it together.

For this expedition I secured a remarkable chauffeur. As children John Owen Wilson and I had been brought up in Cranbrook, neither of us suspecting that he was to become the greatest judge and best-loved citizen of British Columbia; and also the closest friend of my life, which he had saved from drowning in Kootenay Lake. Our boyhood friendship was brief. Jack moved with his family to Prince George and, at sixteen, to the trenches of the First World War. Almost fatally wounded he came home and practised law with his father, the memorable Pete.

Legal fees were hard to collect in the Depression years, and were often paid in cordwood, poultry, and vegetables. But Jack's young wife, Ruth, kept a comfortable house in good times and bad. The family even had an automobile of sorts and I had an expense account with the Vancouver *Province*. A thrifty bargain was negotiated. Jack would provide the transportation; I would generously pay the hotel bills — at no cost to myself. So we set forth westward in an autumn blizzard and a carefree state of mind.

Wherever we stopped with the local election candidate the community hall or schoolhouse was filled by voters, assembled less to hear a speech than to find some human company and refuge from loneliness. They were bent on an evening's entertainment, not on revolution, and usually voted for the same politicians who had served them so ill, not for the new Co-operative Commonwealth Federation, which promised to do better by the magic of Socialism.

After the candidate had delivered the same weary speech that we had heard in the last town, and would hear again at the next, the hall was cleared, someone played a piano, the younger folk danced, and the older women prepared supper in the back room. How they paid for the coffee, sandwiches, and cake I never knew. The world appeared sick beyond cure, a comical German mountebank with Charlie Chaplin's mustache was making speeches as meaningless as those of the local candidate, but the people in the hall gave scant attention to either. They were out to enjoy themselves, and they did.

At one of these towns the meeting was chaired by a man more seedy than the rest, unshaved, unwashed, and taciturn, but wearing a greenish bowler hat, his badge of respectability. Without removing his hat he announced that he was campaign manager for Mayor L. D. Taylor of Vancouver and introduced him as an independent candidate for the historic constituency of Omineca (all constituencies being, of course, historic).

Taylor, then a wizened relic of his early days, muttered a few irrelevant remarks, but they made no impression on the audience. It knew that he was a carpetbagger from the metropolis running in an old blood feud only to spite his enemy, Attorney General A. M. Manson, Omineca's veteran political boss.

When Taylor sat down the chairman, still wearing his bowler, leaped up. Without a word he pulled a concertina from under the table and began to pump it vigorously. He pumped long past midnight while the audience danced, the eminent Mayor of Vancouver forgotten. In the pause for supper, assuming that the solitary musician must represent the rustic political cunning of the hinterland and knew how to elect Taylor, I asked whether he had a good chance of winning.

"Not a snowball's chance in hell," said the campaign manager who had been hired to say just the opposite.

"Then why are you managing his campaign?"

"Taylor pays good. And it's better than my last job."

"What was that?"

"Garbage man at Burns Lake."

Whereupon he began to pump the concertina again and the dance went on.

In these dismal years another curious experience awaited me. I encountered Gerald Grattan McGeer and have never quite recovered from the shock. No one who didn't know Gerry in person can understand how an ignorant boilermaker could make himself a King's Counsel, a Biblical soothsayer, a scourge of Canadian politics, a piercing thorn in Mackenzie King's side, and for me an invaluable teacher (though his teaching was frequently wrong). Nowadays McGeer is not much remembered, even in his native town where he ended his life as Mr. Vancouver, far short of his ambitions and talents. But to some old-timers his huge body, his round Irish face, empurpled nose, deafening voice, and primitive eloquence are unforgettable.

He might have been nothing more than a back-bench Liberal legislator in Victoria if he had not stumbled by accident on the science of money. Inflamed by the discovery, he perfected a foolproof monetary system of his own, a universal cure for human ills. The Depression could be reversed overnight and permanent prosperity guaranteed for everyone by a quick and easy device. The state had merely to create and spend enough money, and control wages, prices, investment, and all the levers of the economy. Then there would be no more depressions.

My economic illiteracy, my enthusiasm for any heretical idea, and a certain knack of oversimplifying it for the newspapers were useful to McGeer. Like some Ancient Mariner, he held me with his glittering eye, his charts, diagrams, and statistics, his torrent of words. I became his unpaid press agent and travelling companion, a third-rate Boswell to a second-rate Johnson.

Soon Gerry was wheedling, bullying, perhaps even educating the provincial Legislature and alarming the Liberal Party in Ottawa. When I told Mackenzie King that the monetary heretic planned to run for Parliament as a Liberal candidate in Vancouver, the Party leader blanched. "Tell McGeer," said King, "that his place is in British Columbia politics. Tell him he has a great future there." The prospect of Gerry in the Liberal caucus at Ottawa, with all those dangerous notions of money, was frightening and King's fright comical. Nevertheless, Gerry would soon reach the House of Commons and attack his own party until King, in desperation, elevated him to the Senate, where he could do no more harm.

Meanwhile King was leading the Opposition and still regarded the new economics, especially Roosevelt's New Deal, as dangerous nonsense. About that time, in another conversation, he informed me that he had recently met Thomas Dufferin Pattullo and had been deeply disturbed by the British Columbia Liberal premier's revolutionary views.

"Why," said King, "that man thinks there should be a washing machine and an electric refrigerator in every home! Sometimes I wonder about Pattullo," he added, tapping his head to indicate, I presumed, his doubt about the sanity of all British Columbians, and not yet seeing himself as the highest bidder in a Canadian New Deal.

Gerry had no doubts about anything, no limits to his ambition, and no scope for it in the Victoria Legislature. To achieve his destiny, he had gone into hard athletic training, forsworn alcohol, reduced his weight by a rigorous diet, and got himself elected Mayor of Vancouver in 1934. There he started to clean up the criminal underworld and, fearing its revenge, was accompanied everywhere on his long night walks by an armed bodyguard of a towering bulk equal to his own. Now he decided to carry the flaming torch of monetary reform across the nation — with me as excess baggage and Calgary as our first stop.

Since the CPR was disrupted by floods, we had to go to Seattle by ship and travel eastward on an American railway. The ship was to leave Vancouver at midnight. I had retired early in my cabin because I knew that in Gerry's company sleep would be scarce. Just before sailing time a soft knock awakened me and a hoarse whisper asked me to open the door. Half asleep, I admitted Gerry. With a finger on his lips, he warned me not to speak aloud or turn on the light. Still in a whisper, he explained that on the wharf he had seen some underworld characters who undoubtedly were plotting to shoot him in his bed. Could he sleep in my cabin and elude the assassins' bullets?

The first magistrate of Vancouver rated the more comfortable lower berth but I didn't propose to leave it. So Gerry undressed silently and heaved his mighty frame into the narrow upper berth, where his snores kept me awake most of the night. The assassins, if any, had been foiled.

We arrived safely in Calgary, Gerry doing push-ups on the railway platforms whenever the train stopped, to the delight of the natives. Now, for the first time, I learned that he had expanded a monetary system into a religious dogma and that a leading churchman of Alberta had invited him to share it with a distinguished congregation. To my amazement, that night I found myself in a crowded cathedral and Gerry in the pulpit. He wore a frock coat of square, Edwardian style, a colossal white bow tie, and, on his crimson face, a look of holiness, unquestionably sincere — the true believer.

His sermon was eloquent, pious, and pure. The reform of the monetary system, he argued, had always been central to the Christian faith since Jesus drove the money changers from the temple. Abraham Lincoln, too, was a monetary reformer and financed the American Civil War on the sort of credit which Canada should use to finance prosperity for the poor. In that sermon Gerry, the politician turned evangelist, lifted economics out of sordid politics, transformed finance into mysticism, and money into a sacrament. I was shaken.

Having also shaken Calgary, Gerry soon moved on to Ottawa. There, with the same dexterity, he introduced the new economics to the old politics in his finest hour. As a witness before a baffled parliamentary committee he cross-examined the nation's private bank managers and proved beyond doubt that they had never grasped even the fundamentals of their own business. It was not difficult to make them, and their friend, the

Conservative government, look pitiably stupid when their system had curtailed the people's purchasing power instead of enlarging it to finance the sale of goods in surplus supply. But presently a different type of witness appeared and it was no longer easy for Gerry. He had confronted the new Bank of Canada's first governor.

Graham Towers was then in his mid-thirties and the most chilling personage I had yet observed on the public stage—a tall, lean, strikingly handsome figure, a brain-machine on wheels. Hour after hour, day after day, he answered Gerry, the prosecutor, in such perfect diction that it could have been published verbatim as a book. Gerry used his blustering questions like a club. Towers' thrusts were delivered with a rapier. A western giant and an eastern giant-killer had met in death grapple while the committee watched in admiring stupefaction but without comprehension.

Or so it seemed to me, and I was entirely wrong. The two Homeric protagonists before the walls of Troy (as my feverish imagination pictured them) would fight all morning. At noon they lunched together and refreshed themselves on martinis for the afternoon's battle.

My opinion of Towers as a cool devil was totally reversed years later when I became his friend. I judged his mind the most penetrating and spacious of his time in Ottawa, and that opinion stands today. But Towers also turned out to be the kindest, most humorous, and delightful of men, a bon vivant and a raconteur extraordinary. The lovable human being behind the banker's grim visage and clipped idiom patiently taught me all I know about money, which, through no fault of his, doesn't amount to much.

Two other men important only to their region stand out in my memory of those years. Against his will and despite his protests, Dr. Simon Fraser Tolmie, as honest and fine a gentleman as I had ever known, became the Conservative premier of British Columbia in 1928, but the Depression inevitably wrecked his government. With his Liberal successor, T. D. Pattullo, who had much superior abilities, I enjoyed some curious little adventures, one of which always puzzled him.

He had arrived in Ottawa, a ruddy-faced, dapper, and dauntless man, to meet Prime Minister Bennett and seek a loan from the federal government, since British Columbia was closer to bankruptcy than the public knew. The two men met *in camera*, argued furiously, exchanged financial memoranda—or rather ultimata—and promised to discuss them with no one. My job, as the *Province* reporter, was to get these documents if I could, by hook or crook, because they would make a major national news story. But the assignment looked hopeless until an unbelievably lucky break came from an unexpected quarter.

Though Stanley Moodie, Pattullo's executive assistant, was a loyal man of all work, he believed that the confidential documents should be published to show that Bennett had treated British Columbia outrageously. I didn't know Moodie's views and was waiting, helpless and desperate, in my Château Laurier room when he and Pattullo returned from Bennett's office. They told me that no word, absolutely none, would be released. An hour before deadline in Vancouver the news desk clamored for my story and bombarded me with increasingly urgent telegrams. I could not answer them. My mission to Ottawa had failed.

Suddenly, by a ruse which belonged to some cheap detective story, I was rescued. Moodie came into my room, gave me a hard look, and asked if I had any carbon papers. He needed them to make several copies of the documents. I handed him a sheaf of new carbons and gave up hope. Half an hour later he brought back the carbons with thanks and another hard look. Nothing more passed between us but I think we understood each other.

Without a scruple, or much hope either, I held the carbons against the window pane. To my delight I found them easy to read, the words neatly punctured on the black paper. I had the full contents of the Bennett-Pattullo memoranda. Or so I assumed. But dare I use them? Were these, perhaps, some memoranda relating to other business or preliminary draughts already changed? Was I being trapped? No, that could not be. Pattullo and Moodie were honorable men and my friends. Besides, Moodie had used a clean new sheet of carbon for every page of his typing, obviously to make sure that all were legible.

Reading them against the window pane, I saw that Bennett had offered a loan to British Columbia but on terms that Pattullo had indignantly rejected. The provincial treasury was left bare. Bankruptcy loomed ahead. Here was a national sensation. To print or not to print it? The struggle in my conscience lasted a long time—two seconds at least. Then I picked up the telephone and, with the carbons still pressed to the window, dictated them verbatim to the *Province* desk.

The news printed in Vancouver quickly bounced back to Ottawa. Bennett telephoned Pattullo and accused him of betrayal. Pattullo in turn accused Bennett, who declared in that roaring apocalyptic voice of his that a royal commission would be set up immediately to investigate the outrage with me as the star witness, or prisoner at the bar. I was properly terrified. Pattullo knew me too well to ask any questions and boarded a train for New York where he hoped to borrow money in Wall Street. I slunk home. Bennett forgot his rage and royal commission in the worse financial disasters already endangering his own government.

From that day onward Moodie never mentioned the affair to me, nor I to him. Back in Victoria, as we were enjoying a drink together in his office, Pattullo said he had heard the carbon-paper story but of course it was absurd. What had really happened? I promised to tell him some time, once he was out of politics, but neglected my promise.

Some two years after this silly incident I saw Bennett up close for the first time and the sight was tragic. He had reached Victoria in his hopeless election campaign of 1935 and drawn a capacity crowd to the Royal Theatre. Arriving late, I groped my way through the gloom backstage to the press table. In the wings a large figure slumped on a very small chair, and for a moment I did not recognize him. He was no longer the lusty, vibrant Bennett I had watched so often as he hurled his thunderbolts across the House of Commons. The man on the chair looked ill, almost unconscious, his face as white as the familiar stiff collar, his hands dangling limp beside him. But it was Bennett all right — the Prime Minister of Canada alone in a dark corner, deserted, drained, and friendless at the end of the road.

The curtain went up at last. The listless figure sprang to life and strode to the centre of the stage, majestic in tail coat and air of defiance, master of himself and the crowd. Then, as the hecklers began to shout, he shouted them down, the almighty voice booming out like a cannon to hush the clamorous theatre. This triumph of the spirit over the flesh was heroic, unnatural, and, as I supposed, unlikely to be repeated.

On the following night, in Vancouver, Bennett faced a much larger and more hostile crowd, which seemed disposed to turn the meeting into a riot. But again the spirit triumphed, the hecklers were silenced, and if votes had hung on speeches Bennett would have won the election.

Victory went to King, who distrusted bravura and could not achieve it anyhow. On the same Victoria stage he offered his hand, "the hand of the physician", contrasting it with Bennett's, "the fist of the pugilist". Now Canada's family doctor was safely installed at Ottawa for the next thirteen years of peace and war.

As leader of a corporal's guard in Parliament, Bennett relaxed, all anger and ambition past. When I was taken to meet him by his honest idolator and my old friend, Howard Green, I found the last true Conservative in a genial mood. His old physical strength had ebbed, the plump moon face had shrunk into lines of age, but the pipe-organ voice seemed as strong, the mind as roving, restless, and insatiable as ever. The black clothes of antique cut were immaculate and usually changed twice a day. The shirt collar was high, white, and stiff. The soft hands pounded the desk for emphasis, the eyes twinkled, the words gushed out as from a clear mountain stream in purring cadence and chuckling ironies—a speech for my sole benefit, worthy of the most distinguished audience anywhere. Though he knew I was a reputed Liberal and an enemy, Bennett had ceased to care about such things. Enemy or friend was welcome to his store of knowledge, wisdom, and advice.

For two full hours he lounged in his easy chair and never stopped talking for a second. Of that torrent I recall little except its vast and disjointed sweep, the old man's memories of youth in New Brunswick, his verdict on Cromwell's revolt and King Charles's execution, his opinion of Ming pottery, his cheerful reflections on the comedy of mankind.

Like a schoolboy in front of his teacher Green listened to this liquid burble. I listened, too, in dumb fascination, realizing that the man whom I had been taught to regard as a pompous phony and sinister agent of oppressive capitalism was quite different from his legend. Clearly, he was Mackenzie King's equal in the mechanics of thought but a comparative child in his judgment of great affairs and ordinary human beings, the final test of politics. Still, Bennett struck me as a big man by any other test and an unlucky one. Depression, not Liberalism, had ruined him.

As Green and I rose to leave his office, Bennett fixed me with a prophetic glare. "Young man," he said, "you have a long time to live. You will see Canada split on the line of the Ottawa River." Wounded by his own tragedy Bennett was brooding (wrongly as I now believe) on the future tragedy of the nation and, though I didn't know it then, already planning his exile in Britain. That, it seemed to me afterward, was the final tragedy of an almost great man. I never saw Bennett again, but after his death our paths were to cross in a strange place, and this time in farce.

While Bennett was Prime Minister I had talked, for the first time at length, with his Senate leader, Arthur Meighen. The two old Conservative rivals were united late in life, if not by agreement on policy, at least by a common detestation of King.

The Meighen I had watched in Parliament some ten years earlier, and met briefly outside it, was changed in body but not much in mind. His skeletal frame had taken on flesh, which improved his appearance. The once lean face of pale austerity was softened, and affable, as if Meighen had learned from his own mistakes and forgiven the mistakes of others. In fact, like the Bourbons, he had learned nothing and forgotten nothing that concerned his arch-enemy; for King he had only contempt.

Meighen's return to the Conservative Party leadership and his last defeat in York South were then unforeseen, and I rashly asked him about his notorious Hamilton speech of 1925 when he seemed to reverse his lifetime's thinking—the conscription law of 1917, his "ready, aye ready" response to the Chanak incident of 1922, his whole theory of a united Empire foreign policy. Despite that consistent record, he had suddenly proposed, in Hamilton, that any Canadian government's decision to enter a war must be submitted to the voters at a general election, a kind of leisurely plebiscite while the enemy advanced.

By the time of our conversation Meighen doubtless had recognized this speech as one of his worst blunders, a constitutional monstrosity, a denial of the parliamentary system itself, designed not for actual use but solely to win an immediate by-election in Bagot, Quebec, where the French-Canadian voters promptly rejected its author.

He offered no serious defence of this astounding mind-lapse. How could he? Instead, he brushed it off, rather hurriedly and sheepishly, I thought, as an attempt to heal old sores, to reassure the Quebec people, and to make certain that in case of another war the nation would enter it united (as if a plebiscite would not have produced exactly the opposite result). He could hardly have expected me to believe such a weak rationalization but of course I made no comment. After all, he was Meighen and I was a brash reporter, still worse, a suspected Liberal.

Nevertheless, having long admired him from a distance as the very soul of logic, I felt some disappointment. Even more disappointing because it involved the nation's safety and Britain's real interests, too, would be Meighen's dismissal of the Canada–United States defence agreement negotiated by King and Roosevelt at Ogdensburg, 1940, as mere "twilight twitterings". That too facile mastery of the quick, corrosive phrase was always more of a liability than an asset.

Until Meighen's death, and afterward, I continued to marvel at the heroic myth built around him by his friends and the drab, dwarfish myth built around King by his enemies when in truth neither man was as large or small as the myth-makers pretended.

That Meighen had a superb factual intelligence, a poetic vein, an unquestioned personal integrity, an unfailing courage, and an unequalled power of speech I had known from my earliest days in Ottawa. That he was a greater man than King, indeed the greatest and least appreciated Canadian of his day, the victim of unjust fate in battle with the gods, as his myth-makers still imagine, I could not believe. The myth was bigger than the man.

Yet it must be said that Meighen had a magnetic quality lacking in King. The Conservative, whose *laissez-faire* economic views were unconsciously rooted in classic Liberalism, could hold his friends throughout his life and beyond it. The Liberal, whose Liberalism was consciously evolving toward a hazy Socialism, could not find such friends and did not seem to need them. Meighen was worshipped by those who had broken through his glacial exterior. King was grudgingly tolerated, and re-elected again and again, by a people who never understood him just as he probably never understood himself. So stands the double myth — entirely misleading in politics, partly valid in human nature, and in any case more durable than the facts.

Among the lesser myths of the thirties, I encountered, at his capital of Edmonton, the newly elected Premier of Alberta and the evangelist of Social Credit. William Aberhart was busy that day, had no time to spare from his crushing problems, but kindly received me after office hours, delaying his dinner. Encouraged by my synthetic sympathy, he talked grandly about his mission. I could see that to this obese and glistening figure, like some Buddhistic statue in white porcelain, oddly misplaced on the alien Prairies of Canada, the mission was already a cruel burden.

With disarming candor, Aberhart said he did not profess to understand the Social Credit theory in detail. He understood only its broad principles, which experts from Britain would refine for use in Alberta. But a man who had taught school, and presumably had received some education, nourished a unique constitutional theory of his own. The money system, he explained, was under the control of the federal government. The credit system, however, was controlled by the provinces and Alberta would manage it for the good of the people. Since money and credit were the same thing, a bookkeeping entry in the ledger of the central bank, I could only blink at Aberhart's discovery and write a mean piece about it, a poor return for his kindness.

Soon afterward, on a transatlantic liner, I met one of the imported British Social Credit experts whom Aberhart had dismissed for referring to him, in private, as "the stranded whale". This man told me that Mrs. Aberhart usually sat beside her husband at cabinet sessions, knitting energetically, like Dickens's harridan at the Paris guillotine, and if the Premier became too angry, would whisper reprovingly, "Now, now, William!" The conjugal warning always improved the cabinet's temper, but nothing could make Social Credit work according to plan, even though its basic objective of increased purchasing power was as sound as the prevailing system was crazy.

The Depression also brought me into touch with one of the truly noble figures of Canadian history. No doubt the bearded, ascetic face of J. S. Woodsworth, like a saint on a stained-glass cathedral window, the small, fragile body, and the deep melodic voice would distinguish him anywhere. But his true distinction was a spirit of charity and inner anguish which all men instantly recognized, even if they disagreed with his politics. And most men, myself included, felt unworthy, almost sinful, in his presence. For he was not satisfied, like the ordinary run of politicians, to rail at the human condition and weep for the victims of an unjust society. Nor, as a Christian minister, would he tolerate the evils of this world until they were cured in the next. To him it was the now, not the hereafter, that counted.

His long fight for social justice and his destruction in politics belong to the history books. The Socialist movement, which only he could have brought through its frail infancy, belongs to the present and the future. It is wrong, however, to suppose that Woodsworth had any clear or practical design for the reform of Canada.

Coming to know him well, often receiving his confidences, I did not accept all his theories but increasingly admired his character. I saw that he fought against evil without knowing how to replace it. As he told me in his house of honorable poverty, he must first achieve office and analyse the existing situation before he could begin to change it.

Woodsworth was a secular saint, as even his opponents agreed, but too decent, compassionate, and tortured to govern a greedy nation. As prime minister he would certainly have failed, lacking any coherent program or the necessary killer's instinct. In the utterance of burning protest he was a magnificent success. By his refusal to vote for Canada's entry into the Second World War he deliberately ended his public career, sacrificed ambition to conscience, and received from Parliament a silent tribute of respect for his lonely courage. To him Canadian Socialism owes its political birth and that soul which, under later custodians, has lost some of its idealism while increasing its vote. If Woodsworth had no possible chance to govern — and that was his good fortune — he changed the whole course of politics more than he ever knew. Few Canadian lifetimes have been better spent.

His successor in the leadership of the Co-operative Commonwealth Federation, M. J. Coldwell (known to everyone by his initials only), was a very different sort of man, but he was as courageous as Woodsworth in a life beset by personal sorrow always hidden from the world. As a political leader he was Woodsworth's superior. Alone among the early socialists, Coldwell would have made a successful, perhaps a great, prime minister (as King knew when he tried, and failed, to lure him into the Liberal cabinet). At one point in 1943 the opinion polls suggested that Coldwell might come to office, but King, seeing the threat, crushed it by lunging leftward.

Coldwell did not look or think like a fanatic of social reform. This pink-cheeked, chubby, jolly, and gregarious man of numberless friends looked like a country gentleman from Devon, and so in fact he was by birth. By chance—and deep study—he became a rebel of Saskatchewan politics but never a radical, much less a Marxist. Coldwell loved mankind far above ideology, hated the world's injustice, did his best to temper it, and held a simple, old-fashioned religious faith. When his Saskatchewan electors defeated him they robbed our public life of a primary asset. No socialist of such talent and breadth has yet succeeded him.

After King won the election of 1935 his dumpy figure bestrode the politics of Canada like a self-made colossus, and now, safe at home, he was forced to consider foreign affairs, which he had long neglected. The election had taken place in the middle of the Ethiopian crisis while the League of Nations was imposing sanctions on Italy, and the Canadian delegate, Walter A. Riddell, pleading for the new Liberal government's instructions and getting none, supported a last serious attempt to halt Mussolini's aggression. King, resting in Georgia, heard of Riddell's initiative at Geneva, was horrified, and through Ernest Lapointe in Ottawa repudiated it. King's famous or notorious act had just been announced when he returned to Ottawa and agreed to see me in his office.

Nothing was said about Ethiopia. The talk concerned domestic affairs only until, without knocking, Lapointe strode into the room. Always in the past I had found him friendly, jovial, Gallic. Now he was scowling, sullen, and obviously under strain.

Why the conversation turned to Ethiopia I forget, and why Lapointe should have discussed it in front of me I can't imagine. But suddenly he launched a fierce attack on Riddell and a laborious defence of the government. His argument, as I vaguely remember it, was that the odious Hoare-Laval deal had paralysed the League, made sanctions unworkable, and Canada's position, as represented by Riddell, impossible. Hence the government had no alternative to the repudiation of its delegate.

At this outburst King, his little hands gesturing abhorrence, lamented the immorality of the British and French statesmen. Lapointe stalked off, apparently forgetting why he had come. Young and innocent as I still was, and not in the least disturbed by Canada's ultimate act of isolationism, it occurred to me that Lapointe had protested too much, that his mind and King's were more troubled than they chose to admit, even to themselves.

Neither of them (nor I, of course) realized then what a watershed had been crossed in the improbable region of Ethiopia, what worse turning points lay ahead, and how both men would look back with useless regret on their own record. For my part, I misunderstood everything but fortunately was responsible for nothing.

After Lapointe had left us, King asked my opinion on a certain western politician whom he thought of taking into his new cabinet. Was the man fit for office? Brash as usual, I said he was not, for various personal reasons. King nodded solemnly. Yes, he feared that my objections were only too true. A few days later that man was a member of the government.

Not long after, I began a lasting friendship with King's new handyman, J. W. Pickersgill, whose upbringing in poverty on a prairie farm had given him the feel of the grassroots—and Jack would never lose it. Oxford University had educated him, but failed to tame an exuberant nature, a passionate Canadianism, and a hatred of snobs. When, as a young apprentice, he joined the Department of External Affairs, it viewed him with respect for his obvious intelligence, but his saucy manner and cherubic look seemed likely to bar him from promotion in the sedate Ottawa hierarchy. That estimate of Jack, typically snobbish, was grotesquely wrong.

The Prime Minister was the first to recognize superior qualities in this assistant who amused, angered, and often baffled him, but who never hesitated to question his judgments. In Pickersgill the master craftsman had found his indispensable Jack-of-all-trades.

At the beginning I saw in my friend only a youth of earthy wit and extravagant imagination, and above all of courage and honesty. Behind his brassy public image he was a romantic and a sentimentalist, but his intuitive sense of politics, his mastery of the rough and tumble in the game of Parliament, his invention of extraordinary remedies were almost as good as King's — sometimes better.

For Jack, Liberalism (or his private vision of it) was little short of a religion. Among his talents it carried him to the summit of the party and the government, where he certainly belonged and brilliantly succeeded. In times of deep trouble and high comedy I came to understand the real man—as he understood me—but the public always misunderstood him, even when he was front-page news and the prey of every cartoonist in the land. The barrage of ridicule did not worry him at all. He laughed at his enemies because he could laugh at himself.

Jack's early and growing influence with King must have produced my invitation to dine at Laurier House in 1937. That was an exciting night for me and a tedious public-relations chore for my host, the Prime Minister.

We sat alone in a murky dining room lighted only by candles and decorated by shadowy portraits of eminent Liberals now departed. A ghostly setting, I thought, out of some inferior movie. King, a good trencherman, attacked his meal with ravenous appetite, downed half a dozen glasses of white wine, doubtless needing extra nourishment for his chore, and talked without interruption for six hours. The guest ate and drank sparingly to keep his mind on the precious monologue. Concentration was not easy when King's Irish terrier, Pat, sprawled across my feet and nibbled my ankles in a cordial fashion.

Even when we were lifted to the third floor in an elevator recently donated by one of King's rich friends, the monologue continued. His hide-out, and Canada's real hub of government, was unknown to the contemporary public and had yet to become a national shrine. To me it was fascinating in its contrived and costly ugliness, the litter of tinsel bric-a-brac, the array of royal photographs and other trophies of the chase, the illuminated portrait of King's mother beside the fireplace, the cougar skin on the floor, and next to the big desk a small table which, its owner explained, had once belonged to the English poet George Meredith. (Every man should have such a table, King remarked, to hold a cup of tea and some biscuits for sustenance in long working hours.)

He was working hard that night on public relations, not on government. While his cabinet conducted the business of the nation in the Commons he seemed quite indifferent to it. With heavy sarcasms, mischievous leers, and sudden boyish grins, varied by passing sighs and moral dicta, he rambled from the unfortunate weakness of the Conservative Opposition and the follies of his younger colleagues to the excellent state of his own health and the prospects of the world.

The prospects, he believed, were favorable, despite all the current rumors of European war. After talking to Adolf Hitler a few days previously, he pronounced a verdict which was confidential then but has since become notorious. The German dictator, he had found, was "a simple sort of peasant" and not very bright, who wished only to possess the Sudetenland of Czechoslovakia. That insignificant prize would satisfy him and the theft of foreign property did not seem to disturb King. No, he said, Hitler did not intend to risk war. And to those peaceful motives King undoubtedly felt that he had made his own valuable contribution.

At midnight, having finished his chore, the Prime Minister accompanied me to the door and saw me safely into his limousine with the best wishes for my future. I was exhausted from listening, he apparently refreshed from talking without pause since six o'clock. If I had seen something of a secretive little man in a hermitage forbidden to the public, it was not much after all. He would die before the nation discovered the real motivation of his life. Leaving him that night, I had no hint of the truth. The practising spiritualist and amateur mystic in communication with the dead of another world still seemed to me only a political genius in this one. Like everybody else, save a very few lip-sealed confidants, I was always to misunderstand the living King.

9

The Great Guy and the King

A few weeks after his inauguration in March 1933, President Franklin Delano Roosevelt glanced across his desk at a stranger who was obviously out of place. By some discreet wangling I had managed to squeeze into the Oval Room with a crowd of American reporters and had wriggled my way to the front row. Only the desk separated me from the most powerful man in the world.

He did not look much like the Roosevelt I had seen pictured in the newspapers. He was not grinning for the photographers or acting his public role of the Great Guy. He was staring straight ahead and through me, the eyes cold, the heavy Dutch chin out-thrust, the massive torso erect, the whole manner bleak, hostile, impervious. Even sitting in his chair Roosevelt seemed to overtop the men standing beside him. I could hardly believe that he was a cripple with legs paralysed, the athlete's body propped on steel braces. His affliction well concealed, he had a look of vibrant health; more than that, an air of serene authority and invulnerable strength.

It may have been my awe in finding myself here, or just one of the actor's many parts, but I felt penetrated, scorned, perhaps hypnotized, by those stony eyes. Hypnotism, magnetism, charm, charisma? The words don't matter. I simply assert, without expecting anyone to believe me, that a current of some sort flowed from the man as from an electric battery. I felt it at first hand as countless millions had begun to feel it from a distance.

If all this sounds absurd now, when the myth has faded,

Roosevelt was truly hypnotic in the early days of his power. Like all successful leaders he even hypnotized himself if necessary. He accepted power as a natural gift to be used as he chose, enjoyed, exuded, and exaggerated—always, as he undoubtedly thought, for the benefit of his people. The sincerity, yet untested, was flawed by manic ambition but redeemed, or so I came to think, by a curious innocence. The unquestioning egotist had a faith not only in himself but in mankind, a hope to sustain him when all hope seemed lost.

Of course no such thoughts crossed my mind until I had watched Roosevelt in the subsequent years of agony. At the moment a young man from Canada could not suspect that the man behind the desk really didn't know what he was doing to his nation or the world. Much less could I suspect the sinuosities and ruthless methods of his public life, so slyly hidden by his apparent candor, or the courage, contradictions, and failures of his private life, the agglomeration of opposites, of greatness and meanness, that historians have never sorted out and probably never will.

None of the flaws, only his strength, was visible at that noonday of 1933. Still staring blankly through me into space, Roosevelt waited for the reporters to fill the Oval Room. Then instantly, the seasoned actor on cue, he recognized his friends of the Washington press corps, grinned that grin of flashing teeth already known throughout the world, fumbled for his cigarette holder, an invaluable stage prop, inserted a cigarette with clumsy fingers, and said he had some items of news to announce. I forget what they were and barely listened. My eyes were fixed on his, my mind fascinated by a scene familiar to my companions but almost magical to me. Better men would have been hypnotized.

After the rotundities of R. B. Bennett and the tortuous speeches of Mackenzie King, Roosevelt's diction sounded colloquial, careless, slangy, the patrician of Hyde Park speaking the language of the man on the street, the Great Guy among his cronies. But just as suddenly as it had appeared the mood changed and the grin vanished.

Some question infuriated Roosevelt. In a new tone as cutting as a scalpel he asked the questioner if the word of the President was doubted and, on his swivel chair, he turned his back to the audience and glared out the window. Hushed by the presidential wrath, no one spoke until Roosevelt swivelled around again and the actor's face wore its Janus mask of laughter. A few more questions and cheerful replies and then someone murmured, "Thank you, Mr. President." We filed out, the Americans to write their hot news stories, the Canadian to walk in Lafayette Park and recover from something close to magic.

It *was* magic, too, a bogus stagecraft magic blurring Roosevelt's inner confusion, but magic all the same when his courage alone stood between his nation and despair. He had no real answers to the Depression, though he pretended to have them, and like most politicians, no original ideas. He depended instead on those of other men whose advice he rearranged, regurgitated, and ornamented to fit his needs. Already his financial naïveté had dumbfounded Maynard Keynes and amused Mackenzie King. Even now his election promises of old-fashioned budgetary thrift had been turned upside down and he was about to torpedo the World Economic Conference in London. Yet he had, like no other man, the one thing needed in the trough of the Depression. He had faith in Roosevelt and his people.

During the next dozen years I attended many of his press conferences. My first feverish impressions cooled as the workaday routine of the New Deal emerged. I followed it eagerly, instructed by some of its senior mechanics, and began to understand it in a vague fashion without foreseeing its consequences. They were delayed for a whole generation and foreseen by no one. Even Keynes, the inventor and master mechanic, could not imagine them. But I was always more interested in Roosevelt than in his economics, which he never understood. And in the autumn of 1937 I saw him at last outside his stage setting.

He had come, unexpectedly, to my home town for a day's neighborly visit. When his destroyer was tied to the Victoria wharf I stood at the bottom of the gangplank, admitted there with a pass from my friends in the local police department but unapproved by the American secret-service men. If they were present I could not see them, only a limousine parked beside the gangplank and a grim, husky fellow standing near by. As I watched in the dim shed, with two or three policemen, while thousands of Victorians waited outside for a sight of Canada's illustrious guest, a tall figure appeared on the destroyer's deck.

For a moment, having always seen him at ease in his White House chair, I did not recognize Roosevelt. The man grasping the two rails of the gangplank seemed limp, feeble, helpless. It was horrifying to see this giant descend, like a wounded gymnast, on parallel bars. Only his hands and bulging arms were of any use now. Hand by hand, inch by inch, he lowered himself down the gangplank, his legs in their steel braces dragging beneath him. When he reached the bottom his face was streaming with sweat and contorted in pain. A journey of about twenty feet had exhausted him.

The burly man beside the limousine seized the President under the shoulders and dropped him, like a doll, to the floor of the car, his legs dangling outside it. Then the attendant, leaping in from the other side, pulled Roosevelt up to the seat, unfastened the braces, and adjusted the useless legs. All this happened so fast and smoothly that no one but the little group on the wharf had seen it. Now, as the President wiped his face with a handkerchief, thrust his cigarette into his mouth, and put on the happy public grin, no one could have suspected his terrible infirmity. A moment later, the car moved out of the shed and the crowds cheered their idol. He waved and laughed at them.

After an official luncheon in Government House I spoke directly to him for the first and last time. On the arms of his wife and his son James, Roosevelt stumbled from the door of the mansion and, surrounded by his secret-service men, was quickly lifted into his car. One of the secretaries had promised that I could question him through the window on behalf of the Canadian reporters for a single minute, no more. The question agreed among us sounds preposterous today, but it was considered urgent, a major news story, in those simple days. When, I asked, would a highway to Alaska be built by Canada and the United States?

Roosevelt looked at me with the cold, bleak face that I had sometimes seen in the Oval Room. Biting hard on his cigarette holder, he replied: "It will be built when the governments of Canada and the United States decide to build it." That was all, and it meant exactly nothing, as he intended; the car drove off.

My brief skirmish with the Great Guy at the peak of his powers was the least of that year's events for Dot and me. To us, 1937 was altogether a magical year.

In the spring we had taken our first look at the Old World as tourists and country bumpkins, innocents abroad, and very fortunate at home where the two Grannies remained to care for our children. Our goal was a king's coronation in London, our itinerary indirect, back and forth across Europe by winding mossy ways. To avoid all the trunk routes we drove a hired English car on the side roads. With my cousin, Archie McVittie, and his sister, Margaret Pressey, we jogged slowly through France, Belgium, Holland, Germany, Switzerland, Austria, and Hungary.

We were still young enough to be impressed by the hackneyed candle-light and wine and castles on the Rhine, the scenery, art galleries, cathedrals, and ruins that the European hucksters know how to peddle with ingratiating courtesy and private leers of contempt.

Every noon we stopped for a picnic in the woods — bread, cheese, local sausage, and the *vin du pays* at about twenty cents a bottle, if you brought your own bottle, as we did. (One of them, filled with robust Chianti, exploded with violence and dyed the car's upholstery a noble, permanent crimson.) Every night, in

1. The Leslie home at Prescott where Bruce Hutchison was born in 1901

2. BH in a moment of serenity rare for a four-year-old

3, 4. BH's parents, John and Constance Hutchison

5. BH, a fire-eating nineteen-year-old reporter for the *Victoria Daily Times*

6, 7. Mr. and Mrs. F. A. McDiarmid, father and mother of Dorothy Hutchison

8, 9. The Hutchison family home just outside Victoria, B.C., and young BH lounging on the steps of the cottage at Shawnigan Lake

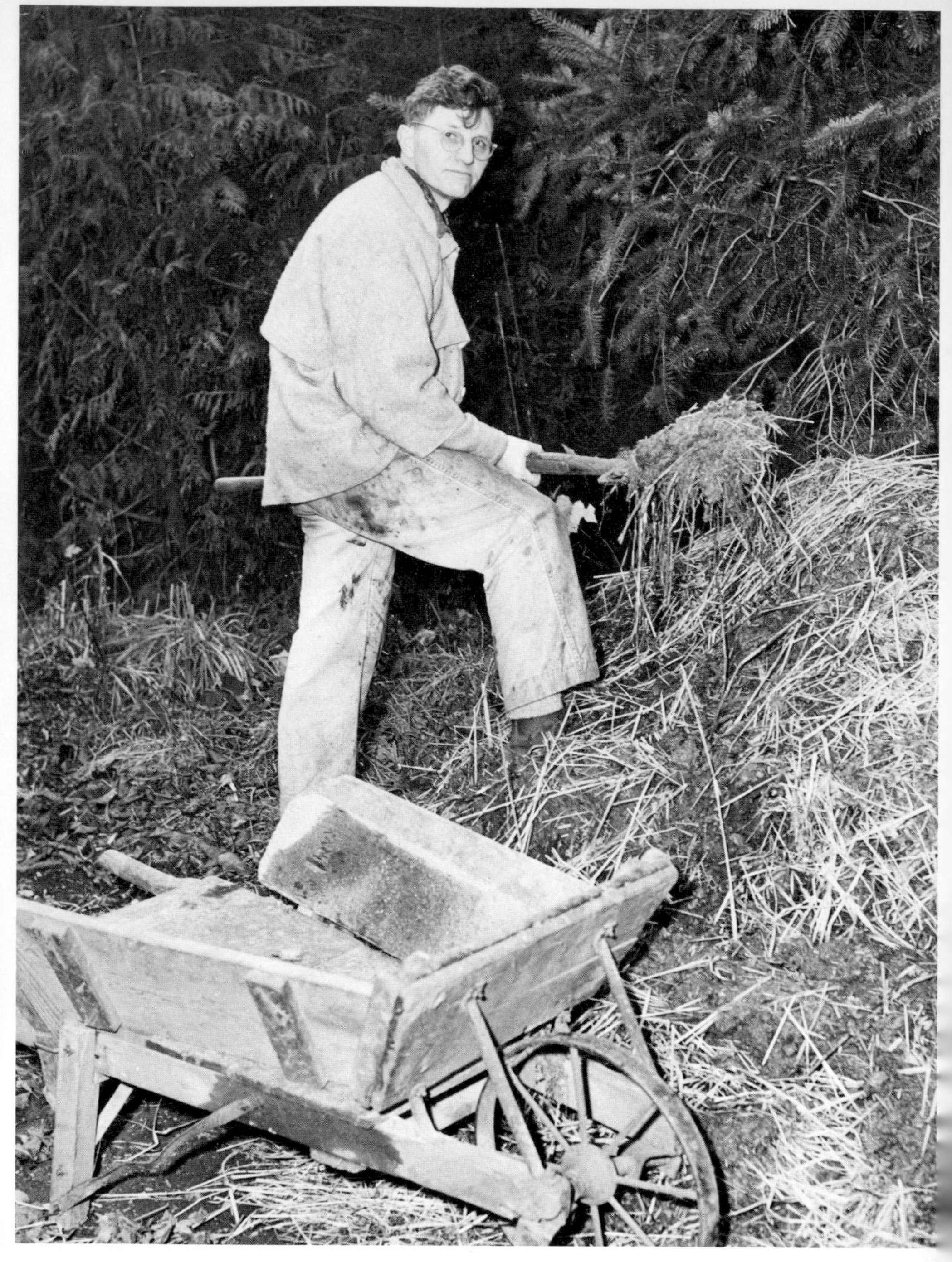

10. BH giving a new twist of meaning to the term "a muckraking journalist".

11. Arthur Meighen. "His voice was calm and metallic,... his arguments marshalled clause by clause in neat syllogism, his irony corrosive, his loathing of King naked, contemptuous, and self-destructive."

12. R. B. Bennett. Despite hopeless odds in the election of 1935 Bennett campaigned relentlessly. In Victoria he "strode to the centre of the stage, majestic in tail coat and air of defiance, master of himself and the crowd."

13. Mackenzie King and German Foreign Minister von Neurath in 1937 at the time of King's interview with Hitler. Shortly after the meeting the Prime Minister confided to BH that "the German dictator was 'a simple sort of peasant' and not very bright, who wished only to possess the Sudetenland of Czechoslovakia."

14. The Coronation of King George VI in 1937: "...the whole Empire and Commonwealth on a parade that continued for most of the day."

some hotel bedroom, dark and dirty because it was cheap, I tortured out a travel piece for the papers, or an interview with some quaint local character whom I made even quainter, knowing that he would never read my regrettably over-colored version.

Thus working our passage, we finally burst into the great poppy-flecked plain of the Danube and followed it to Budapest. There, at the five o'clock rush hour, our car inexplicably died on the main bridge of the city, blocking the traffic in a national Hungarian emergency, until half a dozen policemen, brandishing clubs and screaming in an unknown language, pushed us into an alley and left us. When at last the engine cooled down the car started again. Having inspected the handsomest civic façade in Europe and the loathsome slums a few blocks from the river, we drove down to Italy, explored by gondola the canal-sewers of Venice, which we thought romantic at the time, despite the stinking garbage, escaped through the snow of the Swiss Alps, and headed back to England, broke but content.

In all those European countries I travelled with a mixture of relish and alarm; unlike my bolder companions, I was alarmed at every border where the guards inspected our official papers, looked us over with suspicion, and seemed likely to arrest us as spies. My imagination, as usual, worked overtime, but already Europe was beginning to sense the first chill of the freeze before the volcanic eruption.

In Germany dark columns of troops marched everywhere. Nazi youth clubs, gathering strength through joy, paraded with shovels in work parties, well indoctrinated in the faith by Dr. Goebbels. In comparison, the listless boy soldiers of France, said to be the strongest army in the world, did not look it. Even the supposedly gay Italian temperament was now strangely cool; a stout hotel keeper of Milan informing me that "our big boy, that Mussolini", had defied the League of Nations in Ethiopia, taught England a lesson, and would teach others. Most of all, I was alarmed by those bony women, ageless and immortal, who presided in a dank cavern at every French inn, observed every visitor with a witch's eye, read his thoughts, and doubtless conveyed them immediately to the secret police.

I don't mean that I felt the imminence of war. Assuredly I did not, just as next year I was to fail to see the meaning of the Munich deal, which I welcomed along with Mackenzie King and most Canadians, who a year later denounced Neville Chamberlain for making it. My blunt antennae perceived only the superficial mood of Europe but an old reporter's nose caught a distant whiff of trouble. Dot, who feared nothing in this or any other world, laughed at my alarm, set me laughing, too, and enjoyed everything. All the same the cliffs of Dover looked like home and the English accent, though odd in our ears, was a welcome sound.

A still warmer welcome awaited us in the Surrey house of Grant and Alice Dexter. As the London correspondent of the *Winnipeg Free Press*, Grant introduced me to Vincent Massey, the erudite and exquisite Canadian High Commissioner in whose presence, it was said, the ordinary man always felt like a naked savage. More interesting to me was his pink and youthful factotum. I saw him only for a few minutes but liked his breezy manner, his lack of official gloss or diplomatic pose, and I recognized even then that he had much greater qualities than his secondary job required. The young man's name was Mike Pearson.

After completely encircling the island in the season of Wordsworth's daffodils and finding a beauty beyond any poet's descriptive power, I had learned that this was my father's country, not mine. Then, and in all our later journeys there, Dot and I came to love the British people, above all the Scots, our true ancestors. But the more we saw of Britain the more we realized that North America was our only home. And gradually, over the years, the profound transatlantic gulf, far wider than geography, language, or culture, began to widen for both of us.

To our foreign eyes, the British and the Europeans were

people of secure streets and authentic civilization, of ancient life lived together in immemorial cities, of houses inhabited, fields plowed, and gods jointly worshipped for centuries in a mystical companionship which we could never join — yes, civilized, despite their wars, as North Americans are not yet and may never be.

North Americans are still, at bottom, a people of the wilderness, soul-shadowed by its immensity, loving it, fighting it, ruining it, hiding from it in their flimsy skyscrapers but never escaping it, always aware of its dark menace beside them. With all their economic agreements and military alliances, the street people and the wilderness people, we thought, were almost two different species—an absurd idea, I dare say, but there is something in it.

For the most part the street people of Britain in the late thirties were doing very well. The worst of the Depression was behind them, the war ahead, unforeseen. But in places like the Rhondda Valley, no longer green, life seemed to have run out. The coal miners had no work and existed, without really living, on the dole. Their rows of bleak gray houses, wall to wall between mountains of slag, lacked even the poor comfort and companionship of the city slums. Over their daily glass of beer, the last consolation left to them, the townsmen looked sickly, apathetic, dehumanized by idleness. The pubs were full but silent.

In this climate of apathy we could see no hope, no future. Yet twenty years later we found the valley green again, the towns spruced up, the miners at work, the pubs noisy with laughter, the women crowding all the shops, the children well dressed, the Depression and the war distant memories.

The dumb patience and durability of these people was an old legend, but it was their legend, not ours. In good times and bad we would always be strangers among them, moved by the indescribable beauty of Britain's landscape, awed by its Gothic cathedrals and even comelier country churches, but irritated by its smug orderliness, its fussy official interference, its ineffable superiority so honest, sincere, and deeply rooted, so much a part of nature itself, that it could not be called snobbery. Dot, who expanded the English language to suit her needs, compromised on the less abrasive word "snobdobbery". It served well enough for a class structure so impervious as to make ours in North America seem like a sieve.

For Britain the year 1937 was to be the last great celebration of imperial glory, a time of bitter-sweet nostalgia. In truth, as we had observed them all over the Kingdom, the British people were not much concerned with the Empire or the Commonwealth which was replacing it. Few of them could have listed the members of that amorphous club, and Canada was generally regarded as a cross between Kipling's Lady of the Snows, a second-class Britain, and a colony of the United States.

As Canadians, no doubt we were unduly sensitive to this genial ignorance of our country, and didn't enjoy being taken everywhere for Americans because of our queer transatlantic accent. But we suspected then, and were quite certain in later years, that the British people (as distinguished from their statesmen and better journalists) were interested almost exclusively in themselves, just like other peoples. Beyond the mannered and stuffy offices of Whitehall, the Empire had become for the average Briton a name in the history books, the Commonwealth only an omnibus, generic term, embracing some very decent outsiders like Canadians, and some lesser breeds who, if not without Kipling's law, were not inside it, either; not inside the real arcanum anyway.

Trying to learn that law, Dot and I wandered through London with a camera, photographing the usual sights. One day, we stumbled into an outdoor market where second-hand stuff of every imaginable sort was sold among a crowd of clamorous Cockneys. Always, until then, they had treated us kindly, as if we were lost creatures of the world. But when I raised my camera to record this jolly scene, a dozen fierce and screaming women turned on me in fury as if I had invaded their parlors, or bedrooms. There would be no picture of a strictly private affair. We retreated in disorder, a final imprecation following us. "Look at 'im!" the largest woman bellowed. "Wot's 'e doin' 'ere, 'im and 's bleedin' dreams?" Those were her exact words, mysterious and barely intelligible, yet somehow more expressive than all the sleek jargon of Whitehall. From Cockney dreams, long ripened in the streets of London, a Canadian was forever excluded.

On the other hand, when we needed help, it never failed. One day we drove, too late, into a railway station at some Kentish village where our friend Dorothy Crerar was to catch the train for London and be presented at Court. The train had moved beyond the platform and was gathering speed. Dexter shouted at the station guard: "This young lady has an appointment with the King!"

"Has she indeed, sir?" said the guard and, at the mention of that magic name, he blew his whistle and flashed a signal light. The train stopped and moved back to the platform. Dorothy, as the monarch's guest, reached Buckingham Palace on time. Such a thing could not have happened on any North American railway. In a pinch, and regardless of the rules, the British don't let you down, even if you are a stranger.

Nothing in our experience could match for deadly horror an evening in the lounge of an English country hotel, while the village pub was full of life. Yet I dare say the guests, who seemed like walking mummies, were alive if you could only reach them. Sometimes, not often, we did, and then the drawbridge was lowered, the stranger admitted to the castle, and the mutes amazed us with their friendly, rash abandon.

Odd folk, the English, so pitiably shy, so fearful of their own emotions as they are of no foreign enemy, and, behind their protective sheath, so wildly romantic. Still, they were practical, too, earthy and highly independent in their assessment of the nation's rulers, the monarch always excepted because, under a sublimely illogical and workable system, he did not rule but merely reigned.

When Edward VIII ceased to reign even he was much criticized for prefering an American lady to his crown. While the memory of the abdication hurt, George VI's coronation soothed the family wound in the delusive pause and imperial twilight that had the outer look of a new sunrise. The crowning of an excellent and modest young man, however, must be strictly a British sacrament to which outsiders from his overseas dominions and colonies came as guests — honored, welcomed, occasionally liked, and, by officialdom, studiously flattered, but outsiders all the same.

Since the Romans discovered a ford on the Thames and built their town beside it, London had seldom witnessed such a spectacle. The flags, banners, flowered arches, and polished statues, the bands, the laughing crowds, the kissing youngsters, the bobbies who herded them with tolerant discipline, the whirling patterns and colors of a vast phantasmagoria made us so drunk on pleasure that we needed no wine, or not much.

Since various newspapers at home expected to hear from me, I interviewed the Canadian statesmen who had assembled for a Commonwealth conference of more than usual unreality. Then, on the eve of the Coronation, I suddenly entertained what, in the prevailing mood and the traffic congestion, seemed a stroke of genius. After a full-dress party, I found one of the last hackney cabs in London, bribed the driver in his high pulpit, stuffed five companions into a space designed for two, and with doors flapping open we toured the Strand and Piccadilly Circus at three o'clock in the morning.

None of us felt any pain, nor did the crowds that still swarmed through the streets. Taking us for mad and drunk Americans (which was inaccurate on two counts out of three) they waved and cheered us on, until the coachman announced that he and his mare, whose name was Daisy, were tired and thirsty. He halted the cab and dumped us out, we didn't know where, and disappeared into a pub, leaving Daisy to drink at a watering trough. We found our way back to the hotel on foot. But not to sleep.

Already daylight was breaking on Coronation Day. We had just time to change our clothes and, breakfastless, again on foot, to set out for Trafalgar Square where Admiral Nelson, on his pillar, emerged slowly against a pale dawn.

From our observation point in Canada House everything appeared to go off precisely on schedule — the multi-colored uniforms, the gaudy robes of Asia and Africa, the royal coach, a crawling beetle of gold, its two passengers bravely smiling and gesturing, the diminutive figure of Mackenzie King lost but beaming and bowing in a coach of lesser majesty, the whole Empire and Commonwealth on a parade that continued for most of the day.

Taking no chances on my inspiration, and knowing the sort of sodden sentimentality expected by Canadian editors, I had written a "lead" for my story in advance. It must have been a dreadful story but it was easy to finish, with a few last-minute flourishes, and dictate by telephone to the cable office. Apart from starvation, because the throng in Canada House had eaten all the food while I wrote in an upstairs office, the day passed without accident.

Regrettably, I was not touched by proper royal emotion, only by the Mounties whose scarlet tunics brought a brief flash of Canada, hardly noticed in that multitude. For Dot and me all this was sheer holiday. For the crowds it was a form of worship — worship of an idea that could not be articulated otherwise, and understood, in the full sense, by the British alone. Dimly I recalled Carlyle's dictum, in the French Revolution, that no people was ever great when it proclaimed its greatness aloud, only when it was silent in its daily task. But my mind was fastened on a practical job of work and it terrified me.

The infant Canadian Broadcasting Commission had offered

the magnificent fee of twenty-five dollars if I would describe the Coronation for its listeners on radio that night. Though the honor meant even more than the money to a reporter of my conceit, what was I to say? In the stage fright of my first big nation-wide moment, would I be able to say anything?

All the late afternoon and evening I sweated over my typewriter at the hotel, sustained by sandwiches, coffee, cigarettes, and desperation. At midnight, Dot and I walked along empty Whitehall to some building near the Houses of Parliament in which the British Broadcasting Corporation had kindly promised to provide a microphone. Then the whole imperial apparatus, and, more important, my hopeful career, seemed to collapse.

We found the building all right but it was in total darkness and the front door locked, just fifteen minutes before I was to go on the transatlantic air. What to do?

We dashed down the street to a public telephone booth. It was occupied by a drunken gentleman who obviously intended to conduct a prolonged conversation. At last, by shouts, gesticulations, and a pretty good pretence of violent lunacy, I drove him out, seized the telephone, and found that I had a hundred paper pounds sterling in my pocket but not a single coin to pay for the call. At this crisis in the Commonwealth's life and mine, I threw myself on the genius of Britain. It did not fail me.

When I told the telephone operator that I had no coins, that I must somehow reach the inmates of the locked building, and that, in exactly seven minutes, I was to address the people of Canada, a brisk Cockney voice replied: "Don't worry, sir I'll put you through." So he did, in seconds, without payment, and another Cockney voice, rather peevish and half asleep, said we could enter by the back door but should beware the slippery steps in the darkness.

There were only two minutes left as a sleepy janitor admitted us through the back door and led the way upstairs, a candle in his hand. Three BBC broadcasters, exhausted by the day's work, were relaxing over beer. They said maybe, just maybe, I could use one of the microphones in a glass booth glued for the Coronation to the outside wall of the building.

We dashed in there. I fumbled with my manuscript, beheld with panic a red signal light glowing beside me, and started, breathless, to read my report. That it would ever reach Canada from this cubicle far above the inky, silent street I could not believe. But again, as I heard later, the apparatus worked perfectly. Our children in Victoria heard their father's words and, against all the rules, a personal message to them. So maybe, after all, I had earned my twenty-five dollars. However, as Wellington had said of a somewhat more important occasion, it was a damned close run thing.

We finished off the night swimming in champagne lavishly distributed by a millionaire from Vancouver at Ciro's, where Rudy Vallee entertained us with song and fortified himself at our table. Under his disguise as a crooner he appeared to be a pleasant and intelligent man.

Such was our first Coronation. The second, in 1953, came easier, except for a momentary and purely Canadian hitch in the old apparatus. As before, I was to telephone my report from an upstairs office in Canada House, but when I tried the door, with only minutes to spare, I found that it had been locked by some zealous clerk. There was no time for appeal to the High Commissioner and I could not have reached him anyway in his crowded mansion.

With an audacity which horrifies me as I remember it now, I climbed through the window of an empty corridor, stepped on a narrow ledge outside, three storeys above Trafalgar Square, and crept to the next window. I could not open it from the bottom but managed to pull down the upper glass and hurl myself over it to land on my head inside. It was a bruised and shaking reporter who dictated something, I forget what, to the cable office.

This would be our last Coronation and we were sated with

grandeur. Yet there was more to it than that. By then I had become old and sceptical enough to note a change in the mental climate of Britain, which seemed to find its token in the drenching rain on Coronation Day. The crowds were as large as before, the parade longer, the young Queen as stately and gallant as her father, but after those years of standing alone in the demented world of the second war, Britain seemed to know that nothing would ever be the same again.

The Empire had been given back to its original owners. Most of the Commonwealth belonged to non-white and non-British peoples. Britain itself was not a great power now beside the American and Russian giants—not great in terms of military or economic power but still great, perhaps greater, in its peaceful acceptance of a very different place among the nations that its courage had saved. Where else could such a transformation have been achieved without a bloody revolt?

Touring the whole island again, we liked the new Britain better than the old. The little people, the best people, in the pubs and fields were interested in Canada for the first time, now that it had become truly a nation of its own.

On a third tour later on, all my confused thoughts about Britain were crystallized in final truth when I found myself among the bombed ruins of Coventry Cathedral. There in the rubble stood a crude wooden cross of charred beams, wired together by some unknown man on the morning after the first saturation raid of the war. On the cross hung a rough sign with two scrawled words that seemed to utter the ultimate message of the British folk. Two words—"Father Forgive." I turned away, eyes flooded. "Father Forgive." What other folk in all the world would have invoked that forgiveness on their enemy? Such human beings, and such a nation, I judged, were indestructible.

10

The Halcyon Days

The Depression gave me a smattering of economics, just enough to be dangerous, and certain unalterable views that I would soon change and change again. But in those gloomy times something of more interest and keen delight had occurred, with results never to be changed—the rediscovery of the Cariboo country. I say rediscovery because that rolling inland plateau of British Columbia had become known to me some ten years earlier, thanks to the latest whim of Benny Nicholas.

In the autumn of 1921, on the spur of the moment, Benny decided that he must go north, for reasons unexplained, before winter closed the roads (which he had seen only on a map). As companions on a desperate lunge into the unknown he chose Charlie Shaw, the brains of the rival *Daily Colonist*, Cornelius Moriarty, Victoria agent of the Canadian Press, and myself.

Boarding a ship in Seattle for the voyage to Prince Rupert, we must have looked an odd foursome — Benny fat and shining with cosmic benevolence exactly like Mr. Pickwick on his immortal pilgrimage; Charlie, tall, blond, and handsome like some Nordic god; Moriarty short, swarthy, and mischievous, an Irish leprechaun; and I, then passable in appearance, the youngest member of the Pickwick Club, and second-rate Sam Weller.

All went smoothly until we reached Prince George by rail from Prince Rupert and prepared to move south in easy stages, literally on a stagecoach of some sort. To our amazement we found that there was no road out of Prince George, no stage, no means of travel except a river boat grandly named the *Circle W*.

This craft, moored to the bank of the Fraser, seemed to be hardly more than a flat barge some forty feet long. It was made of rough boards loosely nailed together with an old automobile engine at the stern and a flimsy pilot house at the bow. But her master, a squat round man of grizzled, melancholy face and few words, apparently knew his business. Captain Foster, the veteran of many proud ships and northern rivers, promised that if we were aboard at six o'clock the next morning he would take us ninety miles down the river to Quesnel for a modest fee. Of course, he said, we would be in no danger. Still, when I learned that he had wrecked his own splendid stern-wheeler on a rock only a year ago and lost his life savings with her I began to wonder if the voyage was as safe as he pretended.

Feeling very brave, and very cold in the sleet of late October, we boarded the *Circle W* at dawn. After many failures, Captain Foster got the automobile engine started. The crew — a scarecrow well disguised by an enormous cowboy hat and a Mexican bandit mustache — cast off the lines. We were floating on the brown current that had once carried the birchbark canoes of Alexander Mackenzie and Simon Fraser to the Pacific, and to glory.

The canoes, I suspected, were probably safer than our motorized barge. At least we had a stove, a rusty kitchen range, on the uncovered deck. This was tended by a scrawny Chinese cook who spoke no understandable English but fed us a breakfast of steaks and fried potatoes and kept us plied all day with hot coffee, may God rest his generous Oriental spirit. Before long I was privately expecting to need the same posthumous benediction myself, especially when I saw the rotting bones of Captain Foster's steamboat, and other wrecks, along the shore.

At first we suffered only from the icy wind and driven sleet as, huddling around the stove, we watched the high banks of the Fraser slip by, all gold now, spangled with autumn poplar. Soon

I forgot the temperature in the stress of more urgent anxieties. We had entered the long defile of Fort George Canyon which had frightened even Mackenzie and Fraser.

The *Circle W* wallowed through this stretch of white water, bobbing like a cork. Captain Foster shut himself in the pilot house, spun the steering wheel, and aimed his vessel from one side of the current to the other, evidently familiar with every shoal and hidden rock.

Surprisingly, we emerged without damage from the Canyon and, fortified by a second round of steaks, assumed that the worst was over. But suddenly the river narrowed ahead to pile up on an island of bare stone and spill through two constricted guts. Surely no boat could live in either of them? This, I guessed, was the Place of Wild Onions noted by Mackenzie and Fraser in their diaries with more than usual alarm.

Captain Foster had come on deck and carefully studied the alternative channels. As if he could not decide between them, he stopped the engine and allowed his barge to drift aimlessly, crosswise to the current. I asked myself, but not him, whether he had any notion of what he was doing. It seemed improbable.

The island was less than a hundred yards away and we moved toward it at terrifying speed. Which channel would the Captain choose? Or, more likely, which would engulf us? The crew appeared equally dubious. He picked up a long boathook and brandished it like a spear. I judged that our Mexican bandit had gone quietly mad.

The white torrent on the left looked dangerous enough but better than the foaming vortex on the right. To my horror the *Circle W* was drifting rightward and the Captain still stood moodily on the deck, undecided, as I thought, and helpless. Then, with a single bound, he was back in the pilot house and swinging his wheel. The barge trembled with a creak of straining boards and surged down the worse channel, so close to the rocks on both sides that I could have leaped ashore and was tempted to do so.

This, I told myself, was a queer ending to a short, blameless life, at the Place of the Wild Onions.

Benny, his plump cheeks ashen, gazed at the scene like an idol cast in concrete. Moriarty, that good Irish Catholic, was praying silently. Shaw had lost his look of Nordic grandeur.

Now we lurched abruptly to the left and were a scant yard from the island when the crew, with magnificent nonchalance, thrust out his pole and pushed us off. The *Circle W*, her hull screaming, listed to her gunwales and seemed bound to capsize in another moment. But the moment passed. She was in calm water again, the rocks behind her.

At nightfall we tied up at the little village of Quesnel, found sanctuary in the red-plush Victorian parlor of the Stranger's Rest, and were served a lavish Cariboo dinner by two wonderful old spinsters straight out of Dickens. The new Pickwick Club had survived its first trial. Others, even more unlikely, would soon confront it.

Next day Shaw and I decided that we must ride on horseback to Barkerville, once the capital of the Cariboo gold rush and later on an officially maintained ghost town. It lay some sixty miles to the eastward at the end of a sodden dirt road but this distance could not daunt two romantic and inexperienced youths, thirsty for adventure. Hiring a pair of skinny horses, we set out with no food, blankets, or other necessities while Benny and Moriarty remained in the comfort of the Stranger's Rest.

All day we rode, soon aware that we had not ridden for many years and that our tender thighs were becoming raw from the saddle. A mixture of rain, snow, and wind soaked through our thin clothing. Our healthy young stomachs cried out for nourishment. At one stride came the dark but along that twisting, endless road we saw no human habitation or any glint of light. In the literal sense of the word, we were benighted, God knew where, between the Stranger's Rest and Barkerville. Romance died within our shivering bodies.

At last, around a bend, we beheld a gleam through the trees.

Our tired horses saw it, too, and broke into a gallop. The light came from the window of a ramshackle log cabin but to us it was the illumination of a palace. Answering our knock, an aged man with white whiskers opened the door and gruffly invited us to come in. Our host showed us where to stable our horses in a shed, produced some hay for them and presently a mountain of bacon and eggs for his guests. Under shaggy eyebrows his wise old eyes watched us keenly, as if he was debating whether we could be trusted. Deciding, apparently, that we were deranged but harmless, he began to talk and talked until four o'clock in the morning.

Exhausted as we were by the day's ride, sleep was forgotten. For this man was no other than Harry Jones, one of the three men still living who had marched with the gold rush from Yale to Barkerville in 1862, the last of the original Argonauts. As reporters we also had struck gold on Lightning Creek.

If Jones's talk had been put on tape it would have made a genuine historic document—his memories of Billy Barker, who first hit the riches of Williams Creek, took out $600,000, gave his name to the largest town in the Canadian West, and ended destitute in the old men's home at Victoria; of Cariboo Cameron, who amassed a great fortune, carried the bodies of his wife and baby in a lead tank filled with alcohol from Barkerville to Ontario for burial at home, and returned to be buried beside his claim; of Matthew Baillie Begbie, the terrible Hanging Judge who, in truth, seldom hanged anyone, often scribbled his court orders on horseback, interpreted the law to fit his rough sense of justice, and, mostly by solemn bluff, compelled the lawless American miners to obey him.

All these men, and many others, Jones remembered as friends and described in language the more vivid for its simplicity. Any Canadian historian would have given his eye teeth (or even his Canada Council grant) to hear and record that night-long monologue. We gave only our chance to sleep.

What of Jones himself? How had he come here, old, poor, and

deserted, to this cabin on Lightning Creek where a thousand miners had bored their tunnels and death traps through the shifting mud, but had never reached the final treasure deep down on the bedrock?

The answer was as simple as the tale. Yes, Jones had found treasure enough for any man a few yards from the cabin, had returned to his home in Wales, spent his money on wine, women, and song, and come back to the Cariboo, hoping to find a second stake. He did not find it. Now the Argonaut was ending that Odyssey as the watchman of some unworked mine with nothing but his cabin, his memories, and, beside his door, the gurgle, or perhaps the ironic chuckle, of Lightning Creek in the dark.

Charlie and I set out at dawn and rode into Barkerville at night. The ghost town was a true ghost then, before the government painted, primped, and strumpeted it for the gaping tourists. Its single narrow lane, between Williams Creek and a naked hill, had once been crammed with ox teams, pack horses, miners, gamblers, and dance-hall girls, the human tailings and detritus of the gold rush. No one moved on the street that night but most of the creek seemed to flow across the rotting wooden sidewalks.

Our horses splashed through the water toward the only visible light and we dismounted at Kelly's celebrated hotel, a brave relic of the great days. As Jones had told us, Judge Begbie used to stay here and, one afternoon, when he overheard three miners plotting his assassination on the porch below his room, emptied the contents of a chamber pot on their heads and resumed his siesta. Chilled and soaked, we had no time for these historical footnotes but lurched into the warmth of a lobby as scrubbed and polished as if the gold rush had never ceased.

The man behind the antique desk was not a Barkerville native. He was the ineffable Benny. Somehow he and Moriarty had got there ahead of us in a hired automobile. Now they denied all knowledge of our acquaintance. If we desired a room, Benny said, we must pay in advance, which, in the spirit of the joke, we did; and Moriarty, asking an advance tip, carried our dripping haversacks to an upstairs apartment splendidly furnished with mellow oak and supplied with very welcome feather quilts.

Benny's joke failed to amuse an old man who sat so close to the red belly of the drum stove that his Santa Claus beard was in danger of conflagration. Bill Brown, another of the three last Argonauts, had come in from the hills for a night on the town. But, seeing four strangers, a mass invasion, he left us, grumbling in disgust, resaddled his horse, and rode into the night.

The Chinese cook having revived us with a meal fit for the best hotel in Vancouver, we borrowed a lantern and groped our way through a maze of muddy paths and slippery bridges to the home of Fred Tregillus, the town's sage and philosopher. This determined man had arrived here from England, long after the rush, not to pan placer gold but to discover the ore of the mother lode. Of course he had not discovered it but, as we could not foresee then, he finally hit a rich vein and ended his life of toil in comfort.

Meanwhile his numerous family welcomed us to a cosy house, and since it was Sunday we sang hymns around a queer old-fashioned organ, Mrs. Tregillus pumping the foot pedals with Christian zeal — all this in the year of 1921, in the booming province of British Columbia, in a world already marching toward the Bull Market and the Bust.

Through Benny's influence, elaborate preparations had been made for our return. Premier John Oliver had arranged a special train for us on the provincial government's half-completed Pacific and Great Eastern Railway running from Quesnel to Squamish, on the coast. Sure enough, when we reached Quesnel, after our two-day ride back from Barkerville, the special train awaited us at the station. In the freezing half-light of dawn we boarded the only passenger car. But this dirty and battered vehicle of wood was so jammed with free-riding and very unwashed hoboes that we retreated to an open flatcar and sat on a heap of gravel, cursing the Premier and his government.

Though he was cold, hungry, and half covered with gravel, Benny rose to a lofty height of eloquence and editorial threat, but he cheered up considerably as we arrived around noon at Williams Lake and found indifferent nourishment in a ghastly Chinese café. His choler soon turned to mischief, ingenious and diabolical.

On the railway platform he had noticed an impressive figure who wore a dingy bowler hat, a pointed Vandyke beard, and an air of authority. Sidling up to this gentleman, Benny engaged him in small talk about the weather and the crops. Then, lowering his voice and glancing about to make sure that his words were not overheard, he introduced himself as John D. Rockefeller, Jr., travelling, naturally, incognito. Moriarty, he said, was the powerful Senator Julius Goldstein of New York and a partner in the Morgan Bank. Shaw, whose Nordic glamour fitted him perfectly for the role, was in fact Crown Prince Axel of Denmark, while I was the nameless secretary of this distinguished group.

"Of course, sir," Benny added, in a confidential tone, "I saw at once that you were a man to be trusted, a man of discretion, a man of the world. Otherwise I wouldn't have disclosed our identity. No one else knows it. You, I'm sure, will keep it to yourself. But I must have your pledge of secrecy before I ask your advice on a great matter, a very great matter."

The Vandyke beard quivered and the dim eyes glowed with excitement. Nothing like this had ever happened before in the Cariboo.

"You can trust me, Mr. Rockefeller," the discreet man whispered. "I won't say a word to anyone, not a word."

"On that understanding," Benny went on, "I want your opinion, sir. A consortium of American and European interests, which I am not yet at liberty to disclose, is about to purchase the Pacific and Great Eastern Railway from the government. Then we shall invest large sums, hundreds of millions, in the development of the mineral, agricultural, and timber resources of the

Cariboo. Why, it will be an empire of wealth, a veritable empire."

The ancient gasped and tugged so hard at his beard that I thought he would uproot it.

"I knew this was a-comin', oh yes, I've waited for this day!"

"You won't wait much longer," Benny assured him. "But, sir, in your judgment is our scheme financially sound? Will it pay?"

"It'll pay all right. Sound as a bell, the Cariboo. I always said so."

"Very well, but not a word, you understand," Benny warned. "If this information leaked out everything would be ruined. The stock market would go wild. All our plans would fail. Remember, the whole future of the Cariboo hangs on it. Not a word."

"No, no, not a word. You can count on me, Mr. Rockefeller."

"I'm sure of it," said Benny.

At that moment the train bell rang. We scrambled back to our flatcar and Benny, a finger pressed to his lips as a pledge of silence, waved farewell to his confidant. Then, at a safe distance, he collapsed in gravel and guffaw.

Benny knew precisely what would happen and it did. Within the hour the telephones of Cariboo were buzzing on their open party lines from Williams Lake to Prince George and out across the far Chilcotin range. The intended purchase of the railway, British Columbia's perpetual budgetary nightmare, was quickly reported in the newspapers of Vancouver. By the time we got there Benny's empire had become a sensation and even the government began to hope that the white elephant might be unloaded before it consumed the treasury.

In the meantime, however, we were far from the coast, on top of Pavilion Mountain. Here, after a dizzy climb, our locomotive shuddered and expired a thousand feet or more above the Fraser, which from the train looked as wide as a ragged brown thread. When darkness fell, with heavy sleet, we found that there was no food or drinking water on the train, only the cars of gravel and the passenger coach full of hungry, thirsty hoboes. Two charitable brakemen took us into their caboose and, around a hot stove, they shared a pot of their coffee and the remains of a sticky cake. It tasted like ambrosia.

We slept on the floor of the caboose and felt lucky to escape the gravel and the gale now raging up the wind tunnel of the Fraser's canyon. Unwashed, unshaved, and unfed, we faced the dawn and waited for another locomotive to rescue us. It arrived from Squamish late in the afternoon and slowly hauled us down the mountain to Lillooet. By now we were somewhat disenchanted with the Pacific and Great Eastern Railway, its special train, and the government. Benny's reviving eloquence again shattered the chilly autumnal air, loud enough to reach Mr. Oliver's ears in Victoria, but when I saw the Premier soon afterward and told him of our journey he almost choked with laughter. Still, he wished that the Rockefeller fantasy had been true.

The train stopped for two minutes at the lovely resort of Craig Lodge, on Seton Lake. We leaped from the flatcar and, despite the conductor's protest, refused to go another mile with him. The Lodge, its food, clean beds, and hot baths, looked to us like a pretty good imitation of heaven, as the Pickwickian tour had been a reasonable facsimile of hell.

Next day we hired a car, drove to the CPR mail line at Lytton, and caught a train for the coast. It did not occur to me that, a few years later, I would learn to love the Cariboo country above all others and on Pavilion Mountain, where our locomotive had died, would meet two of the dearest friends in my life.

I found them in 1928 when a provincial election brought the Conservatives to power in the Legislature and installed a new member for the riding of Lillooet. His name was Ernest Carson and he struck me at first as a cold, unapproachable fellow—tall, muscular, with a bronzed outdoor look, reddish hair, clipped military mustache, and a laconic manner. Judging that he was of my age but not of my sort, I had no time for him, nor he for me. Happily that mistake on both sides did not last long. Thrown together in the daily scramble of politics, we soon came to terms of intimacy. I found in Ernie (as everyone called him) one of the half-dozen men to whom I could ever give my total friendship. I also saw that the distant bearing was a thin veneer to hide his shyness and his silent courage under much adversity.

While I had heard of Ernie's wartime service overseas, his reputation as the best horseman in the Cariboo, his esteem among white ranchers and Indians alike, it was not until he invited Dot and me to his ranch that I began to understand the whole man in his own setting. Then I realized that such a man could come only from the Cariboo, with all its distinct character, strength, prejudice, and folk superstition bred in his bones. He had learned all its skills, too, from breaking horses to fixing machinery, irrigating his haylands, and cutting lumber in his little mill. In the rough political game he played fair and won because everybody, in all parties, trusted him without question. These qualities were indigenous and natural to the solitary heights of Pavilion Mountain, which I had first seen from that ghost train as a barren cliff dropping straight down to the Fraser.

Now, as we drove from Lillooet through the first springtime greenery of bunchgrass and faced the narrow zig-zags above the Indian village of Pavilion, we could find no sign of any ranch, not a yard of arable land, and Dot said we must be on the wrong road. Suddenly, rounding the last bend, we beheld a geological freak. The mountain top was, in fact, a valley, a saucer raised close to the sky within a ring of higher mountains streaked with snow and draped in misty blue curtains. There may be nobler sights somewhere, but we never discovered them. It was easy to understand why Ernie's father, escaping Indian massacre on the Oregon Trail and heading north for the Cariboo gold rush, paused and remained here to plow a pocket of rich, black soil, and graze his cattle over five thousand acres.

Beside an immense barn stood his log house, enlarged room by room to accommodate a growing family, and at the door to greet us were Ernie and his wife, Halcyon. This was not the man I had known in the Legislature, nor the woman I had met at cocktail parties in Victoria.

Ernie, in his battered cowboy hat and overalls, was a different man, the shyness forgotten, the patina of the city dissolved. Halcyon, in her kitchen apron, hands white with flour from the day's baking, was no longer the petite society belle but the Cariboo housewife, the range rider, the guardian angel of all the ranch hands, Indians, and animals of a more select society in the clouds. By lucky choice, her name, in the original Greek meaning, accurately expressed her nature.

In the big sprawling kitchen, with its stove about the size of a railway engine, its goodly smell of cooking, its mighty roasts of beef, and its wild raspberry pies, in the barn with the work horses chomping their night-time oats, in the meadows with their irrigation ditches whispering under the stars while incense oozed from the new-cut clover, or looking down on the brown snake of the Fraser to the westward and, to the eastward, on three blue lakes dropped like tears in a canyon of marble — here we lived our own halcyon days, all too short.

From Pavilion, year after year, we made sorties across the Chilcotin plateau to the edge of the Coast Range, to Likely, Horsefly, and Barkerville, to the rodeos of Williams Lake and the cowboy dances of Clinton, to the autumn fairs of Lillooet, and to secret fishing streams where Ernie and I caught innumerable trout and our wives cooked them over the camp fire.

In the dust and heat of summer, or on the glare ice of winter, we travelled the rough, twisting Cariboo Road until we knew its every curve and pothole, and most of its inhabitants. That road of gravel and history is gone now, replaced by a straight line of blacktop. The cosy Mile Houses of the gold rush are gone, too, replaced by sleek motels of neon and chromium.

All the old ways of the Cariboo and its separate civilization—a high civilization by proper measurement—are gone. Even Pavilion Mountain, which had seemed immune to progress behind its stone ramparts, has been scarred by electrical power lines. No travellers pause to notice a lonely hill where Ernie, his parents, brothers, and sister are buried. The man who was the Cariboo's finest product, and then British Columbia's most respected cabinet minister, went too soon, dropping dead in his Victoria garden at the height of his career. After that, we never wanted to see the mountain again.

Halcyon, true to her name, lived on, overcoming sorrow, solitude, and sickness. Beside the ocean in Victoria she made her new home a snug anchorage for many lost ships and human derelicts. Such a woman needed no charity but gave it to all of us.

11

The Secret Agent

The outbreak of war in 1939 began to change the world and Canada forever, but it made no great difference to our domestic arrangements. I was still working with Roy Brown for the *Vancouver Sun* on a comfortable routine, and in late May 1940 he sent me to Washington.

When I reached the American capital it was hot, steaming, sweating, insufferable — a city built for reasons of politics on swamps and sand bars. But there was more than heat, steam, and sweat in the air. Even from the remote banks of the Potomac the vibrations from a tottering Europe could be felt, at least among my friends in the government; felt with a mixture of relief and desperation, relief because the overseas tragedy must soon end, desperation because that end must mark the beginning of tragedy, in some form, at home. After the months of the "phoney war", Norway, Denmark, the Low Countries, and France had been overrun by the German blitzkrieg. The end was in sight already.

Washington seemed to be in state not of shock exactly but of somnambulism. It went calmly about its business, the ranks of bureaucracy marching to their offices in the morning and out again in the afternoon. The White House glistened in the sun, but no one stopped in the street to observe it, as if its resident — or prisoner — and the nation were safe from war behind the moat of the Atlantic. But Roosevelt must have known that his capital and people were walking, working, talking, and playing in their sleep.

I did likewise, though my sleep was troubled. And at that time a young American had written a book entitled *Why England Slept*, the irony of it still hidden from sleeping America, the name of John F. Kennedy still unknown.

For me real sleep was impossible. In a fine hotel, not yet air-conditioned, I rose, sweating, three or four times every night, stood in a cold shower, and lay down under a wet bath towel, waiting for the slight chill of dawn. Or, with an American newspaper friend, I drove around the city in his car, observing the parks full of people physically asleep on the grass to escape their fiery homes, and into the Virginia farm country where it was a little cooler and the air sweet, sickly, almost carnal with the perfume of wild honeysuckle. After dawn, came the blazing, merciless day.

As in previous visits, I lunched with one of the most intelligent in the upper echelon of the New Deal. Jerome Frank, later to become a high-court judge and respected philosopher of the law, was then head of the Securities and Exchange Commission, an intimate of the President, an idea man extraordinary, his mobile, potent face aglow with new ideas every hour. No man of my acquaintance thought so fast, talked so brilliantly, joked so hilariously, or soared into such dizzy heights of imagination and error. But at this particular luncheon, Frank talked only of immediate, serious things and regarded Canada (of which he knew little) with more sorrow than anger because it was already in the war. In his grotesque misconception of my country and its monarch, he actually told me: "You folks are fighting for your poppa in London." Remembering the young King and his lovely Queen as I had seen them land at Quebec, a year earlier, and the sudden, homely rapport they had established with the Canadian people, I realized that Frank did not understand either side of this subtle relationship. But I was here to listen, not to argue.

The United States, Frank went on, would not make Canada's mistake. If I wanted to know why, he advised me to read his recent book, *Save America First*. I read it that night and found in it probably the best argument yet made for total isolationism, as only a great scholar and original mind could make it. He wrote, for example, that there might be some use in the United States fighting to unify Europe "but in such an enterprise England will not be our friend or ally but our enemy."

Even the honest Frank, as he would candidly admit to me after the Japanese roused him, had been sleep-walking in that springtime nightmare of 1940. "It's simple," he said. "I was just wrong. Just utterly, damnably wrong, that's all." For the moment, however, he and his friends were determined to save America first and believed they could. Surely an America which had conceived the New Deal could do anything?

Among some politicians on the Hill the same impossible notion went still further. Key Pittman, the ageing, sickly chairman of the Senate Foreign Relations Committee, assured me, with the authority of his powerful office, that Britain would soon surrender. Since it was only a question of days, the British Navy should be moved at once to the United States, which sometime, possibly, might rescue Europe (though Pittman seemed rather vague about that). A genial old man, a scarred veteran of many battles in politics, he was eager to share his wisdom with any wandering reporter and now sleep-walked toward his own final sleep a few months later.

By this time I had struck up an improbably close association with a more important man. Adolf Berle had become not only an Assistant Secretary of State but a special crony of Roosevelt, who was fascinated by his mind, as anyone would be. For Berle's mind, in its sweep, scintillation, and subtlety, was one of the New Deal's most fascinating phenomena. Why he should have welcomed me whenever I sought him out in the cluttered rookery of the old State Department, and why he should have talked to me with the wildest indiscretion, I was never able to surmise. Maybe it was because I listened with rapt admiration while his colleagues, weary of his cosmic speculations, would not.

A tiny person, not much over five feet tall, with pale, expressionless face and a voice seldom raised above a whisper—himself almost an incorporeal whisper on legs—he talked as if time was of no concern to the State Department. Standing before a wall map and pointing to the battle lines, he said that France already had fallen, that Hitler was in full control of western Europe when official propaganda in London, Ottawa, throughout the Commonwealth, and even in Washington, still pretended that France, unconquerable, would yet rally. Oh no, Berle whispered, the situation was hopeless. Just look at the map. France must surrender within days. This little man, a mind wearing a body as mere appendage, did not walk in his sleep.

After surrender, I asked, what then? Berle fell silent with thoughts, I supposed, too stark for utterance. A mind of his rare excellence, unlike the mind of Jerome Frank, could not expect America to save itself first. Probably he was wondering if it could be saved at all.

During the next week nightmares in wide variety colored my private somnambulism, though I seemed to be awake.

At the Press Club eminent newspapermen, returning from foreign parts as internationalists or isolationists, argued bitterly over their iced mint juleps. The most famous of all these strategists explained, with peanuts and pretzels on the bar to show the hemispheric geography, that the United States would be absolutely secure so long as it held the North American coastline (including Canada, of course) and the Brazilian Bulge of South America.

At the State Department, every noon, Cordell Hull, now old, white, and enervated, whispered to his press conference, saying nothing though he knew everything. One quiet evening in the home of a Canadian diplomat, a young British major, wounded in France, told us of the panzers and the roads jammed with refugees and strafed from the air. I spent what should have been a peaceful Sunday in the Virginia countryside picking gallons of wild strawberries and listening to a peculiarly noxious fellow who laughed with contempt at Canada for playing at war, until even my timid disposition rebelled and we came nearly to blows before friends separated us.

On the morrow at a press conference in the Oval Room, Roosevelt sat coatless, his shirt plastered with sweat to his skin. Then the inevitable question — Mr. President, what is your response to the latest appeal from Premier Reynaud of France for "clouds" of American war planes? Roosevelt slowly shook his head. No planes were available. And, as he did not add, he could not have sent them even if they were, being still imprisoned in legal neutrality and facing, five months hence, an election by no means won in advance.

No planes. That scene was unforgettable, in a tragic sense historical — the man of so-called supreme power helpless, as crippled in his politics as in his limbs, the world and even the nation, for vital purposes, beyond his grip. The old laughter was gone, the actor's role of the Great Guy suspended. Across that stubborn Dutch face, ravaged by seven years of toil, something like despair was written.

Or so I thought, perhaps because I was myself despairing, yet still unable to shake off a spurious sense of continental security on the far side of the street, behind the Atlantic moat.

While I recognized, with half my mind, that all such hopes were futile, things were moving too fast for me, a Canadian sleep-walker. I did not know then that Roosevelt was already planning secret measures of aid to Britain, and would soon sign the Ogdensburg Agreement, without benefit of constitutional authority, binding the United States and Canada together in joint defence and thus preparing for co-operation in war or, if it came to that, for North America's survival alone. In the stifling Oval Office the President could add nothing to mitigate the chronicle of disaster. But everything was soon to change as the German tide paused at the Channel.

Unaware of that change and its meaning, I came back to our camp at the lake confused, tired, still asleep except in body, my opinions quite worthless. It was absurd, I knew, to think that there could be any true escape from the horror beyond our peaceful woods, as absurd as escaping death in the end, but one could thrust these thoughts from the consciousness for an hour or two.

Thus trying to forget reality, I had just thrown myself into the construction of a small guest house, the beams cut from our own trees, the lumber taken from a neighbor's rotting garage, when a messenger arrived from the village with a telegram. It was signed by Dexter and did not invite but ordered me to meet him at Toronto within twenty-four hours, for purposes undisclosed.

Such an order could not be disobeyed. I left the newly skinned beams on the ground where they lay for two more years, packed my grip, and prepared, not without alarm, for my first journey in an airplane, little suspecting that it would lead me all over the United States, in the wildest goose chase imaginable, for purposes known only to Mackenzie King.

At the start it appeared unlikely that I would even reach Toronto. The sturdy Dakota, Canada's first transcontinental plane, struggled over the Rockies, while the passengers and crew nervously breathed oxygen from their masks. Near Lethbridge we were caught in a storm which terrified us all. As the plane flipped and fluttered like a dry leaf and swung deep into Montana to avoid the black front rushing down from the north, everyone, including the hostess, was vomiting freely—all except me, perhaps because my terror transcended my stomach. I expected a crash at any moment and reflected that I alone in this company would die healthy and hungry. It also occurred to me that I would never fly again if I reached the ground alive.

Finally the brave Dakota came through the storm and, eighteen hours out of Vancouver, still unfed, I landed in Toronto where another message from Dexter awaited me. He had started already on a mysterious mission and I was to join him immediately in Barrie. Barrie? I didn't even know its location, but I knew Dexter and assumed that he was reasonably sane, despite all evidence to the contrary. I assumed, too, that expenses were unlimited in wartime and hired a taxi for a drive of some fifty miles at a fixed price of fifty dollars.

At Barrie the mystery was resolved. There I found a splendid railway train parked on a siding and, within it, an assembly of distinguished American newspapermen, the guests of the Canadian government. It proposed to brainwash them, though gently, and let them see with their own eyes that Canada was indeed at war while their own country was not — a first clumsy but honest propaganda effort.

My job, along with Dexter and half a dozen other Canadians, was easy and innocent enough. We had merely to explain for our guests the military encampments, air fields, naval establishments, and munition factories which Canada had built, and about which I knew precisely nothing. It was hoped the Americans would tell their readers that the small nation beside them was fighting not for Britain, not for imperial sentiment, but for the survival of North America entire. According to a subtle plan misleading no one, the propaganda train, with two dining cars, gourmet food, and the finest liquors for the comfort of the guests, moved through Ontario, Quebec, and into the Maritimes while I, as a propagandist, boned up on wartime statistical facts and pretended to know what I was talking about.

Evidently there were watchful secret-service men on board, disguised by army uniform, for at Halifax Grant and I were told by some anonymous official person to watch a certain American magazine writer and never let him out of our sight for a minute. This man had been altogether too inquisitive in the munition factories; he was a trained naval expert and very likely a spy. All his movements, when we embarked on a destroyer, must be observed and instantly reported.

As counter-espionage operators Grant and I soon demonstrated that we were the worst in the profession. We boarded the wrong vessel, the spy was unobserved on another to do his deadly work, and, as it turned out, he wrote the best pro-Canada, anti-German, and unneutral copy produced by the whole propaganda exercise. Canada was new to psychological warfare in those days.

However, Mackenzie King must have been satisfied with this preliminary experiment, though he seldom trusted any propaganda except his own and regarded the new business of public information, or news management, with suspicion, unless he was the manager. At any rate, under his indirect orders, never admitted publicly, I was launched on the craziest adventure of my life.

A group of five leading Canadian newspapers undertook to pay my expenses, no matter how exorbitant they might be, if I would travel in Wendell Willkie's campaign retinue, ostensibly to report the presidential election of 1940. Behind this flimsy cover, my real assignment was to see the local editors wherever Willkie stopped, ask them about the politics of their own areas, and, as a mere afterthought, in a casual, off-hand fashion, tell them why Canada had involved North America in the war, to the outrage of Americans like Charles Lindbergh. Then, perhaps, the editors would become more friendly to Canadian policy and less neutral.

The whole notion of such unofficial diplomacy struck me as ridiculous, and no worse candidate could have been chosen for it — a secret agent out of some farce by Evelyn Waugh, a script written for James Bond. But since I was doing nothing of use to my country in wartime I agreed to attempt this mad mission.

So, with five thousand American dollars in my wallet and no plan in my head, I stood, one bitter autumn morning, on the railway platform at Albany, New York. When the long Willkie train drew into the station I climbed up the steps, half expecting to be thrown off by some palace guard. Instead, the conductor accepted payment for my fare, no questions asked, sold me a lower berth, and wished me a pleasant journey. For all he knew I could have been an assassin, and I was, indeed, a spy of sorts.

Doubtless Willkie was well guarded in his private car at the rear end of the train, but during the next month, day after day he made himself an easy target for any killer.

To me, those days became an endless trance, a film out of sync, a giddy spectacle of vast crowds, strange cities, nameless little towns, and always the tall, chunky figure of Willkie in perpetual speech, his voice reduced to a hoarse croak, his clothes rumpled, his face twisted in an agony of hope, ambition, and dejection.

At first I listened to him morning, noon, and night, as he spoke from the platform of the train, in noisy auditoriums, in squalid movie theatres, or on street corners. But there was no use listening when he repeated his single speech everywhere and the American reporters tried desperately to contrive new "leads" for their stories, a futile task.

Always he began with the same words, appealing to the same American horror of the European war. "I know wah!" he would cry, recalling his own experience as a soldier. Then he would accuse Roosevelt of plotting to seduce the United States into foreign entanglements. And always he referred to Roosevelt, in a curious, slurring accent, as "the presidenunitedstates", or "the third-term candidate", to remind the audience that his opponent was breaking a sacred political convention. The election had become a contest between two men outbidding each other for the anti-war vote, each soon to be ashamed of his fraudulent promise to keep the boys at home, and each secretly admiring his enemy.

As I watched Willkie at first hand and saw his volcanic vigor, his first-rate mind, and his passionate belief in his own misty American Dream, I thought he would make a good president (and so did Roosevelt). But still under the spell of Roosevelt's magic, I never supposed that Willkie could defeat him.

The wily Democratic President knew better and saw that, for the first time, he faced a real challenge from a supposedly conservative Republican who, in fact, was already changing his life-long philosophy and becoming a liberal. Roosevelt, suddenly grasping his danger, was compelled to abandon his pose of a leader above the battle, to fight back, and redouble his promises of neutrality.

All this was no business of mine and, among the horde of American newspapermen, I preserved a strict neutrality, with a fair pretence of interest in the election. To hide my diabolic motives I wrote occasional dispatches for the Canadian press. They merely duplicated the regular news services but provided some useful red herrings.

No one suspected what I was doing on that train and I was no longer sure myself. All I can remember now are vagrant snatches and disordered fragments of New York, Boston, Philadelphia, Louisville, Chicago, Denver, St. Louis, San Francisco, Seattle, a myriad of blurred towns between them, and, more clearly, the great heartland of the central plains where the frozen corn stalks swayed in the wind like an army in retreat, symbolic of the election itself. By a kind of osmosis, through eye, ear, nose, and pores, I was getting my first real sense of the continent—its vastness, its infinite diversity of land and people, the achievements and failures, the contentment and the fury.

Here a thinker, unlike me, could discern a philosophical antinomy, sad or comic, inherited from the Pilgrim Fathers, by which worldly accretion was not only essential to Christian other-worldliness, but a virtue in itself; the American living standard not only the reward but the final proof of piety in God's eyes; even more remarkable, the assurance, firmly installed in the American subconscious, that God, with a little help from the Founding Fathers, had established a Republic of His own design in the first place.

Yet the American people, with all their childlike pride, far short of the true arrogance in older peoples, had also acquired, somewhere on the march, a gnawing conscience, a guilt complex, a canker of self-criticism unique among the successful nations. No other nation so anxiously examined its morals in private while protesting its morality in public documents, statues of stone and bronze, and sculptured mountain cliffs, and in ringing Self-Evident Truths, all the more vehemently asserted because they were inwardly questioned.

All I saw from Willkie's train window was the outer spectacle that neither he nor anyone could fully understand—a cheering, frightening, enlivening, deadening, and ever-changing spectacle. It lived and breathed and moved like a single creature, a collective organism—but where was it going? It gestured, articulated, and squirmed in painful cerebration—but to what end? It adored, elected, contemned, and destroyed its leaders—but for what purpose? It adulated rich men, pitied the poor, revered money as the just reward of merit, punished the malefactors of great wealth, exulted over its classless society, steadily crystallized its classes, demanded equality in law and denied it in practice—but by what logic? It built ideal cities, left them to rot at the core, and fled to the suburbs—but what permanent refuge was to be found there, what hope for those who could not flee? It glorified, expanded, and constantly bedevilled its free enterprise system by state decrees—but on what economic principle? It celebrated, improved, advertised, and vulgarized the American Way of Life—but what did that resounding cliché mean?

And how could a Roosevelt or a Willkie hope to personify in himself all these contradictory impulses and passions known as public opinion and consensus? How to control the demonic energies, the unequalled skills, the mechanical genius, and the old streak of frontier violence pulsating an inch below a frail surface of law and order?

Not by the Constitution, by any statute, government policy, or economic system, only by some centripetal impulse which no stranger could truly share—the will to union, however imperfect, because the alternative already had been tried, and vetoed, by civil war. In this respect, to be sure, the nation was not different from mine or others. They all had their native impulses stronger than their laws but here they were peculiarly open and egregious—a striking proof of myth over matter.

These impressions might be helpful in the future when Canadians would fail to understand their neighbors and blame them for misunderstanding Canada but at the moment, in the dust of the campaign trail, I had no time to think, or even to see that the election hardly touched, much less governed, the convulsive forces moving with it, at home and abroad.

Every day we stopped at a dozen towns, hurled ourselves through the crowds like a football team, hoped that the hoarse voice would say something new, and fought our way back to the train as it was already moving. Every night, while the others attended Willkie's meeting, I called on the local newspaper editor, inquired diligently about the politics of his region, and clumsily led the conversation around to Canada. My sales pitch must have been pathetic. It was usually received with indifference, sometimes with hostility.

A distinguished editor in St. Louis told me that as a boy in the First World War he had delivered telegrams announcing to their parents the death of American soldiers overseas; this, he said, must not happen again, whatever my misguided countrymen were doing. Clearly, I was not welcome in his office and soon left, but a year later that angry isolationist had become a powerful champion of internationalism — and so had Willkie.

A few editors like "Stuffy" Walters, a legendary figure in Minneapolis, treated me with kindness, even ran an interview with me or let me write my own piece. Still, I was bitterly discouraged and thought my mission a total fiasco. What had been accomplished in the peaceful United States by my ludicrous mission while better men from Canada were fighting and dying in the war overseas? Nothing, so far as I could see, beyond the expenditure of about five thousand dollars in precious Canadian foreign exchange, and possibly some education for the spender.

Some months later when I saw Willkie again, across a table in the packed Senate office building, he was a changed man after his electoral defeat, his foreign travels, and his book celebrating *One World*. He was now Roosevelt's ally as an outright internationalist. And when a still-isolationist senator asked him about his former speeches against war he confessed, with a blush, an honest blush, that all those statements had been merely campaign rhetoric. The inquisitors fell silent. What could they say to a man so honest in his mistake and so big in recovery?

The Japanese had yet to rescue Roosevelt from neutrality and, as it turned out, the world from disaster. Meanwhile Willkie, in public defeat, had won his own personal victory. He had grown overnight into maturity and grasped the meaning of the One World. Then he left it, all too soon.

12

The Communicators

In 1941 my experience as the clumsy, unpaid chore boy of the Canadian government took a turn comical and bizarre. Instead of a respectable war job, I accepted the minor role of voice off stage in a farce more hilarious and even less useful than my mission to the United States. But the business on hand was deadly serious.

Having rejected his experts' advice to impose a freeze on all prices, King suddenly adopted it and announced this anti-inflation policy as his own. In Donald Gordon, a shaggy bear of a man, he chose the best possible administrator of the wartime economy and Gordon chose the worst possible press officer.

When, knowing nothing of my capacities and little of the press, he invited me to join his staff I could not refuse. But I asked for a few hours to think it over and, as always, sought Dexter's counsel. My friend flew into an almost believable rage, said the whole idea was idiotic, telephoned the Prime Minister's office, and demanded an interview with King, who received us ten minutes later.

With an air of patriotic indignation Dexter told King that in the national interest, at a moment of deepening crisis, I could not be spared from my duty of reporting the work of government to the people of British Columbia. Otherwise, it appeared, they would be left in black ignorance, close to anarchy on the dark side of the Rocky Mountains. God alone knew, he implied, what that mad province might do without accurate news from Ottawa.

It was a good speech, though a trifle hyperbolic. I listened in the silence of admiration and hope. King listened, too, nodding his bald head in solemn agreement. If he doubted that I, as a reporter, was vital to the war effort, he thoroughly understood that the *Vancouver Sun* was the only important Liberal newspaper on the Pacific Coast. That man had a sure grip of essentials.

Yes, yes, he said, of course I must remain in the Press Gallery and keep the far western public informed on the affairs of state. Without mentioning the affairs of the Liberal Party, he picked up his telephone, called Gordon, and in a voice of sweet reason suggested, merely suggested, that my appointment to the Prices and Trade Board would be a mistake.

That fixed it. I had escaped, and I left King's office like a prisoner released from jail. It was easy to assuage my conscience by remembering that I was entirely unfitted to help Gordon and that he would find a better man, but I knew that my attitude was unheroic, selfish, and typical. As usual, I preferred my freedom, convenience, and outdoor life to any official job if it could be avoided, and this job was far outside my experience. Though I avoided it, with dubious motives, the escape was not yet complete.

Gordon did find a better man in Charles Vining, who moved fast and boldly, as I would never have done. On his recommendation Gordon summoned all the leading newspaper publishers to meet him in Ottawa, at their own expense, to hear a lecture on the menace of inflation. Since Gordon and Vining were too busy for such a routine chore, they asked me to write the lecture—as if I knew anything then about inflation.

No matter, I wrote the lecture anyhow and, on a night train to New York where we were going for reasons now forgotten, showed the draft to Vining. He said he would make a few small corrections and while I slept he hammered on his typewriter until dawn. At breakfast he handed me a new text, not a single word of mine in it. I had seldom read a finer piece of advocacy, dire prophecy, and horrendous warning. When Gordon delivered it to the shocked publishers, with all his own rough eloquence and panache, I knew for certain that Vining was the better man.

Meanwhile King was being hard pressed to establish a central information service that would serve the newspapers and keep the public in touch with the war effort. He had no faith in the experiment but agreed to risk it, believing that it would do little harm or good. At any rate it might satisfy the press and his impatient colleagues. Vining, who had long been a brilliant journalist and lately a daring operator in war, was appointed manager-in-chief of information with no clear instructions, a free hand, and unlimited money. The results astounded everyone, probably even King.

Vining seemed to think, when he had time to think at all, that his assignment was to set up a grand council of the nation, a hotbed of ideas in a cold climate, almost a super-government which, consulting the best minds and sounding the depths of public opinion, would report its verdict to the constitutional government. Then, presumably, this collective wisdom would issue in national policy. The arts of modern communication had come at last to Ottawa.

With no motive but patriotism and no expectation of the consequences, Vining conscripted a veritable army of journalists and advertising types to help him educate the people for war. I was among those thus summoned for purposes never explained but so secret that even my wife was not to hear of them. As we were soon saying in the crowded back rooms, all letters should be burned before they were read, and that would not have been a grave loss. In fact, the operation was about as secret as a circus parade with no known destination.

Probably because he could think of nothing else, Vining instructed me to write not a memorandum but a full-scale book on Canada, its government, history, culture, geography, politics, and economics, the whole works. This factual masterpiece would be distributed throughout the world for the edification of our ignorant allies.

The project seemed quite insane, but it was not for me to reason why. I pestered every government agency in town, collected masses of irrelevant data, and finally produced a swollen, worthless manuscript. It was never published and was read by no one except the author, and a good thing, too. At least I had not damaged Canada's reputation abroad. But somewhere in the clammy basements of Ottawa my first stillborn book must be mouldering among other ruins of the unremembered wartime information empire. As soon as the manuscript was finished, I was back in full-time journalism.

Vining, the patriot, had exhausted himself to the point of physical collapse. King, the inexhaustible emperor, had demonstrated that no empire but his own could work and wisely appointed Herbert Lash, who was also inexhaustible, to bring some order out of the chaos, which he did with his usual quiet efficiency. Thenceforth King communicated what he wanted known to the public, no more, no less.

During the autumn of 1941 he visited his friend Roosevelt in Washington and, on his return, agreed to see me briefly. I found him in such a state of panic, not far short of paranoia, that our talk, or rather his monologue, stretched to a full hour.

He began by saying that things looked very bad. The United States would soon be at war with Japan, war that would doubtless spread across the Pacific to endanger even America itself. I did not venture to ask whether he had received such intelligence from Roosevelt and I knew nothing about the critical negotiations then under way in Washington or about the broken Japanese code. Much less could I imagine the attack on Pearl Harbor, only a few weeks distant. But King plainly knew something, and Roosevelt must have told him.

While I did not grasp the significance of King's gloomy premonition and took it as just another groan of self-pity, I mentioned it to no one except Dexter. In any case, it was not the war overseas but a threat to the nation at home, and to his government, that mainly worried King and reduced him almost to hysteria. I had never seen him in this mood before and I noticed how his face had lately aged, the wrinkles deepening, the old plumpness shrinking.

He paced up and down the office and muttered more to himself than to me. Did I understand what Meighen was doing? Yes, I understood that Meighen had resigned from the Senate, resumed the leadership of the Conservative Party without benefit of any convention, and was running for the House of Commons in South York, Ontario. Ah, but there was much more to it, said King, than the pending by-election. Meighen planned to smash the government and divide the Canadian people by advocating conscription for overseas service, which King had rejected and would always reject. If Meighen re-entered the Commons, life would become "insupportable", the nation disrupted. "Insupportable, I tell you," King repeated.

All this sounded rather childish to me. I put it down to his personal dread of the one man who had dogged his career from the beginning and now might break it. That long blood feud apparently had been settled, Meighen defeated, King vindicated. Yet suddenly, maddeningly, the old spectre had descended again out of the night. Yes, insupportable.

As he went on muttering I saw that King sincerely feared for the nation as well as for himself. With him sincerity was a movable feast, an appeal to higher ends when the means were repulsive, a private accommodation between the faithful servant and his God. Nevertheless, he was sincere. He believed, beyond question, that Meighen (equally sincere) would split the nation between its two languages, cultures, and ethnic regions with damage irreparable, perhaps fatal. After all these years I am convinced, given the conditions of that particular moment, that

King was basically right even if he exaggerated the danger for political purposes and for deeper reasons within his own tortured spirit.

He was wrong, of course, in telling me that Meighen represented the worst and most reactionary elements of society. He was simply distracted and no longer King when he pounded his little fist on the desk and declared that Meighen's return to politics would mean the introduction of fascism to Canada. Fascism? I tried not to smile and said nothing. What could be said when the Prime Minister was raving? And he was not finished even yet. I can still see him clearly now as he paused in the middle of the room, raised his fist above his head, and cried out: "The people, mark my words, will have their rights!"

What those words meant I had no way of knowing. Nor did I know that already King had arranged to give the people of South York their rights by refusing to nominate a Liberal candidate, letting a Socialist win the by-election and finally destroying Meighen.

Before I left him that day King had calmed down and I never witnessed his hysteria again. Besides, I had other things to think about.

On a visit to Washington I had met for the first time a young man then administering a system of loose and partial price controls. The world had yet to hear of John Kenneth Galbraith and he had yet to conceive his Affluent Society, his New Industrial State, and other heresies. Nor had his self-esteem grown to the full dimensions of a physique rising to a height of nearly seven feet.

His explosion of grandeur was some years away and I could not suspect the genius that would ignite it. All I saw was a very tall, very thin, and very modest fellow who informed me that the horizontal freeze on Canadian prices would never work and that the United States would never imitate it. The next year, still disarming in his modesty, he admitted that he had been entirely mistaken and the Canadian example imitated because it did work.

Toward the end of 1941 I called, at the State Department, on my strange patron, Adolf Berle. As always, he was cryptic but more candid than he should have been with a foreign reporter.

Doubtless knowing from the broken Japanese code how near the United States had come to war, he discussed the world situation at length in his calm, whispering voice and polished paragraphs. And then, quite casually, he referred to the current negotiations with the two Japanese ambassadors in an office near by and added: "We're just waiting for the second shoe to drop."

His meaning did not immediately register with me. I went home to Victoria no more excited than usual. On the morning of December 7, I was pruning an apple tree in my garden when Dot shouted from the kitchen door that the Japanese had bombed Pearl Harbor. I heard the news and went on pruning. What else was there to do?

13

The Old Lion

Having found my trade through one of Benny Nicholas's accidental whims and the supreme happiness of my marriage through blind luck, I have never believed that any man is given much control over his fortunes in this world. To be sure, there are no real accidents, only the inevitabilities that move in patterns beyond our sight, the grand logic that we cannot decipher. But for practical, mundane purposes I have always acted, in so far as I could act at all, on the assumption that about ten per cent of my small affairs were controllable, the rest outside my grasp. Beginning in 1942 this rough hypothesis was confirmed by an improbable course of events, leading to a more improbable conclusion — whether good or bad I have never been certain.

In New York I had many friends and jolly interludes before that city abandoned civilization in favor of steel and concrete barbarism. My cousin Archie McVittie, with whom I had been brought up almost as a brother, was now prospering in Wall Street and about to serve on General MacArthur's staff in the Pacific. Archie and his lively wife, Meg, made their big apartment a second home for Dot and me, introducing us to some remarkable characters who ranged from wealthy brokers to impoverished actors, writers, and delightful, miscellaneous lunatics — a cosmopolitan assembly that only New York could muster.

Among the sane members of this group was Meg's brother, Quentin Bossi, an executive in the publishing house of

Coward-McCann. One day, as we were lunching in our favorite den on 45th Street, Quentin received a minor inspiration. Why, he suddenly asked, didn't I write a book about Canada? That idea had not previously crossed my mind and I thought it crazy. What did I really know about Canada apart from politics and statistics? How could I possibly write a book about it? And who would read such a book anyway?

Nevertheless, Quentin stuck by his inspiration, hurried me to his office, summoned his colleagues, and thrust a contract under my nose. I signed it and only then inquired what sort of book the publishers wanted. They couldn't say, being totally ignorant of the subject. The book was my responsibility, not theirs, and like publishers everywhere, they considered it a soft, easy job. All I had to do was write. They would take care of the important business. So we adjourned to a bar and drank to my success as an author.

It was only when Dot and I were on a night train, bound for Ottawa, that the enormity of the commitment to Coward-McCann reached my conscious mind. The first link in the chain of improbable events had been forged. Too late to break it now.

In Ottawa in early 1942, we had rented a nineteenth-century house of some twenty rooms and furniture which, we guessed, had been old before Queen Victoria chose the lumber village of Bytown, without ever seeing it, as the capital of her Canadian colonies. The size, gloom, and chill of that house depressed us but the rent was low, and we remained there until summer.

By day I worked in the Press Gallery, telling no one of my other employment. By night I pored over books, pamphlets, and clippings supplied by the library of Parliament, making elaborate notes, learning a good deal about Canada at second hand, but becoming increasingly panic-stricken about my book. The likely contents were unknown to the publishers and to me alike because the contents of Canada were equally unknown to us all. That thought struck me one evening in the kitchen of the haunted house (where we mostly lived, because it alone was warm), and while vague, it looked promising — an unknown country described by an unknown author for an unknowing audience. Maybe, after all, I could do something with my unknown theme. At least I had a title, though not much else.

When Parliament briefly adjourned at Easter we set off for Quebec, New Brunswick, and Nova Scotia, not because I expected to get any useful information but because it seemed the thing to do. A man who undertook to write about an unknown country ought to take a personal look at it. Then, still as ignorant as before, he could write with an author's sublime prerogative, the cold, black authority of print.

Our little adventures in the stone houses of French-Canadian farmers (perhaps the most impressive people we ever met, with a natural dignity that came from the earth and the crops of three centuries), our sleigh rides through the Laurentians behind horses almost as ancient, our journeys by bus along the Maritime shore, and later across the Prairies, our sense of travelling foreign lands, all of them different but all Canadian, were recounted in my first book but I did not take it as seriously as the reader might suppose.

In a serious sense *The Unknown Country* was not written at all. Its disjointed fragments were thrown together in a period of about six months, in my spare time, while I scamped my full-time newspaper work quite scandalously. My sole purpose was to get shut of the job and return to normal life, since Dot and my children could not stand the strain of a peevish, over-worked author for long.

Somehow, working for the most part in our summer cabin on Shawnigan Lake, I managed to complete the manuscript just before the publisher's final delivery date; it would have been no irrevocable loss to the nation if I had missed the deadline. Until I started to write the present book I never ventured to read *The Unknown Country* in print and now I see the results of haste, ignorance, and carelessness. Worse than that, the shouting, hyperbolic, and naked style of the writing makes me cringe in my old age. Perhaps, however, this slipshod method had its advantages. At least I felt free then to say what I wanted to say, without the nagging dubiety of age, what I thought then but do not think now. I painted my own primitive picture of Canada when my eyes were innocent, my mind uninformed but still pliant, the world as yet unspoiled.

In that first book the times gave me a lucky break. The nation was at war, its energies were concentrated on a single purpose, its achievements already had exceeded its hopes, and it had begun to wonder about its own nature. For this reason a book that tried to explain Canada, even by obscure hint and wild guess, was received more kindly than it deserved. It was even introduced into the House of Commons by R. B. Hanson, the acting Conservative leader and a ponderous man of limited vocabulary, who had stopped me on the steps of Parliament to say that I had written "a racy book" (whatever that meant) and then had solemnly asked Mackenzie King in the Commons if it were true, as I had asserted, that he often cut the throats of his friends and enemies. To which the Prime Minister solemnly replied: "That is the only way to treat certain classes of enemies." If Hanson took me "as an authority for my character, I am ready," said King, "to abide by Mr. Hutchison's decision."

This was heady stuff and I became inflated, smug, and dizzy from my momentary success. As the publishers had told me, anyone could write a book. Now I knew exactly how to do it. What I didn't know was that someone had read the book in New York and seen a certain possibility. The second link in the chain of events was forged.

In my book I had tried to draw a rough likeness of John W. Dafoe, the great editor of the *Winnipeg Free Press*, whom I had long admired from a distance but did not yet know very well. Over the years I had met him occasionally, always in awe, and he was not impressed by the bumptious young reporter from Victoria. Now the editors of *Fortune* magazine, reading about him for the first time, decided that he was worth a serious study. Was

I prepared to write it? In those days of flattery and hubris I was prepared for anything. When I telephoned Dafoe from Ottawa he agreed to see me and explain his editorial views, which through his long lifetime had powerfully influenced and often shaken the politics of Canada.

A few days later, I found myself in the lion's den at the *Free Press* building—an old lion with a shaggy, reddish mane, a huge body, and a weary look. Before a coal fire, Dafoe was sprawled in a leather chair specially designed to fit his bulk. The office and campaign headquarters of endless political warfare was lined solidly with books and small wooden drawers in which he kept his higgledy-piggledy files, the ammunition of battle. Though he had not yet retired, his last battle had been fought, his work finished.

Because he felt sorry for me in my ambitious assignment or because he wished to state his case before departing, Dafoe said I could ask him any question and he would try to answer it. For the next two days we sat together at the fireside, lunched together in the Manitoba Club, and dined together in his old-fashioned house, surrounded by his numerous family of wife, sons, daughters, and grandchildren, the patriarch worshipped by his tribe and, in return, heaving with quiet laughter and domestic jokes.

This was not the Dafoe of the legend, the bitter Liberal partisan, the scourge of governments, the ruthless guerilla fighter of the scorched prairie earth. It was the other Dafoe of private life, of peace at sunset, of tolerance for all humankind, the real Dafoe. After those long battles with his peers, he was near the end and knew it. But, as he had written of his friend Wilfrid Laurier, there was in the closing scene "nothing for tears, nothing to wail". And yet it saddened me. I had come to know Dafoe too late.

If the Canadian public had misjudged the man it had also misunderstood many of his ideas. They had been growing and changing with the times but, as he told me, he lacked the will and strength to argue them. Besides, in the midst of a world war, who cared what he thought? For him victory in the war was all that mattered.

Dafoe wrote so much himself in his clean, unornamented style, and so many books have been written about him, that you might think no area of his mind had been left unexplored. The exploration, as I soon perceived, was still incomplete. Unobserved by his friends and enemies, Dafoe had been moving into new areas. Already he had made himself a great man by any definition, the greatest Canadian I ever knew intimately, and so most historians, friendly or hostile, have judged him. But they have not recorded, because he did not publicly express, his final thoughts on the nation's society.

In younger days Dafoe was a rigidly partisan Liberal, his party's sheet anchor in the West, his power always respected and feared in Ottawa. He was also a philosophical liberal of the Manchester School, a follower of Adam Smith, the economics of *laissez-faire*, the Darwinian theory applied to politics. In his last years I was surprised to hear him denounce the contemporary Liberal government of Canada for its failure to reform a brutal and unjust society.

Slumped by the fire, or lumbering restlessly around his den, and speaking in a plain, earthy idiom quite unlike his written language, he told me that Mackenzie King (whom he never trusted) was managing the war much better than he had expected. But King had made no preparations for peacetime and seemed to have no understanding of the people's needs. Long before now, Dafoe went on, the government should have planned an entirely new system of social security, including adequate pensions for the aged, medical insurance for everyone, full employment for the able-bodied, help for the weak and the poor.

Moreover (and this really astonished me) the government should realize that the basic wealth of the nation belonged to all the people, not to a few rich proprietors. The forest and the minerals, for instance, could be exploited most efficiently by private enterprise but the enterprisers should hold these resources under some system of lease, granted by the state, and the public, the true owner, must have its full share of the profits.

This doctrine of vigorous competition, but with a floor under society's living standards and a ceiling over its rewards, was not classic Liberalism, as I understood the word. It was almost the reverse, or at least a new synthesis of opposites. In his social thinking Dafoe, whom the younger Liberals of Ottawa regarded as a reactionary immune to new ideas, stood far to the left of King. Dafoe seemed to be the modern Liberal, King the antique.

Just as King had misjudged Dafoe, so Dafoe had misjudged King. At that very moment, though Dafoe did not know it, King was already preparing in secret the kind of social-reform program that Dafoe impatiently demanded. It would be unveiled for a postwar election, but Dafoe would not live to see it.

Certainly he had not changed his general view of the world and Canada's proper place in it. During the First World War he had never doubted that a second must follow if the League of Nations failed. Against King, a Liberal government, a Canadian people almost solidly isolationist, and even his own readers, he had fought his lonely battle for the League and, in personal anguish, had watched it fail and the second war follow inevitably. Now he believed that a third war would destroy civilization entire if the League, in some form, was not revived and made to work.

All his predictions so far had been fulfilled. All the critics of his internationalist convictions (including King, "the appeaser from Appeaserville") had been discredited. For himself, as he told me, there remained no assurance of human sanity or a livable future, only a blind faith.

Dafoe had not changed his free-trade principles, either, the economic underpinning of his political internationalism. He still believed that abundant commerce between the nations alone could ensure their prosperity, but he did not expect them to take down their tariff walls for a long time yet. He would be satisfied if the barriers were gradually reduced. Always practical, pragmatic, and willing to compromise in detail, he would gladly accept half a loaf.

In retrospect Dafoe's creed may appear antique and naïve. In his own time he was a daring pioneer, a leader of the Canadian march. But now he could march no further. I listened to him in wonderment and asked again why he did not clarify his thoughts in print. He repeated that he was too old, that no avoidable controversy should interfere with the nation's war, that younger men must do the work beyond his energies.

For myself I had neither the knowledge, the temerity, nor the time to argue with the weary lion. My job was to report him as honestly as possible in *Fortune*. Meanwhile I began to grasp what later historians usually overlook—that Dafoe had never ceased to grow and change even when his body would no longer obey his mind. In the history books, as a result, he is measured by the public writings and private letters of his active years, not by the unwritten conclusions of his age. The legend overtops and distorts the man.

At the end of our two-day conversation I asked him if he wished to see my *Fortune* article for correction before it was published. He blinked at me for a moment over his spectacles. "No," he said. "I don't want to see it. I'll take a chance. Go ahead and publish."

So I did, after weeks of toil at home, and *Fortune*'s camera crew pictured Dafoe as no Canadian had every been pictured in any American magazine. He seemed to like the piece, but all he said to me was that it looked pretty good, though maybe a little too flattering. I did not suspect, because he never hinted at them, that he already was meditating certain plans for my future. The third link was being forged.

That work would take another year or two. In the interval he introduced me to the august company of western magnates known as the Sanhedrin. It met in the Manitoba Club at noon every Saturday and often sat in talk until dusk. The strange sodality had no written rules, no records, and no limits on its wandering debates, but it was very strict about its membership. Only half a dozen men, with occasional out-of-town visitors, were admitted to the inner circle, which over the years had become a kind of secular communion, almost the invisible government of the whole region between the Lakes and the Rockies.

Winnipeg was still the single prairie metropolis, Dafoe the uncrowned philosopher-king, his *Free Press* the Bible of the West, his editorials a primary factor in the nation's politics. In his special easy chair (which no one else would dare to occupy) the monarch was surrounded not by courtiers but by equals. While I did not suspect it then, three of these men were to have a profound impact on my affairs.

The ablest of them, with a mind as good as Dafoe's and possibly more subtle, was Edgar Tarr—a lean, pale wraith of a man, reinforced by invisible steel, who had made, lost, and remade his fortune in law and business but cared nothing for money and, late in life, had beheld with anger and compassion the misery of mankind. Since he said little and mostly listened, an outsider like me could not realize that his views were a potent yeast working not merely within the Liberal government at Ottawa but among Conservatives and Socialists as well.

Men of all parties confided in him their deepest doubts and sought his advice in times of trouble. He advised, helped, warned, and sometimes rebuked them, and he sought nothing in return. Tarr was listless in his manner, ascetic in his habits, and almost saintly in his thoughts (though he carried forty ounces of the best Scotch whisky on his travels and an odorous pipe hung perpetually from his lips).

He could move with speed when necessary, often with ruthless candor. His voice was never raised but it was always heard in Ottawa, most clearly by King, who tried to make him a cabinet minister or ambassador. Tarr wanted no office. Without it he held a unique influence, and much sooner than his friends of the

Sanhedrin he had seen that the existing Canadian society must be drastically altered. In that tight little assembly he was the most ardent reformer, the most realistic observer, and the least ambitious for himself.

George V. Ferguson, the second man of consequence to me, had long been Dafoe's managing editor, amanuensis, and alter ego in the *Free Press*. He was a dour Canadian Scot of bulldog face, rough tongue, and cynical, bantering speech in public. In private, once you got to know him, he was a matchless raconteur, a sentimentalist easily wounded, a wildly generous friend, a dogged enemy, and a writer of rare talent.

Dafoe, who now wrote hardly anything himself, talked with George every morning for about five minutes to suggest some line of argument. Without a note or need for it, George would instantly grasp the old man's purpose, retire to his own dingy office, and in half an hour at most produce an elegant editorial so accurately modelled on Dafoe's style that no reader could guess its authorship. As a journalist George had few competitors in Canada.

The other man who would most affect my future was Victor Sifton, owner and publisher of the *Free Press* and, as I judged, the exact antithesis of George. Then in his middle forties, Sifton's face was like the marble bust of a Roman senator, his body tall, lean, and powerful, his mind always clear, his speech precise, his manner courteous but, with strangers, remote. The youngest Canadian colonel of the first war, he had lost the sight of an eye in battle, had received the Distinguished Service Order (when, as his companions protested, he should have been given the Victoria Cross), and had come home a Puritan in his habits, a true believer in the virtue of business profits, and one of the world's best horsemen.

Victor was a man of uncompromising principle, a victim of his own logic, the product of merciless self-criticism — a highly intelligent but lonely man, eager for friendship, dissatisfied with all the wealth, success, and power that he hoarded jealously, the most ambivalent and least understandable man who ever crossed my path.

The men of the Sanhedrin called themselves Liberals in both the partisan and non-partisan sense. So they were, according to the definitions and political climate of the time. So was I, their apprentice. According to the definitions and climate of the present time, they were conservatives, except for Tarr. To all these men the problems of the day seemed immensely complex and intractable. By today's standards they seem wonderfully simple. While Tarr saw more clearly than his friends the conflicts of the future society, he thought they could be relieved, if not cured, by wise governmental action at the top, not to destroy but to improve private enterprise and thus save it from self-destruction.

For the time being the economic rationale of the Sanhedrin seemed unanswerable. In fact, it was already becoming highly dubious, if not obsolete. At its heart stood the market of unlimited competition and free entrepreneurial enterprise, the unerring mechanism that would reconcile discordant elements and provide justice for everyone if it were allowed to work as God and nature intended, as governments refused to let it work. Back of the market stood the ghost of Adam Smith, the nostalgic memories of British Free Trade in the golden Victorian age, and the bitter memory of the Reciprocity agreement defeated in 1911, that fatal Canadian blunder and sacred lost cause which somehow must be reversed, or at least modified, when the nation returned to its senses after the current war. With certain quiet reservations on the part of Tarr, and somewhat fewer on Dafoe's, the Sanhedrin was a remote temple of classic Liberalism and maintained the ancient faith long after the Liberal Party of Canada renounced it.

In that temple, however, there was much more hope than confidence. These men were too shrewd, realistic, and battle-scarred to expect quick miracles. They were gradualists, pragmatists, men of an imperfect world who hoped for the best, would not be surprised by the worst, and, with all their misreading of the future, probably read it more accurately than the politicians in Ottawa.

I listened and advanced no serious views of my own, having none to advance. But if I had repeated to the Sanhedrin members Dafoe's talk with me I was sure they would have disbelieved it. So I said nothing. Their affairs did not seem to involve mine. That was one of my worst misjudgments. Already Dafoe and Sifton had begun to forge the next link.

14

The Exiles of Fort Garry

Like the flame to the moth, Ottawa is the ultimate target of ambition, the making or breaking point, for all Canadian public men. Even for me, a stubbornly private man, the capital has been such a point, with decisive consequences, happy and otherwise. But these thoughts, and all thoughts of any importance, had yet to enter my mind when I went to Ottawa toward the end of 1943, a man as jaded and frightened as he was private.

For the first time in my life, I had just escaped a brush with lingering death, or so it seemed. The doctors suspected the worst, put me in hospital, conducted their unpleasant tests, and concluded that the symptoms were not fatal. Since there evidently was some doubt about the diagnosis, I suspected that the kindly doctors were shielding me from the truth, and I set out for the east still in pain, fright, and a temper of darkest hypochondria. At the crunch, real or imagined, my courage was disappointing. In Winnipeg I got through a speech of safe platitudes, as long planned, without serious damage to myself, if not to the audience of businessmen, and arrived in Ottawa. There Grant Dexter, sometimes an over-candid friend, greeted me at the railway station with the announcement that my appearance shocked him.

As I brooded over a lonely dinner in my hotel room one evening, too miserable or weak-minded to venture up Parliament Hill, a sharp knock on the door announced the last visitor I expected to see. Victor Sifton sat down at the table, accepted a cup of coffee, and said he had a problem on his mind.

Since Dafoe had once told me that Victor was a more gifted man than his dominating father, the great Sir Clifford Sifton, I received my visitor with appropriate awe. He crept up to his proposition rather slowly and awkwardly — my first glimpse of his shyness.

Dafoe, he said, would soon be gone. To prepare for that inevitable blow, the *Free Press* must find new journalistic muscle. At last the proposition emerged and to my surprise I found that it involved me, more deeply than I could yet guess.

With a mind at once spacious, educated, and powerful, but oddly limited in the mechanics of our trade and in the comprehension of other minds, Victor had devised a triumvirate to replace Dafoe. Ferguson, Dexter, and I would carry on the old man's work, all of us equal. For which purpose would I move, without delay, to Winnipeg, there joining Ferguson, while Dexter remained, as he obviously must, in Ottawa?

My mind, usually hesitant and over-cautious, was made up at once (perhaps because I was still sick and frightened of the future). No, I would not move to Winnipeg. This seemed to flabbergast Victor. The masterly horseman was not used to horses that refused to jump. The rich businessman could not understand a middle-income reporter refusing the generous wages and bonuses that he had offered.

But Victor was not a man to give up so easily. As I was to learn afterward, he already felt confident that my decision would be reversed when I had more time and normal health to think about the practical facts of life. In the end, he was sure, the horse would jump, into Winnipeg. Under this delusion, he suggested, in the most benevolent way, that I could remain in Victoria if I wrote regularly for his paper and, with George and Grant, accepted responsibility for its policies after Dafoe's departure.

Thus, in about half an hour, the deal was made. It suited me well. By this time I had seen that my own departure from the *Sun* would suit its new publisher, Don Cromie, equally well, and I realized, too, that he needed a man who would live in Vancouver, a sacrifice of convenience that I was not ready to make.

Besides, Cromie's idea of journalism and mine were separated by several light years, at least.

Victor's invitation had come at exactly the right moment, as perhaps he knew, and without it I don't know to this day what would have happened to my affairs, my numerous household, and my scanty bank account. So my latest of many bosses left me with these profitable arrangements complete, a future apparently safe, and, more important, a sudden return of confidence in my health. As Dr. Johnson might have said, a man's mind is wonderfully revived when he hears that he will enjoy a good breakfast, instead of a gibbet, tomorrow morning. I had won a reprieve; and, with it, the unbelievable chance to work, for a while anyhow, under Dafoe.

When I stopped off at Winnipeg on the way home, the grand old man met me in George's house and casually remarked that he had heard from Victor of my appointment. "I'm cheering," he said. That was all, except for a sly twinkle in those eyes of ageless wisdom (as if Victor would have made any important move without his editor's approval, or instigation). At the start of the new year, then, I would join the circle of which Dafoe must always be the centre and kindly autocrat so long as he lived.

Apparently he expected to live for some time yet. He was shaggy, rumpled, and tired but his spirits had recovered from the black pessimism, almost despair, of the first years of the war that he had long foreseen. Now that the tide was beginning to turn, his mind turned also.

Having rejected every demand for his memoirs, a unique and essential fraction of Canada's secret history, he told George and me that he had decided to write them after all. The last job of his life, he thought, would take maybe a couple of years. In preparation he was putting his papers together. This news delighted us. I went home in excellent bodily and mental health.

The new year had hardly opened before my telephone rang and George, in honorable tears, said Dafoe was dead. The secret history would never be written. The *Free Press*, and Canada, too, would never be quite the same again. The paper must be published without its maker, the editorial policy set without his sure hand to guide it, the circle maintained without its centre.

Though crying on the phone, and cursing his tears, George was ready, and well equipped, for that long task. Still, I felt surprised and a little shaken when he asked me to telegraph, within the next three hours, an article on Dafoe's life and work, an immediate task for which I lacked both the knowledge and the right. I managed it somehow, but George's second request had quite bowled me over.

He said (not expecting me to believe him) that he had been working too hard of late and wanted a holiday. As he would be absent for some indefinite time, would I take his place in Winnipeg and edit the paper? There was no serious problem, he added, since Victor would be with me, and no special hurry, either. I need not come for a couple of days yet.

So George left for Europe and I came, with Dot, to Winnipeg. George's substitute arrived in a state of profound misgiving, not to say panic. I was not yet forty-three years old by the calendar or more than half that age by disposition, a late bloomer, if I was to bloom at all. The boy must undertake the man's errand and try to fill Dafoe's shoes. Long before it was solemnly codified as the Peter Principle I had grasped the fact that most men were unfit for their jobs. At the beginning of 1944 the Principle was given a vivid demonstration in the *Free Press* where, against all expectation and common sense, I found myself editing the paper, and the staff found a highly suspicious character in the editorial chair.

That our association would continue for more than three decades to the present day; that I would churn out, by conservative estimate, some six thousand articles, signed and unsigned; and that I would outlast all the veterans of Dafoe's time, thanks mainly to my safe remoteness from the arena of events—these prospects did not occur to me as I sat down in George's cluttered cubbyhole. But I knew that I was there by accident, not by plan.

My lifelong theory that mere chance governs most of any man's affairs was confirmed again. And I also knew by instinct more powerful than reason that I would never be at home in Winnipeg.

Victor did everything possible to make us feel at home. He installed Dot and me in a fine suite in the Fort Garry Hotel, expenses unlimited. He entertained us lavishly in his mansion on Wellington Crescent. He drove us in his sleigh, bundled in buffalo robes, behind four splendid horses, through Assiniboine Park at temperatures that almost froze our thin Pacific blood. He let me keep my own office hours, never interfered with my work, and seldom suggested any verbal change in my copy when we met for ritual afternoon tea in his office (and he sheepishly borrowed a cigarette because he had given up smoking). As he told Grant, I would eventually settle down on a nice little farm, which he would buy for me to suit my quaint rural tastes, along the banks of the Red River. Poor Victor, with all his intelligence, power, and money, had miscalculated his new recruit as I had miscalculated him. The horse wouldn't jump.

That was a queer winter for Dot and me. While the daffodils sprouted in our Victoria garden and the two timeless grandmothers looked after our house and children, we fretted in the Fort Garry suite, with brief sorties outside for air, and envied the lusty natives who throve on their ferocious climate. We were both too soft in body for Winnipeg and too hardened in our habits to think of living there.

The friendly matrons of the town took Dot in hand and she helped them with their wartime charities. Only for the exercise, I forced myself to trudge every morning to the office in a monstrous overcoat and a mangy fur hat inherited from a long-dead uncle. Often, doubting that I could survive the half-mile, subzero walk, I would lurch into a store on the way. Then, partially thawed, I made a last dash for 300 Carlton Street.

Once through the revolving door of the *Free Press*, at about eight in the morning, I was physically warm but still mentally frozen. Before me lay the dummy of next day's editorial page—eight empty columns to be filled, and filled only by *Free Press* writers, according to an inflexible rule. No word of outside, syndicate stuff (even if it were much better than our own) could be admitted to this hallowed ground.

Fortunately Dexter was in full spate at Ottawa. His clean copy (often containing news scoops within the deadpan comment) required no revision. George sent some typically smooth and penetrating pieces from London. At Washington, Chester Bloom, a reliable work horse, was filing his rough dispatches on the blunders of American politicians and annoying even President Roosevelt.

In theory Victor had made me responsible for the whole paper but I had the sense to leave everything except "The Page", as we reverently called it, in the hands of the competent staff. I rarely visited the newsroom, where I was looked upon, quite naturally, as an interloper, perhaps a conspirator who coveted George's job.

Even young Jimmy Gray, George's assistant and one of Canada's best journalists and authors, as the future would prove, shared the general mistrust. This victim of the Great Depression, whose riven face, subdued manner, and sceptical mind still showed its imprint (and whose later books vividly recorded its horrors), watched me for a few days with obvious suspicion. Finally he put his own job boldly on the line. If I had come to replace George, he announced, I had better understand right away that he would have no part of the intrigue. Jimmy was George's friend, not mine.

At this I didn't know whether to laugh or cry. The notion that I was conspiring against George was laughable enough, still more laughable that I would ever wish to live in Winnipeg. But I had taken an immediate liking to Jimmy, admired his courage in a life of hardship, recognized his talents, and was deeply hurt by his suspicion. Somehow I kept my temper, told him to forget all such nonsense, and asked his help until George returned, when

I would instantly leave. Jimmy seemed to believe me, we became fast friends and managed, often by the skin of our teeth, to fill the daily vacuum.

Without his writing and editing skills I would have been lost. Without Grant's unfailing and unequalled reportage from Ottawa The Page would have lacked its backbone. Without Edgar Tarr's advice and knowledge of affairs at home and abroad I would not have been able to discuss them seriously in print. Without Victor's backing I would not have dared to commit his paper on many controversial issues of which I knew little. Without a pretty good opinion of myself at the age when arrogance normally reaches its peak I would not have undertaken this task at all. And without physical energy, brashness, and speed amazing to me as I recall them now, I could not have produced the torrent of factual debate, criticism, and sober appeal to reason that gushed into The Page, irritating and possibly illuminating the *Free Press* readers.

It was all great fun, spiced with a sense of invisible power. For I understood, and felt awed by, the weight of my responsibility, that I was no longer working in an ordinary newspaper but in Dafoe's national institution, a big wheel in the machinery of government, and a respected Canadian voice among foreign nations.

Every "leader", or main editorial, of the day must not only comment on some public issue. It must try to analyse and simplify the facts and figures in exhaustive, and exhausting, detail after they had been dredged out of official documents, bluebooks, *Hansard*, and Grant's secret memoranda — homework that no reader was likely to appreciate. Facts, figures, and undeviating principles were our business, or obsession. And rather comically, as I now remember those days, we almost felt that we were speaking *ex cathedra* like a mediaeval Pope or carving our message in granite for eternity.

Comical, yes, but useful training. If we were often wrong, we were honest in our mistakes and prejudices. As newspapers go, the batting average of the *Free Press* in discussing Canada's immediate problems was, I still believe, the highest in the country—only because Dafoe had made it so. Following his editorial line, a well-blazed trail, we felt reasonably safe. It was not too difficult to learn the idiom if not the force of Dafoe's writing, much harder to break out of it and produce what we hopefully called "light pieces". How easily one can demolish a government's policy and devise a perfect alternative with a sleek, unsigned "leader". After a little practice any experienced hack should be able to do it drunk, and often does. Sir James Jeans's celebrated monkeys could do it if they had enough time and typewriters. Even they would be lucky to stumble on a real joke. Yet we always tried to season the dull, daily argument of The Page and hold the reader with a whimsy for the evening fireside. Jimmy and I switched from one style to the other, perhaps without grace but without strain, at a speed now unbelievable. We were instant experts on politics, international, national, provincial, and civic, on finance, commerce, economics — everything. Or we churned out lampoons, limericks, and jingles as occasion and space required. Pundit or buffoon, Mr. Hyde or Dr. Jekyll, it was all the same to us.

With Victor life was a dubious battle, the democratic process an unending contest between good and evil, the economic system sound when governed by the infallible market, unsound when it yielded to human weakness. Knowing that folly was epidemic, he held, in his favorite credo, that a free society seldom moved in the right direction until a fire was lighted under its belly. He insisted that the editorial fire be kept at maximum temperature, and we piled on all the fuel that we could find, or invent.

As I see now, it was mostly straw of brief combustion. Our debating points, valid at the time, and influential, too, because they carried the Dafoe tradition and trade mark, were directed at a world already in the first stages of decay, or at an imaginary future world beyond human reach. Like liberals everywhere, we had been caught in the old trap of impossible expectation.

It was all very well to puncture the stuffed shirts of politics, to criticize the Liberal wartime government (the ablest, by far, in Canadian history) while supporting its policies in general, to denigrate the wretched Conservative Opposition, to ridicule the amateur Socialism of the CCF, and to preach the ideal of postwar peace and prosperity under some kind of world authority. But how pathetic these noble hopes look today! They were not wrong, not even impractical, given a minimum of human intelligence. They were, in fact, much more practical than the practicalities that soon became the solemn lunacy of all nations. Only the necessary intelligence, or morality, was lacking.

If we did not understand where mankind was really going, Jimmy and I worked hard. We had several assistant editorial writers, good men whose names are forgotten, but sometimes we wrote the whole contents of The Page between us when copy was short, seven or eight separate pieces, heavy and light. Once, with Jimmy sick, I wrote them all in a spasm of energy and conceit. They were not much good, and this was no way to run a newspaper, but someone had to fill the gaping white vacuum. Somehow Victor must be satisfied and apparently he was. In my moments of sleepless night-time clarity I was not. Despite the boundless hospitality of the town, I yearned for home. So did Dot, though she never complained about our fortunes, uphill and down, to the end.

George Ferguson returned from England in the spring. Now there would be solid fuel for Victor's fire. It was badly needed. And I knew already that the triumvirate of equals could not work. Clearly George was and must be more equal than Grant and I, because he alone had been trained in editorship by Dafoe and he alone was prepared to live in Winnipeg where final decisions necessarily were made.

This unequal arrangement suited Grant and me admirably. We could pursue our carefree lives and rustic hobbies on the fringe while George, who was hobbyless, sweated it out seven days a week at the centre. My affection for him and Mary, his gracious wife, grew steadily with my debt for the unlimited freedom of their home.

Something else besides the unworkable theory of triumvirate was going wrong. I had begun to sense that the temperaments of George and Victor, because both were able, strong, and proud, and each held a different view of life, must collide sooner or later.

In the meantime our joint business seemed to go well. Jaded by the work and, more, by the hectic social life of Winnipeg, where the natives played hard after working-hours to beguile the loneliness of their prairie fortress and fierce climate, Dot and I came home to our garden and family. That was the summer of the allied invasion of Europe, but it must have passed quietly for us, since I remember little about it. As always, we were remote spectators. By autumn, however, things started to happen even in our isolated affairs.

After a visit to Washington I stopped off at Baltimore for lunch with the editors of the *Sun*. We had just sat down at their table when I was called to the telephone. George's gruff voice informed me that a political crisis had erupted in Ottawa and I had better get there right away. Next morning I was with Grant who filled me in. King's cabinet had split on the issue of conscription for overseas military service. The public knew nothing of the split so far, but the government might fall within days, or hours. This could be the nation's trauma of 1917 over again, or worse.

Grant's pipelines were in their usual good working order. His cabinet friends, all of them inclined to enforce conscription now that it seemed necessary to the nation's war effort, told him everything they knew, the oaths of official secrecy ignored. But at this point they knew only half the story and would not learn the other half for a long time to come. I, of course, knew nothing, though my reporter's nose twitched when Brooke Claxton, the youngest and brightest of King's ministers, came to lunch in my room at the Château and admitted that the situation was truly desperate.

King, he said, was using him, as a skilled negotiator, or extemporizer, to buy time, to draft alternative options and hypothetical formulae, above all to keep the cabinet arguing and postponing any decision. For such work Brooke was well equipped. He had one of the best minds in Ottawa, strict personal integrity, and absolute loyalty to King. Yet he could not be sure what the Prime Minister really wanted or intended. Did King himself know? Brooke, the most buoyant of men, was sunk in perplexity and gloom.

A waiter had just brought in the lunch table as the telephone rang. The call was for Brooke. Recognizing a vaguely familiar voice, I handed him the receiver. He listened in silence and his face suddenly turned pale. "Yes, sir," he said, and hung up.

"That was King," Brooke told me. "By God, I can't make out what the old man's driving at."

The Prime Minister, he explained, had instructed him to cease all his work and say nothing more to anyone. An entirely new situation had developed. Brooke would learn about it later in the day. For the time being, mum was the word.

"I can't make it out," Brooke repeated, tramping up and down my room. "Something's happened, but what?"

Usually a good trencherman, he ate little and soon left for the House of Commons in deepening alarm. Neither of us knew that King had telephoned most of his colleagues during the lunch hour with the same instruction — silence and suspended judgment until the cabinet met. A snare had been laid for his only possible successor. Before that evening King would spring it.

Grant dined with me at the Château, both of us excited, and hungry more for news than food. About eight o'clock a bellboy called Grant to the telephone in the lobby. He returned in a state of extreme shock, hardly able to speak. King, he said, had fired Colonel J. L. Ralston, the leading conscriptionist, and appointed General A. G. L. McNaughton as Minister of Defence.

"Its the damnedest thing," Grant muttered, "the God-damnedest thing I ever heard of," and he hurried away to see his cabinet friends on the Hill. Around midnight he came back with the facts of that famous and ugly incident. The snare had been sprung but not even King knew then that it had caught the wrong quarry.

On my typewriter upstairs Grant wrote his dispatch and it was a blockbuster. All his affection for Ralston, all his detestation of King after an unforgivable outrage, were poured into the copy. At the end of it, Grant asked me, with comical anxiety, if he had gone too far at the risk of bias in the news columns.

"Hell, no," I said. "Let her go the way she looks."

So she did, doubtless burning the wires to Winnipeg. I followed on the train next day to find Victor and George as furious and perplexed by King's move as everyone else.

Several times a day Grant telephoned from Ottawa as the government's political crisis deepened and our own editorial crises deepened, too. McNaughton had promised to recruit adequate overseas reinforcements without conscription. Ralston, in his finest hour, had refused to break the cabinet, as he could have broken it with a single word of encouragement to his friends, and made himself Prime Minister with Conservative support. McNaughton's campaign of voluntary recruitment seemed to be failing. The cabinet meeting in almost continuous session, the Commons restive, uninformed, and ready to explode, King at the end of his tether and apparently near physical collapse—here was the biggest Canadian news story of our lifetime, and we thought that Grant, if anyone, must be on top of it. But he was not. He could not be. For only three men in the cabinet knew what was really happening and they had pledged one another to silence. The pledge would be faithfully kept for almost a decade.

Our editorial crisis, like the crisis of politics, had long roots, old memories, and new complications. Dafoe had supported conscription in 1917 and was among the chief architects of the Union Government that enforced it. After a shattering quarrel between the Anglo-Saxon and French communities, he had determined, if possible, to avoid any repetition.

As he wrote to a friend not long before his death, the nation might be divided again, but if so let it be divided between parties, not by ancestry and blood. Such was the policy, or rather the general philosophy, that Dafoe bequeathed to Victor and his queer triumvirate — conscription, yes, if it became essential for victory, but not otherwise. Of all this Ralston and his friends had been confidentially informed. In the crunch they could count on the *Free Press*.

As veterans of the first war and responsible opinion-makers of the second, George and Grant accepted Dafoe's guideline. Victor, likewise a veteran and a man of strong martial instincts, accepted it, too, but always with grave doubts, his mind torn between his warrior's patriotism and his civilian responsibility as a publisher. Having no experience of war, I was ready to follow my seniors, whatever they decided. And now I began to fear that the split in Ottawa might split the triumvirate from Victor in Winnipeg.

For a week or so Victor, George, and I lived in uneasy editorial partnership, awaiting news from Grant. George wrote and Victor reluctantly approved the leaders that appeared to say something but really said nothing decisive until we could see the success or failure of McNaughton's campaign for voluntary recruits. Under this strain Victor's iron nerves obviously were close to the cracking point. They would have cracked, I thought, if Tarr had not been with us — a wise and placid counsellor, a man you could always tie to in a storm. George and I tied to him, avoided Victor as much as we could, and waited for King's other shoe to drop. Like the cabinet, the *Free Press* couldn't stand the strain much longer.

The first break came late one night as George and I sat in his office with a forbidden bottle of rye, which he kept in his filing cabinet for emergencies, indexed under the letter "R". Without warning, Victor appeared at the door. But it was not the Victor of working hours. He stood resplendent in full evening dress, tails and white tie, white gardenia in lapel, his face of Roman sculpture wearing a look of quiet fury. In our fevered state of mind, the absurdity of this scene struck George and me together —the two shirt-sleeved laborers with their whisky, the gorgeous, dramatic character in the doorway who made me think of the hero in some antique melodrama or possibly the ambassador from Ruritania. For no reason, except our cracking nerves, George and I laughed hysterically.

Victor ignored our idiot guffaws and even the forbidden whisky. What, he asked in a glacial voice, had happened that day in Ottawa? Nothing, we said. Then Victor's nerves cracked, too, without laughter. I forget his words but they meant that he doubted our loyalty to him. We seemed to be stringing along with the anti-conscriptionists, equivocating on the crisis, leaving the paper's policy in confusion and discredit — something like that. His face as white as his gardenia, Victor strode into his own office.

For a long moment George and I looked at each other, speechless. Then some dam inside me broke almost audibly. Before George could open his mouth to stop me I leaped up and followed Victor through the door and found him at his desk.

"Victor," I said in the voice of a stranger far away, "if you don't trust your editors you'd better get some new ones. Right now."

That tore it. Victor blushed like a schoolgirl. The ice in this tempestuous man melted instantly and he seemed close to tears. His apology was awkward and mumbled but it was total and generous — no question of trust in us, no offence intended, merely a misunderstanding, all doubts removed. Let us get on with the job.

Victor had showed himself a big man. Drained of anger and feeling physically sick, I left him without a word and returned to George's office and gulped some rye. I could hardly believe my own temerity and it gave me no satisfaction. For I realized that my first breach with Victor was unlikely to be the last.

George had overheard the conversation in the next room and he, at least, was satisfied.

"Kid," he said, "I could kiss you."

I dissuaded him and we put the paper, and ourselves, to bed.

In the morning the night's clash was not mentioned. But the editorial decision was still unmade, and Victor, for patriotic reasons, nothing else, could not tolerate the indecision. His nose began to bleed and would not stop bleeding. His doctor ordered him to bed, flat on his back, bandaged and seething with impatience. When George, Tarr, and I visited him in his bedroom at home we were alarmed by his appearance. This was a sick man. We told him what we had heard from Grant, which wasn't much, only that the cabinet remained in deadlock, McNaughton's recruiting campaign apparently had failed and King had reached the ultimate crunch.

As George and I could not have done, Tarr soothed Victor. We must wait another day or two before the *Free Press* declared for conscription, the wise old counsellor urged, and Victor grudgingly agreed. He, too, was wise enough to trust Tarr's judgment above his own, for a day or two, no longer. But he worried mostly about his intimate friend, Ralston. Why was Ralston silent after his dismissal? How long would he wait for the government to act? Had he let King's outrage go by default? No, impossible. Ralston must have some plan. So the conversation went over and over the same beaten ground.

On the following day the three of us attended Victor again. He was still on his back but had just reached Ralston in Ottawa by telephone and was addressing him affectionately as "Boss". What's happening, Boss? What are you going to do? Victor listened to the Boss for several minutes, but evidently Ralston had nothing definite to communicate or suggest.

Victor hung up the telephone beside his bed. The Boss, he said, had advised us to keep our shirts on and await events as Ralston himself was doing. That advice suited George, Tarr, and me. Victor accepted it because he trusted Ralston more than anyone else in politics. We left the house a little easier in our minds.

Victor must have been easier, too. His nose stopped bleeding.

The doctor let him come to the office next day. That night Grant phoned to say that the government had imposed overseas conscription. The political crisis was over. Ralston, out of office, had beaten King. The snare had caught McNaughton.

Our own editorial crisis had also passed, Victor was happy, George and I worn out. But we still did not know what had really happened in Ottawa. Neither did Grant, Ralston, nor any member of the cabinet except King and the two others, who would say nothing for more than eight years. By that time the affairs of the nation and the *Free Press* were to be drastically changed and my own disordered.

15

The Party Line

For mankind the next year, 1945, was one of the most momentous since civilization began, the year of agony and victory, the year when a brave new world seemed to be in birth and was not. For the triumvirate in Winnipeg, however, it was a year so smooth and quiet that I remember almost nothing of its passage, except the United Nations' founding conference at San Francisco.

Grant and I, pigging it in the attic of a third-rate hotel, spent our days watching the world's masters on parade, reported their noble rhetoric with innocent enthusiasm, and failed to see, even in the stone face of Vyacheslav Molotov, the pending veto of their dream. But dining one night in a loathsome beanery with Mike Pearson, then ambassador to Washington (who never knew or cared what or where he ate), we saw that his doubts had begun. Prime Minister King, who wore a statesman's confident air in public and invented the typically vague, Kinglike status of a Middle Power for Canada, had passed the stage of doubt and written off the United Nations in favour of writing his own election speeches for early use.

Grant and I had no time for doubts, snowed George under with a blizzard of copy, and enjoyed ourselves until a bout of influenza and a kindly doctor sent me home to Victoria. Like Lincoln Steffens in the Russian Revolution, we had seen the future but didn't know that it wouldn't work.

The triumvirate, urged on by Victor and Tarr, continued to assume that it would work. The old, eternal verities had been reconfirmed at San Francisco, the basic policies of the *Free Press* and Dafoe's hopes vindicated. We went about our job of building an editorial strategy for the new world as we believed that Dafoe would have built it. While we had not yet grasped our real prospects, we had encountered, after the second war, his exact dilemma after the first. Now, as then, the attempt to create at least the embryo of a future world government capable of maintaining the immediate peace was swiftly showing itself to be an obvious failure.

Nevertheless, since Dafoe would not desert the League of Nations while there was a spark of life left in his "brat", we continued to support the United Nations — not because we thought it was yet working but because we hoped that it might work, somehow, someday. The second brat must be kept alive, if possible, through its ailing infancy until, perhaps, the world understood that the alternative was a third war. Since the United Nations could not enforce collective security on a worldwide basis, we strongly approved the North Atlantic Treaty Organization and its two Canadian architects, Louis St. Laurent and Mike Pearson, even if such regional arrangements were a holding device, an essential tourniquet, no more, pending the return of the world's health and sanity.

We denounced the whole balance-of-power theory and the wiser men like Walter Lippmann who advocated it. We applauded King when he repudiated Lord Halifax's impossible plan to make the Commonwealth a "Titan" of centralized power beside its peers, the United States and Russia. And in our own minds we never questioned Dafoe's warning that without a larger international authority to reconcile the divergent interests of its members, the Commonwealth would explode or quietly wither away.

We were generally right, I think, about the long-term hopes

and dangers, though wrong in our timing and our estimate of human possibilities. For the integration of the world, beneath the surface of politics and the cold war, was moving faster than we could see, not by plan but by unplanned economic and technological necessity. It was also moving toward a new and unique crisis that we could not imagine and the wisest men would not recognize for another two decades.

Theoretically we were right, too, in arguing for expanded trade between the nations, if possible free trade eventually, in bullying the Liberal government at Ottawa to abandon its Conservative tariffs, in exposing its protectionist sins. Here again we expected too much; John A. Macdonald's National Policy could only be modified, not repealed. But if we were editorially naïve and boring in our daily protests, we were much more realistic in our private thoughts than we looked in print.

Dafoe, always the realist, had known and written that Canada's vote against Reciprocity in 1911, his great lost battle, would not be reversed in his time, or any foreseeable time. He believed, however, that far short of the free-trade ideal, the tariff might be reduced marginally and systematically. He compared it to a dam which, cut down even by an inch, would release a massive extra flow of water.

Our strategy, therefore, was to demand tariff reductions far more drastic than practical politics could allow in the hope of getting an inch or two off the dam and an increasing current of trade. We asked a lot but expected little, and little was what we got. The commercial structure built by Old Tomorrow still stands, modified only in detail by his successors, Conservative and Liberal alike.

While I must have written a thousand editorials over the years on this oldest Canadian political controversy, Adam Smith's efficient division of labor, and the other pieties of classic Liberalism, they never touched my emotions, aroused my passions, or disturbed my sleep. Besides, I was learning slowly to question and then to abhor the whole economic interpretation of human affairs. George likewise could take the historic ideal or leave it alone. Victor and Grant, the idealists of *laissez-faire*, pined for free trade as the universal solvent, the breeder of worldwide affluence, the road to the good society.

For these men, the tariff was a monster, the snake in Eden. My idealism, and George's, could not reach such heights, except in our writing. But we admired our friends who could. Of course we knew, too, that Victor and Grant, as practical men, did not confuse principles with facts, not often anyhow. They knew in their hearts that economic Liberalism was not an immediate prospect, that the tariff debate, in politics, was a grimy contest between the beneficiaries of the tariff and its victims—strictly a cash-register operation, part of the never-ending struggle of an agrarian West against an industrial East, which, as we all knew, was only one part of a larger struggle for power in the market place.

Victor and Grant believed that, despite its occasional blunders from day to day, over time the free market alone possessed a collective, automatic, almost mystical wisdom unknown in government and elsewhere. It was not only the most efficient method of production, distribution, and consumption but it had a moral aspect as well. It permitted the maximum use of men's highest talents, rewarding the worthy and punishing the backslider. It preserved the chance of a personal freedom more important than the wealth that the rich men produced incidentally.

The poor, unfortunately, seldom understood these benefits or their corollary, which I later discovered for myself—that few rich men, none of my acquaintance, seemed to be truly content. Of all fables the tragedy of King Midas tells the deepest truth. Among my rich friends that golden touch has never failed to have the same result. But then, my friendship in these exclusive circles is limited and no doubt colored by envy. For all I know many rich men enjoy private lives of sublime satisfaction, both material and spiritual, that money alone can buy. If so, they hide it well.

To me, ignorant of economics and totally inexperienced in business, the market is a useful and for the most part an inescapable mechanism under any social system because the law of supply and demand must prevail in the end, no matter what the state or any other power does to obstruct it. There, in the invisible millstones of the market, most collectivist theories like socialism are ground exceeding fine by the millstones of a rapacious human nature. But to argue, as some of the old-time Liberals and Conservatives do, that these harsh and often unfair arrangements contain an ethical sanction, a nearly divine authority, a sacred Christian essence, seems to me the direct denial of the basic Christian doctrine which, if it means anything, means that man stands above the market and the brief economic concerns in this world, far below his destiny in the next. The young Carpenter's opinion of rich men, camels, and the eyes of needles, and his quarrel with the money changers in the temple, were clear enough on those points.

However that may be, none of us then realized, neither the true believers like Victor and Grant nor the half-believers like Tarr, George, and me, a fact then concealed by accumulated layers of legend, the stratified rock of nostalgia — the fact that the free market was no longer free as it may have been, relatively speaking, in a few countries in the nineteenth century. The emergence in the twentieth of three gigantic power blocs, the Big State, Big Business, and Big Labor, already was distorting the market, unbalancing its whole delicate machinery, and making a myth of a former reality.

Yet we worshipped the myth and so did the men of Government, Business, and Labor who were destroying the reality. Government preached, and still preaches, the glories of the market while deranging its decisions by tariffs, taxes, and regulations innumerable. Business preached and still preaches the creed of competition, attacks government's interference, but demands its help and, through vast corporate agglomerations, seeks to strangle the market and protect itself from competitors at home and abroad. Labor preached and still preaches the natural justice of free collective bargaining for the good of all the workers while demanding in wages more than the economy produces in goods and, by inflating the medium of exchange, brutally damages the old, the poor, and the weak whom it professes to love and protect. And as I now believe, this struggle of the three giants, in their secret or subconscious partnership, must finally endanger human freedom itself, the declared objective of them all.

These heretical notions had not yet entered my mind, or the political mind of the nation. The old myth survived and blurred the new reality. Perhaps it always does, the state lagging behind events, our species behind the insoluble problems of its own creation, the whole theory of progress behind the march to planetary ruin.

At any rate, as editors our minds were on current politics where the *Free Press* undoubtedly exerted more influence than any competitor of that time, mainly because it did its homework. By Dafoe's method it moved like a turgid, relentless river, heavy with silt, slowly building up the alluvial delta of public opinion. It might bore the reader but it impressed him by its perpetual motion. If they disliked its views they trusted the printed current to flow as surely as the Red and the Assiniboine past their doors. The newspaper had become almost a geographical fact on the Prairies. While it had long been linked organically with the Liberal Party, it was by no means a government organ. It was just the opposite — a critic, gadfly, and self-appointed conscience that the government feared, tried to mollify, and, for the most part, hated.

Viscount Bryce, the acute British observer, once wrote that "Party seems to exist for its own sake. In Canada ideas are not needed to make parties for these can live by heredity and, like the Guelfs and Ghibellines of mediaeval Italy, by memories of past combats." Dafoe used to quote that phrase gleefully and argued that a party was a nation within the nation. It had its own secret laws, rewards, punishments, and ethical gloss, but its real purpose was the aggrandizement of its power. To that objective all others were subsidiary, except in public rhetoric.

Dafoe knew, too, that very few of the dedicated partisans, not one in a hundred, understood why they supported a party. Most of them were satisfied with their ancestral prejudices, which they flourished like Tibetan prayer wheels, never asking what the prayers meant or how the party's program worked. For them it was enough that the sense of belonging to a group, a sort of expanded and warm household, appeased some natural craving for company in the loneliness of a cold world—a herd instinct, if you like, but also a necessity of politics if the democratic system was to work at all.

From the Liberal Party the *Free Press* sought and received no rewards. Nor could the government punish it, and it had its own zone of power, jealously guarded from the politicians of all parties. If the paper had detached itself from the Liberal Party altogether, life might have been easier for Mackenzie King and for us as well. Dafoe had believed, however, and his successors agreed (with increasing doubts on my part), that an uneasy marriage of convenience or loose liaison, a continuing wrangle between members of the same ideological family, would give the paper an influence for good denied to outsiders.

There was more to it than this considered strategy. For Victor, Grant, and even for George there was an emotional attachment to the party that I could never feel. The party's sins distressed them personally, as they did not distress me. By association and accident I was a Liberal and sometimes contemned, quite justly in those days, and only those days, as a Liberal propagandist. But for me the party held no innate, subliminal virtue, no long memories, no magic. For me politics (though none of my friends would believe it) held no interest comparable to my interest in my home, my little plot of earth, the forest and the mountains where alone I found my nourishment. This I husbanded with a miser's avarice, often with crude deception.

When George called me at Victoria, asking for some editorial by telegraph, in a hurry, he did not know that I came panting to the telephone in my garden clothes and gum boots but supposed that I was interrupted, in deep thought, at my typewriter. With experience and a trained slipperiness one can lead a double life quite successfully, provided that the boss is half a continent away. This had been my invariable operating method, with gains and losses about equal. Keep away from the office as much as possible is my counsel to young journalists, and it may not be as crazy as it seems.

In truth I was not too wise but too selfish, too fond of my privacy, to be a good editor or a reliable partisan. My colleagues made up for that deficiency and between us we argued our case thoroughly, sincerely, and interminably.

Whether the general public read it mattered little. Our target was the political establishment at Ottawa. The Page had no serious interest in circulation, only in argument. Had not Dafoe declared that a newspaper's readership, like a rose bush, needed frequent and drastic pruning? Yet somehow the circulation grew despite us. On the whole we seemed to succeed mainly, I suppose, because our argument was sound, given the mental ambience of the day, the premise of a sane world, and a workable democratic process—given, in short, that creed and core of the liberal faith, the Reasonable Man.

Not for a long time yet was I to question those holy givens. But as early as 1944, when Victor and I toured Saskatchewan and watched the current provincial election campaign, we should have seen that something more profound than the destruction of an old Liberal government and the arrival of Premier T. C. Douglas was under way. We should have seen it but didn't; much less did we see a future socialist government in Manitoba, the invulnerable bastion of free enterprise.

Something else had happened closer to home. To our *Free Press* omelet of four eggs was added a fifth, the most potent and durable of all, though we didn't then regard Richard Sankey Malone as such. At this early date we could not guess that he was to become the manager not only of the *Free Press* but of a coast-to-coast newspaper apparatus built by himself, single-handedly.

I had met Dick Malone in Ottawa for a moment during the war. He was on leave from overseas service as Ralston's confidential military aide and I had taken him for a blond stripling rather too handsome for his own good, a mere prince charming. Among all my mistakes of personal judgment this was the most absurd, but my colleagues seemed to share it.

To all of us Dick was the nice guy, the perfect adjutant to Ralston in war, to Victor in peace, the diplomat, fixer, and trouble-shooter extraordinary, and no more. Because he seldom talked of his experience we hardly realized, on his return to Winnipeg, that he had probably seen more of the war than any Canadian—in Britain, North Africa, Italy, Normandy, and the Pacific—had been Montgomery's intimate, and had come home with cruel wounds, the rank of brigadier, and certain plans much larger than our own. But it was not long before we began to see that Dick's gay banter disguised an exceedingly tough mind.

When the *Free Press* was struck by its mechanical unions in a dispute not over wages but over contractual authority, Dick emerged at once as the indispensable man, the universal joint of the machine. Victor had the courage and the money to face the strike, whatever its merits may have been. Dick alone knew how to set type, cast metal, operate a press, and somehow publish a newspaper without the unions.

It was, to be sure, a ghastly little paper at first, four mean tabloid pages a whole day behind the news, produced by typewritten copy, pasted on cardboard, and photographed, but it kept the *Free Press* alive against all probability. And without

Dick's knack of improvisation, his cool military head, which he kept while others were losing theirs, the thing could not have been done.

Amid that scene of apparent chaos—girls typing and pasting, reporters writing stories already out of date, desk men whittling them down to pointless paragraphs, George supervising and gruntling the staff with sandwiches, coffee, and his endless repertoire of unprintable jokes, Victor sleeping in his office, and Dick seldom sleeping at all — my job was insignificant, though not easy.

The *Free Press* and its competitor, the *Tribune*, which was also struck by its printers, combined in a joint edition. This allowed each paper about half a dwarf column of editorial comment, and in it, the wan ghost of Dafoe's Page, I was expected to discuss the affairs of the world, the state of the nation, and the civic business of Winnipeg. The contents, by the time I had written, rewritten, and written them again, not for quality but for size, must have been even more pathetic than I realized. Fortunately no one cared so long as a paper of some sort, even a ghostly symbol, issued every day from Dick's machine of haywire.

Within a few months he had rebuilt the machine, hired and trained new printers and mechanics, and had the shop operating normally again. The circulation of the *Free Press* was undamaged. But in Vancouver the *Province*, whose printers struck in sympathy with the Winnipeg unions, lost its first place to the *Sun*, with delayed and curious results for all of us, especially me.

Shortly afterward, the triumvirate, if it had ever really existed, was broken by George's resignation. No doubt it had been inevitable from the start. He and Victor shared a mutual respect for each other's abilities but never a true friendship, or even a clear understanding. Their natures, both strong, honorable, and talented in different ways, simply could not be meshed. Grant and I, who were too young, or maybe too self-centred, to understand either of these men, made clumsy efforts of conciliation and failed.

Unlike us, George did not fool himself. Without a word of complaint, another job in sight, or any substantial savings, he told us one night, and Victor next day, that he was leaving a newspaper that since his college days had provided not merely his employment but the focus and habitation of his life.

This was an act of high courage, all the more courageous because it was done so quietly. None of us appreciated at the time what his separation from the *Free Press* must have meant to George, what risks he was taking with his own future, or what a talent we had lost. That knowledge did not come to me until much later, with infinite regret. By then George's craftsmanship had been recognized more clearly in Montreal than in Winnipeg and he had begun a second and even more successful career as editor of the *Star*. But I dare say it could never hold the joy and witchery of the days with Dafoe, who had treated him as a son.

After his departure and the end of the artificial triumvirate, Grant became editor of the *Free Press* against his will, his happiness, and his whole life scheme. In this appointment there was a harsh but irresistible logic, and a tragic price had to be paid for it.

Grant had come to the paper from a Manitoba bush farm, had started as an office boy, graduated to the reporting staff, and caught Dafoe's attention. The older man saw the makings of a journalist, maybe a successor, in the eager youth who worked by day, read by night, and was devoured by curiosity about everything.

When Grant returned from the First World War Dafoe sent him to Ottawa for the next step in his education. There he was soon the best reporter in the Press Gallery of his time, or any time. But he was much more than a reporter — he was Dafoe's eye and ear at the hub of events, his personal ambassador, and, like George, almost his son. While Grant's scoops amazed the news desk and crammed the front page, his flow of secret memoranda was Dafoe's chief interest. On Grant's conversations with Mackenzie King, the cabinet ministers, and their officials, Dafoe founded his editorial leaders and they often contained, in some oblique, casual paragraph, if you knew how to read it, the most important news of the day, its source always well hidden, the confidences never broken. The editor and the correspondent perfectly complemented each other in thought, trust, and affection.

As the third stage in his education Grant was sent to London where his range widened from Canadian to world affairs and where, incidentally and accidentally, he received from a new friend, Mike Pearson, a world beat on the Munich deal. By now, however, hard news had become a minor concern. What Dafoe wanted and Grant delivered was a constant analysis of events, then rushing toward war, backed by those memos of conversations in the strange brotherhood of Fleet Street and Whitehall.

After this invaluable training Grant came back to Ottawa and settled down as an unofficial member of the establishment, which he accurately reported and often bitterly criticized on The Page. He was a kind of inconvenient but unavoidable *amicus curiae* at the judicial bench of politics and always the Liberal Party's link with Dafoe.

To Grant, on George's retirement, the prospect of leaving his cosy home in Rockcliffe, his vast library, his week-end sanctuary in the Gatineau, and the fascination of his work on Parliament Hill for an editor's office in Winnipeg was heart-breaking. He had no alternative; Dafoe had prepared him, Victor needed him, and the paper could not do without him.

So the rustic office boy of the *Free Press* returned as Dafoe's natural heir for years of grinding executive work that he detested, to power that he did not want, in a town no longer his home, and to a strain that finally destroyed his health. I was now perhaps his closest friend, but not a good enough friend to join him in Winnipeg and share his burden. While I momentarily considered that sacrifice, and Victor's lavish financial offer, I rejected them, with a too brief twinge of conscience, partly because I knew that I could never work in any office, much less a Winnipeg office, but mainly because the roots of my life in the earth of the Pacific Coast were too deep now to be broken. Besides, I owed everything of ultimate value to Dot, and her happiness was not expendable.

Grant understood and never asked me to come. Victor did not understand and never forgave me for refusing. Our break, like Grant's promotion, was inevitable. So, I like to think, was our reconciliation in friendship after Grant had gone.

In old age, however, my conscience sometimes troubles me yet. Everything would have turned out differently if I had been willing to join and succeed Grant, as Victor hoped. But given Victor's temperament and mine, everything would have turned out badly for all of us, no doubt in some shattering explosion. Anyhow, there was a factor in this equation that none of us understood at the time. There was Dick Malone with plans much more daring and thoughts much longer than ours.

16

The Prairie Town

The cold winter of Winnipeg is justly celebrated, a timeless Canadian family joke, a proud boast among the natives. The summer, though warm and genial, is worse. Or so I found it in my August banishment. Never had I felt so miserable, lonely, and lost as in those months when I had complete responsibility for the *Free Press*. I loathed every moment while Grant was at his Gatineau retreat and Victor at his place on the St. Lawrence. The whole paper had been placed in my nervous hands, but I didn't want it, managed it indifferently, and grudged that precious time away from Shawnigan. Fortunately I had beside me some good men, Winnipeg men hardened by the climate, who remained in their city by choice as the best of all possible holiday resorts. Maybe it was, except for soft strangers who wilted in the heat.

On large financial and economic affairs I talked with Edgar Tarr several times a week by telephone or, in the evening, drove out to his country home beside the Red River with a copy of next day's editorial for his judgment. The pale, gaunt sage puffed his pipe, sipped his whisky, and ticked off my mistakes with a deadly pencil.

When Canada lurched into the currency crisis of 1947 most editors were bewildered, but Edgar, as a director of the Bank of Canada, understood it at once. Patiently, through long night sessions, he got the facts through my head. The resulting series of learned explanation contained my words and his ideas. The paper was given credit for acute perception, but the real author sought and received nothing more than my gratitude and devotion. That friendship was short-lived. Edgar's death came suddenly before he could see the failure of his hopes for a better world. In sweep of mind I never met his superior. In perception of other minds I seldom met his equal.

To him I was a youngster but to the coterie of three younger men in the office I already showed the plain signs and bad temper of age. The invaluable Jimmy Gray turned out a mass of excellent copy and managed all the housekeeping chores. Frank Walker, a breezy wartime officer of the Canadian Navy now home from sea, brought some of its flavor with him and a writing talent that later took him far from Winnipeg to succeed Ferguson as editor of the *Montreal Star*. Max Freedman, a Winnipeger of diminutive size and large intelligence, was our only scholar. Max had apparently read every book in the English language, collected a voluminous library, and modelled his style on Thomas Babington Macaulay until it was difficult to tell the pupil from the teacher. Later as a Washington correspondent he became the friend of Presidents Kennedy and Johnson, and a recognizable contributor to their speeches.

Unlike the rest of us, Max neither smoked nor drank and, as a result, was hopelessly addicted to sweets. When the craving overwhelmed him he would sneak out of the office and smuggle in a five-pound bag of cream puffs, chocolate éclairs, and other sickening confectionery, which he consumed at leisure — and then complained of a mysterious indigestion likely to prove fatal. But Macaulay's style survived even these orgies.

The hot summer working day, from 8 a.m. to 6 p.m., passed quickly in the scramble to fill and, at the last moment, trim The Page. It was the evening that left me alone and homesick as I walked the streets of Winnipeg until I seemed to know every building in it and despised them all — not because Winnipeg was ugly, for in fact it was for the most part handsomely built, roofed with green foliage, and bright with flowers, but because a man raised among mountains and forests could not be at home on this flat prairie or comfortable in the downtown gorges of concrete.

Winnipeg, to tell the truth reluctantly, was a great city, if not yet great in population then assuredly great in character. A squalid village at the junction of two rivers had defied climate, geography, and the eastern economic system to make itself a citadel always under siege, a warm refuge, a brave glimmer of light in the darkness of the plains. But its shape and spirit were not mine. Its people were not my people, either. No man can be as solitary as when he is surrounded by a multitude of friendly strangers.

So I walked, night after night, observing with envy the countless little homes where the natives retreated from the night and the appalling void around them to seek the company of their kind, the blare of radio voices, the electronic echoes of the distant world until daylight came again. Though Winnipeg was the most hospitable of cities, I could never be a part of it, only a passing guest, eager to depart.

As I began to realize, or imagine, the outdoor men and the indoor men of streets — two distinct breeds the world over, the basic division of humanity — are eternally separate even when they appear to mix. And with my outdoor disposition I thought (but did not say aloud) that the men who inhabit Charles Lamb's sweet security of streets, their feet on pavement instead of earth, must lose some of their vital juices. Mine were running out too.

On week-ends, however, I sometimes escaped from the city with a couple of my colleagues, to voyage on a hired boat up the Red River, a miniature Amazon walled by rank jungle, or to drive across the endless croplands of southern Manitoba where the grain was fattening for harvest. I began to discover the three governing dimensions of the Prairies: the sky, the land, and the loneliness. They reduced any man to less than a cell in this vast breathing organism. Yet, in another sense, he was enlarged and reoriented not only to his own minor planet but to the space and mystery beyond it.

Under the pink sky of dawn, the blazing sky of sunset, or the night sky of stars, his feet on soil urgent with summer growth, his eyes confronting the ultimate reality of things — here a man understands that he was born alone, lives alone, and will die alone. All this has been said by every philosopher and poet, but on the Prairies it becomes real to ordinary men like me.

I have always believed, as one of the few consistent beliefs of my life, that the land itself, not man's grimy marks upon it, had shaped, colored, and nurtured the total mind of Canada — a crude theory, to be sure, a mere hunch and vagrant notion good enough for books or newspaper columns but denied by all the economic figures, the best sociologists, and the ant-hill society of our time. Still, the fact of the land has endured, pervasive, inescapable, and dominant, as it will be to the end after our scratches have been expunged.

Against its three dimensions, the prairie town, as I now came to know it, is a Canadian prodigy unknown to most Canadians— prodigious, yes, and somehow heroic in its dusty squalor, its survival against the withering sun, the blizzard, and the impact of sheer space. From the window of a train the town is a mean clutter, a thin façade of boards and paper, a poor mockery of civilization. From the airplane it is a fly speck by day, a minute gleam by night. But if you walk its single street at dawn, before it awakens to the day's work, when only the birds break the silence and the starveling trees are awhisper, then the contents of human life are open to the imagination if not the eye.

So Wordsworth looked from Westminster Bridge on London when the very houses seemed asleep and all that mighty heart was lying still. Even mightier, it seemed to me, were the hearts of men who, far past the shelter of London's stone walls, dared to face the emptiness of the Canadian West and raise their frail wooden towers, the native Gothic of their grain elevators.

As a microcosm of the whole human experience the prairie town will serve. Wordsworth would have seen it and written a sonnet from some bridge of planks across a muddy creek. For if the site is different the meaning is the same. By the Thames or by the creek the beauty of the morning is like a garment worn, and the village sleepers are the same, too, as the sleepers of London, each alone in his own night world but all common in their waking humanity, and helpless under the same mandate of dawn and toil.

Thus it appeared to me when, at daylight, I looked down the empty street to the sky, the level earth, and the circular horizon far away. In this immensity stood the town, a mere encampment of men who had marched toward an unknown destination and paused here, momentarily, for rest. As the sun rose the street doors would open, the day's work would begin, and the town, immaculate in dawn silence, would look mean again, to anyone but a Canadian, or a poet.

Lacking poetry, I was content to see the town in my private version and watch the crops surge up at its edge with the greenery of spring and the gold of autumn when the clamorous geese were flying south. And long before the world's hunger confirmed the fact, I had come to realize, or guess, that the vacant central plains, not the crowded cities, were the heart of Canada because here the crops grew, the grain ripened, and man's food emerged surely from the earth.

The men who plowed the earth and reaped the crop would receive the lesser part of this treasure. The larger part would go to the middlemen of the cities, the brokers and hucksters who, throughout all ages, battened on the craftsman, the original producer. But he had his reward. He had the land and felt its virtue coursing through his own veins. He had the cool morning, the hot noon, and the fire of sunset as a personal possession. And unlike the street man, the countryman, as Washington Irving once wrote, might be rough but he could never be vulgar; he might not know much but what he knew was in true proportion, measured by the horizon line, balanced between the three dimensions.

Such were my reveries in the villages of the central plains, and if they are less valid nowadays they remain more vivid in my fancy at twilight than at noon.

After a week-end outdoors, Winnipeg, like all cities, looked unnatural and temporary, a huge agglomerate heaped up by man and likely, some day, to disappear with him while the earth remained to absorb both. But the *Free Press* building, square, solid, and functional, would outlast most of man's handiwork. Meanwhile it relished its moments of fun, pranks, and intramural gags that must have been somewhat puzzling to an outsider. It also fostered some wonderful eccentrics who scrounged on the payroll and made the city room their communal roost.

Every morning I found beside my door a venerable and shrunken creature on a bench, clothed in magnificent white mustache, frayed bowler hat, and overcoat of enormous dimension, even in summer. For most of the day he just sat there, silent, motionless, alert. No one knew his name or questioned his purpose. But his fixed stare so unnerved me that one morning I made the mistake of inviting him to my office, whereupon the story of his life poured out in a flood — his birth as an English gentleman, his education in the best public schools, his ruin by fraudulent advisers, his theories of social revolution, his radical poems and prose which publishers were too cowardly to print.

I was foolish enough not only to lend him a few dollars but, worse, to accept his bulky manuscripts for criticism. After that, he watched and beset me, like a faithful dog, and I contrived numberless lies to excuse our unfortunate inability to publish his works. He generously accepted my small loans and returned next day with more manuscripts, quite illegible. He was still sitting on his bench when I left Winnipeg and doubtless still living on minor loans from the staff or Victor.

Every night without fail, year after year, a nameless woman of Slavic appearance would march into the newsroom, discard three overcoats and several sweaters, appropriate a typewriter, and type until dawn. Then she would disappear — a witch, perhaps, fleeing from the daylight. Who she was or what she was writing no one asked. Like the revolutionary poet, she had her title deeds to the *Free Press*. Even Victor, the thrifty executive, never questioned them.

That other side of a shy and vulnerable man did not appear in working hours, and I began to see it only when Victor offered me the highest compliment in his gift. One winter, I forget just when, I was invited to go riding with him.

On a cold Sunday, cold even for Winnipeg, many degrees below zero, with a cutting wind, we met at his house where I found a splendid equestrian outfit laid out for my use. It belonged to his absent wife, Louise, a masterly horsewoman, almost as tall and skilled as her husband. Unfortunately my legs were too large for her breeches and my feet for her boots. By main force I wriggled into them, my limbs soon numb, my blood circulation apparently suspended.

At Victor's stables outside the city we inspected a herd of horses gigantic, powerful, and nervous enough to scare me out of Louise's boots, if they had not been so tight. I had ridden many ranch horses in my time, always in a western stock saddle, but I had never seen, much less ridden, any animal like these proud steeds. They eyed me with contempt.

As a final token of friendship, Victor insisted that I mount the biggest, finest, and, I suspected, the most dangerous of the herd. I protested that it was his own special horse, that he alone should ride it, and, besides, that I had not ridden for years and never in an English saddle.

Nonsense, said Victor. This horse was a family pet, a veritable rocking horse for children, and safe for anyone. I looked with dread at those towering buckskin flanks, the withers so far from the ground that no one could mount to that elevation unaided. What would happen if I managed to reach the saddle I dared not think but the risk must be taken. Victor was watching me with an unspoken challenge and, in honor, or bravado, I could not turn back now.

His hand under my left boot, I heaved my right over the saddle and sat there without any feeling of life in my legs and nothing but terror in my thumping heart. My hands and face seemed to be frozen already in the prairie wind-chill. Holding the bridle, Victor surveyed me and said I looked comfortable.

Then, with a lapse strange in such an expert horseman, he carelessly raised his riding crop. The horse reared, a bridle strap broke, the bit and reins dropped to the ground, and I felt my body shattered by an explosion. That horse did not leap. He detonated like a bomb. As he burst out of the stable yard I heard behind me Victor's calm military voice saying, "Dismount, dismount."

Dismount! As if I could detach myself from my rocket of pulsating flesh. Or, if I fell off, the frozen earth must break my neck, if I escaped the horse's mighty hooves. The reins and bridle dragged beneath him and he was sure to trip over them at any moment. His somersault would be the end of me. Bubbles of foam drifted from his lips and smeared mine. They tasted salty. I clung to his mane, balanced on the stirrups, and thought of my wife and children. My only hope was that the horse would tire before he tripped.

We were aimed straight for the prairie skyline at a speed unequalled in the British Derby. To the rear, I heard shouts and the pounding of other hooves. Victor and three grooms were in hot pursuit, but they could never catch up to my living projectile.

At last he began to swerve in a long circle and was soon headed back to the barn, without slackening his pace. Suddenly I perceived that if he leaped the corral fence or, worse, if he halted beside it, at this speed I would certainly be thrown to instantaneous extinction. There was only one small chance of survival. I must anchor myself to the saddle and hang on to the mane.

After what seemed miles and hours, we thundered across the stable yard toward the high fence. Would the horse jump or would he stop? I gripped the mane harder and thrust Louise's boots forward in the stirrups. He stopped. I was astride his neck, my head between his ears when Victor lifted me to the ground.

"You should have dismounted," Victor said. "Oh well, no harm done."

He forgave me, which was handsome of him. I had no breath to express my thanks, and no sensation in any part of my body, nothing but thirst for strong liquor. There was no liquor, of course, in Victor's stable and he saw no reason to rest after our gallop. Instead, he mounted me on a slightly smaller horse and announced that we would now enjoy a proper ride. Of this ride I have no recollection, except that it lasted a long time until Victor headed for some hurdles in a field and showed me how to jump them. The jumping lesson, I fear, was not a great success but, miraculously, I did not fall off in mid air. Victor said I was learning fast. A few more lessons and I would get the hang of it.

At dusk, with the thermometer down to about thirty below, we returned to his house and I tried to detach Louise's breeches and boots from my lifeless legs. They could not be removed and seemed likely to remain as a permanent outer skin. Finally, with a desperate heave, Victor managed to tear them off me, taking some real skin as well, and I plunged into a scalding bath. Then tea was served by the butler. But still no liquor. That, I thought, was carrying the cause of temperance a mite far.

After this inadequate stimulant, Victor drove me to the hotel, said we had enjoyed a grand ride, and promised to take me for another next week-end. He did, too, fortunately on a different horse. His riding crop, the cause of my day's adventure, was never mentioned between us.

17

The Vagrant's Return

After one of my week-end jaunts I noticed, at breakfast in the Fort Garry Hotel, an old gentleman of unlined, florid face, benign temper, and rumpled tweeds who, like me, seemed lonely and out of place. I took him to be English, a retired professor from Oxford, perhaps, or a country squire visiting the Canadian colony for the first time and finding it a bore.

His look reminded me of someone but I could not put a name to him. At breakfast and dinner every day we exchanged polite nods but no words until Philip Chester, the manager of the Hudson's Bay Company, asked me to lunch with a friend of his in the Manitoba Club. Arriving there, I found the old gentleman from the Fort Garry, whom Chester introduced as Field Marshal Lord Alanbrooke.

Like everyone, I had seen newspaper photographs of the austere and chilly personage, a kind of brain machine, who headed the wartime British Imperial Staff. But the stranger bore slight resemblance to the public Alanbrooke. What had become of the starched military bearing and scornful eye recorded by Yousuf Karsh's camera? Where were the clipped speech and stiff upper lip of the ruling class? Chester's friend was merry, indiscreet, and talkative, a man of wit and laughter, the world in his eyes a wonderful joke. From noon he talked and laughed steadily until four o'clock. We did not interrupt him.

His memories of war are preserved in his diaries but they omit some delicious episodes, among them the pantomime scene at

Number 10, Downing Street. As Alanbrooke recounted it for us, with winks and chuckles, he had been summoned to Winston Churchill's residence at midnight, the usual conference hour because the Prime Minister, well rested by an afternoon nap, always arranged to meet a chief of staff too tired by a long day's work to resist him.

In the darkness and din of a German air raid, Alanbrooke arrived at the garden entrance, opened the back door of Number 10, but could find no one inside. The house was as dark as the garden. Then he heard an unmistakable voice shouting, "Clemmie! Clemmie! Where are you, Clemmie?" and a dim figure lurched across the hall to disappear through a doorway. It was followed by another, shouting in a woman's voice, "Winston! Winston! Where are you, Winston?" and it, too, disappeared. A third figure, apparently female, now emerged, also shouting, and was gone in the blackness.

Standing at the entrance, Alanbrooke remembered the Christmas pantomimes of his boyhood where the actors dived through the scenery and he waited for the climax. It came when Churchill, his wife, and daughter, Sarah, collided violently in the hall and someone turned on a light.

At last, thought Alanbrooke, the midnight conference could begin. But Churchill had different plans. He seized Alanbrooke's arm, explained that they must go to Regent's Park on an urgent mission, and hustled them all into a limousine. Why the hurry, Alanbrooke demanded, and why Regent's Park in the middle of a bombing attack? Because, said Churchill, his daughter was to man an anti-aircraft gun and he must see her in action. Alas, when they arrived at the park the raid was over, the sky clear, the guns silent, and Churchill bitterly disappointed.

"Come, Alanbrooke," he said in a mysterious whisper and led the Field Marshal down a gloomy path, evidently for a conversation of utmost importance and secrecy. So, at the supreme crisis of Britain's war, its two chief managers walked alone in the darkness and reached a great beech tree. There Churchill paused and informed Alanbrooke that he was observing a memorable scene. Yes, here in this place Churchill's nurse had often brought him as an infant and set his perambulator under this very tree. Alanbrooke should mark it well.

At the moment, however, he was too exhausted to care about Churchill's infancy and hoped that, for once, he might go home without a long conference at Number 10. Unfortunately, Churchill was not in the least tired. He drove Alanbrooke back to Downing Street and the conference continued until dawn.

In later years when both men were dead, it would be said that Alanbrooke, in his diaries, had resented Churchill's domineering ways and his amateur conduct of the war. In his luncheon talk with Chester and me the Field Marshal expressed nothing of this sort. On the contrary, he thought that Churchill had been the greatest Englishman of all time, the architect of victory, the unique genius. He loved that man.

True enough, said Alanbrooke, they had often disagreed, sometimes with anger, on strategic questions. Churchill had often been wrong in overestimating Britain's resources and planning impossible operations. He had used all his arts of persuasion and seduction to change Alanbrooke's mind, had broken into theatrical tears, and lamented that even his closest adviser had deserted him in his extremity. Those tears, and the overpowering eloquence of the man who paced up and down his office, had been hard to resist, especially when Alanbrooke was numb with midnight fatigue, but, when necessary, he had resisted them and gone home feeling like a traitor. Now, in his age, he looked back on his memories with nothing but affection.

All that afternoon in Winnipeg the memories gushed forth in sparkling freshet—the wrangles in Downing Street; the working holidays in North Africa; the airplane journeys when the Prime Minister and his companions narrowly escaped death by mountain or bullet; the grotesque spectacle of Churchill in his bed wearing a dragon-spangled robe, secret dispatches littering the quilt; the useless, crazy flight from Marrakech to Cairo at

15. John W. Dafoe. "Already he had made himself a great man by any definition, the greatest Canadian I ever knew intimately, and so many historians, friendly or hostile, have judged him."

16. R. S. (Dick) Malone. "Dick gave [F. P. Publications] his drive and imagination. He alone could manage nine newspapers — and even more remarkable, their cranky editors — while maintaining their individual, often contradictory, characters."

17. Victor Sifton, owner and publisher of the *Winnipeg Free Press*. "Sifton's face was like the marble bust of a Roman senator, his body tall, lean, and powerful, his mind always clear, his speech precise, his manner courteous but, with strangers, remote."

18. George V. Ferguson "had long been Dafoe's managing editor, amanuensis, and alter ego in the *Free Press*....In private,...he was a matchless raconteur, a sentimentalist easily wounded, a wildly generous friend, a dogged enemy, and a writer of rare talent."

19. Grant Dexter, the Ottawa correspondent of the *Free Press,* was a lifelong friend of BH and "the ablest political reporter that Ottawa had ever known and perhaps would ever know".

20. Louis St. Laurent, then Secretary of State for External Affairs, with Prime Minister King at the San Francisco Conference, 1945. "...King, who wore a statesman's confident air in public and invented the typically vague, Kinglike status of a Middle Power for Canada, had passed the stage of doubt and written off the United Nations in favor of writing his own election speeches for early use."

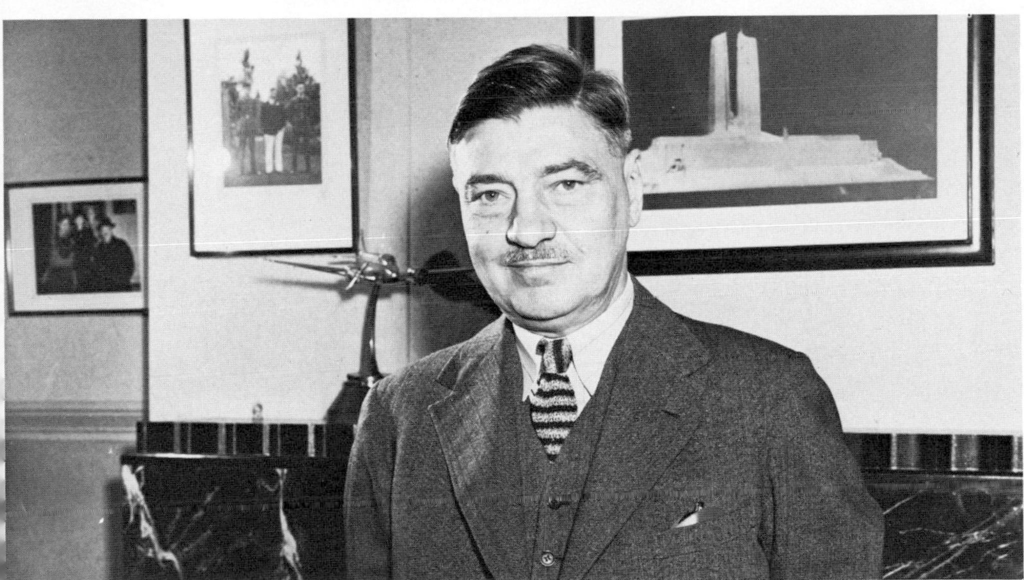

21. C. G. "Chubby" Power resigned from the King cabinet over the conscription issue. Later Senator Power generously allowed BH to read his private diary of the crisis as the basis for his account in *The Incredible Canadian*. Power "understood his Quebec compatriots probably better than they understood themselves."

22. Shyly celebrating with his wife the 1950 publication of his book *The Fraser*

23. Dean Acheson, U.S. Secretary of State, 1940–53: "...his legend of arrogance and austerity was false. In fact he was one of the kindliest and most humorous men I would ever know."

24. Walter Lippmann, eminent American author and journalist: "...more than any contemporary journalist he made the American people think systematically about foreign policy."

25. William Putnam Bundy, Assistant Secretary of State for Far Eastern Affairs, and his wife, Mary, became close Washington friends of the Hutchisons. "By most certain knowledge and personal test I also know that no finer and few abler men had served the nation, or his friends."

26. BH engaged in the important business of life, cultivating his Victoria garden

27. BH and his wife in their Victoria garden in 1960

28. Dorothy Hutchison

Churchill's sudden whim when the night weather was unfit for any plane; his dawn arrival at the British Embassy, unshaved, dirty, and famished; the startled butler in pyjamas; the demand for instant breakfast of bacon, eggs, buttered toast, and, of all things at that hour, white wine. Alanbrooke never learned the reasons for that flight, or for many of Churchill's other vagaries, but they were, he supposed, the price of genius—a low price.

Such jolly interludes in the doldrums of the Winnipeg summer were rare and I was bored. Though I had not yet fully realized it, Victor's patience with me had worn thin. Quite logically, he wanted a colleague who put the paper above personal convenience and was not so eager to decamp from the office at first chance. He liked my work but not my elusiveness and he simply could not understand me, nor I him. While nothing was said, our friendship had begun to cool. Much worse, and tragic for all of us, Grant's health had deteriorated and his talents were being wasted under the strain of executive responsibility that he loathed.

None of us admitted the plain fact but we were heading for a break. It came when Grant's doctors told him that if he wished to live any longer he must get out of the office and preferably out of Winnipeg. After giving most of his life, and now his health, to the *Free Press*, he had richly earned his leisure in Ottawa, his real home, where he now settled down to resume his old and natural work.

Confronted by a vacuum at the top, Victor could think of no Canadian equipped to replace Grant. As the new editor he chose Tom Kent of the London *Economist* who had written some admirable pieces for the *Free Press*, visited Canada occasionally, and liked it.

Among all the journalists of my acquaintance, this pale and icy young man was the most facile, a wonder of speed and self-confidence. Where we old-timers might take two hours to write a leader he could dash it off in ten minutes, letter-perfect, in the *Economist*'s bravura style of metaphor and sarcasm. A few months before this time, in a London restaurant, Victor had introduced Kent to me as his editor-designate. I was certain at once that the deal would not last long because the two men were antipathetic in disposition, poles apart in their political and economic views, altogether mismatched. But I held my tongue. By now Victor and I were in polite, professional communication only, and I anticipated the early end of our prickly relationship; also bleak prospects for myself and my dependants.

In my recollection the sequence of events from then on is confused because they happened so fast and improbably. One absurd scene, however, remains clear.

At Shawnigan I was at the bottom of a deep hole that I was digging for a privy when Donald Cromie wandered up the trail and, looking into the hole, invited me to become editor of his *Vancouver Sun*. Hardly pausing in my work, I declined with thanks. I continued to decline for the next several days as Cromie and his wife stayed at our camp and he continued to press me. Even if I had been willing to replace my old friend and mentor, Roy Brown, I had no intention of moving from Vancouver Island to Vancouver. Besides, though friendly, Cromie and I were as incompatible as Victor and Kent. And in my demented scale of values, a good privy, symbol of the outdoor life, stood far ahead of any office job on the mainland.

Curiously enough, the privy still stands, a noble structure built of hand-hewn beams, a monument to the Canadian identity, and in the builder's dream a royal throne of kings, a Pharaonic temple sited by astronomical calculus so that the occupant is lifted to the zenith of cerebration. Three generations of our family, and some renowned guests, have conducted their meditations in that sacristy, warmed and inspired by the sun as it rises over the bare flank of Mount Malahat. Even more curious, Cromie is out of the other *Sun* while I am back in it and out of the hole.

Most curious of all was my meeting with a second publisher who changed my entire prospects. When Maxwell Bell, of Calgary, turned up in Victoria, bought the *Daily Times* in 1950, and asked me to publish it, he looked like a college undergraduate, dressed like one, and, I thought, spoke in the accents of youth, mixed with an economic jargon out of a textbook. My judgment of him was typically erroneous. This breezy, tanned, athletic fellow with his crew-cut hair and gaudy sports clothes had superlative business gifts, a mind for figures and balance sheets, and a daring imagination that would carry him to wealth and power. He generously shared both with his friends until his life ended, far too soon, in undeserved suffering.

At first I felt attracted to his offer, since I saw no other way of making an adequate livelihood, but I had enough self-knowledge to see that I was unqualified to publish the *Times*, or any paper, and hated the routine of an office. Anyhow, Max's plan to buy the *Colonist*, add the Victoria papers to his Calgary *Albertan*, and make a fortune appeared grandiose and sophomoric. That was another of my mistakes.

With Scottish caution I did not refuse Max's offer until I had telephoned Victor and received his promise that my job and wages at the *Free Press* would remain unchanged while he owned it. Thus insured, as I wrongly supposed, I told Max that he must find a different publisher. Surprised and disappointed, but with thoughts longer than mine, he asked me to suggest a candidate.

Without much thought, because this was not my problem, I recommended Stuart Keate, a Vancouver native son, whom I had known and liked in earlier days but had seldom seen after he came out of the wartime Navy to work for *Time* in New York and later in Montreal. Max had never heard of him and I knew little of his abilities, but more by guess than judgment I had recommended exactly the right man. Max hired him and became his bosom friend.

That was a happy stroke for all of us, especially for me. Stu's instinct for news, his zest for life, and his natural gifts as a leader of men were soon to establish between us not only an intimate personal friendship but also a daily working partnership. Both have continued all these many years, outlasting the arguments of policy and turmoil of newspaper life, and today are as firm as ever.

In Winnipeg, Kent understandably did not want me as more than a casual contributor to the *Free Press*. He wanted younger men by his side who could be trained in his luxuriant writing style and the new, foolproof economic theories imported from London to enlighten Canada's darkness. Since his methods and views were the precise opposite of Victor's, I didn't think that their association would last long. Nor did Grant Dexter and Dick Malone. But at first Victor was delighted with his brilliant young editor, left the paper's policy to him, and, in failing health, lived for the most part on his St. Lawrence River estate.

Perhaps I should not have been astonished, but I was, when Kent informed me that my wages would be cut to a third of the sum guaranteed by Victor and my editorial contributions to some light pieces now and then. As Kent put it, I could write about the woods, the birds, and the flowers — easy work as he imagined, never having descended to such trivia. I assumed that he did not know of the guarantee and said nothing, but decided to quit as soon as I could find an alternative job.

It almost seemed as if a scenario had been written in advance for my special benefit. I found the job at home. One rainy night in the summer of 1952 Stu Keate came stumbling down our trail at the lake, that day's edition of the *Times* burning in his hand as a makeshift lantern, and offered me the editorship of his paper on my own outrageous conditions. I could work, he said, in my house or the office, the hours unspecified, my rural habits undisturbed, the pay handsome (and quickly doubled by Max). After long absence I was back where I had started, and sitting in Benny Nicholas's old chair. I occupied it with gratitude, but without his faith and passion.

Everyone seemed happy with this queer deal, except Grant and Dick. Both insisted that I must not break the frayed thread joining me loosely to the *Free Press* even if I wrote only light pieces about woods, birds, and flowers. The situation in Winnipeg, my friends assured me, would soon change, the good days return. That seemed improbable but I owed Grant and Dick too much to ignore their advice. So I continued to write some light pieces at a ludicrous wage, and without knowledge of a larger plan involving us all that Dick and Max were already pondering.

Their opening move, conceived and executed by Dick, was the purchase of the *Ottawa Journal* by Victor and Max jointly. The Sifton interests of the *Winnipeg Free Press* and the young but growing Bell interests that owned the Calgary *Albertan* and the two Victoria papers were combined to form F.P. Publications, which was later to acquire control of the *Vancouver Sun*, the Toronto *Globe and Mail*, the *Montreal Star*, and the *Lethbridge Herald*. Victor and Max supplied the money needed for this chain. Dick gave it his drive and imagination. He alone could manage nine newspapers — and even more remarkable, their cranky editors — while maintaining their individual, often contradictory, characters.

As the most remote editor in the group I heard nothing of these plans, received no instructions from the planners, and was comfortable in my ignorance. The best years of my life, and Dot's, had begun.

We spent four summer months every year at our Shawnigan camp, with frequent winter travels, and I kept turning out books in my spare time. These cosy arrangements were possible only because Stu regarded me as a sort of historical relic, a museum piece, very frail in my old age, easily broken and needing tender care. Ponce de Leon had failed but Stu had discovered the fountain of eternal youth, a perfect mate in his lovely Letha and the good life in Victoria. He soon won the loyalty of his staff, and he let me work, or not work, as I pleased, in my own time.

I husbanded it with miserly greed. By eight o'clock every morning I was at the typewriter in my house. By eleven I had written a signed column and the leading editorial for next day's paper. I carried them to town and, refusing to accept any separate office lest it trap me, dictated a few letters to Elsie Edwards, Stu's charming secretary. Then a chat with Stu and a feet-on-desk conference, or so we called it, with my excellent, long-suffering colleagues, Brian Tobin and Arthur Stott, who somehow endured my vagrant habits. By noon I was driving home again for a couple of hours' work on books, magazine stuff, and those heavy-light pieces printed, without enthusiasm, by Kent in Winnipeg. After that the garden or, in summer, the Shawnigan woodpile.

How Stu tolerated a bird of such erratic flight I never asked, nor did I know what held the editorial apparatus together. Certainly I did not. But the *Times* had more reliable birds than the so-called editor. While Stu presided as publisher, and the well-loved Leslie Fox as one of Canada's ablest managing editors, the paper appeared regularly day by day and, for the size of its constituency, was among the best in the country. Its management received scant help from me but I provided a lot of copy, most of it indifferent, some the best I ever wrote because it was written on the wing.

18

The Scoop and the Yawn

When he succeeded Mackenzie King in 1948, Louis Stephen St. Laurent changed not only the methods but the whole mental climate of Canadian politics — not that the new man was more talented than the old but that he was more kindly, generous, and human. For practical use St. Laurent's mind was superior to King's, and quicker. As a piece of machinery it may have been the best mind ever to govern Canada, though it lacked King's fourth political dimension, that premonitory warning system more reliable than all the facts assembled afterward to justify some vague impulse and sudden act.

St. Laurent's understanding of the Canadian people came to him very late because his life had long been remote from theirs, but when it came it was mutual. Power also came to him without his preparation or ambition. It came, you might say, by accident, and by accident it was withdrawn.

An accident of war brought him to Ottawa in the first place, for temporary service. I knew him then only by name as the new Minister of Justice until one day, with Dexter, I encountered a brisk little man striding alone down Wellington Street. No other pedestrians seemed to recognize King's latest colleague. When Dexter introduced me to him I was struck at once by his genial manner and, on second glance, by his penetrating, quizzical eyes. They looked right through you. St. Laurent was no longer young then, but he was lean and trim, a crisp terrier of a man, as I thought him, with a ruddy face rather too handsome, a deportment rather too modest.

He had joined the cabinet only to replace the dead Ernest Lapointe and planned to return to his law practice in Quebec as soon as the war ended. So he told us that day on Wellington Street. Of course he was wrong in his expectations and our judgment of him still worse. We considered him an adequate minister, an eminent lawyer, a gentleman of the old school, and in politics a bird of brief passage. At the beginning everyone was wrong about St. Laurent, even King, who seldom erred in judging men.

After he became Prime Minister I often saw St. Laurent, though I never knew him as I had known King. Neither man was easy to know but each guarded his privacy by a different method. King's thoughts slid out of your grasp like jelly. St. Laurent's mind, apparently open to the world, was protected by an iron curtain which he lowered instantly with an audible clang against any trespasser.

It was lowered against me when I undertook to write a piece about him for an American magazine. He answered all my questions with candor, sometimes with twinkling humor, until I came to a famous incident. Did he now regret his decision, as Minister of Justice, to arrest and hold incommunicado a company of alleged Russian spies? The smiling face hardened in a scowl. The kindly eyes seemed to congeal in black opacity. A stronger man than I might shrink under his look. King would have fobbed me off with a long homily and a smoke screen of evasions. St. Laurent paused for a moment, his scowl deepening, his eyes drilling mine.

"Sir," he said at last, "I don't care to answer that question."

In print the incident seems trivial. In life it told me much about St. Laurent. His iron curtain not only excluded the offensive question, it nearly decapitated the questioner as it fell.

Generally St. Laurent's patrician charm was his greatest asset, though the least of his qualities in government. Even his political enemies could not dislike him, as so many had detested King. Equipped with high intelligence and, by his parentage, with the two distinct elements and languages of Canada, he was bound to succeed, for nature had made him the common national denominator, the average man writ large. He governed with no claim to genius but by common sense, the most uncommon asset of all.

Sometimes at a distance, sometimes up close, I was a spectator of his success and his ultimate misfortune. He always spoke frankly to me and in an easy, colloquial idiom unexpected from the erudite scholar of law and constitution, but in his presence I always knew that the iron curtain hung by a hair. After seeing it once, I did not risk a second descent. While our paths crossed in a pleasant and correct fashion, I learned after a time that St. Laurent was not as immune to criticism and the pinpricks of journalists as the public had supposed. A curious episode of his making directly involved me and disclosed another side of his nature. I still shudder to think of this affair.

King had left his papers and dropsical diary to a group of literary heirs, Pickersgill among them. These men were to produce the historic record that the great man had not lived long enough to write. Who, then, could write it? In a moment of friendship, or weakness, Pickersgill suggested my name. The prospect of spending several years with tons of documents appalled me. Besides, I was in no way fitted by training, knowledge, or bent for such a task and had no thought of attempting it. I did not have to refuse, however, because the literary heirs, less partial to me than Pickersgill, wisely chose a much more qualified biographer, the late MacGregor Dawson.

Assuming, quite wrongly, that I might be disappointed, Pickersgill proposed that I write a book of my own on King. The papers and the diaries would not be opened to me but without them I might turn out a rough journalistic job unworthy of the scholars though possibly interesting to the public, even profitable to the author.

Rash enough to grasp the bait, I spent the next two years, in my spare time, among King's printed speeches and the men who had known him in life. Three full days, for example, were needed to read merely the constitutional debate of 1926, and then I misunderstood it entirely, according to Eugene Forsey, who had made that historic controversy into his life's work. He seemed to consider me King's self-appointed, posthumous apologist, as he certainly was Meighen's, and failed to observe that I was trying to do nothing more than report King's views, not my own.

Years later I met Forsey in some Ottawa club. To my surprise, the bitter critic was a jolly, reasonable fellow, an ornament to the Senate. His angry verdict that my book had been far too charitable to King was rather amusing when King's idolators protested that he had been scandalously libelled.

All this would scarcely be worth mention if it had not produced a queer sequel that involved a prime minister, the nation's defence forces, and me. As the reader will see presently, my hack job as an amateur biographer carried me into a morass of politics and personalities far beyond my depth. The escape was to be painful and narrow.

Meanwhile my spare-time labors resulted in a book called, for lack of a better title, *The Incredible Canadian*. The reviewers and the public seemed to think that the book contained some tantalizing secret history and, if it did, the late Senator Charles Gavan Power deserves most of the credit.

Before attempting the book I had never met the well-loved "Chubby" Power, though I had often watched and admired him in the Commons. The delay in our acquaintance was entirely my fault, and a great mistake. Now, when I telephoned his office in the Senate, he asked me to come up right away. I found his office untidy, unlocked, and friendly, like its occupant. The man with his feet on the desk was of pure Irish descent, but with his swarthy face and black mustache he looked French, and he understood his Quebec compatriots probably better than they understood themselves. Ever since 1917, when he came back from the First World War gravely wounded, they had elected and re-elected him, until in 1944 he resigned from King's cabinet, as an opponent of conscription, in what has always seemed to me a splendid act of personal sacrifice and public honor.

What, asked Chubby in his gruff, barking fashion, did I want to know? My instinct told me that it was useless to temporize with this blunt person and I came immediately to the point, hoping for the best, but expecting little. Would he tell me something about his experiences with King in the conscription crisis?

As I was a complete stranger to him, Chubby sized me up at leisure, through his usual cloud of cigarette smoke. Apparently he decided that I could be trusted. Why yes, he had some information and I was welcome to it. With that, he unlocked a filing cabinet and took out a loose-leaf book, his private diary of the crisis. No one except his confidential secretary had ever seen or heard of it, he said, and I could not imagine that he would let me read it. To my amazement, he handed it across the desk.

"You can have it," he added, "until nine o'clock tomorrow morning, and not a minute later. I want to lock it up again before I leave for Quebec. No one but you, absolutely no one, is to see it and you'll never mention it to anybody else. Is that understood?"

It was understood all right but I could hardly believe my luck. To a complete stranger, for no understandable reason, Chubby was committing the secrets that King had taken with him to the grave. I left the Senator's office dumbfounded and incredulous, hurried to the Lord Elgin Hotel at about four o'clock in the afternoon, locked my bedroom door, opened the diary, and found that it was as long as the average book, or longer. Within seventeen hours I must read and note down its contents, if that were possible.

Through the whole night, without food and with only water to drink, I scribbled notes in my rusty shorthand. By eight next morning I was faint, dirty, and famished, but the diary had been well and truly gutted. I took a quick shower, changed my clothes, and staggered up to Parliament Hill just as the tower clock was striking nine. Chubby awaited me in his office, thanked me for returning the diary, trusted that I had found it interesting, shoved it ino his filing cabinet and left for Quebec.

He had not asked me a single question or suggested how I should use, or not use, his record of the crisis. With his secrets in a stranger's hand, I now began to see that Chubby, in his own way, was as incredible as King and much more attractive — a rough operator in party politics but in life and human compassion a better man. Such a man was not given, like King, to public gestures of high principle, but under all the laughter and raillery, Chubby's Irish nature contained a bundle of passionate emotion. King had cried like a child when Chubby refused to withdraw his resignation and break his anti-conscription promise to Quebec. Chubby did not cry. He marched alone into the wilderness, a great career ended by his own choice and without a moment of bitterness.

Until now, long after his death, I have never mentioned Chubby's diary to anyone. Even St. Laurent and Pickersgill, who knew nearly everything, must have wondered where I had found a day-to-day account of the cabinet's conscription quarrel. And even Chubby died without realizing that he, and the diary, had missed the central point of the crisis.

This point was unknown to me as I considered how the record could be used in my book. I decided to report it almost word for word, as the diary of an unnamed author. But when I sent a copy of the first draft to Chubby for comment he was shocked. Surely, he wrote back, I could disguise the source of the evidence better than that? He did not request, merely suggested, that I should not use the word "diary" lest some of his former colleagues trace the material to him. Otherwise he had no advice to offer. My condensed account of the crisis was accurate. Therefore, publish and be damned.

With only the objectionable word removed, the contents of the diary were duly published in my book and in *Maclean's* magazine in 1952, no one suspecting the source, everyone apparently assuming that I had many different sources and had gotten to the bottom of the crisis at last. Like Chubby, I thought so, too, until the spring of 1953 when a funny thing happened to me on the way to Europe.

Dot and I were preparing to catch a train from Ottawa at two o'clock one afternoon and board a ship at Halifax. As we packed our bags the telephone rang in our Lord Elgin Hotel room. I answered it to hear Pickersgill's familiar but now excited voice. Could I do a favor for him and Mr. Laurent? Sure I could but what was it all about?

It was about the real facts of the conscription crisis, said Pickersgill. He reminded me that King had excused his decision to conscript soldiers for overseas service by hinting darkly in Parliament that otherwise trouble in the defence forces might precipitate national anarchy. Did I remember?

Of course I remembered but what was Pickersgill getting at now? Only in the last few hours, he replied, had the real facts been disclosed to him. He had always believed that there was more in King's mind than in his words to Parliament and now the truth behind the words was out.

"Okay," I said, "but that's nothing to do with me. We're catching a train in an hour."

"Listen," said Pickersgill, and I listened.

St. Laurent, he went on, had read my book on King and had no quarrel with it except on one passage touching him directly. My version of the crisis seemed to represent St. Laurent as accepting conscription because he, a French Canadian, lacked the courage to resist the political pressure from King and the English-speaking provinces. Evidently that account of his stand in the crisis had rankled in St. Laurent's mind ever since the publication of the book (though certainly I had not intended to write it in that way and could not imagine anyone so reading it). A proud man, he wanted me to correct my supposedly false impression.

"For God's sake how?" I demanded of Pickersgill.

That was easy, he said. If I called at the office of a certain Army general he would tell me the true story of the crisis and vindicate St. Laurent's role in it. I would learn that St. Laurent had accepted conscription because the alternative was disastrous and unthinkable, just as King had warned Parliament.

Pickersgill gave me the name of the mysterious general but I insisted that there was no time for me to see him. My train would leave in less than an hour and I had a ship to catch.

"Then call him on the phone," Pickersgill urged in a voice of desperation. "This is mighty important."

I saw that it must be important if St. Laurent, the Prime Minister, thought so. But the idea of re-exploring possibly the most complicated political crisis in Canadian history on a telephone, with an unknown general and only minutes to spare, struck me as insane.

"Go ahead and call him," said Pickersgill and rang off.

I looked at our litter of baggage while Dot frantically tried to pack it. My first impulse was to forget the General, slink out of Ottawa, and let St. Laurent skin his own skunks. On second thought I knew I couldn't do it. My friends would never forgive me.

So I picked up the phone and called the General. Obviously he expected the call by arrangement with Pickersgill. Yes, he was ready to tell me the facts. In brief, the members of the Army Council, he among them, had met on the morning of November 22, 1944, and decided to resign if the government did not impose overseas conscription immediately. I gasped. The General was telling me that King and St. Laurent had indeed faced, with Defence Minister A. G. L. McNaughton, a crisis far more alarming than they dared to discuss in cabinet.

While the nation may not have been in danger of anarchy, or anything like it, as King later hinted to Parliament, clearly the resignation of the men who commanded the defence forces at the climax of the European war would have destroyed the government. If that was no great matter the convulsion following it would have shattered both the war effort and the brittle partnership of the two Canadian communities, driving Quebec, for the second time, into sullen isolation. Hence St. Laurent's duty had been plain. He had accepted conscription without believing it to be of any practical use because he alone, as Quebec's leader, could prevent such a rupture, even if acceptance might well destroy his own political career.

All this I grasped at once on the telephone. The General didn't need to explain it. He merely told me, in a few clipped, military sentences, of the Army Council's threat to resign and left the rest to my imagination. It was working at high speed as I asked the General if I could publish the facts. Certainly I could, he said, provided that his name was not connected with them. Like Chubby, he trusted a total stranger, presumably because the Prime Minister's office had assured him that his confidence was safe. Having given me the facts, he hung up his telephone.

Here was a pretty kettle of fish. My shaky hand had jotted down some rough notes on the hotel's pad of paper and now I could hardly decipher them. I had been given the biggest news scoop of my life, a glittering chunk of Canadian history, but I didn't know what to do with it. The Prime Minister wanted the record set straight but who was I to deny the accepted version of the crisis and probably find myself sued for libel? Clearly it would be libellous to report, without proof, that the nation's highest military officers had threatened joint resignation in wartime. Base such a story on a telephone conversation of two minutes, on a tiny page of scribbled notes? Don't be an idiot, I told myself.

Dot had packed the bags and called a bellboy. The train would leave in a quarter of an hour. There was no time to call Pickersgill and plead that I could not help the Prime Minister. We scrambled into a taxi and drove to the station. On the train I tried to think the thing out and the more I thought the more dangerous it looked.

In the first place, if the facts as given to me by the General were true, how had they been suppressed since November 1944, more than eight years? They had been known all this time to three cabinet ministers — King, St. Laurent, and McNaughton — and to perhaps half a dozen military men. Surely someone would have talked before now? If not, no secret had ever been kept so long and well in Ottawa's thunderous whispering gallery.

Yet why should the General misrepresent the facts at this late date? Why should the Prime Minister have taken so much trouble to get them out? They must be accurate, but if I wrote them and they were indignantly denied by some participant in the crisis, where would I stand? Who would come forward to defend me? Probably no one. I was on my own, and the next day, still undecided, on a liner bound for England, the telephone notes burning in my vest pocket.

The voyage gave me a chance to invent a strategy of sorts, a trap door of escape if it were required. Since I could not avoid my obligation to St. Laurent, and especially to my friend Pickersgill, I must write the piece. In our cabin, I set to work while the ship rolled in an equinoctial storm and my little typewriter kept sliding off the table.

After a couple of days I had finished a job of no literary merit, a rather sloppy job, but it was loaded, I thought, with high political explosives. Then I wrote a covering letter to Ralph Allen, editor of *Maclean's* magazine, explaining some, though not all, of the facts and omitting, of course, the names of the General, St. Laurent, and Pickersgill. As I told Ralph, he must take my word for it that the story was valid and, if any libel suit or other trouble came of it, must take full responsibility because I could produce no legal proof. Or if he decided not to print it, that would be fine with me, too. I had done my best for my friends.

So I dropped the envelope into a post box as soon as we reached London and called immediately on the Canadian High Commisioner, Norman Robertson, who took me to lunch at his house. There I related to him what I had heard in Ottawa but mentioned no names, nor St. Laurent's interest in the matter.

Robertson was flabbergasted. To all the events of the crisis he had supposed himself to be privy. King, he believed, had told him everything. Indeed, Robertson had always been the chief idea man behind the wartime government, the central cog of the whole machine, and yet he had heard nothing of the decisive facts. I doubted that he would believe my story but was sure that he would check it through his own unequalled sources.

Dot and I set off on a motor tour of Europe. When we returned to London for Queen Elizabeth's coronation I learned from my newspaper pals that the piece had been printed and the great scoop had been received by the public with a great yawn. Elizabeth, and the dawning second Elizabethan Age, were the only interesting news at the time. That disappointed me as a reporter but as an easily terrified fellow I was delighted to escape any trouble.

Whether St. Laurent was satisfied I never knew. In all our subsequent meetings the subject of conscription was unmentioned. No thanks, no hint, no smile or wink suggested that the Prime Minister knew anything about our remote and silent collusion. Even Pickersgill did not mention it again. Whether the General who gave me the facts by telephone is still alive I don't know. I never saw him. I have never repeated his name. For me the only regret in this odd business is that my book on King was published before the key fact was known to anyone outside the circle of three cabinet ministers and a few soldiers who had so long and so honorably sealed their lips. Strangest of all, that circle had not included J. L. Ralston, Chubby Power, or Angus Macdonald, the pre-crisis defence ministers.

Having won the election of 1953—an easy personal triumph—St. Laurent, though ageing, still looked healthy, durable, and serene. The once diffident and formal lawyer from Quebec had been transformed into the folk figure of Uncle Louie, everybody's friend and next-door neighbor, who without the least visible effort had somehow made himself one of Canada's greatest prime ministers. Such an unnaturally comfortable time could not last. By 1956 St. Laurent's time of sorrows had come suddenly, brutally, perhaps inevitably. And the sorrows came not as single spies but in battalions.

The story of the rancorous and generally misunderstood pipeline debate needs no retelling, and in any case I did not witness it at first hand. Those who watched the daily spectacle of passion and disorder, the pipeline scheme itself forgotten in the wrangle of procedure and debating rules, could not understand why a man long master of the Commons had lost control of it. Even the cabinet (except Pickersgill) did not know that St. Laurent was exhausted, sick in body, and stricken in mind by a private grief. His manner was quiet and polite, his interventions brief and sensible, but the old strength had ebbed. He seemed almost indifferent to the storm raging around him.

When it subsided as quickly as it had arisen no one in the government realized that the Liberal Party had already lost the next election. Arrogant, as always, unable to imagine their own defeat, the party managers refused to see that their chief, after a magnificent record, had earned retirement, peace, and health. While he was a little weary for the moment, and his ministry bruised, both would soon recover. At the age of seventy-six, St. Laurent remained the party's most precious asset. Uncle Louie could surely win one more election. So, against his judgment and all his inclinations, he agreed to fight it in 1957. The result, in the literal meaning of the word, was tragic.

Until he reached Victoria on his last campaign tour I had not seen him for some months and assumed, like most reporters, that he was the same man I had known in earlier, happier days. One glance at his face, when we met in the wings of a local theatre, told me that he was not. He seemed unable to recognize his friends or remember their names. He nervously smoked an endless chain of cigarettes. He read a very dull speech on foreign affairs, obviously written for him, when the party stalwarts expected and needed a slam-bang attack on John Diefenbaker, who recently had whipped the Victoria Conservatives into a mood of euphoria.

With more courage and more anguish than the public ever realized, St. Laurent went through the motions of a campaign from coast to coast but they were motions only, the motions of a somnambulist—dignified, courtly, and modest, but lacking any of the old sparkle and fire, the will to victory.

Nevertheless, his party had no doubt about the victory, no sense of its leader's bone weariness, no idea that the Canadian people might be bored with Liberalism after its twenty-two unbroken years in office. The wonder was not that St. Laurent won fewer parliamentary seats than Diefenbaker but that he won more total votes and robbed the Conservatives of a majority. Even in his physical weakness and mental strain, he might have won another majority of his own but for the famous rebuke to European "supermen", an angry spur-of-the-moment response, instantly regretted, to a grossly unfair attack on his position in the Suez crisis.

He took his defeat with outward composure, decided on election night against any attempt to govern with a minority, as King undoubtedly would have done, and sat silent in the Opposition benches. But the defeat was shattering to a man who had known up to then only public acclaim and private happiness. He blamed himself alone for his government's misfortunes, and he brooded on them alone in bitter self-reproach, to the alarm of his intimates. It was many months before his spirits and health slowly recovered from the shock.

When I last saw him in his Quebec law office, two years later, the recovery seemed complete. This man was old but he was St. Laurent again. He told me that he should have retired before the 1957 election in favor of a younger man and had so intended. The arguments of his friends had persuaded him to stay — a grievous error but his own.

That manly admission was typical of St. Laurent, but inaccurate. For in fact his selfish friends had committed the error and dragooned him into service to win an election. However, he uttered no word of complaint. Toward Diefenbaker he expressed no bitterness. For his Liberal successor, Mike Pearson, he held high hopes. For the nation's future and the abiding partnership of its two communities he had no fear. As to his own work of unity, the historians could judge for themselves. He would write nothing. Nor did he in the years of serenity left to a very perfect gentleman.

19

The Lost Leader

It was during St. Laurent's period of office, and my own occasional editorship of the *Free Press*, that I first collided with John George Diefenbaker. Neither of us suspected the horrendous adventures awaiting him.

Our intermittent relationship went back to the year 1926 when, at a British Columbia Conservative convention in Kamloops, a guest was introduced as the party's most distinguished member, thinker, and orator in Saskatchewan. Few British Columbians had heard his name before he appeared on the platform. Diefenbaker was young then and unknown to the nation, a leader without followers, a gangling, twitching figure whose black, metallic curls accentuated the deadly pallor of his face and the feverish glare of his eyes.

For a man apparently so frail in body, a short physical life, and an even shorter life in politics, might have been safely predicted —until he began to address the convention. He said nothing that anyone remembered, but no one was likely to forget the rumbling, rasping voice. It sounded like a brass trumpet out of tune. It carried the heat and wind and acrid fumes of a prairie fire. With that speech Diefenbaker emerged momentarily as a phantom, a will-o'-the-wisp from the Conservative swamps of Saskatchewan, only to disappear, as all of us supposed, forever.

I did not see him again until 1942 when he had entered another convention in Winnipeg to seek the national leadership of his party. By this time he was middle-aged, less emaciated, and more polished in his oratory — much too polished. He looked now as if he had been taking elocution lessons from some incompetent village instructor. He gestured, he postured, he struck heroic poses like a hoofer in some third-rate vaudeville show, or a competitor in amateur night at Prince Albert. The convention was not impressed.

In any case, Arthur Meighen, executing his last great political blunder, had already decided that John Bracken, the Manitoba Premier and a Liberal who called himself a Progressive, must be the new Conservative leader. Against this misguided battle plan Diefenbaker had no chance, and poor Howard Green, also a candidate, fainted from hunger and tension in the middle of his speech, falling backward to the floor, the lectern on top of him. I thought for a moment that my old friend had died, but he was soon revived for many years of faithful service to the public.

Shortly after the convention I met Bracken, for the first time, in the Ottawa office of the non-elected, unofficial Opposition leader and was astounded by his ignorance of national affairs. He had been an expert agriculturist and a good Premier in Manitoba. His lean, wholesome outdoor look, iron-gray locks, and quiet voice seemed to invoke the earthy wisdom of the prairie farm. Since few words came from his lips, and those reluctantly, it followed that he was storing momentous thoughts in his head. This sort of deduction often fooled me, and the public, in more important men — but not in Bracken.

Possibly because he was too honest, certainly because he was too ill-informed, the politics of Ottawa bewildered him from the start. He refused to enter Parliament in a by-election and tried to lead his party outside it, an impossible task. He told me that the debates under way in the House of Commons just below his office were of no real significance. I left him with respect for his character and his patriotism in wartime but with no doubt of his inevitable failure at the summit.

King held the same view, even more strongly. He assured his

colleagues that the Conservative Party had chosen the worst of all possible leaders. Anyone would have been better. To rub it in he wrote Bracken regretting his conversion to Tory principles, adding that he had intended to offer him a portfolio in the Liberal cabinet. Of ironic mischief King was a master.

While Bracken's star sank finally in the postwar election, Diefenbaker's was rising slowly but surely in the West. By 1948 the time had come for his second lunge at the national Conservative leadership. Only then did I see him face to face, in strange circumstances which he has probably forgotten long ago.

In the late summer of that year, with Grant absent on holiday, I was editing the *Free Press*, assisted by my clever young colleague Max Freedman. Max knew Diefenbaker intimately and learned that he was coming to town. Would I like to meet him? Of course I would. Max arranged for the three of us to breakfast in my Fort Garry Hotel room on a Sunday morning.

Diefenbaker arrived punctually. At first, in the company of two notorious Liberals, he was glum, defensive, and uncommunicative, quite unlike the flaming theatrical personage I had seen on the platform, and noticeably older, the black curls now streaked with white, the face growing fleshy around the gills. A large and lengthy breakfast seemed to relax his mood. An unplanned luncheon further eased his suspicion. By mid-afternoon he was sharing with us the inner secrets of the Conservative Party.

The party was soon to meet again for a leadership convention and he was already a major candidate. But he had reason to fear that the convention would be pre-packed against him by the baneful Ontario interests supporting George Drew. The mechanics of this plot were complicated, as Diefenbaker explained them, and I cannot recall the details. I only recall that, with his anonymous encouragement, I proceeded to make a fool of myself and the *Free Press*.

Next day I wrote an unattributed piece under the florid headline — "How to Pack a Convention". It looked great on the editorial page. Max and I felt that we had struck a blow for democracy.

Our triumph did not last long. Before night J. M. Macdonnell, president of the Conservative organization, had sunk me and the paper without trace. All our facts were garbled, all our charges false. Knowing Macdonnell as a man of unquestioned honor, I saw at once that his facts and counter-charges were undeniable.

We tried to reach Diefenbaker by telephone, hoping that he would publicly confirm our statements and rescue us from our self-made trap, but we heard nothing from him before the convention opened. He was too busy, I suppose, to worry about so small a matter and he may well have believed what he had told us, as we had believed him. Anyway, the convention, packed or unpacked, chose George Drew.

For a time I felt angry with Diefenbaker but gradually cooled off when I ran into him, now and then. After all, an occasional misunderstanding was to be expected in politics, or in show biz, which he had thoroughly mastered. We became quite friendly and confidential.

The man was easy to like, or to hate, depending on your taste. I liked him, and in his courageous grief in the death of his first wife I pitied and admired him. He fascinated me with his dramatic talents as he spun his tall yarns of the pioneer West and his legal coups in dusty courtrooms, or perfectly mimicked the speech, idiom, and mannerisms of St. Laurent, Pearson, Pickersgill, Drew, and all the prominent Members of Parliament. Striding up and down his narrow office, chuckling, winking, leering, he could people it with the whole House of Commons. Diefenbaker's commitment to political life deprived the world's theatre of a superlative character actor whose repertoire included sermons and wisecracks, prophecy and banality, sense and nonsense, tragedy and comedy, sometimes farce.

What had Canadian politics gained? It had gained in drama

and in certain human qualities of passion, revolt, and sympathy, all sincere, mixed with a corrosive hatred of enemies and often mistrust of loyal friends. In opposition the small-town courtroom lawyer was at his best. (Later on, in a Vancouver criminal court, Justice J. V. Clyne was outraged when Diefenbaker, clutching his own throat and gasping, dropped to the floor to illustrate how his client, accused of murder, had been assaulted by the real murderer.) In personal contact he was modest, chummy, delightful, the best of companions for a dull day. In his work, study, and reading he was almost too industrious. In his humor, as a story teller, he had few equals. In his ego, not yet revealed to the public or probably even to himself, he had none.

But in political philosophy the man, as I knew him then, was wildly confused; among friends he frankly admitted his confusion. That humility, I thought, was a plus mark in his tortuous personal equation. Often we discussed the imponderables of democracy, both of us equally uncertain, although he was always ready to learn from anyone, however unlearned.

On a long train journey, for example, I once expounded to him my homemade theory that the voters in a free society seldom had enough information to comprehend, much less to decide, any complex issue, especially an economic or financial issue, that they could deal only with the broad fundamentals of government, the sovereign simplicities. On the other hand, I argued, the people's collective judgment of a public man, if they had watched him in action long enough, was infallible, their unspoken hunch more to be trusted than any court. This seemed to strike Diefenbaker as a new and startling idea and he kept returning to it afterward. Whether my theory was sound or not in general, it would be vindicated with peculiar force and brutality in his own case.

That grim story had yet to be told. For the present I was concerned with Diefenbaker only as an odd exhibit in the museum of politics, and my own judgment of him was all too fallible, distorted, no doubt, by his friendliness and modesty. At least I saw that his thoughts, like those of most thoughtful men, could not be fitted into any neat pigeon-hole. A Conservative by label and accident, he was anti-conservative in half his instincts. A liberal by nature, he spent his life fighting a Liberal Party that, by similar illogic, was half Conservative. By rough definition he could be called a prairie populist, with a generous compassion for the underdog because he had long been one himself. But his radicalism was tempered by a nostalgic British imperialism and his love of humanity tinctured by a latent egomania. He had magnificent courage under fire, a profound faith in God and God's servant, John Diefenbaker. Like King (whom he secretly admired) he knew that God had chosen him for high service to the people.

Preparing for his mission, he was a voracious reader of history, an ardent scholar of politics, a midnight drudge among his daily *Hansard*s, his bluebooks, royal commission reports, and official statistics. While economic arguments bored him, and he finally concluded that they never won elections anyway, he never ceased his studies of everything within the range of his profession. For, above all, he was a professional politician. When I sometimes met him on a western train he was always poring over his bulky files but he would drop them and listen solemnly to my flippant gossip or changeable notions of government as if my knowledge was superior to his own. No man could have been more amiable and humble — before the explosion of his ego.

In short, Diefenbaker, though a unique mutation of the Canadian breed, a creature *sui generis* in politics, remained, in ordinary life, typical of many human beings less gifted—articulate and power-hungry, consistent and contradictory, generous and mean, suspicious and forgiving, large and small, briefly triumphant and, at the end, lost.

Such a man could arouse the nation, but could he govern it? I never asked myself that question in his early Opposition days because it seemed pointless. To us in the *Free Press* the Liberal Party, though flawed and often infuriating, was the natural party of government, the alternative much worse. That Diefenbaker would have the chance to govern did not cross our minds or, up to then, the public's. All of us were wrong; none so wrong as the Liberal managers whose underestimation of Diefenbaker, even when he had reached his apogee, was stupid, arrogant, and fatal, of itself guaranteeing his victory in advance. If I, too, was wrong in the beginning and here plead my belated *mea culpa*, I had privately changed my mind on the eve of the 1957 election and bet a dollar that the Liberal government would defeat itself.

Still, our original mistake was less foolish than it seemed at the time. For Diefenbaker, as events soon proved, had not been equipped for government. He had been equipped, and superbly, for opposition as a critic, agitator, and scourge of evil. But in the days to come it was surprising, and a little frightening, to see the Canadian people embrace him as their governor and swallow, as coherent policies, his noble and misty visions, his grotesque financial arithmetic, his economic grab bag. Only a future Liberal government could match that hodgepodge of promises and defaults to make Diefenbaker look, in retrospect, almost rational.

To my ears he was not even a good orator, yet oratory in the public ear was his supreme asset. As Malcolm Muggeridge wrote of Ramsay MacDonald's speeches, Diefenbaker's were tolerable because no one could understand them. Anyone who tried to analyse their convoluted digressions and sly intimations must also find them unbelievable; but the speaker believed every word when he uttered it, if not afterward. The words didn't matter. What mattered was the hypnotic effects on the listeners. They were powerful effects but could not last long because they had no substance, only words and passion.

Knowing him when he was obscure and humble, I was sure that he must fail if he ever attained real power. My theory of public wisdom in judging leaders failed, too, for the time being. Diefenbaker's partial victory in 1957, and his nation wide sweep in 1958, seemed to prove that the public could grossly misjudge the man. The theory was sound nonetheless, even if the time frame was temporarily warped. After two or three years the public reversed its judgment.

The electoral wounds of 1962, the defeat of 1963, and the Conservative regicide of 1967 were all foreshadowed by the laws of politics and, more certainly, by the nature of the man. His end had been written in the beginning. He could endure his early failure with stoic patience. He could not endure his later success. As the years went by I began to fear that the same might be true of the nation as well.

20

The Night of Debacle

In January 1958 Canada spawned one of those legends that politicians love to recount over their drinks and journalists to embellish on their typewriters until Mike Pearson's parliamentary fiasco on the Ottawa has become almost the Canadian equivalent of General Braddock's Fatal Mistake on the Monongahela. The facts, as I know them rather intimately, and painfully, differ from the legend. They are much more improbable.

John Diefenbaker had formed a minority government after the election of 1957, St. Laurent had retired, and the Liberal Party was assembling in convention to choose a new leader. Everyone knew that Pearson would be chosen, though Paul Martin pretended to his friends (and possibly even to himself) that he had a chance. But leadership was not the party's immediate problem. It had to answer a tantalizing question of political strategy.

Should the Liberal Opposition pose a want-of-confidence motion, word it to ensure the support of the Socialist members, defeat the government, and precipitate an election which the Conservatives were likely to win? Or should the Opposition frame a motion which would *not* attract the Socialists? Voted down, such a motion would give Diefenbaker no excuse to dissolve Parliament, and would force him to govern with a minority and live in peril from day to day until he discredited himself. The quarrel over strategy raged within the élite of the Liberal Party and split it down the middle.

On the one hand, an influential group, with Chubby Power as its angry spokesman, insisted that the government must be defeated in the House of Commons, that the Liberals must fight a snap election and take their chances on the result. Better to lose with honor, said Chubby, than flee in cowardice. Ever since he had fought the Germans in the First World War and come home terribly wounded, Chubby had always favored the attack. He didn't know how to retreat.

On the other hand, a more cautious faction argued that if Diefenbaker were forced to call an election it would not produce a Liberal defeat, it would produce a rout. Therefore, he must be kept in office while his magic waned and the Liberals awaited the right moment to destroy him. Urged by Sifton, and not because we had any firm view of our own, Dexter and I found ourselves in the second group. Actually the entire dispute was academic because Diefenbaker was bound to win whenever he chose to call an election, but Sifton's hired hands carried out his orders in their usual clumsy fashion.

On the day before the convention opened we met Pearson in his parliamentary office. He looked pale, weary, punch-drunk, and quite unlike his usual self. Obviously, after two nights without sleep in New York, he was in no proper state of mind to decide a subtle strategic question. When we appeared he was just leaving his office to meet and gruntle some convention delegates in the Château Laurier.

"All right, say what you have to say and say it fast," he growled and flung his overcoat on a chair. "I'll give you exactly two minutes."

Dexter needed only a minute to make the familiar case for the survival of the Diefenbaker government. Pearson listened impatiently and cut the conversation short.

"It's no use, Grant. I've made up my mind. We're going to force an election. That's final."

He picked up his coat and left us. The grand strategy was decided. We reported our failure to Sifton but to no one else.

When the convention met next day Mike's secret was still safe. Neither side in the party's quarrel seemed to know what he intended to do in Parliament.

His selection as leader was no more than a formality, amid the customary clamor and tribal rites. At the press table in the evening Dexter and I listened to his acceptance speech and judged it adequate, considering that the speaker was physically exhausted. Busy with our notes and deafened by the cheering, we were irritated to find our old friend Jack Pickersgill beside us in a state of high excitement.

That very morning, he whispered, he had awakened at six o'clock with an answer to the Liberal conundrum and, like Archimedes, had cried "Eureka!" By following a simple plan, Jack explained, Mike could unite the two party factions and put the government on the spot without risk to himself. He had merely to move that Diefenbaker should resign and allow the Opposition to take office. Then the Socialists would vote against the motion, an election would be avoided, and the Liberals could not be accused of cowardice. The circle was squared. Eureka!

Since we knew, or thought we knew, Mike's real strategy, the cunning Pickersgill formula made no impression on Dexter and me. Dismissing it as a harmless whimsy, we listened again to the new Liberal leader's speech, wrote our reports, and about three in the morning went to bed in Dexter's house, the formula forgotten. No more, we supposed, would be heard of it.

Early in the morning Dot and I flew to Washington, happily leaving the Liberal conundrum behind us. After all, what Mike did or did not do was none of our business.

As we sat down to dinner in a friend's home that night, an urgent long-distance call brought me to the telephone. It was Dexter. Next day, he said, Pearson would move his non-confidence motion and, after a momentous debate in Parliament, would go on a coast-to-coast television network to celebrate his triumph. This was to be his first appearance as Liberal leader and a historic occasion. No, Dexter had not been told exactly what the non-confidence motion would say, though he assumed that it would ensure the support of the cross benches and the defeat of the government.

What about Pickersgill's formula, proposing that the Opposition replace the government immediately? That, said Dexter, was too fancy and unrealistic to be considered when the government had more members than the Opposition. We could forget about the formula but I must return at once to Ottawa. Pearson wanted me to interview him on television.

This invitation should have flattered, but it only enraged me. I had made many engagements in Washington and next night was to meet Dean Acheson—a meeting I had long hoped for and did not intend to miss.

"Tell Mike," I said, "to find someone else. He can get lots of better guys."

"Maybe, but he won't have them. He wants you. And you can't refuse Mike."

"Oh yes I can. Tell him I'm not coming."

"Okay," said Dexter, "but you'll regret it."

He rang off and I returned to the dinner table. We had just finished dessert when Dexter called again. This time I knew from his tone that he was furious with me.

"Now listen," he said. "Mike asked you and you wouldn't come. Now it's different. Now *I'm* asking you. Get that—*I'm* asking. Are you coming?"

Of course I was coming. To Mike, at this stage, my debt was small, to Dexter beyond repayment. Next morning I was on a plane, my chance to meet Acheson lost, my mood ugly, and my task in Ottawa unexplained.

When I arrived there in mid-afternoon, Parliament was already in session. Still lugging my suitcase and typewriter, I stumbled up to the Press Gallery and joined Dexter. Pearson appeared to be halfway through his speech, the climax yet to come.

What motion would he move? The Pickersgill formula? Surely

not. Yet the formula's author, sitting beside Mike, looked suspiciously complacent. I began to wonder. Diefenbaker, across the aisle, lolled in his chair and gazed intently at the ceiling as if the Opposition's secret were written legibly upon it. Except for Mike's voice, the House was silent, waiting for his gambit. On it hung the fate of the government.

Diefenbaker tried to read the ceiling. I tried to read Mike. And suddenly it seemed to me that he was fumbling, groping for words, no longer sure how to finish. At last he dropped the bombshell. His motion proposed that the Prime Minister resign and hand the government over to the Liberal minority smaller than the Conservative.

The bombshell dropped—but exploded only in the jeers and laughter of the government benches. Even the Press Gallery laughed. Dexter and I were too crushed to laugh, the Prime Minister too delighted. The formula was a dud and Pearson knew it, too late. As he sat down, his cheeks turned white and Pickersgill's crimson. Both of them realized in a moment of bitter truth that there could be no escape now from their fiasco.

It was Diefenbaker's turn to cry "Eureka!" Slowly, carelessly, with almost feline stealth, he rose to deliver the *coup de grâce*, the greatest speech of his life and, to me, the most terrifying. He stood now at the summit of his powers, a regnant leader, his face muscles contorted, jaw outthrust, eyes glaring, the incomparable actor, the master of tragedy and comedy, himself an unconscious mixture of both. This would be his supreme moment, and Pearson's worst.

In a honeyed voice the Prime Minister congratulated Pearson on his appointment to the Liberal Party leadership. Then, turning his back on the Opposition with a theatrical shrug of contempt, he hissed between clenched teeth: "I congratulate him—but not for courage!" The words sounded like a saw beneath a file.

After that opening insult, the Conservative members were his marionettes in a *danse macabre* as he lifted them with a wave of his hand, or hushed them with a scowl. He stabbed his long finger at the Liberals in pious rebuke, he chuckled, he jeered, he tore his passion to tatters, out-Diefing Diefenbaker. The marionettes danced on their strings. The Liberals writhed. Pickersgill leaped up to protest and was shouted down. Pearson slumped in his chair, inert, flushed, stupefied by sound and fury signifying little in English but lethal in politics. Watching him, I wondered how we could possibly appear together on television that night. The taste of terror was already in my mouth.

All this time a thick document had been lying on Diefenbaker's desk. Now, defying all the rules of the game, the code of gentlemen in Parliament, the legitimate confidentiality of government itself, he brandished a secret report from the civil service to prove that the St. Laurent ministry had foreseen a business recession, taken no steps to avert it, and hidden the facts from the people. But he was not quite satisfied even yet. Following the dinner recess he would complete the butchery.

As soon as the House adjourned, Dexter and I hurried upstairs to Mike's office. He was sitting at his desk, aimlessly shuffling a heap of papers. His wife, Maryon, paced the room, muttering to herself. Perhaps better than he, she understood what had happened to him. It was no time for regrets. Within the next hour and a half Mike must go before the television cameras, not to celebrate a triumph but, if he could, to salvage a wreck. And I, of all men, was expected to help him.

For a moment I looked at the limp figure behind the desk, at the heap of papers, the tray of cold food, and I thought that Mike was beyond any help from me. But something must be done and somebody had to do it, right away.

At my signal, Dexter took Maryon aside and they picked at a miserable supper. I sat down opposite Mike and, faintly disguising my terror, asked him what he wanted me to do.

"You've got a script ready?" I suggested. "Some questions I can put to you? We'd better go over them together. There's not much time."

"Well," he replied, "the boys have prepared some stuff," and he pushed the mass of papers across the desk. I glanced at the columns of statistics, the teeming memoranda, the experts' useless brain work.

I swept it away. "Look, Mike, this stuff's no good. Let's get down to business. What are we going to talk about?"

As always in a crisis, he suddenly came to life. Between us we worked out half a dozen simple questions for me to ask him and I jotted them down on an envelope. When we were finished it was a scant half-hour before the cameras would be rolling. All of us scurried out of the office, found a car at the Commons entrance, and scrambled into it.

As Mike started the engine, Blair Fraser squeezed in beside me, for reasons unknown. His granitic Scots face looked more granitic then ever, for he loved Mike. No one spoke but I wished that Blair could take my place. He was long experienced in television, a trained performer as I was not. Why had Mike chosen me? Too late now for explanations, but the choice was another mad mistake on this night of contrived fiasco.

The car drove fast toward the outskirts of Ottawa, in the silence of a funeral procession. I had no idea where we were going, what I would say, or how I would look on the camera. By now I was dizzy, hungry, trembling, physically sick. It occurred to me that I was about to faint. As if that mattered! What of Mike? He, not I, would sink or swim ten minutes hence.

We reached the distant studio of the CBC. Some make-up girls dusted powder on Mike's face and mine, hung microphones around our necks, and seated us in easy chairs around a coffee table. It was to be a homey, intimate conversation in a fake living room, a light-hearted charade against a backdrop of disaster.

I tried to pull myself together, glanced nervously at the envelope of scribbled questions, and could not read them. Mike's expression had not changed. He sat with a stony face, white beneath the make up. Then the studio lighted up and so did he. As the cameras rolled he grinned at me across the table.

"Well, well, Bruce," he chortled, "it's been a grand day in Parliament, eh?"

"Yes, grand," I said and hoped that my voice was not trembling like my legs.

"So let's talk a little about it, shall we?" Mike went on as cheerfully as if he had just enjoyed a holiday of boyish frolic.

What happened after that I can't recall. Mike's grinning face and lively banter mixed with crisp announcements of Liberal policy; Blair brooding somewhere in the shadows; Maryon and Dexter watching us from the wings; the hot, dazzling lights; the burlesque of the domestic scene; the cosy chat between two untroubled friends — all this was a revolving blur, a mirage of horror.

Presumably I said something. Words must have issued from my throat. They were incoherent but Mike had no need of me. He carried through the travesty like a man without a single care. My portrait of him in his worst hour remains vivid, gay, unforgettable. The worst hour, I still think, was one of his finest. What the television audience thought of it I had no means of knowing.

After an eternity the lights went out and I could breathe again. We drove back to Parliament Hill. No one spoke. When Diefenbaker ended his speech late in the evening I flew back to Washington and Mike never once mentioned to me our joint tragicomedy — no explanation of a strategy reversed overnight, no word of complaint to Pickersgill, no excuse for the blunder, no blame except on himself. He would learn to laugh about this dreadful day, but between him and me the rest was silence to the end. Why he had called me from Washington is still a mystery, and I tell the curious little tale now only to show the steel behind the grin.

He soon needed it. In the election of 1958 Diefenbaker won the largest majority since the nation's birth. Mike had reached the nadir of his public life, with a pathetic band of outcasts supporting him in the Commons. But presently the tide turned. Its turning, I believe, began invisibly on the day of fiasco when an amateur of politics became a professional in his baptism of fire.

During his six wretched years of parliamentary opposition I came to know Mike better and yet, like all his friends, I sensed behind his frank speech and intimate manner a deep gulf of reticence. Outside of his family, I doubt that anyone ever crossed that gulf, while the public hardly suspected its existence. His thoughts on politics were shared with all those he trusted, and with men less trusted he used his favorite press-conference trick of talking recklessly about marginal matters to distract the interrogators from more dangerous ground.

Though many men were much closer to him, often on returning from London or Washington he would tell Dexter and me the top secrets of the British and American governments, his conversations with a prime minister or a president, even military secrets which both of us promptly put out of our minds and wished we had not heard. In such confidences he could sometimes be erratic — as, for instance, when he was Minister of External Affairs and mentioned to me, in an off-handed fashion at lunch, that he might accept the invitation of NATO to become its Secretary General and, to my amazement, confessed that he had not yet informed Prime Minister St. Laurent of this possibility.

Or again, when fighting the election of 1963 as Liberal leader, he disposed of an unwanted associate by persuading him to run for Parliament in a remote, hopeless constituency where defeat was certain. "That," said Mike with a grim chuckle, "is worthy of Machiavelli — no, of Mackenzie King himself!" The simple, innocent Pearson of the public image had always been a caricature.

His talk, candid in fact or in appearance, depending upon the listener, was part of the day's work, but another compartment of his mind was hermetically sealed. His personal credo, his view of life and death, his ultimate conception of the universe, the choice between belief and disbelief that every man must make—

this region, the only one that matters finally, was never shared with us, if it was shared with anybody, even by a passing hint. We could not bridge the last gulf.

In another book about Canadian prime ministers, I once tried to analyse the unknown, subliminal Pearson, arguing that a profound religious belief, an unadmitted strain of mystical faith, had been nourished in his father's Christian home and colored the son's life afterward. Mike only laughed when he read my bungling attempt at psychoanalysis but added that his wife seemed to consider the general picture of him accurate enough, however incomplete. Looking back, I think it was, though I have no evidence, only hunch.

Of one thing I am absolutely sure, with ample evidence—the laughing, carefree, often bumbling Pearson familiar to the public was not even half the total man who, toward the end, had come almost to despair of human prospects. Combined with the despair was a desperate hope, no more than that, and the amalgam gave him a coherent political philosophy, or at least a target of outright internationalism which many of his admirers, in Canada and elsewhere, could not accept. To them he was the impractical dreamer whose dream served for rhetorical occasions but not for the world's practical business which, under their management, has achieved a climax of impracticality.

Of course his folksy looks and homespun charm helped to make him perhaps the most successful diplomat of his time, but they would have failed if his flexible, pragmatic methods had not been founded on a base of solid conviction. He succeeded because he believed in what he was trying to do, though he knew that no man could do very much. If the reach exceeded the grasp he still reached. In his own oblique fashion, I think, he knew what a Heaven was for.

In Canadian politics, apart from the new tide of nationalism already flowing throughout the world, the obstacles facing him as an internationalist were greater than the public, or even he, realized at the beginning of his party leadership. A year or so after our television nightmare, I encountered by accident one of these obstacles which Mike himself had not yet suspected.

Until then I had not met Walter Gordon. Mike had assured me that the Toronto magnate was the ablest economic brain in the country, and when the Liberals came to office Gordon would be the Minister of Finance. Without knowing him, I accepted this judgment but in our first meeting I began to doubt it and, later on, so did Mike.

At some point, I forget just when, Mike was to make another broadcast as leader of the Opposition. Sifton had learned, with alarm, that the speech would commit the Liberal Party to prodigal tax reductions, deficits, and inflation when, already, as Sifton saw it, the Diefenbaker government was gutting the treasury (a minor gutting by contemporary Liberal standards). As if he or I could influence Mike's policy, Sifton asked me to see and dissuade him from this madness, with the clear threat that the *Free Press* would never support it.

Well aware that the mission would fail, I called on Mike and made the argument, which appeared sound to me. He listened patiently and then, in one of his typical diplomatic diversions, asked me to write the financial passage of his speech. I refused but he insisted. At least, he said, I should talk to Gordon, and together we might work out a satisfactory formula. Having ghost-written too many undelivered speeches for politicians in my time, I was sure that this one, too, would be stillborn. However, against my better judgment, I agreed to see Gordon in an adjoining office.

He was relaxed, friendly, and sympathetic, but even at this early date I detected in him a certain dilettantism, the amateur's approach to politics. In one way my impression was false, in another accurate. Gordon's casual manner and bland Bay Street face hid a fierce appetite for power, some high abilities in seeking it, and, undoubtedly, a burning patriotism. But as we talked about the proposed speech I realized that Gordon did not belong in any political party led by Mike.

On basic doctrine the two men stood at opposite poles—Mike, the outright liberal internationalist and advocate of the freest possible foreign trade; Gordon, the fervid nationalist and true believer in protectionist Conservative policies. Such code words are unfair to both when, like all men, they nourished a mixture of contradictions and inward doubts, but the disagreement in principle between the leader and his chief lieutenant was clear from the start. Though neither seemed to recognize it then, the gap of sincere conviction must break the partnership, and even the friendship, in the end. As things turned out, it almost broke the Liberal Party.

For the moment I put that possibility at the back of my mind since it was none of my concern. The immediate job was to write a brief passage in Mike's speech and I wrote it, left it at his office, and went away, sure that it would never reach the public ear. Of course it didn't. In collaboration with Gordon, Mike delivered an entirely different speech, Sifton's plea for budgetary restraint ignored.

I had been through the same futile exercise too often to be surprised or irked by the failure of my boy's errand. What alone surprised me was Mike's failure to understand Gordon—and I doubt that Gordon ever understood Mike. Anyhow, the partnership and friendship continued, in mutual misunderstanding, for several years, even after Gordon's first calamitous budget and his honorable offer of resignation, which Mike unwisely rejected.

Still, Mike had begun to entertain his own private misgivings. They were unwittingly conveyed to me in our only serious collision. Just after he had become Prime Minister in 1963 I happened to read in some newspaper an extraordinary article by Gordon, now Minister of Finance. Calling on Mike at his Sussex Drive house one day, I handed the article to him and observed, with more than usual impudence, that Gordon had written a perfect Conservative manifesto of anti-Liberal protectionism.

This time I went too far. Mike's face reddened with anger. He dressed me down in a voice that I had never heard before. I forget his words but, in effect, he said I had no right to meddle in the business of his cabinet and, besides, I misunderstood Gordon. Cooling as fast as he had heated, the Prime Minister added that I needn't worry, he would attend to Gordon. Everything would be all right, never fear. After a drink and a pleasant talk of other things, I left Sussex Drive more than ever convinced that the partnership must dissolve. Mike had protested his confidence in Gordon but he had protested far too much.

21

The Rigor of the Game

A politician, if he only knew it, has much more fun in the shadows of opposition than in the sunshine of government. But he seldom knows it. The lust for office and power has been the driving impulse, and fame the spur, of politics throughout the ages. And when the prize has been won it usually destroys the happiness of the winner; the spur pierces the rider who wears it.

A political journalist, on the other hand, since he cannot have office and power anyhow, finds in opposition the perfect setting and elbow room for all his talents of moral protest, mischief, and destruction. His own party may not fit his ideals, or even his convenience, but the ruling party is always fair game, an easy target, a sitting duck, a source of innocent merriment.

The Conservative government elected in 1957 soon became the easiest of targets, a barn door that the worst marksman could hardly miss. John Diefenbaker's arrival had neither surprised nor personally inconvenienced me (though I was certain from the beginning that it would inconvenience the nation). Now the fun of opposition could begin, too. "A clear fire, a clean hearth and the rigor of the game," said Charles Lamb's celebrated whist player, Mrs. Sarah Battle, were, next to her devotions, the main purpose of life. So, on a minor scale, I enjoyed the game of politics without official cards to play but with some grimy unofficial jokers of denigration up my sleeve.

Actually, the remote editor of the *Victoria Daily Times* was not as irresponsible as he seems to me in retrospect. He honestly believed that the Diefenbaker government was a national calamity to be removed at first chance. While he was not prejudiced enough by party ties to suppose that the Liberals would do much better in office, he supported them in a newspaper that had always been Liberal. It was an automatic support, no doubt, a kind of hereditary tropism, a legacy from Benny Nicholas. But it was a part-time job, far less important than the jobs of garden and woods.

For the next six years my only news source in the government was Howard Green, the Minister of External Affairs, who deplored my Liberalism, misunderstood my views altogether, but forgave me out of our old friendship.

No finer man ever practised Canadian politics than this philosophical, or rather visceral, Conservative. Green was loyal to Canada, to Britain (which he also misunderstood), to the monarchy (which he adored), to his leader, his party, and his friends. His whole life had served the nation. He fought as a soldier in the First World War and as a politician in peacetime, though he could have made a much richer living in the practice of law. But politics was in his blood, together with a wild miscellany of prejudice, a rag-bag of illusions, all overlaid by his honesty and love of humankind. Sometimes he would explode in rage as when, ignorant of the contrary facts, he accused Pearson of knifing Britain in the back during the Suez crisis of 1956. These outbursts quickly passed and their victims could not resent them for long. No man disliked good old Howard, whose political talents might not be of the first rank but whose character retained the nation's respect, even its affection, long after his government had lost both.

Since I felt unable, in decency, to approach Diefenbaker when I had so often attacked him in print, and had met no other members of his cabinet, I often called on Green. His door was always open to me. I could ring him on the telephone at any hour. I trusted him absolutely and he seemed to trust me well enough to speak with an indiscretion that would have horrified Diefenbaker.

On one occasion, for example, I found myself reluctantly

carrying a secret verbal message from the Canadian foreign minister to Mike Mansfield, leader of the United States Senate, only because I knew both of them and knew, too, that they were men of the same honesty. The message concerned some detail in the Columbia River Treaty, then under negotiation, but I forget what Green wanted from Mansfield or what Mansfield wanted from Green. At any rate, the American agreed at once to accept the Canadian proposal, whatever it was, and I so reported by telephone to Green, wondering to myself how Diefenbaker would regard our private relations. Fortunately he never heard of them.

Again, on the day when President Kennedy launched his assault against the Bay of Pigs, Green telephoned me from New York about a different matter and said that, in his own opinion, the assault would end in disaster, as it did. If he was no genius and knew little of the world outside Canada, he had more instinctive wisdom than many men whose brilliance finally consumed them, and much else besides.

In another proof of his common sense, Green saw immediately, as the great brains of the State Department failed to see, that Kennedy would make it impossible for Canada to join the Organization of American States if he publicly urged this controversial step during his visit to Ottawa in 1961. Ignorant of Canada and ill-advised by his experts, the President lurched into a clearly visible trap.

As one who favored and expected O.A.S. membership later on, Green was staggered by such an egregious blunder and told me next day that Kennedy had ruined his own initiative by pushing it too hard, too soon, and too openly. The Canadian government, already doubtful and divided on the issue, could not yield to naked American pressure. A subtle politician at home, Kennedy should have foreseen these consequences in a foreign country, but he did not, and Canada refused to join the hemispheric club.

If Kennedy botched his mission to Ottawa, he had the best of reasons to distrust the Canadian government. So many newspapers and books have told the story of the President's lost memorandum that I shall not repeat it at length here. Sufficient to say that when Kennedy entered the Ottawa cabinet room he carried some notes written by his assistant, Walt Rostow, on a single piece of paper. One short phrase reminded Kennedy to urge O.A.S. membership on Canada, which he did, both in private and in a public speech. After his talk with the cabinet he forgot that paper and left it unnoticed on a chesterfield. Later in the day it was brought to Diefenbaker, who, as Kennedy's host, was bound to return it to the owner. Instead, Diefenbaker locked it away for possible future use.

In the following year, with an election impending, he told the American ambassador, Livingston Merchant, that the missing memorandum might be disclosed to the Canadian voters if the United States ever tried to coerce its neighbor. Unable to believe his ears, Merchant flew immediately to Washington and informed Kennedy of Diefenbaker's threat. Kennedy's reply, delivered by Merchant to Diefenbaker in smooth diplomatic language, warned him against an act of international folly that must disrupt all relations between Washington and Ottawa, but offered him a way out. If Diefenbaker did not release the memorandum the United States government would regard Merchant's report as being unofficial and thus no cause for official reaction. Coming to his senses rather late, Diefenbaker accepted this convenient reinterpretation of the facts. The memorandum was never published. But the President never trusted the Prime Minister again, with results damaging to Canada and, in the end, ruinous to Diefenbaker.

This repulsive incident had two amusing sequels. According to the popular Ottawa legend, Kennedy had scribbled on the margin of his momorandum the letters "S.O.B." in reference to Diefenbaker. Of course he had not but the rumor persisted. According to Kennedy's intimates, they asked him about the marginal note and he replied with a laugh: "How could I have called Diefenbaker an S.O.B. in Ottawa when I didn't know he was — then."

In early 1963, when Kennedy met the British Prime Minister, Harold Macmillan, in Nassau at a critical point in British-American relations, Diefenbaker suddenly turned up, without being invited or expected, to seek some means of escape from his own political crisis at home. He was taken to lunch with the two senior statesmen, who could hardly refuse to see him. Afterward the President was asked how the lunch had gone. "There we sat," said Kennedy, "like three whores at a christening."

By this time the Diefenbaker government was in its death throes. It had split clean on the question of introducing nuclear weapons into Canada, but the split could be hidden temporarily by an unspoken alliance of thought between Green and Pearson. Both of them opposed these weapons and so long as Pearson held that view the government was safe from serious Liberal attack. Green, therefore, could resist his colleagues who argued that Canada was committed to a nuclear policy by solemn agreement with its allies and by its vital interests.

So far as I know, the two men never discussed the matter directly, but Green realized that his position in the cabinet largely depended on Pearson. If the Liberal leader should change his attitude and support nuclear armament, the Conservative ministers of the same view would force it on the cabinet or possibly resign. In the deepening crisis of Parliament, Green watched Pearson anxiously for any sign of wavering. Several times he asked me whether Pearson would stay put. I said I believed so, having no cause, so far, to think otherwise. Pearson's reversal seemed impossible to Green or me. But our imagination was limited and Pearson's flexibility was not, as events soon proved.

In the meantime Kennedy had lost all patience with Diefenbaker, who was desperately trying to hold his cabinet together, or at least to keep its split concealed. When the Prime Minister returned from Nassau and announced in Parliament that the whole strategy of NATO was being revised, and hence that Canada could make no immediate decision on nuclear weapons, the American government was outraged by a total distortion of the facts. It feared, moreover, that its European allies, reading the Diefenbaker speech, would suspect some deal between the United States and Britain negotiated behind their backs.

The President, however, did not write and did not even see in advance the savage official statement issued by his government. This unprecedented rebuke, noting that Canada had proposed no practical contribution to North American defence, was written in the State Department, late at night, and authorized by Under-Secretary George Ball while Kennedy slept in the White House. Next morning the President read it in the newspapers and was shocked by its brutal language. He told his officials that they had gone pretty far, but the job was done and could not be undone. There was no use crying over spilt milk and if the Diefenbaker government drowned in it Kennedy would waste no time mourning its demise.

As diplomatic relations between Ottawa and Washington virtually ceased, Diefenbaker's cabinet broke on the nuclear issue, was defeated in the House of Commons, and stumbled into an election that it could not hope to win. Its ruin was finally ensured when Pearson became convinced that Canada must fulfil its undoubted commitments to its allies and accept nuclear weapons after all. Working through the night in his Toronto hotel room, he rewrote his intended speech to the York-Scarborough Liberal Association, reversed his defence policy, and, by that sudden turnabout, destroyed Diefenbaker's last chance of survival.

All this is well known and clear enough in hindsight but it was not clear at the time and in Victoria I knew nothing about it. The election apparently was being fought on other issues, mainly on the Liberal promise (plagiarized from Kennedy's slogan of 1960) to "get the economy moving again" when, in fact, it was already moving fast out of a recession.

The public saw a Prime Minister doomed, bewildered, and without a policy, yet more courageous than ever in his ruin. It saw a vigorous, grinning, and healthy Opposition leader on the way to victory. What it did not see was a Pearson so physically sick with an undiagnosed infection, and so filled with antibiotics, that his doctor put him to bed in Victoria.

I visited him in his Empress Hotel suite and was jolted by his appearance. Resting in bed before his speech that night, he admitted, for the first time in my memory, that he was really sick and not sure that he could go on with the campaign schedule.

The big news break of the night's speech, Mike said, would be his announcement that the Liberal Party planned Canadian membership in the O.A.S. What did I think of this initiative? I thought it would gain no votes and lose many when his only purpose, at the moment, was to win the election. In office afterward, I added, he could do as he pleased about the O.A.S. but first he must get there.

"Okay," he agreed, "I'll skip it," and he did. In office he left the O.A.S. issue untouched.

Sick as he was in Victoria, he told me a queer story which could not be retold during his lifetime. In Edmonton, a few days earlier, he had spoken from the platform of some veterans' hall. While he was in the middle of his speech one of his secretaries answered a telephone call in the basement. The voice on the long-distance wire said that the call came from the White House in Washington on the instructions of the President, who had a message for Mike. At first the secretary guessed that someone was playing an unfunny joke, but the caller insisted that Mike must come to the telephone at once. The presidential message was top-secret and urgent.

Mystified, but keeping his head, the secretary replied that Mr. Pearson could not leave the platform. He would call back after he had finished his speech. When the secretary informed Mike of the White House call he was amazed and incredulous. If Diefenbaker learned that the President of the United States was communicating with the leader of the Canadian Opposition and intervening in a foreign election, then, of course, Mike would be innocently and perhaps fatally compromised. Already Diefenbaker was denouncing Mike as the stooge of the American government. The telephone call would provide a convincing exhibit in Diefenbaker's case if he ever learned of it. A ridiculous blunder at Washington might well rob the Liberal Party of its electoral victory.

Immediately realizing that even the indirect conversation with some White House aide was dangerous, Mike asked his secretary whether it had been overheard by a group of men drinking beer in the basement. The secretary didn't think so but wasn't sure. Mike told him to say nothing and later called the White House on a private telephone from his hotel. The call was answered by another presidential aide who said Kennedy was otherwise engaged. The President, he added, would be glad to help Mike in any possible way and would issue a public statement of support, if it were considered useful.

The madness of this suggestion took Mike's breath away. Did Kennedy understand what he was doing? Or had he been misled by some idiotic adviser? There was no time to explore these questions, time only for Mike to tell the White House official that the President should issue no statement, make no comment on Canadian affairs, and ignore the election.

When Mike arrived in Victoria he still did not know whether the first call had been overheard and might be reported to Diefenbaker. He was baffled by the President's mistaken offer of help. He could not quite believe that Kennedy had really authorized such a suicidal ploy. And he feared that the story would leak, one way or another, before election day.

It did not leak. Mike got through the Victoria speech somehow, the listeners unaware of his sickness. Next night, in Vancouver, he calmly outfaced a band of screaming hooligans who gave him precisely what he needed and lacked, a public image of courage under fire. Soon he was in the prime minister's office.

The mystery of the telephone call in the Edmonton basement was never solved. An international mystery of greater importance had yet to emerge. It would prove, among other things, that Mike could not be overawed by the American presidency, even when it was occupied by the ferocious Lyndon Johnson.

22

The Professor and the Goddess

As I mounted the steps of an old-fashioned house in Montreal a man of middle age and small stature emerged from the door to greet me on the shady porch. He wore a yellow sweat shirt, unpressed slacks, and sandals. His face was unlike any I had ever seen before—homely at first glance, sallow and deeply grooved, but at the second, mobile, sensitive, almost handsome, a face not easily forgotten. In his left hand he clutched a bottle of whisky. His right, when I shook it, held mine with a surprisingly firm grip, the grip of an athlete.

"Have a drink?"

These were his opening words and they, too, surprised me for they were uttered without a trace of French accent, though the speaker was a native of Quebec. Since the summer day was hot and I was tired, a drink seemed a good idea. We sat down on the porch to enjoy it. My host talked for the next two hours in a soft voice and a scholar's idiom, mingled with jarring vulgarisms. The outward calm, I suspected, might hide some inner furies. About that, if nothing else, I happened to be right.

At my original meeting with Pierre Elliott Trudeau maybe I should have seen the makings of a Canadian prime minister but I did not. To me he was an obscure professor of law, only a name among many, a person of no significance whom I hardly expected to meet again. And yet for reasons that I did not try to analyse then, the man left a vivid impression of strength, subtlety, and, above all, toughness. In mind even more than in language he seemed about the toughest man I had ever met; also one of the most brilliant. But the brilliance, I assumed, was that of a cloistered academic, probably a rich dilettante. No judgment could have been further from the mark.

This was in 1959. Some nine years later, when his personal magnetism and nothing else carried Trudeau to supreme office, his aura of innocence, warmth, and modesty did not impress me. I had seen the other Trudeau, the cold logician, the exceedingly tough guy without his party manners, theatrical attire, and stage properties. At least I knew that the two Trudeaus, public and private, had given politics a new style and a leader totally different from any of his predecessors. Here was a sport and mutation in the political species, a gaudy *rara avis* among a flock of gray Canada geese.

In the long aftertime history will make its own judgment on a complex and many-faceted human being. All I could guess about Trudeau before his life became a major Canadian asset or liability was that he possessed some high intellectual voltage. But I surmised even then that his mind might be too brilliant, too logical, too lacking in the common touch for the rough game of politics.

Since he had not yet entered or considered the game, his character was of no concern to the nation. Nor did he concern himself with his public image: so far he had none. As he wrote later in a somewhat contemptuous credo, "The only constant factor to be found in my thinking over the years has been opposition to accepted opinions"—the surest method of losing electoral votes and avoiding office.

Leaving his mother's house, I said that his scornful comments on the politicians of Ottawa and Quebec presumably were not for publication.

"Hell," he replied, "print what you damn well please. I don't care."

At that time I'm sure he didn't, but in future days he learned to care, to love the game for itself, to know its triumphs and agonies, possibly to know a different Trudeau changed by both. Anyhow, I decided not to print his conversation because it seemed too heretical and bizarre for my immediate job. This was a mistake. I failed to anticipate that these heresies would soon provide the central stuff of Canada's government.

Besides, I had not come here to report the opinions of an undistinguished professor, however blunt and logical, merely to write a piece for *Maclean's* magazine about the second centennial of the English conquest on the Plains of Abraham. Ralph Allen, that great editor, thought it might be useful to recall what had happened to the conquered in two centuries of experience, though we knew, of course, that the word "conquest" was irrelevant and odious.

Some sixty thousand French Canadians, the only true Canadians when Wolfe's soldiers landed at the Anse au Foulon, had survived by a feat of endurance unbelievable to their conquerors and become a third of the future nation, with an undoubted power of veto over its destiny. Both of us knew, too, that as Anglo-Saxons we could not hope to understand the inwardness of Quebec, even if Quebec understood itself, which, judging by Trudeau's reflections, was dubious. We could only report what the French Canadians told us and how their modern lifeways looked to an impartial observer.

Mainly because Dot and I needed the money and always relished a visit to Quebec, Ralph's assignment was undertaken—but with grave misgivings. They increased as I talked to many public men and still more as I found myself in a monastery listening to a Catholic priest declare radical left-wing views on society that most Protestants would never expect from his Church; or again when I dined with a company of irascible lawyers and professors who spoke English at the beginning, for my benefit, but soon lapsed into French and disputed constitutional mysteries beyond a layman's understanding in any language.

Anglo-Saxons of my sort find it difficult, often impossible, to grasp the labyrinthine logic of the French mind, even the half-French Trudeau mind. But fortunately it is not logic, law, or written documents that hold the dual nation together. Instead, trial, error, and illogical compromise serve us well as the working method of national politics. Understanding that much about Canadian government, I ignored the constitution, wrote a superficial color piece on Quebec, and flew with Dot to Los Angeles, from the real world to the make-believe world of Hollywood. There a minor farce and a *femme fatale* awaited me.

How I fell into the company of Miss Zsa Zsa Gabor she does not know and surely does not care. But this enchanting lady might be disappointed to learn that she was the third choice for treatment in *Maclean's* and chosen because two still more enchanting candidates were out of town.

Ralph had conceived a whimsical inspiration and offered it to me as an easy, profitable chore. The old reporter of politics would rise above his sordid occupation, interview a love goddess (any established goddess would do), and write a solemn analytical piece on the most sacred fable of American civilization. I must risk no Freudian overtones, anything remotely carnal. Innocent, romantic love, passion in the abstract, the fable updated—that was Ralph's formula. In plain terms I would retell the oldest fairy story in the world and make a fool of myself to amuse his readers. For money alone, and a bit of fun, I agreed.

The chore was not as easy as it looked and would have been impossible without the help of the late Jim Richardson, the celebrated Los Angeles editor known in newspaper legendry as The Last of the Terrible Men, though in truth he was a woolly lamb and his wolf's clothing deceived no one. Jim made the necessary arrangements and we drove into the hills outside the city, lost our way, and reached Miss Gabor's mansion two hours late.

In countless photographs I had seen her *petite* beauty, immune to middle age, like that of a glazed figurine, but her costume startled me. She wore a modest crimson housecoat from throat to ankle, a halo of golden curls, an excusable air of impatience, and a new engagement ring with a diamond approximately the size and color of a robin's egg. This, I assumed, was her battle dress.

At first she appeared rather nervous, probably expecting me to ask the usual reporter's rude questions about her private affairs. Assured that I sought only some views of life in the best American society, her ideals of womanhood, and the true meaning of Glamour, she relaxed and seated me on a sofa beside her. Then she took me in hand as a mother might comfort a helpless child, or the village idiot. My strategy of bumbling ignorance and senile decay could not fool a superior strategist for a moment. She saw through me at once and knew that I intended to make fun of her in print. Very well, she would play along and pretend an equal simplicity. I was putty in the delicate, manicured hands of the love goddess.

While her official biographer watched us silently from the distance, also aware of the strategy, the Terrible Man paced up and down the room muttering grunts of disgust at my feeble inquiries, and a photographer crawled about the floor exploding flash bulbs, Miss Gabor talked about life in an earnest, homely style, deliciously flavored by her native Hungarian accent.

Ah, life! It was wonderful in America—her own life especially as the frugal housekeeper and trained cook, the athletic outdoor life, the life of art and literature, the simple domestic life best of all. Our dialogue of mock cerebration lasted about two hours, both of us laboring mightily, the biographer bored and groaning, the Terrible Man fuming and muttering, the flash bulbs exploding, Miss Gabor in full command of the battle.

As I was leaving she put her arm around my shoulder in maternal fashion and, with an impish grin, whispered: "I don't mind if you pull my leg, just a leetle." So I did in *Maclean's*, possibly more than a little. She was not amused, which saddened me. But all my commentary on public affairs had never interested Canadian readers so much as that inane dialogue in Hollywood. How could a potential prime minister and the professors of Montreal hope to compete with a love goddess?

Revolted by the whole episode, Jim took Dot and me, next day, through the movie studios to watch the toil of the dream-makers whose names and faces were known throughout the world. It was harsh toil with long hours of endlessly repeated camera takes, the raw material of Glamour processed by hidden machinery, the actors quite incidental. After a weary day in dark caverns, exotic stage sets, and Oriental scenery made of pasteboard, we fled to Jim's house where his truly glamorous wife, Margaret, introduced a remarkable guest.

His face was familiar to us, as to everybody, but in manner and mind James Cagney was the exact opposite of his reputation. Instead of the song-and-dance man, the snarling gangster, or the cunning detective, the man who came to dinner seemed shy, wary, almost timid before strangers. He sat by himself in a corner and said nothing while "Bill", his sprightly little wife, carried the conversation.

We were somewhat disappointed until Margaret fortified us with a good dinner (but no alcohol) and Harlan Ware, a distinguished screen writer and one of Cagney's intimates, persuaded him, much against his will, to show us some secrets of his profession. A short man, he marched across the room as some imaginary hero and looked ten feet tall. Or, acting the villain in some crazy melodrama, he became a dwarf. He danced, sang, and told stories in the accents of a dozen nations.

The cameras of Hollywood had missed a gorgeous one-man tableau, but behind this wild burlesque Cagney was a man deeply read, worried by the state of the world, and well informed of its problems; a farmer, conservationist, painter, and amateur poet who had written that "all is ephemera except soil and soul." He was no artist of the stage, he said, only a showman "jumping up and down and making faces to earn a dollar." We had always enjoyed the Cagney of the screen but we liked the real man better.

Our notion of life in Hollywood was further amended by a visit to Byron and Doro Folger, friends of our youth and veterans of the theatre, who had succeeded in the movies. Observing them and their associates work and study harder than most men of my trade, I concluded that political journalism was a soft way to make a living. But even in politics no man succeeds nowadays unless he is an actor and we were about to see the peerless tragedian of his time.

Jim Richardson had known him since the day a young fellow, then unknown to the world, appeared at the Terrible Man's office to ask his advice. The visitor said he wished to enter public life but how could he begin? Jim told him how and the advice was followed with notable success. Now Jim's original protégé, Richard Milhous Nixon, had arrived in Los Angeles to meet an assembly of California's élite in a huge banqueting hall filled by wealth, power, and Republican euphoria.

This formidable congregation did not awe Jim, who could still look terrible when necessary. He thrust himself through the crowd to the head table, dragging me with him in a state of ghastly embarrassment, and addressed the Vice President of the United States as "Dick". Informed that I was a Canadian, the gifted actor from Washington responded instantly on cue.

Assuming the role of the good neighbor, he greeted me with a quick, flashing smile and a firm handshake as if he had no other business in mind. Canada, he said, was a great country. Its people were great, too. Yes, he had learned to appreciate them when he drove across British Columbia on his honeymoon and saw the beauty and resources of that great province. I was indeed lucky to live there. But he hoped I would like California, another great country. All this was said with a convincing sincerity which may have deceived Nixon himself. Amid the noisy crowd we were like two old friends gossiping over the garden fence of an undefended border. Nixon was as folksy and unassuming as he was sincere.

Then, facing a nationally televised press conference and a corps of dogged reporters, he smoothly changed the act, without pause or written note, into a statesman's earnest survey of his nation's worldwide mission. The thoughts were tightly organized, the words marshalled in orderly sequence, the moral conscience of Americans eloquently invoked, the manner and gestures dignified, authoritative, but modest. I had never witnessed a more impressive performance in theatre or parliament. The man of sincerity looked every inch a future president, perhaps a great one.

After the tragedy of Watergate it is easy to say that in those happier times Nixon had chosen an act that he could not long sustain. But no one in the room that night saw through the act, nor did the actor see where it would lead him. Another make-believe world, a spectacular impossible for Hollywood to produce, was already in the works.

We soon returned to the actual world in Japan as guests of its government. Under such auspices all doors were open to a Canadian reporter, every hour scheduled for interviews with politicians, officials, economists, industrialists, and even Communist Party leaders, the joint architects, despite their family quarrels, of the Japanese economic miracle.

At the moment it was temporarily managed by Prime Minister Nobusuke Kishi, a genial man, all smiles and glittering teeth, who received me like a monarch among his obsequious, tail-coated functionaries and promised to send me written answers to all my questions. I took this to be a polite brush-off, an old Japanese custom, but the answers, six pages of them, remarkably frank and specific, were brought to my hotel by courier a few days later.

If Kishi briefly represented the miracle, one of his predecessors, Shigeru Yoshida, represented Japan's earlier conversion to democracy under American tutelage. The postwar strong man, in his house of intricately carved wood and heavy Western furniture, spoke fluent English with a strongly American accent. His square, belligerent face, shrewd eyes, and salty down-to-earth talk would have fitted any Chamber of Commerce or Rotary

Club in the United States. But this aged portent of the new time wore a flowing black kimono, his servants treated him as a shogun if not a god, and our escort from the Foreign Office, hissing through his teeth, bowed to the ground in the presence of the illustrious democrat.

Having talked freely about Japan's practical business, with many jokes and sly giggles, Yoshida led us through his majestic garden of goldfish ponds and waterfalls. Suddenly he stopped to point at the distant white pyramid of Mount Fuji, framed symmetrically between the towering pines that his ancestors had planted long before democracy's arrival. At that view his eyes narrowed, the hard face softened. "Nice," he said.

What were we to make of the ambivalent patriarch who loved politics and power not less but perhaps beauty and the past even more? What of his people who could not conquer Asia in war but seemed to be purchasing it in peace? What of the American conquerors who were tired by foreign adventure and baffled by the problems of affluence at home while the conquered throve on ruin, knew no weariness, and already had begun to repeat the West's mistakes with superior efficiency?

Of course we had no answer to these questions and in the jumble of palaces, temples, shrines, museums, kabuki plays, geisha houses, teeming crowds everywhere, and the hideous blare of loudspeakers in a country never silent by day or night, Dot and I felt haunted by a sense of isolation and loneliness, a mind-gap almost physical.

Most haunting of all, and tinged, I suppose, by a bad Western conscience, was the pleasant town of Hiroshima. New buildings, parks, boulevards, and tidy streets had erased the horrors of August 6, 1945, except for the twisted skeleton of the city hall, a solitary monument to the nuclear age. Near by a museum of photographs and worse exhibits was too horrifying for our eyes. We escaped into the sunshine and tried not to think of that other man-made illumination.

Some of its survivors remembered and told us about it as they would discuss a quite ordinary event. The mayor, entertaining us at an excellent tempura luncheon, did not mention the only event of importance in his town. But even the Japanese poker face failed to hide those memories. No stranger could penetrate the malice, or forgiveness, still lingering with the old folk on their park benches and the bonny children at play where grass and flowers covered the relics of a spectacle that changed and threatened all human prospects.

"Tell your people," says an ancient man who witnessed the spectacle and took us for Americans, "that we must have no more wars. Please understand, no more wars. Tell them what happened in Hiroshima." With his single remaining hand he presses mine and peers into my eyes, searching for assurance. As if I could offer it or tell anyone what happened in Hiroshima. As if anyone wanted to listen.

This town had marked more clearly than any spot the birth of the American Empire, a worldwide, unadmitted, but unquestioned imperial apparatus of power. Unlike all previous empires it had crowned no emperor, claimed no foreign territory, established no ruling system, always denied its own existence, and, in the nature of its people, desired only to be left alone — the ultimate impossibility. Yet it was the world's most powerful empire because, for a mere moment of historical time, some thirty years, it alone possessed the means of destroying civilization, the records of mankind, and itself. While these facts had been proclaimed in a quiet rural town by a flash of exploding atoms, the empire's birthplace was noted or understood by few men, Americans or foreigners, any more than its end would be acknowledged in the jungles of Vietnam a generation later.

Compared to the overcrowded islands of Japan the island of Taiwan, with its lush farms of green and yellow checkerboard, its floating, dreaming mountains, and its bustling, friendly people, looked small, snug, and comfortable. But for its rulers this was an island of heartbreak not to be concealed even by Generalissimo Chiang Kai-shek.

When he granted us an audience in his vast and gilded throne room, filled with his courtiers and adorned with his flags of victory, he might have been the Sun King at Versailles receiving the ambassadors of a foreign nation, the ritual grave or comic, depending on one's sense of humor. The shrunken figure in neat uniform, the bony, grinning face, the routine, rehearsed answers, the look of a misplaced gnome from a child's nursery tale, his wife's face of mellow ivory and eyes of infinite sadness, all told a very different tale. For these exiles, once regnant throughout China, there could be no return. The game was finished and they knew it.

Was Taiwan also finished as a prosperous independent state? Must it become a mere pawn and fiction in the larger game of international power? For Canadians that question holds a peculiar interest since Canada exists on the principle of self-determination and could not exist at all if our American neighbors broke it. Surely we should be the last to deny the same right to another people, a fine people as I judged them.

Unlike their current rulers, they did not appear in the least heartbroken. In the back alleys of Taipei, among the night-time hordes of merrymakers, the deafening roar of loudspeakers, the pedicab carrying a grand lady in silk with two butchered piglets on her lap, we were hopelessly lost but detected no sign of heartbreak. When the loudspeakers blared out the unmistakable tune of "Home, Sweet Home", we decided it was time for us to go there. Rescued by a policeman with sign language, we went. From the logicians and the future prime minister in Montreal, to the love goddess in Hollywood, and the Pacific islands of enigma it had been a long journey, and for the next ten years heartbreak was behind us.

23

The Elephant and the Mouse

In 1949 when I first saw him, from the outer fringe of a crowded press conference, Dean Acheson, the newly appointed United States Secretary of State, was at the apex of his nation's power and his own. He struck me as the coldest fish I had yet encountered in the ocean of politics—cold, invulnerable, cynical, altogether frightening. Not that his manner or speech was arrogant that day. On the contrary, both were subdued, almost deferential to a group of irreverent Washington journalists. But I detected (quite wrongly) an ill-disguised contempt for his listeners, an aura of superiority, a well-bred sneer.

In his slow, elegant language, his tall, majestic figure, chiselled face, and pointed, belligerent mustache straight out of some Renaissance portrait gallery I beheld the classic intellectual snob, the born aristocrat of the classless society. Here was the symbol and, second only to his President, the custodian of such power as the world had never seen until now. Before this frigid presence, I thought, petty newspapermen of my sort must peep about and find themselves dishonorable headlines.

All of this was nonsense, for later correction. To begin with, Acheson inherited from both his parents as much Canadian blood and tradition as I had. Like mine, his mother was born in Canada. Like mine, his father came there from Britain, but unlike mine at that stage was desperately poor, with no rich family to help him. Acheson, senior, once earned a bare livelihood by running a hotel elevator in Toronto, fought in the Riel

Rebellion, somehow acquired a university education, entered the Church as a curate, and ended his life as the Bishop of Connecticut.

The popular belief that young Dean had been raised in wealth and luxury is false, like so many legends still clinging to his memory. His parents' home was modest and austere, close to the typical small-town American life of those days, and his talents were suspected by nobody. He was remembered by his contemporaries as an independent, solitary boy, a struggling cleric's unpromising heir.

Though his family managed to see him through Groton, Yale, and Harvard, the old breeding grounds of privilege and snobbery, his career was all his own. So was his oddly ambivalent feeling for Canada, which he came to know well — an alloy of fond nostalgia, disappointment, hope, and sometimes anger, just as his nature, like most men's, was a contradiction of vanity and humility.

These eccentricities were not apparent when I first glimpsed the new Secretary of State on public display. Even then, however, I recognized, as I had recognized in Roosevelt, a great man not merely by reputation and official status but by his unspoken impact on everyone around him. The two men, opposites in disposition and frequent collaborators, though never friends, colored and illuminated the four decades of my experience in Washington.

Concerning Roosevelt I had no personal knowledge, but of Acheson, once he befriended me, I learned much. Enough at least to see that his legend of arrogance and austerity was false. In fact he was one of the kindliest and most humorous men I would ever know — a blithe spirit whose flashes of merriment were wont to set any dinner table on the roar. The contrary legend persists, I imagine, because he could do nothing on a minor scale. His achievements and mistakes were always writ large and bold, then exaggerated by his friends and enemies.

Whether he was working with the destiny of nations, making

delicate mahogany furniture, writing books of history or whimsy as his mood changed, he could be nothing less than the master craftsman, the perfectionist. It was the same in large and small affairs. He might seem case-hardened and impervious on state occasions and his irony, among equals, was often withering, but he could be instantly hurt by the sorrows of the humble and weak. They never lacked his help in trouble. He had known many troubles in his own life, public and private, and though he rarely mentioned them, they are easily read between the lines of his books and letters.

One absurd scene, early in our acquaintance but still fresh in my memory, revealed the man unknown to the world. In playful humor Acheson and George Ball, another blithe spirit of a different kind, had conducted a high and rather outrageous debate all evening, half in raillery, half in earnest, both expounding the uses, grandeur, and burden of American power while the rest of us listened in silent awe. Finally Dot could stand no more of it and alone dared to interrupt the two titans.

"What," she demanded as they were leaving the house, "is going to happen when you Yanks get too bloody big for your britches?"

Horrified by her impudence, I expected from Acheson a polite and crushing rebuke, or at least a lethal sarcasm. Instead, he kissed Dot's cheek and murmured, "Yes, my dear, you're right. I'm just an ornery old cuss after all."

The American people never saw that side of Acheson. Their portrait of him lacked its necessary third dimension. Always the two-dimensional caricature blurred the man.

My friendship with him and his family came out of a lucky happenstance. Ever since Roosevelt's arrival in the White House I had visited Washington regularly, spring and autumn, had made more friends there than in Ottawa or Victoria, and had enjoyed more fun. It was not until 1953, however, that I met a young man of extraordinary height, ruddy look, New England accent, a whimsical turn of speech, and, as I did not know then, deep personal misery. His name, William Putnam Bundy, meant nothing to me or to the public. But I liked him on sight and made discreet inquiries about his business.

It appeared that as a lawyer and historian from Yale and Harvard he had served overseas in the wartime intelligence apparatus. Now he held some highly confidential post in government and had married Acheson's daughter, Mary, who was beginning at last to recover from a desperate illness in a remote sanitarium. (Acheson's letters to her at that time are the most poignant passages in any of his books.)

When we next came to Washington, Mary had returned, her illness cured. At our first meeting Dot and I knew that we had found, in a world unfamiliar to us, a woman strangely untouched by all its wealth and shams. She had inherited Acheson's tall figure and her face immediately reminded us of his. She had also inherited her father's intelligence and the artistic tastes of her mother, Alice, a distinguished painter and a great lady of the old school. There was something else in the daughter—not just a dark beauty that arrested every eye but a subtle, almost psychic perception of other minds. A radiant creature, fancy free, as we thought her. She will not like such words in this book but they are accurate.

Mary was loved by everyone, from statesmen in high places to servants working beside her in the kitchen. All of them became her friends. Yet she was shrewd, too, and at times disconcertingly tough in her judgments. Fools she could suffer gladly. Fakes she demolished with smiling ridicule, especially if the fake happened to be rich and powerful. Altogether, Mary was the most remarkable and commanding woman to enter our lives. And I think now that she knew us better than we knew ourselves.

Why the Bundys welcomed us to their house so often and so lavishly we could never quite understand, but it became our second home. Its door opened our third distinct instalment of Washington life after the New Deal and the wartime periods. It also opened a world which we had seen, up to now, only from the outside.

That house, within sight of the Washington Cathedral spires

and the sound of its bells, was enormous, rambling, and, at most times, filled with jolly tumult. Three Bundy children, Michael, Carol, and Christopher, their playmates, and a daily procession of older guests made the house a caravansary where the magnificoes of politics, diplomacy, and journalism appeared for refreshment of body and mind, where the latest gossip was exchanged and generally discounted, where the country mice from Victoria were rapidly educated, even partially sophisticated.

Nothing we heard there, over some twenty years, was ever repeated. After Bill had become Assistant Secretary of State in charge of Far Eastern Affairs, my friends in the Canadian government would ask me what he was saying privately about the Vietman War. They disbelieved me when I told them that he had not discussed it in my hearing. Nor had he. Not once, literally not once, was the business of the State Department mentioned during all our long companionship. We talked about everything else under the sun, we travelled with the Bundys on holiday in America and Europe, but of Bill's job no word was uttered.

All I know even now is that however the foreign policy of his government is argued in countless books, some of them unfair, none complete, Bill did his job seven days a week and frequently through the night until, at the end, he had given the government not only his service but his health. By most certain knowledge and personal test I also know that no finer and few abler men had served the nation, or his friends.

Concerning foreign policy (which Bill, of course, did not make but only served) I learned much from other men in even higher places, nothing from him. The Vietnam War was then the centre of endless, bitter argument in every household throughout the land, the wedge splitting the nation, the ruin of its President. But if I had doubts about it, a sense of approaching climax, things moved so fast that I could not hope to keep up with them. In any case, rightly or wrongly, I felt that it was not for a Canadian reporter to make public judgments on his neighbor's misfortunes whatever he thought privately, when better men were in agony of doubt, men in the same government disagreeing on fundamentals of policy, caught in the same trap.

Some Canadians, more self-confident than I, were making their own judgments, wise or unwise, and professed after the Vietnam tragedy that they had foreseen it from the start; I assuredly had not. Such feelings of moral superiority among my own people, and the pieties often preached in Ottawa, may have been honest enough, even prophetic, but they usually ignored the real facts of power, the awful responsibility that Canada did not share.

Though Pierre Trudeau had yet to express it in the most irresponsible of his early speeches, many Canadians were beginning already to accept the smug, unreal, and contemptible premise that the United States must defend us under any circumstances, on our own terms, whether we carried a minor share of the continental burden or not. This notion seemed to me impractical, unworthy, and humiliating but I cannot claim any wise thoughts on Vietman before it became the first total defeat in American history, and a decisive event in the history of the world, its ultimate consequences still unknown.

If Bill assumed that I had sceptical views on the business of his nation he never inquired about them. Our friendship was, and is, a very private affair. For him and Mary I could do little, in rough times or smooth. For me, in my rough times, they did more than they ever knew, with understanding that must be rare in any times. For a journalist the men, women, and information moving through the Bundy home were beyond price, but to Dot and me secondary. What mattered was a completely different thing, beyond explanation or thanks.

One thing at any rate is clear in retrospect. The people gathered around the Bundys showed no resemblance to those portrayed and glamorized nowadays in a library of smirking best-sellers. Reading these books, the foreigner might suppose that every dinner table in affluent Northwest Washington was a roost of plotters, every house a high-class Mafia den with some political Godfather presiding to hatch conspiracies, arrange bribes, assassinate reputations, debauch governments, and seduce foolish virgins from Kansas. If such a Washington exists outside the books (and the passing horror known by the code name of Watergate) we never came within sight or smell of it.

The Americans of our acquaintance were rather old-fashioned and conservative in their habits, though often politically radical in their thinking; simple and unassuming in their manners, however rich and influential; as approachable and easy to know as our rustic neighbors at home, however they appeared in print. If they belonged to an élite of sorts it was a very loose and fluid élite, its membership unspecified and constantly changing with the tides of politics. Today's most powerful men were gone tomorrow, no one knew where. The democratic process — a fact of life, not a constitutional theory — gave no exemption to this élite or to any of the other unacknowledged élites that govern American society in politics, business, the labor unions, and the smallest town. Whether democracy, here or anywhere, was strong enough to endure the strains ahead we never asked in those carefree days. The ultimate question had not yet appeared.

Meanwhile, we were treated not as foreigners but as neighbors and welcome guests. With the exception of government experts, who knew every Canadian fact down to the last decimal point, our hosts, though otherwise well informed, usually knew little north of the forty-ninth parallel. They always showed a lively, somewhat pathetic, interest in Canada and freely confessed their ignorance. Past the border a blank, white immensity, hospitable, benign, but mysterious, stretched to the Pole, marked here and there by a scarlet Mounted Policeman, a quaint Quebec peasant in gaudy chapeau, and, later on, by the electric personality of Pierre Trudeau, that mystery incarnate, who quite outshone the drab Washington politicians. I exaggerate my friends' ignorance, to be sure, as they exaggerated my knowledge of the United States. Many had visited Montreal, Toronto, or Ottawa, some daring travellers had even reached Vancouver, on the last fringe of civilization, and thought, poor souls, that they had seen a fair sample of the nation. But for the most part it remained a blank.

This didn't matter much since Canada and its reliable friendship were taken for granted like the bracing northern climate—an old grievance with us, a convenient excuse sometimes for dodging specific issues, and really a compliment. So we are beginning to realize now when the carefree days have passed and the continental neighbors, like nations everywhere, are troubled, frightened, and peevish.

While I foresaw none of these things during my third instalment of political life in Washington, I did see (with a mixture of native pride and scepticism) that most Americans, even the well-informed men at the top, usually overestimated Canada's peculiar excellence and minimized its faults without bothering to explore either. The myth of a strong, silent, rustic people inhabiting and conquering the cold, clean North was still alive then and would take an unconscionable time to die.

But the continental fact would never die. A great power and a small one — the twitching elephant and the uneasy mouse in Trudeau's metaphor — were locked into the same land mass from the Rio Grande to the Arctic Sea and, after two centuries of recurring war and a century of struggle just short of war, must somehow live together, willy-nilly. Their marriage of geography, language, culture, economics, and mere convenience will become increasingly troublesome with the shifting power balance of the world, but no divorce is allowed in the court of history.

Acheson had deeply studied the resulting international problems, known Canada at first hand since youth, and learned more about it from Hume Wrong, a Canadian who became one of the closest friends of his life. As relatively junior officers of their governments they had found their duties and dispositions happily intermingled.

It happened that I also had known Wrong some years before he became Canadian ambassador to Washington and, like everybody else, thought him a man of exceptional brilliance, Acheson's equal in mind if not in power. For both nations the friendship between these two men was invaluable. Because they were friends of deep affection their official business must have been intimate, agreeable, but, one supposes, difficult. For each had to protect his own nation's interests regardless of friendship. So they did, with brilliance on both sides and no illusions about the perpetual but ever-changing nature of the North American relationship.

In my early acquaintance with them, Acheson and Wrong told me little of such business. Suddenly, however, in 1966 (to stretch this personal record out of sequence) I stumbled upon the margins of the continental friendship and the natural strains within it.

Livingston Merchant, twice United States ambassador to Ottawa, Canada's good friend in Washington and fortunately mine, decided to publish a book which he hoped would inform the neighbors of their common interests. For this worthy purpose he charmed and coerced three American and four Canadian writers. Aiming high, he even persuaded Acheson to take his formidable, not to say ruthless, pen in hand.

The result was a book of joint authorship entitled *Neighbors Taken for Granted*. Few of the neighbors read it, though the authors, if my own contribution is a fair sample, had sweated hard to make their diverse arguments. Acheson, too, worked diligently and now, for the first time clearly, I understood his mixed sentiments toward the nation of his mother's birth and his immigrant father's early life.

With obvious gusto, as a retired Secretary of State at last free to speak his mind, he headed his chapter: "Canada, Stern Daughter of the Voice of God". When he showed me the manuscript and asked my opinion I thought that the heading, based on a favorite quotation from Wordsworth, was just too clever, or too ironical. For in truth, as Acheson must have known by this time, Canada had long ceased to be stern, Godlike, or anyone's daughter. The old northern bromide was obsolete. Still, he relished it out of his nostalgic Canadian memories and, more explicitly, his memories of official negotiations with Wrong and Wrong's successors.

Acheson opened his chapter solemnly, eagerly, sympathetically, in his highest style of Socratic irony by assuming that Canadians, on their own self-assertion, were quite unintelligible to foreigners, their native culture too mysterious for outside examination. He must depend, therefore, on Canadian witnesses in his attempt to decipher a baffling enigma. As one delicious morsel of evidence he quoted the distinguished Toronto editor Robert Fulford, who had written that Canadians cling to their moral superiority over Americans as "white trash cling to segregation. Heaven help us if it ever vanishes and we must see ourselves naked."

This quotation, without his own comment, and others of like kind, were ample for Acheson's purpose. His judgment appeared only at the end of the chapter in words to be remembered on both sides of the continental border. The durable friendship between the two nations, he wrote, was not a simple matter of goodwill and inspiring rhetoric. Nor was it "foreordinated". And "if it is to be achieved, Americans must not take Canadians for granted. But something else is needed. Canadians must not take Americans for granted, either."

Reading the manuscript, I observed not without amusement that Acheson had reversed, whether he remembered it or not, my wife's harsh warning to Americans. He had told Canadians not to get too bloody big for their britches. Reading further, I agreed with his warning to both peoples, and I consider it more relevant today than it was when written. But I was distressed to find in the text some references to Mike Pearson which struck me as grossly unfair. Now I began to grasp the strange relationship of affection and antagonism existing between two great men who, I think, could never understand each other.

That puzzle could await leisurely investigation. At the moment my problem was to screw up enough courage to question Acheson's judgments. Courage failing me, I decided to let the manuscript go unquestioned, but Mary Bundy, stern daughter of the voice of Acheson, would have none of it. She insisted that I beard the lion in his den and Dot, who feared no lion or man, egged me on.

Sustained only by my fear of womankind's contempt, I told Acheson that he had mistreated Pearson and, in some cases, misconstrued Canadian foreign policy. Having recorded this stuttering caveat, I prepared myself for an explosion. Instead, Acheson remarked, quite casually, that I might be correct and could revise the manuscript any way I pleased. So I did (the details now forgotten) and he accepted my revision without another word, if he even read it, which I doubt—this from the man of legendary arrogance and inflexible bias.

Such a minor episode would not be worth mention if it had not led to something much more significant in Canadian affairs. As I now realize, Acheson was slowly warming up for his masterwork, *Present at the Creation*, the complete and often devastating memoirs which, he had often assured me, would never be written. When that prodigious book appeared, three years after the joint book produced by Livy Merchant, I saw immediately why Acheson as Secretary of State had good cause, as he thought, for his ambivalence toward Canada and Pearson.

The clash of principle between the two men was a confused and unhappy side issue of the Korean War while each was the foreign minister of his nation. Since both have discussed this incident exhaustively in their books, it must be sufficient here to recall that they disagreed on the forcible repatriation of North

Korean troops imprisoned in the South. Acheson's book cites in minute, almost hourly, detail the positions taken at the United Nations by Canada, Britain, and India, and describes their delegates, including Pearson, as "conspirators" who tried to block and confound American policy with "sophistries".

In the midst of an ugly quarrel among friends behind the scenes in New York, Acheson was invited to Ottawa. There, in a triumph of understatement, he told Prime Minister St. Laurent and a bewildered cabinet some unpalatable truths. As his book records this dismal meeting, he said that the United States, on the full authority of the United Nations, was fighting the Korean War with its own six divisions and twelve Korean divisions "with welcome but token assistance from others". Hence "it seemed to me that the military opinion that should be listened to was that which bore the responsibility of command."

His shot went home. In Acheson's record "the Prime Minister agreed; so far as he was concerned, he said, there was no answer to that observation. The point had been made where it counted and no more talk seemed necessary." St. Laurent, as always, had said the last word. Pearson, in New York, had been outflanked in Ottawa by a manoeuvre as mild as it was deadly. Or so it appeared at the time. But Pearson's account of the whole Korean affair, in his own book, differs sharply from Acheson's.

As a friend of both men what most interested me was something else entirely. Looking back now, I can see that each represented not only a separate national policy but a separate view of the world; more than that, a separate philosophical view of life.

In my own retrospective and unauthorized speculations Acheson was a stoic realist in the struggle for world power, Pearson a frustrated idealist in the struggle for world understanding. The Canadian fought for one lost international hope after another. The American faced no such soul-struggle because he had never held such hopes. The difference between them was not of the ultimate goals sought by both, but of timing. They disputed the best immediate use of power aimed at the same long-term result.

The dispute outlasted them, of course, but in their closing days of life neither spoke ill of the other. Friendship survived the clashes of policy. The gap of thought was narrowing.

Acheson had come to reassess the limits of American power, as demonstrated by the Vietnam War. Pearson had realized the limits of human intelligence and was dubious, almost to the point of despair, about human prospects, the famous grin, even as he calmly awaited death, masking those doubts and much else besides, unsuspected by his nation.

Acheson, who had the good fortune to drop dead without pain at his desk, the busy pen still in hand, never despaired, never surrendered, and never doubted the manifest destiny of his nation. But that destiny did not for a moment include, as it had included before his time, the acquisition or domination of Canada by the United States. He was far too much of a realist to consider or desire such a possibility. All he wanted — no small thing — was Canada's understanding of the unique responsibility and crushing burden of the superpower, and sole defender, on its southern flank. All Pearson wanted — an even larger thing — was American understanding of Canada's manifest, or rather its self-chosen, destiny.

In the shifting destinies of both nations neither man could hope to get what he wanted in North America or elsewhere. No man ever does. Yet both these men as I knew them were truly great, each in his own fashion. They were also playful and mischievous to the end, as a queer little contretemps reminds me.

After both had left office they conducted some kind of television debate in which Acheson quoted an earlier speech by Pearson to score against him. Pearson vaguely remembered the quote and checked through his records to find it. As he had suspected, the statement was not his but Acheson's. For once the

American's infallible memory had betrayed him. Hoist on his own petard, he apologized handsomely and the old friends enjoyed a hearty laugh together.

My education in these continental matters, so vividly epitomized by two good men, had begun when I first penetrated the Canadian Embassy in Washington (or, as it was then, the Legation) whose marbled Edwardian splendor awed me. Of that visit all I remember now is the jovial Leighton McCarthy, a fine old gentleman from Ontario, who had been appointed Minister in 1941 because he was a close family friend of Roosevelt. While a direct channel to the White House was thus opened, McCarthy's young assistant ran the affairs of the Legation. Mike Pearson ran them so completely, indeed, that McCarthy once said to me with wistful laughter that it would be nice if Mike sometimes told his boss what he was doing.

The other Canadian ministers and ambassadors whom I came to know were all professionals and, according to my friends in the State Department, as able as any in their profession. Their average ability, by common consent, was far above that of their contemporaries from overseas. Their contact with American officialdom was unique, not only because they were respected as individuals but because the United States and Canada enjoyed uniquely close ties.

That never meant subservience on Canada's part. The Canadian ambassadors, without exception, were very tough guys in defending their nation's rights (or wrongs) either at the official bargaining table or, more frequently, around private dinner tables where their governments could not hear them. Their American counterparts and personal friends responded with the same candor in those always rugged exchanges. Such was the working machinery of the unique relationship—an asset envied by other nations and little appreciated by Canadians or Americans at home.

None of Canada's ambassadors agreed with all the policies laid down in Ottawa. Some were highly critical of their government's blunders and often succeeded in forestalling or salvaging them. But once they were finally instructed, after intramural argument, all the ambassadors carried out their orders faithfully, whether they agreed with them or not. And what a galaxy of talent that embassy produced over the years.

Hume Wrong, as I have said, possessed his own singular distinction of mind, his brittle energy, his impatience with fools, his occasionally sharp language, cutting like a razor, and yet a warm, sensitive side disguised by incurable shyness.

Equally intelligent, a sprawling, untidy man and certified genius among his peers, Norman Robertson was, or at least appeared, much more relaxed, leisurely, and patient than Wrong. In Ottawa, Washington, or London he prefered listening to talking and listened with an ear wonderfully acute. He picked up all the nuances as they floated by and then drafted some brief memo which usually became Canadian policy — the government, of course, claiming full credit for it.

Pearson, as ambassador, was perhaps less intellectually brilliant than the other two but he had a surer human touch, a better political instinct. Otherwise he would not have become the master of all Canadian embassies.

Arnold Heeney was another kind of man, strikingly handsome, modest and charming, but more stubborn than any outsider would suspect in business with the American government. His smooth surface concealed most of the time an exceedingly hard inner core; also his rigid self-discipline and deep religious convictions. He had no side to him, no public act, no stuffed shirts in his wardrobe. When, on a midnight of blizzard, Arnold dashed out of his mansion in pyjamas and slippers to rescue a cargo of lost newspapermen whose car was stuck in the snow, he was not acting the part of an ambassador. As one of those rescued, I thought he was just being a competent snow driver from Ottawa, another ordinary Canadian. No wonder everyone liked him and mourned his too early death.

Then there was that deceptive and generally misunderstood

personage, Charles Ritchie, with his loping gait, absent-minded professor's look, rumpled clothes, and the best jokes in Washington. Charlie could have given lessons in comedy to Chaplin himself, or the Marx Brothers, as he reproduced, with wild gestures and shrill sound effects, his ceremonial approach to Queen Elizabeth's throne in shoes that were suddenly glued to the palace floor by wads of discarded chewing gum.

That tale may have been slightly exaggerated, but anyone who knew Charlie also knew that the winking comedian of the dinner party was by day a cold-blooded negotiator of worldwide experience, subtle insights, and, in Canada's affairs, grim tenacity. What no one knew then was that he wrote a daily diary of such witty discernment in exploring other men's foibles and his own that when *The Siren Years* was published at last in 1974 it hit Ottawa like a well-guided missile. And yet, behind his giggles, I detected a rather sad fellow.

No man who represented Canada in my time was mentally bigger, more efficient at his job, or more fully equipped with common sense than Edgar Ritchie (Charlie's namesake but not a relative). In Ed, a giant of physique, and in his darling, blunt-speaking wife, Gwen, I found all the finest qualities of the Canadian breed. For me they were Canada exactly personified. No other land could have produced this pair and no luxury, privilege, or pomp could spoil them. Around their table, with Gwen in full control, Dot and I felt as much at home as in our own kitchen. Ed's performance in Washington and Ottawa was never surpassed by any of Canada's servants but he seemed to get things done without the least strain or flourish until his labors broke his health at the peak of a magnificent career. That cruel mischance brought equal sorrow to both capitals.

On first sight his successor, Marcel Cadieux, seemed to me a neat-minded, flawless French-Canadian bureaucrat, a typical Ottawa mandarin. As I soon discovered, he was nothing of the sort. But perhaps my mistake could be excused since he wore in public a cloak of discretion, silence, and austerity—the mechanic of diplomacy to perfection. Off duty, however, among trusted friends, the Gallic fire, the mordant wit, and sometimes the ancestral poetry of Quebec erupted from this man like a sudden volcano. I felt that in him and Ed the two sides of Canada's nature were fused to final definition.

All these ambassadors grappled with the same perpetual problem so vividly symbolized by Acheson and Pearson. All understood—usually better than their bosses in Ottawa—the wise uses and definite limits of Canadian power in the continent of elephant and mouse. All could easily have made themselves millionaires in private business, all served their nation for small reward, and none was corrupted by rank or temporary affluence. This record, I thought, said something pretty important about Canada.

24

The Shadow Line

Man's history is an unbroken continuum without known beginning or end, too long, complicated, and inscrutable to be measured by the rudimentary apparatus which he calls his mind. For practical use he must cut human experience into neat, minor segments and even these he is unlikely to understand.

That curious segment nowadays called, in Washington, the age of Kennedy and Johnson was generally misunderstood by the participants and outside observers alike, myself among them, and celebrated mostly for the wrong reasons. The imaginary Camelot beside the Potomac, the New Frontier, the Great Society, the ever-growing American economy, the perpetually rising standard of life, and all the other clichés served well enough for their time. But they hid the flow of the continuum.

As we can see in somewhat longer perspective, the Kennedy-Johnson age was not the age that its makers or interpreters supposed. It was not the age of rising American power abroad and durable affluence at home, despite all the exciting military and economic statistics. It was not the age of advance but of pause, in some areas of retreat, despite Kennedy's hopeful beginning. It was not the age of discovery but of disappointment, despite Johnson's furious energies. It was not the age of wise historical judgment, but of almost unanimous error. In short, it was the age of adolescent euphoria soon followed by the age of adult disillusion, and then by the age of total reassessment.

The assassination of two Kennedys, the abdication of

Johnson, the violence on streets and campuses, the underlying fragility of the long business boom, the drastic shift in the ownership of the world's capital assets — these and other portents should have warned everyone that the contemporary age must soon end whether its governors survived or not. Except in a few minds, then disregarded, all the warnings failed to register.

If that age, like all ages, was misunderstood until it had passed, much less could the succeeding age be predicted. Watergate was still only the name of a luxurious hotel for rich travellers, not a code word for infamy. Richard Nixon was a private citizen practising law in New York. The men who would accompany him in disgrace were still innocent of any crime. But if the next age was unpredictable so, for most outsiders at least, was the untapped vitality of a nation able to survive all these men and miseries.

About this time I was given a forgotten book by Joseph Conrad entitled *The Shadow Line*. I read it then without perceiving its obscure symbolism in the lives of governments and ordinary men alike. Now I can see that under Kennedy, Johnson, and Nixon the American Republic had crossed, without noticing, its own Shadow Line from youth to maturity, from illusion to reality, from abundance to scarcity, from strength to weakness, and perhaps from weakness to a new strength. In my own affairs I, too, must cross that line without advance knowledge of it, and make the passage in a single instant, alone.

While the Republic was unknowingly in midstream, and frequently changed horses, the men who governed it could not reckon either its weakness or its strength and they pursued the customary business of any capital, in any time or place. They sought personal power for its own sake, a legitimate ambition but in Washington peculiarly ruthless. For this town is an economic parasite thriving on the wages of a swollen bureaucracy and power is a way of life, supported by millions of remote taxpayers who will never see its public monuments or its secret feuds.

In one form or another, of course, the same appetite drives all capitals and all the living cells of society everywhere, from the largest metropolis to the smallest village. Washington is unique among North American towns only because it has more power and uses it more nakedly.

The epicentre of politics and news offered me nothing but fun. For any journalist it was and remains the most open town in the world, like a candy shop where a boy could gorge himself at will, even though it had a back room and a stock of goods undisclosed, the door sealed against the likes of a Canadian reporter.

Occasionally, however, I caught a tangy whiff of these hermetic regions when, for instance, one of the most powerful men in the State Department informed me, with bitter indignation, that Canada had sold the pass and "crawled on its belly" to recognize the Chinese communist government. The United States, he said, would never humiliate itself by such a craven surrender of principle. And within the week Henry Kissinger landed at Peking to woo Chairman Mao Tse-tung.

Near the top of the pinnacle the right hand did not always know what the left hand was doing. Between the first and second layers of a supposedly coherent organism the gap might be as wide as the Pacific, as dark as the mind of Richard Nixon. But apart from the back room the big candy shop stayed open day and night, its managers willing to talk indiscreetly with the visitor, provided that his discretion had been tested over a reasonable length of time. With four men of primary power the test was short and easy.

Long before the Kennedy-Johnson age Senator Mike Mansfield had opened his office and thoughts to me. At first his candor seemed reckless, or deceptive, and in truth the Senate majority leader was a deceptive man — deceptive, I mean, because he never learned how to practise deception. A political reporter accustomed to half-truths, platitudes, and evasions could hardly believe that Mansfield's look of innocence and a serenity almost Oriental were more than a well-rehearsed public act. As I soon discovered, they were automatic, compulsive, and unconscious.

The tall, sinewy figure, the taut, leathery face, and the crisp idiom of the Montana range land marked a diverse apprenticeship as miner, soldier, university professor, scholar of politics, and always the devout Christian believer. I judged that this man had won the only struggle of consequence in any man's life. He had mastered himself. While he could not be a wily Senate boss like Johnson, few Americans of his time possessed so much power and in the exact sense it was moral. He possessed it because he never sought it.

Our meetings over the many years followed an invariable routine. Mansfield received me in his modest suite outside the Senate chamber, relaxed in his old-fashioned armchair, lighted his pipe, and answered any question I cared to ask. Every answer was a blunt yes or no, or a brief, staccato outline of his views. He gave the same impartial advice to presidents of both parties and they all trusted him even when the advice was ignored, often to their later regret. One by one they disappeared. Mansfield remained, serene and unshakable. He had become almost an institution of government and, as I saw him, the democratic process incarnate.

My second good friend was Senator Henry Jackson of Washington State, a compact, tireless man whose lean outdoor face, folksy manner, and common touch explained in part his continual re-election; only in part. Jackson had made himself one of the dominant figures in national politics by concentrating a very tough mind and very fine antennae on practical issues, domestic and foreign. In the outward arts and flourishes of his profession he had small talent. Lesser men but more skilful actors outshone him on the platform and on television. None of them had a surer grasp of the facts or a wider network of friendships and information, at home and abroad. Never had I met a more likable, frank, and unpretentious man. At our first meeting he insisted that I call him Scoop and so did everybody from coast to coast. Besides his unlimited capacity for hard work he had his own kind of serenity, as unruffled as Mansfield's, and maintained it by daily swims in the senators' pool, lunches of half-raw hamburger, and fishing holidays in the other Washington.

I doubted, however, that even Scoop's trained muscles and cool nerves could have borne his load if he had not shared it with an equally tireless assistant, a friend of his family, a forthright critic and handywoman-in-chief. After long experience in the State Department and the Congress, Dorothy Fosdick knew every gear and lever of the governing machine. She worked overtime for Scoop but thought for herself with canny opinions of men and events.

In one respect Jackson and Mansfield resembled each other. Both were natural politicians, craftsmen of government, their competence and honesty unquestioned. But the irreconcilable differences between them were more important than the men themselves because they identified two currents of American thought diverging or comingling from the Revolution onward.

While they remained loyal Democrats and generally agreed on domestic issues, Mansfield and Jackson could not have been further apart on foreign policy. Under the more rigid Canadian political system they could not have belonged to the same party. In the shorthand of the day Mansfield was called a Dove, Jackson a Hawk. The shorthand was accurate enough for the Vietnam War, since Mansfield opposed it from the start and Jackson supported it to the last day. Beyond that specific issue the labels were unfair to both.

Mansfield's critics suspected him of a latent isolationism, or at least of views that would ultimately lead to it. In fact he considered himself a strong internationalist. He did not suppose for a moment that the United States should withdraw from the world — to him a ridiculous notion — only that it should keep its commitments within its real means.

Before most of his colleagues he had realized that the means were less than Americans usually assumed. Nor did he exaggerate his own people's moral virtue. On the contrary, he was dissatisfied with the nation's prevailing mood, its lack of self-discipline, its demand for rewards physically and economically impossible. But he believed that its even less realistic allies should carry a fair portion of defence costs as some had failed to do.

In his judgment the gulf between the Western and the Communist societies must be narrowed, step by step, if it could not be soon closed, or it would swallow them jointly in the end. To the work of reconciliation he devoted his calm authority and infinite patience, expecting no quick success, content with one step at a time, and sure that the Communists, unless they were totally insane, would take it also.

Jackson did not share his friend's confidence. Though a liberal and reformer in domestic affairs, he was a conservative protector of the nation's security abroad and often of the Pentagon (where the newly elected President Nixon had vainly tried to place him as Secretary of Defense). Much less than Mansfield was Jackson ready to trust the long-run motives and designs of Russia. Indeed, he barely trusted them at all unless every bargain was backed by sufficient American power to enforce it.

As for the nation's inherent morality he seemed to have no doubts. The United States might not be perfect but in his eyes the old Dream of its founders still glowed and his life, personal and political, was built around it. From that faith in the people, the system, and himself came his ambition, always candid, and finally thwarted, for the presidency, but why he, or any man, should want the world's hardest, loneliest job I could not imagine. Neither, I dare say, does any candidate. In all of them the impulses, hopes, and penalties are too mixed for knowing.

George Ball, my third powerful friend in the Establishment, and then Under-Secretary of State, was also a friend of Canada, though he sometimes expressed his friendship with a bluntness likely to irritate many Canadians. A little-known episode demonstrated his concern for improved neighborly relations. After he had watched their periodic spasms Ball devised, and persuaded Johnson to approve, a joint study of the continental fact by the American diplomat Livingston Merchant and the Canadian Arnold Heeney. Their report, a classic document of its kind, was almost unanimously misunderstood in Canada and completely overlooked in the United States. The authors got little credit for their work and Ball none for originating it.

Few statesmen of my acquaintance possessed Ball's soaring imagination. No reverse could discourage him. No task was too big to daunt him, no problem insoluble, no accident beyond repair. This physician of statecraft, always on call to prescribe midnight heart stimulants, radical surgery, or mild placeboes as diagnosis indicated, was gifted not only with an inventive mind but with a physique seemingly exempt from strain. A tall, brawny man with square-jawed rosy face and cheerful disposition, Ball had become an incurable work addict. Seven days a week he reached his office at eight in the morning and left it twelve or fourteen hours later to write some official paper or speech at home.

When I suggested that his working habits were crazy and would ruin his health, he said he worked best under maximum strain. Obviously he did but the strain broke some of the men around him. When, for example, he introduced me to Dean Rusk, the Secretary of State, I beheld a courageous, intelligent, and exhausted man who defended American foreign policies mechanically, by rote, his argument dulled by too much repetition, too many hopes deferred.

At that time I did not know that these two men, intimate friends and colleagues, disagreed basically on the central issue of the Vietnam War. As Ball and I became better acquainted he told me, long before his retirement in 1966, that he must go. He stayed longer than he wished only because he hoped that the attitude of the government might be changed if it were questioned at the top level.

That was a doomed hope but Ball continued his versatile

career in business, journalism, and the higher counsels of the Democratic Party as a sort of roving, unofficial ambassador-at-large. His abilities, I thought, could have been still more usefully employed. Among the contemporary candidates he appeared to me well qualified for the presidency, but men of his independent mind, bold ideas, and blunt speech seldom appeal to party conventions.

A very different type of man, though equally inventive and irrepressible, had showed me much kindness together with the contents of a dazzling mind. Walt Rostow was widely accused of genius and, in good conscience, felt unable to disclaim it. If he had become mayor of Johnson's palace by the accident of McGeorge Bundy's departure, there was nothing accidental about Walt's instinct for power or his use of it. He needed power as ordinary men need food and he received it from a President who needed his vast economic knowledge, his literary flair, above all his eternal optimism in a time of deepening gloom.

Coatless and perspiring in his White House basement office, Walt filled and nearly drowned me with background stuff, part of it red-hot and unprintable news, some merely his warmed-over musings and historical predictions. Or in his own house, of a Sunday morning, he strode up and down the room, his round, potent face flushed by the labor of cerebration, one hand gripping a Bloody Mary, the other reaching for salted peanuts as he delivered, in flawless, bubbling prose, a lecture well worth a large admission fee.

Before this man, as before some spectacle of nature — a hurricane, landslide, or flood — outsiders would sit in dumb shock and admiration. It was useless to argue with him, no matter what you thought of his opinions, his incandescent sparks of fancy, and his unfailing confidence of victory in Vietnam. As well argue with the Mississippi or Halley's Comet, which in motion and fire he closely resembled. But all his hopes and power collapsed in Johnson's ruin. Of their joint triumph and tragedy I remember Walt only as a constant friend.

Next to Johnson the most celebrated Washington figure of those days was the second of the three brothers whose separate misfortunes had a common ring of fate. Senator Robert Kennedy, recovering at last from the trauma of John's assassination, surprised Dick Malone and me. Instead of the loud, frenetic Bobby pictured by press and television, we found a quiet man of small stature, neatly whittled face, cool manner, and soft speech. He looked older than his photographs, sadder and surer of himself. As the insignia of his youthful constituency, now overflowing his anteroom, he wore his hair long, uncombed, and in urgent need of a barber. On his office walls a still younger generation was self-pictured in the rough crayon drawings made by the Senator's own children.

Meeting us at the door, Kennedy moved across the room in a hurried, loping gait as if he had many miles to go before he slept — the miles fewer and shorter than he could know. In his shirt sleeves, dwarfed by a massive desk, the immediate political heir of the dead President answered all my questions in clipped, abrupt sentences, hardly above a whisper, allowed me to take notes for direct quotation, and only once, on second thought, asked me not to print his low opinion of a certain government in Europe.

This was routine. He had said the same thing over and over again, including the assurance, no doubt sincere at the moment, that he had no thought of contesting the presidential election in 1968. A few months later he was the leading Democratic candidate. Then, like his brother, he was murdered. Reading that news I remembered those childish pictures on the wall.

The third brother, Senator Edward Kennedy, received me some months after the latest murder and again the man denied the public persona. Like Bobby, Teddy was cool, quiet, and thoughtful, but, unlike him, tall, physically impressive, plumply handsome, and immaculately dressed — a man of distinction anywhere, a man of intelligence also, and a talented actor who knew his lines, though not the plot of his private drama.

Since all newspapermen had asked him about his presidential ambitions, I asked his views on the future relationship between the United States and Canada. He discussed it with gravity and deep concern, but I saw that he knew little of my country. Having said nothing worth quotation, he ushered me into the corridor where a swarm of idolators, young and old, waited to meet, touch, and worship the last Kennedy, who surely must be president some day. At once the persona was donned like a well-tailored suit. Smiling, hand-shaking, and back-slapping, Teddy posed for photographs beside the ecstatic strangers and retreated, as soon as possible, to his office. There, I suppose, the persona was doffed and the dull business of politics resumed.

Among such men of power one is memorable, though I talked with him for only an hour at a wedding party. Justice Felix Frankfurter, whose tortuous legal mind and waspish *obiter dicta* shed radiance on the Supreme Court and deeply influenced the policies of Franklin Roosevelt, was a sprightly little fellow off the bench, full of gossip, jokes, and mischief. But at our single meeting, not long before his death, Frankfurter turned solemn and gave me a lost footnote to Canadian history.

Mackenzie King, he said, had come in his latter days to Washington, unnoticed by the press, and made an impromptu speech at a gathering of old friends, a farewell speech, as they guessed. Frankfurter, who had heard many famous orations, considered King's short, confidential chat the most perceptive, prophetic, and moving of them all—this from the grand equivocator and notorious public bore! No record was made of the aged man's final conclusions, but if the Canadian people could have read them, Frankfurter believed, their posthumous opinion of King would be greatly changed.

From a natural prejudice of my trade, however, I was less interested in the men of official power than in certain men who possessed it outside politics and office.

25

The Men of Words

In my youth the trade of journalism enjoyed a reputation of high glamor compensating for its low wages. Since then, glamor, like many words once respectable, has been debauched and driven into the streets, a poor slut betrayed by Hollywood and Madison Avenue, her seducers. One hesitates to call any trade glamorous nowadays, but even without glamor the press is still mysterious to the public and suspected of motives, designs, and cunning unknown to its workers.

As for journalism, the old-timers of the trade seldom used that word, either. In our vocabulary a journalist was a broken-down newspaperman who bummed small loans from us on pay day, boasted of apocryphal scoops, and smelled of whisky. Though we claimed no honorific title, we laid one flattering little unction to our souls. For us newspapering was a true and special craft unlike any other, a kind of witchcraft; even better than that, a game.

It had its own argot, passwords, rites, heroes, triumphs, and disasters, all jealously guarded within the brotherhood. A successful newspaperman might lack money but among his fellows he had a status in the separate world of print. That world was imaginary, of course, but it served well enough. It bred a loyalty to the paper, any paper employing us at the moment, an esprit and craftsman's pride which may have been pathetic, or comical, and yet was rather fine in its way, almost mystical, when we were given little else to keep us going.

The old fiction, alas, withered in the enlightenment of the modern, practical world. Who, among the young, can remember those newspaper dramas of stage and film that used to thrill the public before facts more thrilling and unbelievable marched nude across the television screen every night? Presses rolling, telephones jangling, typewriters clattering, hard-boiled city editors with raw nerves, stomach ulcers, and hearts of gold cursing reporters on to the scene of some bloody crime; sleek foreign correspondents, gentlemen all, like John Barrymore, Errol Flynn, or Clark Gable, drunk but clear-headed, with one arm around a glamorous female, probably Myrna Loy, Norma Shearer, or Marlene Dietrich, the spare hand punching out a news story to shake the world—these were the *dramatis personae* of a cast long superannuated, mostly forgotten, and sad to think on.

A loss of fiction has been outweighed by real gains. The better newspapermen have turned a trade into a profession and sometimes acquired more power than most statesmen. The newspapers have vastly improved in scope, quality, and honesty, as anyone can see by looking over their musty files. The skills, ethics, manners, and self-respect of journalism have risen with the wages. But the excitement of the game has paled since the great days.

Even sadder to think on, the great days may never have existed at all in more than our imagination, the single place where anything of importance can exist. Our fulfilment (yet another grandiose word then unused) looks bogus now, as our material rewards and working conditions were tolerable only because we knew nothing different.

We worked fifty or more hours a week, with no overtime pay for additional night assignments, as against forty hours or less today under union contract, but the craft was easier to learn then. Any young man of average intelligence and strong constitution could follow the fire brigade to a fire or the police patrol to a murder. It takes education and much reading of small print to follow a national budget, a trade balance, an economist's chart or a prime-ministerial shrug.

These are matters of intramural concern, worrying all editors and under constant scrutiny by men usually self-hypercritical. The larger truth of their trade, and every institution dealing with the body politic, is that none has kept abreast of society's needs. All have fallen behind in the race between necessity and comprehension. If this fact seems obvious to everyone (and almost everyone thinks he knows how to change it) the institution of the press and the other so-called media gives its workers certain advantages denied to their contemporaries.

The media's product, written or spoken words, arrives instantaneously, out of thin air, to compete in the market of ideas months or years before a new physical product can reach the market of commerce. Hence the person of talent is likely to advance faster in journalism than in other trades. For the product is personal, visible or audible, and in general demand. Every producer is assessed on his or her work and no one with a special ability need wait for dead men's shoes. But the masters of the craft are a breed entirely distinct from the performers.

Among many such men I encountered in various countries, five based in Washington and New York particularly impressed me, not just for their mastery but for their benevolence to a stranger. Everywhere newspapermen, though ruthlessly competitive, are still a brotherhood, united against their natural adversary, the rulers of the state.

Like all my fellows I had long admired the most influential master in the English language. But I had never expected to meet this man until one day in Washington Hume Wrong, the Canadian ambassador, phoned to ask whether I would care to watch him pick a bone with Walter Lippmann at lunch in the Metropolitan Club. Would I! Wrong did not often ask such foolish questions.

The bone was Lippmann's campaign for a disengagement of NATO troops in Europe as a means of encouraging the Russians to do the same. Wrong thought the whole notion ridiculous and dangerous, and since his mind was the equal of Lippmann's, his tongue sharper, and his logic unanswerable, the bone got thoroughly picked at the lunch table.

I listened in silence. If Lippmann said anything I forget it, but not that pale, thoughtful, and melancholy face, the brooding, speculative eyes. It was a one-sided bone-picking contest because Lippmann did not try to argue with a trusted friend. What he thought of Wrong's argument I had no way of knowing but afterward, as I remember it, the campaign for European disengagement ceased.

In great affairs Lippmann frequently changed his mind. While the shift of gears in print was so smooth that the public rarely noticed it, the mistakes were gleefully dissected by the cognoscenti whose own judgments, usually no wiser than his, went safely unrecorded. Thus he saw no promise in the young Franklin Roosevelt, no harm in the early Hitler, and he supported the first election of Richard Nixon, once telling me (long before Watergate) that the man showed no sign of greatness, only technical competence. On the other hand, in a last campaign requiring all his courage, Lippmann opposed the Vietnam War when most of the nation approved it, and he accurately predicted its end in American defeat.

After that lunch with Wrong it seemed improbable that I would meet Lippmann again but fortunately I did, many times. Our intermittent association gives me no right to judge his judgments beyond saying that more than any contemporary journalist he made the American people think systematically about foreign policy. That was a unique contribution to his time whether he happened to be wise or unwise on specific issues. The books and articles written about Lippmann by men who knew him intimately are so numerous, fair and unfair, that I can add only some personal recollections, not to gauge his wisdom but to show the kindness and modesty of a private person surprisingly unlike his public image.

In his big house near the Washington Cathedral I used to find him wearing a frayed sweater, baggy slacks, and a look of weariness. The nation's Delphic oracle was getting old now, his face furrowed by sickness and regret, his manner gentle, but his eye as speculative and sharp as ever, his ear welcoming information from any source. The lofty prose of his books and columns was replaced in conversation by the plainest idiom. His latest view of politics was expressed in jerky, casual phrases as if he were airing it aloud before he committed it to print.

Nothing had turned out as he had hoped in his young days. The Good Society of his best-known book had failed to appear. What had gone wrong? Many things, he replied; above all, the politicians' impossible promises.

The boy prodigy of journalism had helped Woodrow Wilson draft the Treaty of Versailles and heard him promise to make the world safe for democracy—ludicrous, crazy, but Wilson had said and believed it. Then Herbert Hoover's two-car family with two chickens in every pot, Roosevelt's New Deal, Truman's Fair Deal, Kennedy's New Frontier, and Johnson's Great Society, all promising impossibilities. How could these able men suppose that the political resources of men in the mass, or the physical resources of the planet, were enough to sustain their wildly exaggerated hopes? And why, said Lippmann, should anyone be surprised when they produced the age of disillusionment?

He did not fit that age. He belonged to the Age of Reason. An eighteenth-century man had been born by unhappy accident into the twentieth. To him as a worshipper of Reason it was a god betrayed by human folly, but perhaps his own youthful expectations were hyperbolic, too. Raised in wealth and privilege, not among common men, his understanding of them may have been less than that of much smaller minds. Had he been poor, forced to struggle for a living, and known that ordinary men often behave not as reasonable units in society but as unreasonable human beings in ceaseless muddle, he might have suspected that the god of Reason was, at best, a second-rate deity, not the betrayed but the betrayer.

In New York, where he lived his last years because the odious environment of Johnson's Washington repelled him, Lippmann looked ill, burned out, and more gentle than ever. The ardent social reformer of Wilson's New Liberalism ended as a sceptical conservative, a wry Stoic, all passion spent. He looked despair in the eye and did not flinch or whine. He only sighed, with now and then a gleam of irony, a remembered spark of feuds and battles long ago. To me he was more than a master of the craft. He was a symbol of one age already dying, of another in tormenting birth, its shape unknown to him or any man.

James Reston, who alone could be compared to Lippmann, his close friend, in knowledge and power, was of an almost opposite nature and method, but he showed me equal generosity. Though his deadline might be an hour away, his telephone ringing, and visitors waiting, Reston never seemed to be in a hurry. Nothing, not even the convulsions in the White House a few blocks distant, ruffled a man of Scottish birth, American upbringing, and worldwide experience which could not shake his faith in the blundering human species. Scotty, as everyone called him, seemed to me a born romantic, a shrewd but always hopeful and never cynical spectator at the tragicomedy of the world.

Smoking his indispensable pipe, speaking slowly and quietly, he would tell me the news of a leaky capital, some of it for publication next day in the *New York Times* column read by anxious governments at home and abroad, some unprintable because he broke no confidences. Without breaking them, his column, like a reliable barometer, usually forecast every change in the political climate, often before his own reporters had sniffed it.

Reston never claimed or tried to imitate Lippmann's profound scholarship, but in his own way he, too, was a philosopher and closer than his friend to the earth, the folkways, and the visceral twitches of America. Besides, his copy was livelier, easier to read, contained less Reason and more of human nature's daily food. The lad from Scotland had become the confidant of the world's statesmen but all his fame and power could not detach him from his origins and his Presbyterian conscience. This was no Stoic in despair but a happy covenanter who, in dreams, might still behold the Hebrides. At least he beheld the American Dream, somewhat battered and yet a reasonable hope if you worked hard enough at it, as Lippmann's dream of pure Reason was not.

The boy reporter who had first covered baseball games now watched the deadlier game of politics with the same discerning eye for strikes and errors. At any moment he could take a mass of contradictory news and, with no visible effort, crystallize it into a thousand words, sparkling like the sports page. How much invisible midnight oil was needed to polish these minor gems of colloquial wit and historical quotation one could only guess. A lot, I suspect.

Of Reston's knack in simplifying a complex theme I had a rather painful experience of my own when, for the *Reader's Digest*, we jointly undertook at his house a taped discussion of various issues and disputes pending between the United States and Canada. I knew, because it was my business to know, more about this subject than Reston did, but he handled it with a crisp, convincing authority that I could not match. To me the exercise had been a morning of agony, to Reston an easy warm-up for the day's work. Yet he also knew agony of a nobler sort. Behind the drawl, the grin, and the pipe smoke he agonized for his nation and humanity.

Robert T. Elson, another great journalist, had worked with me on the Vancouver *Province*, later headed *Time*'s Washington bureau, and then reached the pinnacle of Henry Luce's empire in New York. This quick rise could not spoil the youth from British Columbia or change his Spartan habits of professional and private life. Both lives were clearly recorded in the clean-cut handsome face, the perpetual motion, the lean writing style, and the stern view of society. Bob's drive, physical energy, and unquenched thirst for news might intimidate any stranger who had not seen the benign, doting *paterfamilias* at home, far from the empire.

In mistaken friendship he wanted me to join it. But when the two of us met *Time*'s celebrated managing editor, T. S. Matthews, and the imperial though strangely nervous Luce himself, the offer of a job and more money than I could ever earn in Canada was no temptation. Time, both the magazine and the real thing, moved too fast for my speed and New York was unthinkable at any price.

The fourth man of higher journalism who befriended me was unlike all the others in his origins, methods, and old-vintage urbanity indigenous to Europe but now transplanted to America. Henry Brandon, of the London *Sunday Times*, had been born in Czechoslovakia, schooled in England, and matured in Washington. The world of American politics soon became his oyster, his house a safe retreat where politicians, ambassadors, and officials of the first rank swapped their secrets without fear of leaks.

Henry spoke several languages in his silken English voice and always seemed idle and carefree when he was under heaviest strain, listening with an air of polite attention, almost indifference. But he missed nothing of use to him in his enormous flow of newspaper copy and frequent books. For him the political extravaganza never lost its fascination, the oyster its relish.

In earlier years, New York being still fit for human habitation, I often visited it and encountered there perhaps the most gifted, certainly the most amusing, craftsman of my trade and, above journalism, of true literature, About politics he knew, and wanted to know, less than the Washington correspondents. About life in the round, its measureless absurdity, its laughter, and its pain, he knew, or imagined, much more.

Christopher Morley was born too late and died too soon. He belonged to Shakespeare's age. His nature, his antique language and gleaming satire, even his splendid beard, were made for the company of the Mermaid Tavern where he could have held his

29. Hard at work on the legendary woodpile at Shawnigan Lake

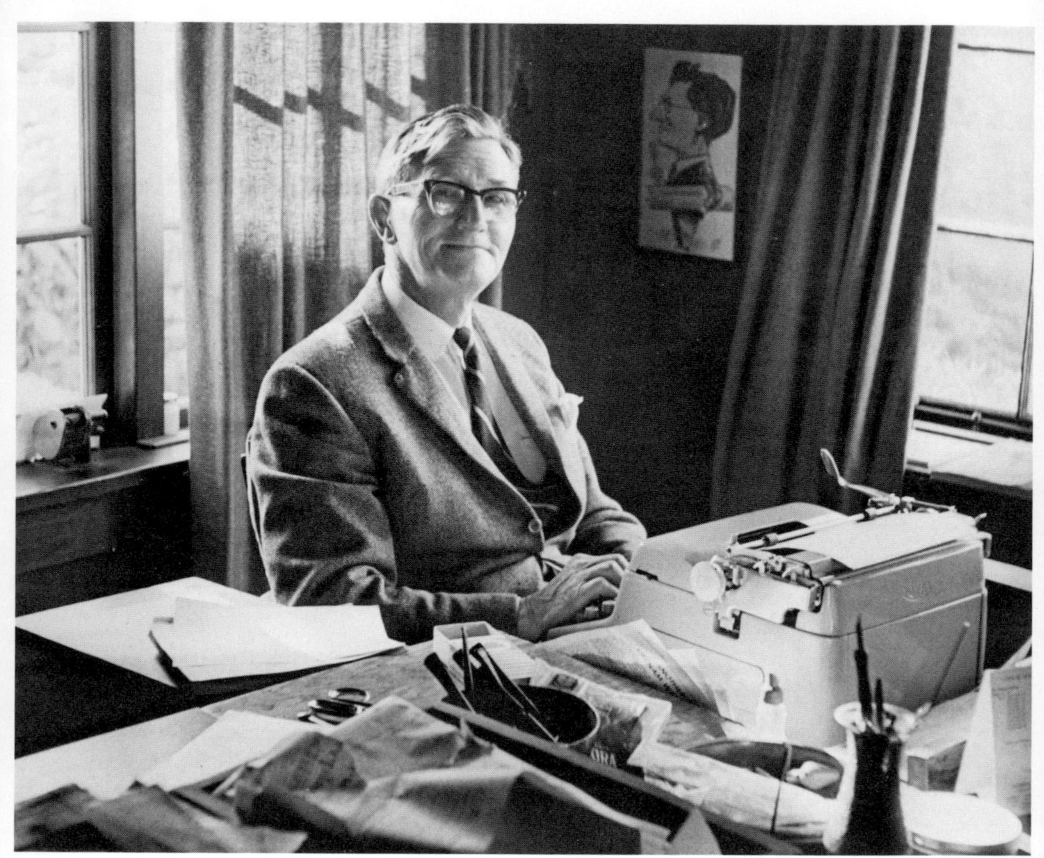

30. The working newspaperman at home in his Victoria study

31. ...and on foreign territory, interviewing Zsa Zsa Gabor in Los Angeles

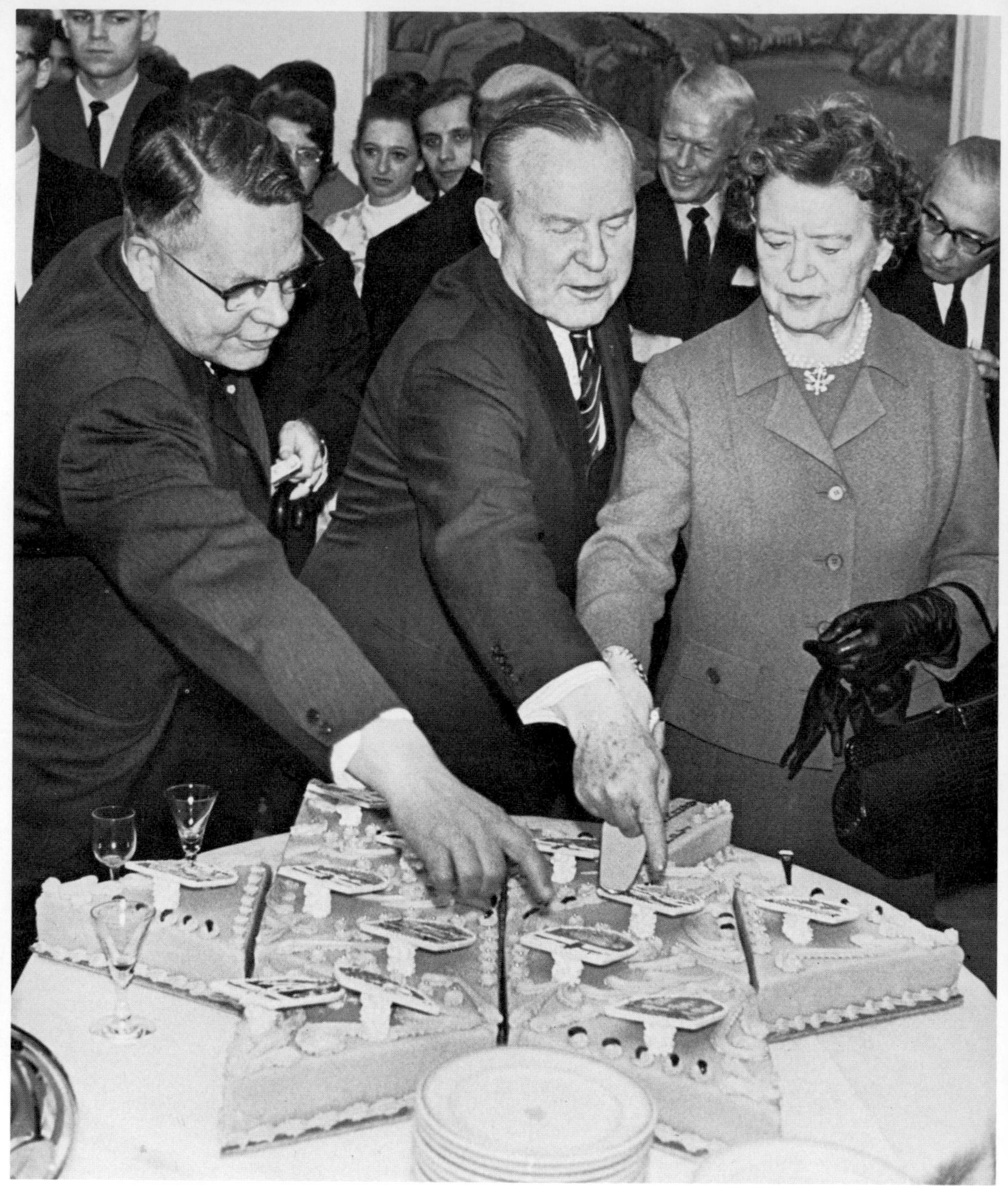

32. Prime Minister and Mrs. Pearson admire a special centennial birthday cake presented to Mr. Pearson on his seventieth birthday in 1967, assisted by Transport Minister Jack Pickersgill. "For Jack, Liberalism (or his private version of it) was little short of a religion."

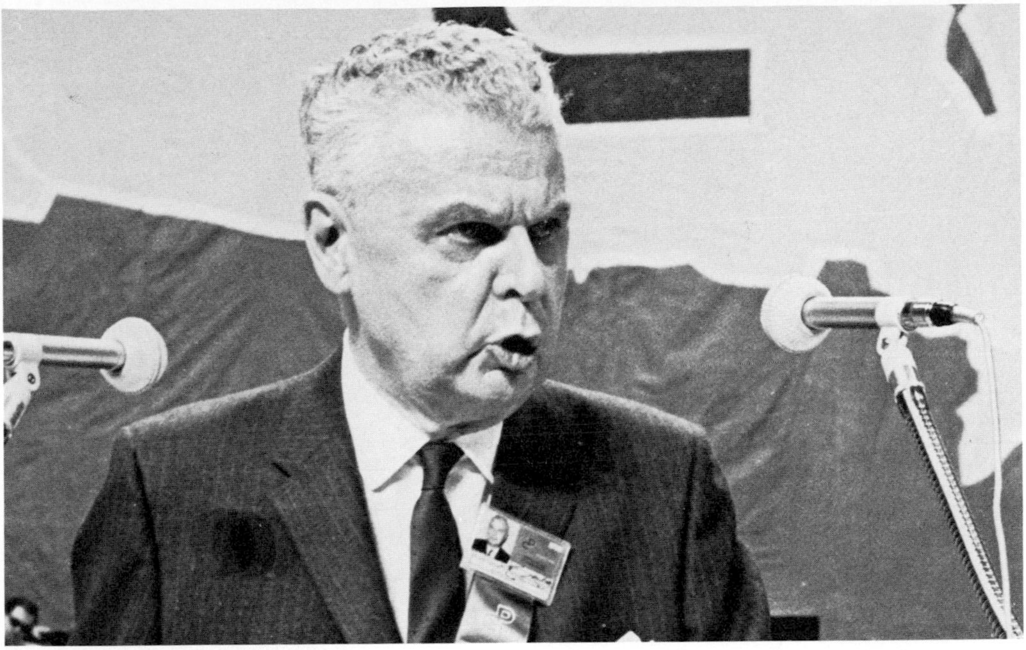

33. John G. Diefenbaker. "A Conservative by label and accident, he was anti-conservative in half his instincts. A liberal by nature, he spent his life fighting a Liberal Party that, by similar illogic, was half Conservative."

34. Pierre Elliott Trudeau: "On his arrival in Ottawa, rather like an Unidentified Flying Object from outer space, some of us wrote that the Canada existing until then would not have accepted such an exotic leader, different from any before him."

35, 36. Two celebrations. The first shows a banquet held in Vancouver in 1970 to mark BH's fifty-two years in journalism. Left to right are Lester Pearson, BH (apparently about to suffer a self-inflicted axe-wound), *Vancouver Sun* publisher Stuart Keate, and Chief Justice J. O. Wilson of the B.C. Supreme Court and the Shawnigan Lake woodpile. The second photograph shows BH receiving an honorary degree from the University of Victoria.

37. BH at home in 1975 flanked by his daughter, Joan, and his son, Robert. Daughter-in-law Corinne completes the family group.

38. BH and Brock Chisholm relax by Shawnigan Lake.

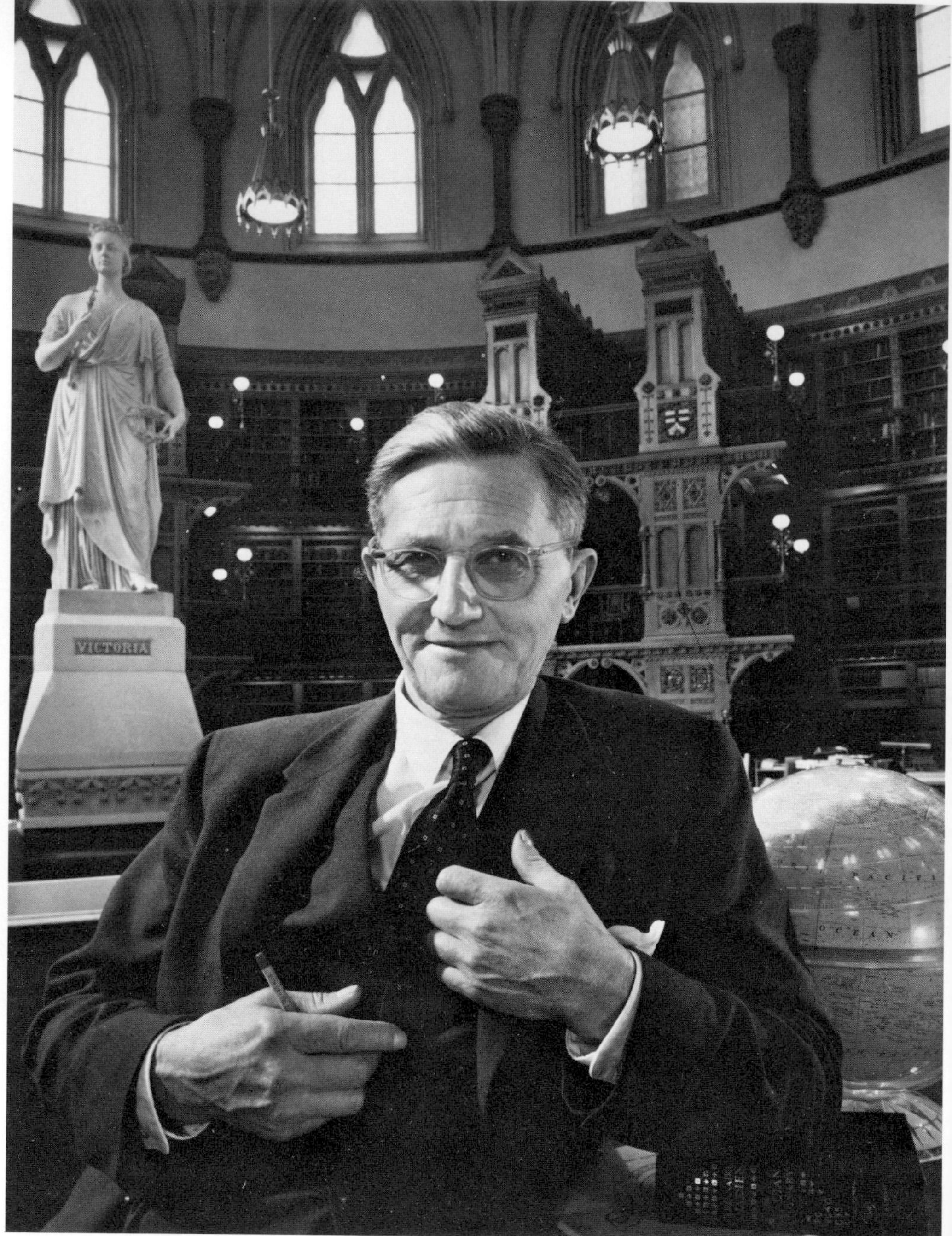

39. BH in the Parliamentary Library in Ottawa

own among all the assembled wits and poets. Yet all his sly jest, his twinkling prose and droll rhyme, filled only the downstairs, public rooms of this illusive creature's strange household. He kept the attic, with its treasures, well guarded and haunted, like the bookshop of his well-loved tale, by genial ghosts and innocent whimsies.

His masterpeice, *Thunder on the Left*, for instance, was a ghost story, if you knew how to read it, and the title, more remembered than the book itself, had a curious origin, characteristic of the author, unknown to his readers. In his New York snuggery (where I found him hiding behind a mountainous rubble of books, newspapers, magazines, and neglected correspondence) he told me that the title swam into his ken as he watched the French countryside from a train window. He had written the book but didn't know what to call it until, suddenly, he saw an electric storm in the distance. Then, with his own lightning flash, he had the magic words. Of course! The thunder was coming from the left side. The title was ready-made.

Unfortunately, however, it bore no relevance to the book. A moment's pondering at the window of the train solved that semantic dilemma. If title and book were strangers, Chris would marry them by historic invention. Under his precious title, in small print, he quoted an imaginary sage of ancient times who had declared that when the Roman gods had momentous tidings to communicate they always released their thunderbolts leftward.

Having explained this pardonable fraud, and donned a railway engineer's cap to direct a toy train over the littered landscape of his hideout, Chris said we must put our minds to serious business and two essential books. We walked across town and in a grubby second-hand store he purchased a new record of English ghosts, authentic ones, the genuine articles. A second work, he insisted, was equally important to my future.

Had I read *The Shadow Line*? No, I had not. Incredible, said Chris, since this book, long out of print, alone contained the ultimate essence of Joseph Conrad, the distillation of his life and philosophy. A single copy remained on sale. Chris bought and presented it to me. The appeal of the ghost record to a man who believed in ghosts, or invented them if necessary, I could understand. But why Conrad's obscure volume? As we walked back across town Chris shyly admitted his worship of the Polish author and warned me that every man must cross a shadow line in life's journey.

That worship was expressed in more than words. Some years previously Chris had learned of Conrad's last ship, rotting on a Tasmanian beach, and acquired its steering wheel. The sacred relic was brought to New York and Chris rolled it all the way uptown from the Battery like a child's hoop, with pauses for refreshment in sundry bars among sailormen who drank appropriate toasts. Then he attached the wheel to that of the *Queen Mary* and was allowed to steer the liner for a few minutes in mid-Atlantic, Conrad's ghost doubtless beside him. After the voyage the relic was placed in a royal marine museum. Chris had paid his tribute to the supreme master.

When I next saw him, in his roomy Long Island house, he had just emerged, as crimson as a boiled lobster, from a steaming bath where he wrote his finest poetry. Forgetting ghosts and Conrad, he asked whether I had read much of Kant (or it may have been Schopenhauer). Again, regrettably, I had not. Chris acknowledged that, until yesterday, he hadn't either. Now he was excited by a wonderful revelation. The dull German philosophic stuff could be ignored, but did I know that Kant devised a special kind of braces to suspend his trousers without irritating his shoulders? Imagine it—the learned mystic pondering pant suspension! Glorious, eh? And it was only by chance, browsing through his library, that Chris had made this astounding discovery. A man, he said, should pay no attention to literary critics, educators, and philosophers but read wherever fancy carried him. Otherwise the works of real virtue, like Kant's suspenders, would be missed.

He put me on the New York train, still laughing at his discovery. Not long afterward I read in the Victoria newspaper that he was dead. But with his friends the old thunder will keep rumbling and echoing, on the left.

From all these men and many others, I must have learned something about the newspaper business, though I was no longer concerned with news as news, had ceased to write it, and sought only its meaning, a very different thing and much harder to understand. Often the meaning appeared in the most unlikely places, to be caught on the wing or lost forever, as the passing glint in a friendly or hostile eye may tell more than hours of talk.

At Washington men of inside knowledge had given me the news of the Watergate tragedy now approaching its climax, but nothing I heard there moved me so much as the words of a cook in a friend's kitchen. Quite unconsciously, this poor black woman, her own life tragic, uttered the heartache and the faith of all good Americans, black and white.

"The trouble," she said, "hurts mighty bad. Sometimes I can't sleep nights, thinkin' of it. But trouble always brings a family together. And it's goin' to bring us together again like a family. Just you wait and see." Then, with sudden tears and a meaning that no words could utter, she added: "Oh God, how I love this dear old country!"

The heartache was real, the faith simple, their impact lost, of course, in meaningless print. I reported what she had said, without comment, in a routine piece from Washington, supposing that few Canadians would understand and no Americans would read it. But Mike Mansfield, a man of quick perception, immediately placed her words in the *Congressional Record*. He understood them. He knew that they came from the nation's depths, from the trouble which might yet bring it together. Much more had still to come, in heartbreak and perhaps faith.

26

The High Places

For two days the October mist, like a wall of concrete, imprisoned us in a narrow canyon. By linear measurement we were about twenty miles from the plains of Alberta, by air travel perhaps three minutes, by our saddle horses at least three days, with good luck and weather. But the autumn weather of the Rockies is always unreliable and our luck had run out.

At dawn on the third day James Riviere, whose huge frame and gaunt face seemed to be encased in durable rawhide, sniffed the air and announced our immediate departure. The mist, he said, would soon lift . Since James knew every pass, wrinkle, and chasm in the mountains as a city man knows his own street and, besides, held our safety, even our lives, in his hand, we trusted him. Here, without legal ownership, his suzerainty was undisputed.

Within the hour his big roan mare, her neck bell jingling to warn off grizzlies, had climbed an avalanche of loose shale and topped a ridge of naked rock, some minor vertebra in the continental spine. A dozen pack horses followed, gulping the thin air with lungs fit to burst. Behind them came half a dozen amateur riders, also gulping, wet, and scared.

On the ridge the concrete ceiling hung low. Dot's horse, a yard ahead of mine, was a blur of dark steam. James and the pack train had disappeared. Suddenly a wind from the east hit us with the force of a bullet, almost lifting the horses from the ridge. The sun drilled through, the walls of mist collapsed, and far beneath us the torn cloud rack whirled like a blizzard of gigantic snowflakes.

Through them we looked down a good half-mile into a bubbling cauldron. The earth's solid substance had melted. All its colors oozed out and ran together, the green of spruce, the gold of poplar, the blue of an inky tarn, as if some monstrous kaleidoscope were changing its pattern every second. Here, I thought, was an authentic re-run of creation's first day, before the planetary flux had time to cool.

Dot's horse snorted and reared in terror but she hung on somehow. The pack train bolted across the ridge, spilling most of its baggage. James, now visible beside us, had dismounted and held his plunging mare by the bridle. Above the wind, faintly, I heard him name his Saviour with reverence. The remark seemed appropriate. For a Christian, it occurred to me, this must be like dying in agony and going in bliss to a Heaven of radiant sunshine.

In less than a minute, the spectacle ceased, the wind dropped, the ceiling closed, the walls of mist surrounded us, and the earth was solid again. We had witnessed only an optical illusion but not even James remembered its like. He repeated his pious oath and began to collect the lost pack train.

Mist-blinded, soaked, and miserable, we descended the ridge through a jungle of charred logs and, long after dark, camped in the next valley. Whereupon a moon of yellow Canadian Cheddar swam out, the sky was bravely spangled, and the Rockies, reef on reef, turned to sterling silver, inlaid with diamonds. We gasped at the day's second spectacle, but briefly, and dried ourselves beside a roaring fire, the single gleam of light in a cavern measureless to man. Then, warmed by Mountain Milk, James's reliable temperance beverage — whisky, sugar, and a drop or two of hot water — we slept well that night.

It was one of many such nights. Our pack-horse expeditions had become, for Dot and me, the most exciting times of our joint life and more instructive, for reasons not yet appreciated, than all our travels in the cities of men. We had found the surest escape from routine and responsibility, with adventures perilous enough in fact, more perilous and satisfying in our imagination. Of course we exaggerated and embroidered them on our return, almost believing our tales of danger faced and overcome. At least we had seen, as no tourist in a railway car, automobile, or airplane ever sees, the lifeless but living stuff of the mountains.

Though motionless, they always had the look of motion as cloud and shadow varied their shape, hue, and texture from hour to hour. Those who travelled them slowly, on horse or foot, discovered some additional treasures, cunningly hidden in that massive bulk — lapidary mosaics of stone and minute lichen, tangled arabesques of storm, frost, and erosion, the marquetry and silent handiwork of ages unimaginable. By such measurements any human was reduced to accurate size in the universal scheme of things, and the scheme of men's politics, power, and momentary consciousness looked mean and insignificant.

We had begun to recover our lost wonderment and to see life, organic and inert, with a truer sense of proportion. In the cleanly upland air, the audible silence, and the presence of danger, the mind is wonderfully clarified, only to be muddled again in the noise and security of streets.

By then we were past middle age, into our late fifties. Most of our contemporaries, who took their vacations on wheels and refreshed themselves in the best foreign hotels, judged us mad, no doubt correctly, because we chose horse, saddle, and tent. But the few friends who came with us were the better for it, we guessed, their bodies often lacerated and stiff, their souls mended and flexible. Like us, they would never be quite the same again.

Our good companions far above timber line were a select group, sharing our wholesome madness. Judge Jack Wilson was rescued, sick and sleepless, from the longest criminal trial in Canadian history and instantly revived by transfusions of sun, wind, and rain. Dr. Gordon Grant, a hand surgeon of worldwide reputation, was a still better horseman, and his wife, Ginny, rode as well as he. Dr. Bobby Hunter, eminent in his science of internal medicine, felt less comfortable on horseback and often preferred to walk, but here, as everywhere, he laughed at saddle sores and the universe. His wife, Cynthia, whose golden beauty was ageless, understood horses and loved them, even when a bay mare rolled over her on a rock slide.

Dot, coming late to the saddle, had never learned to ride as easily as the others, but by nature she was more daring. While the rest of us might hesitate before some impossible climb, a mile of treacherous shale, a slippery precipice, or an ice-cold river ford, she followed James without question and egged him on with corny jokes and genial insults. They got along fine together.

Often terrified, I followed them for very shame until we three alone, on a day of bitter wind, reached a howling ledge where a band of mountain goats eyed us with suspicion, like sober, bearded deacons interrupted at their worship. We did not disturb them but gazed down on the prairies of Canada laid out, flat and geometrically squared, in autumn's yellow carpeting all the way, it seemed, to the Atlantic. Even James, who had seen everything in the Rockies, was silent on a peak of his private Darien.

After we had slithered down to camp, he drew me aside to make a statement for the record. "That gal of yours," he said, "she's a likely little gal." In fact, she was at least ten years his senior. But concerning women, men, horses, and weather, the important things, he had sound views, matured by long experience in unlikely places.

From him we learned some lessons in mountain craft that were useful on the trail, and even more valuable in our memories. He taught us how to throw a diamond hitch, to make a fire of wet wood, to boil tea for ten full minutes, with the flavoring of pine needles and smoke (a fair substitute for alcohol in an emergency), to crush turkey grass and apply it on outward cuts and bruises, an unfailing Indian antiseptic more sovereign than Shakespeare's parmaceti.

When I was attacked by some internal microbe and could hardly ride or walk, our two distinguished doctors, lacking drugs, were no help but James brewed a rancorous concoction of wild strawberry roots. Next morning I felt well enough to start the day's march on a breakfast of a dozen pancakes seasoned with the purple nectar of huckleberries.

James's craft was humble but he had mastered it completely, and it satisfied him. That, I reflected, was the great difference between his kind and the city men of business and politics, whose craft could never be mastered and satisfied none of them in the end.

Over the years Dot and I had followed some strange guides to some strange camp grounds. Now they have been improved by motels and swimming pools, our trails blacktopped, our silent lakes enlivened by speedboats, the loon's haunting cry heard no more. We sought the wilderness year after year not only to please ourselves but to educate our children in disciplines taught nowhere else.

The young learn fast. When Joan was ten years old and Robert seven both could ride like veterans and preferred horses to bicycles. Soon Joan became her mother's equal in outdoor cookery and Robert excelled me as an angler.

Though a simple calculation, wisely never made, would show that each trout we ever caught must have cost about five dollars per pound or more at pre-inflation figures, the investment paid high, uninflated, and untaxed dividends. The children's extramural education, we thought, had been as useful to them as all their years in school and university. So their lives, and their children's lives as well, have demonstrated.

The Cariboo, the Chilcotin, the Dry Belt, the hidden lakes of the North Thompson aswarm with trout in autumn snowstorm, the Skagit River, then undammed and approached only on foot, the Kootenays, the Okanagan, the rain forest of Vancouver Island, the lonely mountains of Wyoming—all these regions and many others now familiar to the tourist we explored at leisure, just following the latest rumor of fish and scenery, maps ignored, time and expense quite incidental.

Before we stumbled by chance on Riviere's ranch near Pincher Creek, Alberta, and persuaded him to take us into the Rockies, our camps had been mostly in British Columbia. Now—an ugly thing for any British Columbian to admit, an act of local treason but in truth undeniable—we beheld a land unique in Canada for its splendor and for the glorious eccentricity, not to say lunacy, of its natives.

The rolling, brown, mammary swell of the foothills against the white fangs of the Rockies, the foaming rivers and erratic weather, were not so well known in those days as they are in the age of oil and gas shortages. But Alberta has always been unique since the days of Sitting Bull, the first Mounted Police, the Whoop-Up Trail, the cattle barons, and the whisky traders. That short and violent history bred a maverick people, almost a separate species, their political affairs erratic like the climate, their ambitions unlimited, their youth everlasting.

In the town of High River a remarkable old man gave us some inkling of these regional mysteries. Billy Henry was as unlike the conventional cowboy as he could be—no more than five feet in height, close to ninety years in age, mild in manner and speech, his gnarled face still aglow with health. This last survivor of the original Alberta breed had lived through the great days, ridden the empty, unfenced range, taken a herd of 150 cattle all the way to the Yukon gold rush without losing a single one, and known the immortal Bob Edwards before his *Calgary Eye Opener* had begun to titillate and scandalize the nation.

Henry's life seemed to him quite commonplace, nothing, as he said, worth writing about. For his companions, however, all now gone, he had a touching admiration, his eyes misty when he spoke of them. Groping for the right words, he finally uttered a comprehensive verdict. "They dreamed big," he told me. But even Alberta's dreams were to be exceeded by its future affluence when it struck oil.

The dreams of High River's most distinguished citizen were somewhat different. We traced Mrs. Hughena McCorquodale to her editorial desk in the office of the weekly *Times* where she was simultaneously reading proofs, talking on the telephone, and fabricating a shapeless bundle of tobacco and paper which might be intended for a cigarette or an incendiary disaster. Though old, she was still beautiful, a dainty china figurine, a lady of culture, elegance, and acid wit, misplaced, as we thought, in a little cow town. We were wrong. She had been placed exactly where she belonged to preserve the muniments of her region, among them and most precious, the only complete file of the *Eye Opener*. Better than anyone else since her friend Bob Edwards, and without his occasional lapses, she expressed in print the foothill mores and commanded, like a queen, the worship of the Highwood Valley folk.

We were fortunate enough to meet her often in the home of Bill Mitchell, whose novels were best-sellers, his televised "Jake and the Kid" already national figures, and his three wandering horses a menace to all the town gardens as they committed what Mrs. McCorquodale delicately termed "errors of toilet". Bill's fictitious characters, it soon appeared, were no more improbable than the living inhabitants around him.

Bert Sheppard, on his big spread and bachelor's establishment beside the river, was a throwback to the great days, the finest horseman, bronco buster, and judge of cattle ever known to Billy Henry, himself the supreme judge of those arts. Further up the valley Dave Diebel, with only the help of his wife and children, had carved a model ranch out of the forest on the Rockies' eastern slope and their life, except for some modern machinery, differed very little from that of the pioneers.

These two men disappointed us at first sight, since they bore no resemblance to the cowboys of the old myths or even to the synthetic cowboys of Calgary who wear high-heel boots and have never ridden a horse. Bert and Dave were scientific agriculturists, experts of animal husbandry and practical economists with strong, unconventional views on politics. They regarded the movies of western romance with tolerant amusement, rodeo performers with contempt, and their occupation as a business like any other.

Of course it was not. Their adventures involving frozen cattle, grizzlies, forced winter marches, and sudden death could be extracted from them only by long nights of questioning, and then were told in reluctant snatches not, they warned me, for publication in my bloody newspaper. Dave, in particular, was annoyed by a printed report that he had recently killed a grizzly with a club when, in fact, it had been a small black bear that ate too many calves. But its hide on the wall looked very large to me.

It had taken us a considerable journey to reach the Highwood country — some fifteen thousand miles by automobile from Halifax, with detours too many and absurd to be remembered. I forget now even the year of those wanderings but they were hard work before they ended.

For three months, through the Maritimes, Newfoundland, Quebec, Ontario, and the Prairies, I drove while Dot took notes for my intended book whenever a usable notion struck me. If this was not an ideal way to write a second book on Canada, and a mess of magazine articles as well, it was a good way to rediscover our country some dozen years after the first.

Since the cities, their problems, inhabitants, and future, had produced libraries of books, royal commision reports, and political tumult in sufficient abundance to set everyone off in a comic quest for "the Canadian identity" (which had long been established by the nation's daily life) we avoided the main highways and, with a few accidental exceptions, the men known to the public. Having neither the wish nor the ability to duplicate the work of expert researchers with superior equipment and less aversion to facts, we kept to the side roads, seeking out Canadians as people, not statistics—a distinction often overlooked in government.

Beyond the frail civic boundaries we encountered many such

people whose lives are seldom reported by the newspapers or in *Hansard*. Fishermen in the Newfoundland outports; farmers on the niggard Gaspé coast, the lush Ontario meadows, and the central plains where cities rose slowly from the horizon like approaching ships at sea; oil drillers in Alberta; trappers in the North; ranchers in the foothills; lumbermen, miners, and fruit growers in British Columbia—all these innumerable Canadians, their names and varied accents, are now a blurred montage of the nation, without sound track or technicolor. But perhaps we learned something about the silent minorities that the urban majorities have yet to discover, and will never see from the paved highway.

Two people who had worked long and successfully to make themselves Canadians stand out from this multitude. We found Julius Kratz and his wife, Hanna, in Fort Vermilion and they fully justified our drive of several hundred miles, on rough gravel roads, north of Edmonton.

Both were physicians of the highest credentials in Germany, they had opposed the young Nazi Party, eluded Hitler's secret police, and after narrow escapes at gun point, and too much hunger, poverty, and heartbreak for any lifetime, had settled in a forlorn village beside the Peace River. Now, hardly richer than their Indian patients, they gave them the skills of modern medicine. Concerning their past they said little and counted themselves lucky to be Canadians not merely by naturalization but by a feeling for Canada deeper, we guessed, than that of the average native, because they saw it against a background of human misery elsewhere.

In the tiny but immaculate Fort Vermilion hospital an Indian child, his life saved by Hanna's surgery and restored by Julius's therapy, seemed to us a kind of humble testament to them and their chosen country that I could never put adequately into words. We drove back on that weary road, our car weighted down with mud, the windshield cracked by flying pebbles, our faith in Canada renewed, if it needed renewal, by a piece of evidence obscure and unnoted but more persuasive, to us at least, than all the statistics.

Then a preposterous interlude reminded us that Canada had not only compassion but its own sardonic sense of humor, its deadpan native pranks despite the contrary legend of Canadian solemnity believed by foreigners.

In some dusty Peace River town a meeting had been called by a political party, its name unknown to us. Since a provincial election was under way in Alberta, we attended the meeting, as faithful reporters, to get, if possible, a spot of local color or even a slight understanding of grave public issues.

Our count showed fifteen persons, male and female, assembled in a stifling room above a general store, the local forum of democracy. But the candidate, whoever he might be — a fact never disclosed — had failed to turn up and no substitute was available. Facing this awkward dilemma, the chairman, a friendly, bustling fellow, received a timely impulse. To my horror he announced that I, a visitor well known by everyone present, had agreed to deliver a speech — and then in a hoarse whisper, asked my name.

Possibly because my own sense of humor was touched and Dot dared me to meet the challenge, I stood beside a kitchen table which supported a cracked jug of water, an unwashed cup, and many ancient mice droppings. As Dot informed me later, it appears that I actually spoke for about an hour, though I have no idea now what I said and probably none when I said it. Nevertheless, I registered one vital point. With the vague notion that the meeting was in the Conservative Party's interest, I thought, as a notorious Liberal, that it would be only good sportsmanship and a fair partisan compromise to launch a scurrilous attack on the theories of Social Credit enforced by the government of Alberta.

The practitioners of democracy, like fifteen stranded mackerel, listened without a murmur or movement and when I had finished they filed out and faded into the long June twilight without a word of praise, blame, or thanks. They had their sense of humor all the same. For afterward we learned at the hotel, from its grinning manager, that I had addressed a loyal Social Credit audience.

Such is my scrambled recollection of the proceedings but I may have the political parties confused, my shrewd arguments reversed. It doesn't matter. If I had preached communism, fascism, or anarchy, those sound democrats would have listened, mute, impassive, and mackerel-eyed. Unlike foreigners, they understood a Canadian family joke when they heard it and, within the national family, no comment seemed necessary. The joke was on me.

After we had come home at last it was not easy to sort out our myriad impressions while the publishers set impossible deadlines, insisting, as is their habit, that copy be delivered the day before yesterday. In a half-built cottage at Shawnigan I wrestled with Dot's mass of notes, all neatly written as I had dictated them, but now almost meaningless. The result, *Canada, Tomorrow's Giant*, satisfied the publishers in Toronto and New York, the writer much less.

My second book on Canada was more coherent and knowledgeable than the first because our travels had been wider. It was less flamboyant and gushing because the intervening years had made the country known to itself and also tamed my youthful hyperbole. As that incorrigible word twister Justice Wilson remarked, I had turned to lowperbole.

That, I suppose, is the price that age must pay for a little extra wisdom, or maybe just weak avuncular tolerance — a dubious bargain. As they grow older all men find successive layers of reticence and caution encrusted on them like the annual rings of tree growth, protective covering for the ego.

Only in youth, when he has little to say, does a man dare to shout it aloud in public. My shouting days were past. Anyhow, I had shouted enough already and over-exposed my big Canadian dream without crystallizing it in my own mind. But then, who ever does?

Still, age has its compensations. If I had seen Canada with less panting ardor, I had seen it with more realism from the sobering heights of the mountains and other lonely places, more confidence, and a clearer sense, too, of its fortunate but vulnerable place in the crowded world.

27

The Sun at Its Rising

One morning in August 1963 breakfast was served early to three men on a handsome yacht moored to a Vancouver wharf. For me, hundreds of others, and the whole newspaper industry of Canada that meeting would be critical and, in the end, fortunate. Max Bell, of Calgary, owned the yacht but seldom used it. With him was Dick Malone, of Winnipeg, who now managed F.P. Publications, which he had invented and which Bell and Victor Sifton had financed. Why I had been invited to the confidential breakfast party was not explained — perhaps because I was the oldest horse in the F.P. writing stable, and the least garrulous.

With no advance warning, in his usual abrupt fashion, Max informed us that before noon he would purchase control of the *Vancouver Sun*, Canada's second or third largest newspaper (its circulation and wealth much more impressive than its quality).

While Dick had long ago planned this acquisition, he doubted that the time for it was yet ripe. As the three of us knew, many men had tried to buy the *Sun* and all their offers had been rejected. We had seen Sifton fail some years previously when his bid of a capital sum far less than the paper's future annual profits was accepted by the owners' agent. With the purchase cheque already in the mail from Winnipeg, the deal fell through because Donald Cromie had persuaded his mother, at a midnight family conference, to retain the controlling shares inherited from her late husband. Dick and I supposed that Don, now rich and in full charge of the property, would not sell it in these prosperous times.

But Max was not deterred by our doubts, Victor's earlier disappointment, or any obstacle of mere money. In Alberta he had learned to dream big, spend lavishly for what he wanted, and pay on the nail. As a youngster he had borrowed from friends to buy his first paper, the Calgary *Albertan*, and the loans were repaid exactly twice over, despite the lenders' protests. Max enjoyed money, knew how to make it, shared it with his associates, and called himself a simple promoter, though he was much more than that.

Assuring us that the *Sun* could be bought at the right price, he left Dick and me on the yacht while he met Don to talk business in millions of dollars. We awaited his return, quite certain that, like Victor, he would fail. Within the hour he was back, the necessary stock transfer had been arranged, his big dream, and Dick's, vastly expanded.

It did not seem to concern me. Then, to my amazement, they asked whether I would like to be publisher of the *Sun* when Cromie, as was foreseen, had retired. Knowing my solitary habits and unclubbable disposition, they doubtless made the offer more out of friendship than serious intent and expected it to be declined with thanks. Of course it was, immediately.

At an earlier age I might have grasped such a glittering chance, but now I was old enough to realize that I could not do the job properly, did not want it, and was well satisfied with my cosy editor's chair in the *Victoria Daily Times*. Besides, Dot would never have agreed to live in Vancouver, even if I were willing. For every reason, professional and domestic, the move did not tempt us.

After returning to our Shawnigan camp I assumed that the new F.P. property would get along all right without my help. So I went about the summer's vital business, which, at the moment, was the construction of an extra woodshed. From its incomplete roof Dot summoned me to the telephone to hear Dick announce, politely but firmly, that I would become the Editorial Director of the *Sun* while remaining on Vancouver Island. As I had long watched houses, governments, and nations burn from the far side of the street I could now watch a newspaper being rebuilt from the far side of Georgia Strait. Neither of us knew how this could be done or what my title meant, if anything, but these questions, Dick said, were of no consequence. Everything would work out all the better for being undefined.

Thus casually, almost absurdly, on a rustic party telephone line, the matter was settled with no written word because, between us two, none was needed. It suited me fine and has continued, to my immense benefit (although I cannot speak for the paper), until the present day. But it could not have lasted without a second and more practical decision by Max and Dick. They found in Stuart Keate, my faithful friend and patient boss on the *Times*, an admirable publisher for the *Sun*, who succeeded where I would surely have failed, even if I had been so foolish as to try.

These flimsy arrangements must have looked ludicrous to the men and women of the *Sun*'s editorial staff. Though I had worked for Don's father, Bob Cromie, before most of them were born, and again under the great editor Roy Brown, they hardly knew me. Dick was a complete stranger, Stu a Vancouver native but long in exile.

So they waited, I imagine, for a sudden explosion of hirings and firings, which never occurred, and probably for an attempt to make their gaudy, boisterous paper a dull echo of the sober *Winnipeg Free Press*. This was the last thing that Dick, Stu, or I intended. All we wanted was a *Sun* with more content and less froth, more world news and less local crime, more accuracy and less sensation. In short, we wanted a paper worthy of Vancouver. We knew that such a transformation must take time, and that the public would not observe it until the process was complete, if then.

Any reputation, good or bad, is hard to live down and in a newspaper it always outlives the facts. But once Stu had taken hold and found an able managing editor in Bill Galt a new *Sun* gradually emerged, year by year.

While it fully satisfied none of us in a business where satisfaction is fatal, it was a paper so different from its earlier slam-bang news treatment and feverish headlines as to be almost unrecognizable if you looked over the old files in the library. Since the public did not remember them, the change, and the thought, work, and money invested in it, were little noted. Perhaps least noted of all, except by the men and women directly concerned, was the fact that Dick never interfered with them and never complained of our editorial views though they often contradicted his own as publisher of the *Winnipeg Free Press*.

His instructions to me were vague and rather charming. I would just keep an eye on things, feel my way, and write what I pleased. It all sounded quite simple but in truth it would have been impossible if Stu had not made a second wise choice of lieutenants. With my hesitant approval, he appointed Cliff MacKay to the key job of editorial-page editor. I had hardly known Cliff, but it did not take me long to realize that he was the best all-round newspaperman in my pretty wide experience.

His Scottish descent was proclaimed in a tall, lean figure, a granitic poker face, an habitual silence, and a writing style of stubborn analysis mixed with pungent metaphor and pawky ridicule. Through all the dizzy Sunrises and Sunsets of his long career he had become the most admired man in the shop, a companion for the old, a confessor for the young; also an innocent bigamist after marrying, in his youth, a lovely lady and the paper. To both he was equally faithful.

With him I soon established a routine all the more practical because it was absurd in theory, had no rules, and we alone understood it. If anyone inquired about our methods, as visiting firemen usually did, Cliff and I gave them a stock reply — we operated *in absentia* by telephone, telepathy, and extrasensory perception. Our little joke was substantially true.

Every morning, often several times a day, we talked on the telephone, argued the meaning of the latest news, and set the editorial line for the next day. Unworkable as the system appeared to outsiders, it worked. But it could not have worked at all without Cliff's uncanny knack of taking some scribbled notes, checking any errors of fact, and refining our joint conclusions into letter-perfect copy which, unlike mine, needed no revision. His editorials seemed to flow automatically from his typewriter as if they had been already written by someone else and he merely transcribed them from inaudible dictation. Few of his colleagues, perhaps only I, knew how much study, toil, and sometimes midnight torture went into the finished product.

Our work together looked easy and I dare say the news side thought it so when, after a whole day, Cliff or his excellent assistants, Jim Dyer, Mac Reynolds, and others, might each fill a scant half-dozen inches of space, and I produced nothing more than a couple of ideas or a signed column now and then. But the real work could not be measured in space and was mostly the dull homework of intensive reading.

As in my boyhood, when we boiled a gallon of maple sap to get a cup of syrup, now the meagre trickle of copy was discouraging and, at a time of bitter national politics, it could rarely be sweet. For we had set out from the start to make the paper politically independent, at the sure cost of alienating, often enraging, all parties.

Since the Liberal politicians had long regarded the *Sun* as their unfailing ally, our independence seemed almost treasonable to them. They got used to it after a while and began to understand that a word of approval from a non-partisan paper was worth more than a hundred from the voice of a party, a word of censure more dangerous. Yet the legend that the *Sun* was a Liberal organ lived on even when it had publicly supported the election of a Conservative government in Ottawa. Newspaper legends die hard.

Whatever the politicians of various stripe may have thought of us, they came to the office in constant parade and knew that their confidences, some quite astonishing, would not be broken. Stu, Cliff, and I had made it a rule not to advise public men, only to listen and make our own judgments in print, fairly we hoped. No doubt we were sometimes unfair and our conclusions wrong, but so were the politicians, the best among them, in that endless exchange of truth, error, and groping surmise, which is the essence and justification of the democratic process.

At any rate, the responsibility for judgment, right or wrong, was ours alone. Stu, busy with a publisher's thousand office problems, seemed to trust me and I trusted Cliff. Nobody meddled in our affairs. As a director of The Sun Publishing Company I often suspected that my fellow directors, all practical men of business, disagreed vehemently with our political and economic opinions but they did not exert the slightest pressure on us to change them.

It is impossible, of course, to gauge a newspaper's influence by its circulation or by the number of subscribers who read its editorials, always a minority whose opinions are divided and fluctuating. But assuming an editorial audience even as low as ten per cent, that minority colors the mind pattern of any town and largely determines the political mood of the majority. If it can be reached and influenced, for the most part unconsciously, the slow, accumulating effect is powerful—an osmotic seepage of ideas, a two-way process that influences reader and writer alike. Certainly the newspaper will have no influence at all, however wide its circulation, if it does not vigorously advocate opinions of its own. In the end they are likely to be most influential if they are most unpopular in the beginning.

As Dafoe used to say (and practise), a newspaper should never seek editorial popularity but shoot its random, burning arrows into the air without knowing where they will land. It must be satisfied if, now and then, one of them hits a distant target and lights a minute flame. With a favoring wind the fire may spread. In such unlikely places all the great movements of society have begun.

Whether any arrow hits a target the marksman will seldom learn immediately, but when he finds eminent politicians and humble neighbors boldly advancing, as their original inspiration, a thought that they could have read only in a certain paragraph of type he knows that some minds have been ignited.

I also remembered Dafoe's further dictum that "a journalist is hardly an authority upon anything unless, perhaps, upon the appraisal of the drift of public opinion." Even by that modest standard I did not feel much personal assurance. My worst defect as a newspaperman or judge of opinion, I now realize, was an unfailing ability, or weakness, to see at least two sides of any question, often three, or more. How I longed for Dafoe's certainties, possible in his age of relative simplicity, beyond reach in ours.

Lacking them we tried to keep the paper open to ideas of all sorts, including the most fanciful because they might be tomorrow's truth. Shot by remote and unknown archers, the arrows of patient reasoning, angry rebuke, and sometimes unexpected commendation hit us in volleys day after day. Wise or foolish, they were a sign of any newspaper's health. The most ferocious criticism, however, must come from inside the newspaper, from its own hired hands, if it is to be healthy. On that score we never lacked free medical advice. No icon of politics, economics, or morals, above all, none of our editorial views, were sacred to columnists like Allan Fotheringham and Paul St. Pierre, physicians, surgeons, and soothsayers who amused, informed, puzzled, and infuriated Vancouver by turn.

Len Norris, the *Sun*'s most cherished asset, seemed incapable of hurting anyone, even the editors. As a unique comic genius he had made himself a Vancouver institution but behind the gorgeous social satire of his cartoons the public never saw a shy and gentle soul, cringing from his fame. Len's imaginary world, with its cast of demented politicians, idiotic policemen, raging tycoons, palpitating dowagers, baffled housewives, and helpless taxpayers — human nature spiced and squirming on the half shell — set the town laughing every night. Then, in a quick double-take, it guessed, rightly, that the artist's own laughter was often close to tears, his view of the civic comedy rounded with a sigh.

How all these men and women, and many others with names, jobs, and skills unknown to the public, could put together their huge bundle of news, comment, and entertainment — something for every taste — remained a mystery to me, a minor miracle in any big newspaper and accepted like the sunshine or the rain. I did not understand the mechanics of it, the iron deadlines, the instantaneous decisions, the controlled frenzy, and was careful not to inquire too deeply lest I become involved and put to work.

My absence went unnoticed and unregretted, my job was what I made it, and my time could be used or misused as I chose. Probably my colleagues thought most of it wasted. In fact, I worked harder than ever and produced more copy when, starting at eight in the morning in my own house, I had a long, clear day before me without interruptions. But over the years every column, every editorial for the *Sun* or the *Free Press*, every paragraph and line took more time, just as the tools of garden and forest weighed more. The days and years became shorter, the casual affairs of life speeded up until I felt carried along in one of those old-time movie chases like a Keystone Cop, driven by camera tricks with flickering and terrifying velocity.

This, I suppose, is the experience of all men, though no young man can believe that it will ever touch his life. Actually Dot and I were not yet very old in years, and on Canada's hundredth birthday we still felt young, even if we didn't look it. The nation has its own memories of that proud centennial, but ours were rather different with the vividness that clings to the trivial and absurd after the important is forgotten. Thereby hangs a queer little tale involving two of the world's major statesmen.

Mike Pearson had offered Dean Acheson the Prime Minister's apartment in the jumble of concrete blocks known as Habitat, beside Montreal's Expo 67, and Acheson had brought with him his wife, Alice, his daughter, Mary, and her husband, Bill

Bundy. As there was a third bedroom in the suite, Dot and I were invited to occupy it. On Mike's instructions the hospitality of the Canadian government was liberal but, at Acheson's request, not overdone. No public fuss and feathers were to spoil the American guests' private holiday.

When a discreet official guide led us through the bewildering exhibits only one person in a vast assemblage of all nations spotted Acheson. A bright-eyed woman from England instantly identified him as Anthony Eden and respectfully asked for his autograph. Without a qualm, Acheson accepted the British statesman's name and dutifully signed it in the woman's notebook. As he explained to us afterward, Eden was an old friend and wouldn't mind an innocent forgery. Moreover, in common politeness and international amity, he could not bear to disappoint a loyal subject of the Queen.

It was exhilarating to see and impossible to describe the exhibition's wonders. It was also exhausting, even though we were smuggled quietly into the various pavilions by a back door while the crowds stood in line at the front. "This," Acheson whispered to me, "is privilege, and privilege is wicked. Still, you learn to endure it."

We endured it quite well but sometimes, at the end of the day, were too tired to leave the apartment for dinner. Then Dot and I discovered that Acheson's cookery was as skilful as his diplomacy. The world which knew the statesman would hardly have recognized the chef in a frilly pink apron frying ham, sausages, and eggs, the only comestibles we had been able to find, and serving them with the sleek urbanity of an English butler.

Our housekeeping went along smoothly until, one night, returning from a late restaurant dinner, we saw Habitat roped off, police guarding the entrances, all admission prohibited. A bomb, it was said, had been planted in the building to explode at any moment and kill U Thant, Secretary General of the United Nations, then in residence. Having nowhere else to go, we spent the next hour riding back and forth on Expo's aerial railway and at last, no bomb being found, were admitted to the apartment. But we had no sooner retired to sleep than a shattering blast awakened us. In our night clothes — a memorable sight — we rushed to the window. It was another false alarm. The explosion had come from a noisy, harmless display of fireworks on the Montreal skyline.

Next morning, however, a more serious accident occurred, an international incident Acheson called it. At breakfast I pushed back my chair and it broke a pane of glass, about six inches square, in an empty book case. Acheson fixed on me that wintry eye which had so often frozen the marrow of the world's governments.

"This," he said, "is a very grave affair. You've damaged the property of the Canadian government and it's sure to accuse us, its American guests, of deliberate sabotage. God knows where the thing will end — probably war on the undefended border. There's only one way to stop it. You must write a confession to the Prime Minister of Canada and take the consequences."

So I did, a few days later in England, offering payment for the damages to the extent of five dollars. On our return to Canada after a long absence, I received a stiff official note from Mike in Ottawa. At that moment he was embroiled in one of his frequent parliamentary crises, the minority government faced defeat, and its leader's hands were full of trouble. But he had taken time in the midst of these alarms to inform me that his cabinet had deliberated at length on my crime. While I might plead mere accident, this was no excuse. Besides, I had implicated four distinguished American visitors and embarrassed the friendly relations between Canada and the United States. Nevertheless, to avoid worse mischief, the cabinet had decided to hush the matter up for *raisons d'état* and, out of secret funds, would pay the cost of repairing the book case, estimated at $3.75. On no account, he warned, must this ghastly episode ever be mentioned in public. If he were still present I think dear old Mike would forgive my breach of his confidence.

28

The Happy Breed

Like all successful nations, Canada has nourished itself from the beginning on a rich diet of fables. Many have been imported from abroad, but two are indigenous, home-grown, and long venerated.

As the twentieth century opened, Prime Minister Wilfrid Laurier told his fellow countrymen that it would belong to them, and this fable, a target of boyish ambition, served its purpose well enough until the century reached a disreputable old age when no one cared to claim its ownership.

The second fable enjoyed a longer life and is still in a fair state of health. It holds that Canadians, by virtue of their history, geography, character, and language, are the natural interpreters, honest brokers, and skilled fixers between Britain and the United States, with a unique understanding of both. Churchill's discovery that Canada was the "binder-together of the English-speaking peoples, the linchpin of peace and world progress" has been so well remembered, so deeply imbedded in the national psyche, that even to question it is a kind of sacrilege.

But as I grew older and more irresponsible I began to question it; began to suspect, indeed, that the average Canadian like myself, while knowing the Americans reasonably well, is peculiarly unfitted to judge his British kindred — unfitted by too much hereditary affection or antipathy. He looks at Britain through spectacles too rose-tinted or too dark, with eyes glazed by too much sentiment, nostalgia, and ancestor worship, or else he is convinced that the New World is far superior to the Old, which has always been smugly certain of the opposite. Thus some Canadians, knowing little of Britain, grossly underestimate it. A few others so grossly overestimate it that they move to London and become more British than the Queen — second-class, hermaphrodite Englishmen, just as immigrants to Canada often become more passionate in their Canadianism than the natives, more xenophobic, and more worried about the nation's identity.

Canadians, in short, have suffered from wrenching transatlantic ambivalence, of which Pierre Trudeau is the most vivid symbol. A French-Canadian isolationist in his youth, he becomes in his maturity the ardent defender of the Commonwealth; perhaps, as he thinks, its rescuer at the historic crunch of the Singapore Conference in 1971 when some non-white African nations quarrelled with Britain because it was selling arms to South Africa. Canadians have always ridden on this erratic see-saw of prejudice and counter-prejudice, even if they are unaware of it.

Behind such imponderables the hard fact, sure to color if it does not dominate all future national policy, is that Canada no longer finds a mighty British Empire or a coherent Commonwealth around it to make weight against the power of the United States. The historic equilibrium, if it ever really existed outside mere rhetoric, has disappeared, the weight shifting almost entirely to the American side. Canada has ceased to be a fulcrum, if it ever was, and is now a power in its own right, with all the profits, liabilities, and lonely risks that power, even on a minor scale, must involve.

If these facts had long been clear to Canada's better historians, they were slow to infiltrate the misty region of politics and my own mistier thoughts. But, after some delay, they prompted Dot and me to re-examine a Britain greatly changed since our young days when, for two innocents abroad, it was mostly the dream-stuff of springtime daffodils, cosy village inns, Gothic towers,

London theatres, and, least forgettable to hungry travellers, those prodigious afternoon teas, with sticky tarts and Devonshire cream, the tribal feast of gods and Englishmen.

Anyhow, our investigation of Britain, where we would be neither Britons nor exactly foreigners, made a tolerable excuse for two visits, now intermingled in my memory and reported here wildly out of sequence. If the whole project was ridiculous it justified, in my employers' simple minds, a generous expense account and a heavy drain on our own resources.

As a strategic base we chose a London hotel so antique and genteel, so haunted by eminent ghosts, that it admitted no guest without a personal introduction from some trusted sponsor. Having passed that test, we were kindly treated, with special attention from a soldier of two world wars and, by his looks, the surviving identical twin of the late Lord Kitchener. This faithful servant operated an elevator of Victorian design without mechanical power, only a cunning arrangement of ropes, cogwheels, and hidden, underground gears that worked spasmodically, defying the laws of physics. Here, we saw at once, was a parable of some import if we could read its meaning. For Britain itself, at this time, seemed to defy historical law, above all, the law of economics, and showed every outward appearance of success.

It had now reached what the popular London press, with more than its usual indifference to the obvious truth, called the "Swinging Sixties" or "The New Elizabethan Age" when any neutral stranger could see that Britain, after its age of heroism, had entered an age of trouble and weakness unlike any previous age in its experience. But we were not neutral. We were Canadian. No doubt for that reason it took us longer than it would take a real foreigner to assess the state of the British mind, and then our assessment may have been as stupid as that of the newspapers and the government.

My own first tingles of doubt began, I think, in the most unlikely place, the noble avenue of Whitehall where, with Downing Street and Number 10 just around the corner, the might of the Empire had always resided. From the outside, the stately row of government offices and shiny brass door knobs still looked invulnerable.

In one of those offices, its dinginess planned with care, its curtains faded, its furniture well worn, I found a large rumpled and thickly tweeded man lounging in his chair, feet on desk, the incarnation of the upper class, the rural squire come to town on some disagreeable business and impatient to leave it. Actually Richard Crossman was a left-wing socialist, a gifted journalist, and the Labor government's leader in the House of Commons. He may have had no lasting impact on British history but his ideas shook me.

"The trouble, don't you see," he said, only half in jest, "is that we had the bloody bad luck to win the war."

The fortunate losers, he explained, had found nowhere to go but up, and up they had gone while the British victors, deluded by victory and misconstruing their future, had taken things too easy. And now they talked, even Crossman's government talked, of solving these problems by entering the European Common Market — a mad proposition in theory and hopeless in fact because President de Gaulle would never allow it.

Though Crossman's senior colleague, George Brown, had told me the precise opposite earlier in the day, and said that Britain would and must join the Market, despite Prime Minister Harold Wilson's firm resistance, this breach of the cabinet's fictitious solidarity was not in the least surprising. I had grown accustomed to it in Canada, perpetual war behind the soundproof door being the norm of any cabinet.

What surprised me was Crossman's vision of his people's rightful place in a changing world. They should settle down, he said, forget all the nonsense of European unity, and make some money like the Germans and the Japanese. Britain, I gathered, must become a larger Sweden or Denmark, a snug nest well feathered against the cold winds of competition, prosperous, contented, efficiently managed by a wise socialist government (which had yet to glimpse the economic catastrophe then only a few years distant).

Such, in the clever, frustrated mind of Crossman, was the ideal Britain, John of Gaunt's other Eden and demi-paradise brought up to date, Blake's modern Jerusalem in England's green and pleasant land. After the age of heroism, Crossman wanted peace, stability, and well-earned comfort—a modest goal within Britain's reach if, he added, the labor unions and allies of the government did not destroy it by their impractical wage demands.

Listening to this strange little homily without comment, I thought it more important than it sounded. Here, in a contemporary voice, spoke Walter Bagehot's typical Englishman, the "enjoying man" whose enjoyment was now suddenly in grave doubt. And here also, it seemed to me, was the core of Britain's dilemma, the choice between a sheltered island economy and the brutal competition of the mainland; between Europe's comparatively high living standard and a lower British standard, as reckoned in the questionable measurement of money; between the genial life of Gaunt's happy breed behind their moat defensive and those other breeds newly united, despite their ancient quarrels, in building a miracle of technology if not of happiness.

That choice was quite clear, except in the contrived confusion of politics, and it was inescapable, but it had not been made yet. Britain, in fact, was trying to have it both ways, seeking to preserve, untainted, the old hearty customs of the cricket field, the rich man's long week-end and pheasant shoot, the poor man's jolly pub and summer holiday at the seaside — all the immemorial, neighborly habits and unwritten contracts among members of the breed that, over the centuries, had made the distinct island civilization.

Yet Britain also wanted the domestic conveniences, luxuries, gadgets, and so-called progress that only the machine, the assembly line, the giant business corporation, and the disciplined work force could supply. No matter what enjoying Englishmen like Crossman might say, the contrary ambitions did not fit together. The two-sided proposition was impractical on the face of it and Britain was in danger of falling between the island and the mainland stools.

To be sure, I did not clearly understand these dangers then or foresee the years of controversy surrounding them to the present day. I did see, however — anyone could see — that the dilemma involved much more than economic bookkeeping. For Britain already had felt the results of another choice made by worldwide forces outside its control.

It had lost an empire, long too costly though its costs were long disguised, a military, political, and financial burden too onerous for any nation's strength. It had ceased, in a single lifetime, to be a great power and now, a secondary power at most, observed the American and Russian colossi bestriding the world, and the defeated Germans and Japanese richer and more powerful than the victors of war. It had watched the first, short-lived Commonwealth, governed by white men and their democracy, turn into a loose fraternity of undefined purpose with a non-white majority, much of it lacking democratic experience or even aspiration.

Finally, Britain had undergone, at home, since the war, its own social revolution. It had seen its class structure remodelled on new lines of cleavage, its wealth redistributed, its whole society in flux—all this without violence or loss of civil liberties, a process that, in other societies, had often spawned chaos, dictatorship, and war. In Britain that process could not be measured by economic figures or government policies, only by the temper of the British mind. But I guessed that few democratic societies, perhaps none, could endure such strains without breaking. Britain had made serious miscalculations. It had not broken. A miracle of the spirit, I thought, as great as the European miracle of prosperity.

Having examined the London of politics in regrettably shallow fashion, I ventured into the City, the London of finance.

There, I found myself at the elegant luncheon table of a rich business firm whose hard-working directors had gathered for noon refreshment. Clever men, they seemed to me, gentlemen all, and probably enjoying men, too, after business hours, with the cool manners, the obligatory understatement, and the careless-looking, exquisitely tailored uniform of their kind. Rumpled tweeds and untidy political notions might be accepted in socialist Whitehall, not here.

Though both places were hospitable, sympathetic, even politely interested in Canada (which neither understood), both exuded a sense of natural British superiority, not offensive, never expressed in words, but unquestioned, like the weather. From Agincourt to Dunkirk the gentlemen of England had often saved it and would save it again, with their lives if need be. For the present, however, they were engaged in the peaceful tasks of business where the needs of a new day had yet to be met and, as I surmised, were greatly underrated.

Eating the gentlemen's excellent viands, drinking their costly wine, and hearing their brisk, confident talk, an outsider might suppose that Britain was saved already and required no more heroism, only better economic management and a reliable Conservative government of free enterprise. The socialist aberration would soon pass. Things would get back to normal. The times were out of joint, but who could put them right and repair the egregious follies of the politicians if not the gentlemen turned businessmen?

The luncheon lasted some two hours without any note of alarm, any sense of pressure. While the idea was outrageous, and unworthy in a guest, I began to feel that I was attending a convention of Britain's unconscious and patriotic grave diggers. Possibly more stimulated by the wine than the conversation, I remembered Shakespeare's wry dictum, in the voice of the immortal digger at Elsinore, that Hamlet's madness would not be noticed in England because all Englishmen were as mad as he. But I also remembered what Shakespeare was really saying—

that madness of the native sort had always been England's higher sanity, its true secret of survival against all the facts.

The gentlemen around the luncheon table undoubtedly had some of that old folk wisdom in them. For all their cheerfulness, they were wiser and sadder, they feared more for their country, than they could admit to an outsider. And I knew, in any case, that the City was no more typical of Britain than Wall Street of the United States, or Bay Street of Canada.

There is, of course, no typical Briton, no typical man anywhere. Still, after my exposure to the right wing of British society I thought it prudent, as a corrective, to sample the left. So I dined well and expensively that night with a man reputed to be the most powerful of Britain's labor-union leaders, a burly, earthy, red-cheeked man, emeritus of the Midland soccer field, graduate of union politics, veteran of war. He was just as surprising in his way as the leaders of industry. I could see in him no class consciousness, either of humility or pride, no bitterness against the rich, and, obviously, no understanding of Britain's economic peril.

His duty was to fight the big-business interests, to extract from them all he could get in wages for his unions, but the argument, he reminded me, was within the national family. Its members often quarrelled but they understood one another. As blood relatives, brothers and sisters, they would settle their affairs by their own methods, with maybe a spot of trouble now and then, but nothing very serious.

Yes, some of the rich were fiddling with their taxes and expense accounts, driving their Rolls-Royces, and playing their little games, but what did all this hanky-panky amount to? Not much so long as the workers got their fair share, and they certainly were going to get it. The unions and a sensible government would see to that. Leave things alone, he seemed to be saying, and they would turn out all right in the end. They always did.

When I left him at midnight in Piccadilly Circus he felt little pain, or any alarm for his country, but it amazed me to think that a man so honest and so totally mistaken should speak for the anonymous millions of working people who already had begun to drive the economy toward disastrous inflation. I suspected also that after the Swinging Sixties the class lines would harden with the economic facts, and the real class warriors would emerge to challenge the moderates and punish the rich. These notions required no prophet. They were plain enough already, and depressing.

Piccadilly Circus itself depressed me at midnight. Once the dwelling and shrine of the imperial myth, with a tiny bronze Eros, of all things, to personify a far-flung and ever-loving Empire, the Circus now looked as squalid, tinselled, and cheap as Times Square, twin degenerates, fake symbols of two great civilizations. And Soho, teeming with queers of several sexes, reeking with the stench of alcohol, drugs, and depravity, would frighten any stranger. I had felt safer, and much cleaner, in the nighttime slums of Tokyo and Taipei. London of the New Elizabethan Age was swinging for sure but to what end? A stranger who saw only London's dark, nether side, a small fraction of the whole, might well imagine that Britain was swinging on a frayed rope, over an abyss. Fortunately Dot and I knew better, and our confidence was soon reinforced from the light upper side. At some stuffy cocktail party we met a royal eccentric, a model of all the old-time British virtues and probably the handsomest inhabitant of London, whom we had known slightly when he was Canada's Governor General.

The Earl of Athlone had once regaled a small dinner party in Government House, Victoria, with his considered opinion of Winston Churchill, then leading Britain's wartime government and, by his genius, saving its future. As commander of the Royal Military College at Sandhurst, Athlone had tried to make the young Churchill into a soldier (a "solja" in the Governor General's native accent). That was a hopeless task. Churchill could not be taught the arts of war. Still, he had done his best and succeeded in the lesser arts of government.

"You know," Athlone remarked, "Winston does quite well in politics. Quite well. Makes a very good speech, too. But nevah make a solja!"

That verdict was pronounced with deep solemnity and obvious regret. No, Churchill would never make a soldier. Now, in postwar London, Athlone recalled at considerable length his happy times in Ottawa. He told us that he did not read books, but his wife, the lively Princess Alice, read many and summarized their contents for him. Among them she had lately reported my book on Mackenzie King and Athlone thought that I had portrayed him quite accurately.

This reminded the Earl that his Prime Minister had appeared lonely and miserable in a desolate bachelor's house. Pitying King's misfortune, the Athlones had always invited him to Christmas dinner at Rideau Hall and he had come with pathetic eagerness. A damned sad thing, what?

"Ah yes, King!" Athlone observed in his soldierly drawl, as if he had just made a tragic discovery. "Poor King just missed being quite a decent feller!"

These memories must have stirred the Athlones to unusual depths. They invited us to dinner, perhaps with the same motives of pity that used to rescue the lonely King, but we just missed our one chance of a lifetime to enter Kensington Palace because I had to make a speech on the appointed night to a gathering of exiled Canadians who were as much bored as the speaker. A damned sad thing.

It reminded us of another thing, whether sad or comic we could not decide at the time.

The voice on the telephone that morning, some years earlier, was the gruff, staccato voice of Lord Beaverbrook, the Canadian exile of narrow but undoubted genius who had so long explained Britain to itself through the multi-million brass trumpets of his newspapers. Would we care to dine with him next evening at his place in Leatherhead? The invitation was not explained but of course we accepted it. Few Canadians would be strong enough to resist Beaverbrook's other genius for crude flattery. In our case it had the extra power of mystification. His limousine picked us up at our London hotel and a somewhat ridiculous episode followed.

In the flesh the Beaver closely resembled his photographs in the newspapers — the heavy-featured, lumpy face, the familiar scowl or grin — but he looked smaller, older, and more fragile. None of the dozen guests around his glittering table were known to us. Most of them bore titles of nobility, evidence of wealth, and a languid, well-bred expression of incredulity at our presence.

The host alone was in a sprightly mood. Disregarding the servants, he marched about the circle to pour a precious French vintage into our glasses. For mysterious reasons of his own, the great man unbent. But what were Dot and I doing here? What possible designs could this extraordinary personage have upon us, whom he had never seen before and probably would never see again?

That mystery was still unexplained when the Beaver ushered his company into a private theatre for a showing of the dullest movie ever made, which he escaped by falling immediately asleep in the back row of easy chairs while the rest of us, perforce, endured the ordeal awake. It lasted until midnight, the host dozing peacefully like a real Canadian beaver in hibernation. Then drinks were served and a footman informed me, in a discreet whisper, as if it were a state secret, that a car was waiting to take us home. Still no explanation.

But as we were shaking hands at the door our host drew me aside into a dark corner and announced that I would be given the privilege of writing the official biography of his friend, the late Viscount Bennett. Though flabbergasted by such a ludicrous proposal, I managed to protest that it was far beyond my powers. I knew little of the deceased Conservative Prime Minister, had met him only once, disagreed with his views, and, besides, was branded as an inveterate Liberal.

Unused to disobedience, the Beaver swept my objections aside. I could write exactly as I pleased, without interference from him or anyone. All Bennett's papers in the University of New Brunswick were at my disposal, all my expenses would be paid, and any fee that I cared to ask. Surely I could not refuse this splendid chance? Nevertheless, in what must have been my finest hour, I did refuse. Bennett's loyal friend was not to be put off so lightly. Would I think it over and meet him next day in his London flat? My momentary courage oozed out. I weakly agreed.

The Beaver was alone, except for a majestic butler, in something like an acre of apartment space when I called on him. His wee figure snuggled in a massive couch like a kitten, or perhaps a gargoyle on a Gothic façade. That man was irresistible in his homely charm, his innocent look, his language of sham modesty. But knowing that the Bennett biography would be his, not mine, I somehow resisted. The kitten no longer purred, the gargoyle ceased to grin as I left.

Still, he forgave me after a time, hired a girl reporter from Victoria on my bold recommendation, and sent me a letter of greeting with a curious postscript. For my information, Mackenzie King had been gravely ill on his last visit to London and, realizing that he must soon die, had summoned Churchill to his bedside. As the two men were parting forever, King asked Churchill, his old comrade of war and peace, to kiss him. According to Beaverbrook, "Churchill obliged." I could print this historical footnote if I cared to.

It is printed here not because it has much importance to history but because it may show the combination of kindness, ferocity, and mischief which made Beaverbrook such a paradox, the narrow genius wrong about all the broad events, the dreamer of obsolete imperial dreams, the well-meaning misinterpreter of Canada in Britain, and Britain in Canada. Yet another damned sad thing.

Though London, as always, had alternately enchanted, puzzled, and bored us, it was time for Dot and me to seek the open countryside. There the riddles of politics and economics might fade before the light of common day, the wisdom of inexpert humans. And there, at least, we would never be disappointed.

On our third circumnavigation of the island by automobile we found it little changed at first sight since our two previous tours—the same cold solitude and warm-hearted folk of the Scottish mountains, the Lake Country painted in transparent water colors, the brown and mellow Cotswolds, the sunken roads of Devon, the jagged coast of Cornwall, and, by chance in Brighton, the opposition Conservative Party assembled, the former Establishment aligned on the platform like a family photograph, somewhat faded, Edward Heath orating in fluted Oxford cadence en route to Downing Street for temporary residence—all this fresh and sunny side of Britain, and the look of the happy breed itself, reassured us.

Over the whole island, as nowhere else, hung that luminous glow and vague mixture of sight, sound, and scent which only the English poets could describe, and they in fragmentary hints. But of course Britain had changed, changed deeply and irrevocably, in both landscape and mind. Only our naïve Canadian nostalgia would have made us expect anything different.

Nevertheless, we were still innocent enough to be a little surprised by the screaming, savage football crowds, the empty, silent churches, the narrow country lanes jammed with automobiles, the main highways as loathsome and dangerous as any in America, the lovely village squares and ancient wool markets turned into ugly car parks, Mr. Pickwick's lodgings into brassy motels, the cockney jokes of Sam Weller and the sublime incoherence of Mr. Jingle buried with them.

The latest instalment of the Industrial Revolution was inevitable, a process that had begun right here, on this island. But it differed from the earlier instalments because Britain did not lead it now, was falling behind new rivals in the competitive race, borrowing abroad, no longer fully paying its way in the world.

Less obvious, beyond the stranger's understanding, was the mood of the people. By long-taught discipline they hid their feelings under a mask of jollity, or sometimes of snobbery, their defence of a shyness so vulnerable that it must always be denied. Did they understand what was happening to them and their nation? No, they did not.

The same may have been true of all peoples in all times, but modern Britain could afford miscalculation and indifference to facts far less than most Western nations that were richer in goods if not in happiness. And how much additional happiness was Britain truly gaining by its own accretion of paper wealth, gadgetry, and social welfare? How much was lost to the real treasure of the happy breed?

If the stranger had no right to answer such questions we were perfectly sure of one fact usually misunderstood in Canada — the British people as a whole cared hardly a devalued tuppence for the Commonwealth, despite all ceremonial gestures to the contrary. Why should they when the Commonwealth's non-white majority cared so little for them?

We had looked at them in our shallow fashion and wondered, at the end of a sentimental journey, whether any place was left for Bagehot's enjoying men and women in a world where enjoyment was sacrificed to sleazy affluence, impossible expectations, and the fallacy of the human being as an economic creature. Maybe there was no such place anywhere. Or maybe these strange islanders would find it again at home like archeologists burrowing in a neglected midden.

Anyhow, in all the hard days to come, we never doubted, though we could not prove it, that Britain would pull through, changed but indestructible. The economy might dwindle, the pound and the living standard fall, governments appear and disappear, but the people, Britain's only sovereign asset in a naturally poor island, would still be there. They would endure by no plan, theory, or logic but by their own methods, baffling, often infuriating to strangers.

With these hazy thoughts, and now accompanied by our daughter, Joan, who had been nursing flood victims near London, we flew to Paris, the historic residence of pure philosophers, where logic is faithfully worshipped, and revolutions, as a consequence, are not always peaceful.

It intrigued and bewildered me to watch that worship at first hand. During a three-hour lunch in their favorite restaurant, the French experts of the Common Market argued its problems for my benefit and, with rising Gallic agitation, disagreed about the economic figures, quarrelled over decimal points, wrote sums in billions on the table cloth, and sent me reeling, statistic-drunk but otherwise fairly sober, along the Left Bank of the Seine.

These men's energy, almost their agony, in the hunt for logical answers and exact mathematics, was sobering, even alarming, after the amiable illogic of Britain. Still more energetic, efficient, and dogged in their work habits were the Germans, who, as Crossman had told me, fortunately lost the war and found nowhere to go but up. Anyone seeing them at work could understand why they had gone up so fast. These workers possessed not only the almost demonic strength that came from defeat and despair, but an innate loathing of idleness that made them soul-sick when unemployed, the natural prey for madmen like Hitler. They also possessed their old instinct for self-discipline at the bottom and superb management at the top, centred at that time in the chief architect and technician of the economic miracle.

When I met him at Bonn, Ludwig Erhard had yet to become Chancellor of the Federal Republic, but he seemed to have no misgivings about its future or his own (even if the American government had already christened him "the Rubber Lion").

This rotund and beefy man, with his crimson cheeks, ready

laugh, and cold eye, plied me with his special brand of celluloid-tipped cigars and warm soda water which he relished and I pretended, somewhat unconvincingly, to appreciate. Through a good-looking female interpreter he spoke enthusiastically of the Common Market's past achievements as no more than the preface to larger success and higher prosperity. Britain would soon join it, of course, to complete the European family, but he emphasized over and over again, lest I misunderstand him, Europe's vital dependence on American power. Here, I thought, was the postwar Germany embodied, the marriage between state planning and free enterprise finally consummated, the transatlantic man flushed and chortling at the summit of his personal success and yet, in the highest political office, doomed to failure.

From Bonn we travelled so far by plane, train, and automobile into Berlin, Austria, Holland, Belgium, Spain, and Portugal that I forget where we went and why, all the memories now disordered and homogenized. Eventually we landed in Geneva, and happily, at this point, Mary Bundy arrived to take charge of Dot, Joan, and me. With her as navigator, interpreter, and guide, we drove through the dizzy passes of the Alps down to Italy for immersion in art galleries, cathedrals, treasures, and ruins innumerable until they became, for me at least, only a smudge, a surfeit of culture and history, an exhausting bore.

The ladies enjoyed themselves and improved their minds while I tried in vain to grapple with the scintillating minds of Italian bureaucrats who then appeared to believe that their economic miracle would last forever. When one of the leading official economists informed me that the United States government was clumsy, stupid, and naïve, making every possible mistake in Europe, I felt my North American gorge suddenly rise and I reminded him that Italy, after its era of fascism, was hardly entitled to cast the first stone at its rescuer. In justice to him and his newly democratic government I record that he had the grace to blush scarlet and apologize.

Such chaotic travels occupied much of our own Swinging Sixties and ended our marriage. One day, early in 1969, as I was listening to a dull House of Commons debate from the Ottawa Press Gallery, a friend came to tell me that Dot had just been killed near by in an automobile collision.

That event left a grief unimaginable until then, quite incomprehensible to anyone who has not experienced it, and forever incurable. Enough to say that anything good in my life, and all its happiness, were of Dot's making and without her had no worth or substance. As I write these lines, in a springtime garden that we planted together long ago, I seek some words perhaps half worthy of such a woman. Others have found them but I cannot. Wordsworth's farewell to his Lucy, lacking better, must serve, ". . . and oh, the difference to me!"

29

The Bridge

In saying a last farewell to Mike Pearson as a friend, I knew it would be also farewell to the era that he had personified in Canada, an era of mighty achievements and mean failures, of problems unexampled in human experience and all unsolved. The man of many parts — boy soldier, university professor, diplomat, prime minister, and world citizen, the man whom every Canadian knew and no friend really understood — was dying. I found that fact hard to grasp as I approached his house in the autumn of 1972. But the end, they had told me, was not far off and he knew it.

The end. What, besides his life, was ending? Countless other things, some to be remembered in the history books, some forgotten, some distorted.

Mike's years of political power had ended already, without his regret. The guard not only of persons but of ideas had changed in Ottawa and he could not discern the new guard's aim and purpose, much less fathom the mind of its commander. Pierre Trudeau, though stimulating and highly gifted, was an insoluble conundrum to Mike. Each man respected the other, but between them there could be no deep personal affection, no real meeting of minds.

Contrary to the accepted version, Mike had done nothing behind the scenes to make Trudeau the leader of the Liberal Party in the convention of 1968 that had chosen an untried and little-known successor. The retiring Prime Minister had insisted only that some French Canadian must be a credible candidate and, privately, was inclined to favor Jean Marchand, without indicating his preference to anyone. Marchand was ignorant of Mike's view, did not want the leadership, could not have succeeded in it, and wisely supported Trudeau. From then on everything went well with the party, even better that Mike had hoped.

All this he had told me when, after a flight around the world in 1969, he landed in Vancouver and, by arrangement, we met at the airport. That day, for the first time, I saw him deeply angered.

In Japan the Canadian Embassy had given him the cabled text of a speech recently delivered by Trudeau in Canada and, reading it, Mike was outraged. Trudeau had said, in effect, that until his government revised Canada's foreign policy it had been largely dominated by the thinking of military men — a brutal, unjustified attack on Mike's record, the very opposite of the truth, whether Trudeau knew it or not. Perhaps the speech was written for him and he had recited it without foreseeing its consequences to a friend. If so, that was a lame excuse. Mike as the captive of the generals, a cold warrior, a stooge of the military-industrial complex? The notion was comical but insulting.

In his Vancouver hotel room Mike said that as soon as he reached Ottawa he would confront Trudeau and demand an explanation. But how could such a speech ever be explained? He doubted, anyhow, that the new Prime Minister, in office for less than a year, yet understood much about foreign policy.

Trudeau, it should be remembered, also doubted his own knowledge. As late as December 1971 he described himself to an American journalist as "not even an informed observer" of international politics. Mike, of course, did not anticipate this humble admission. He was thinking then only of Trudeau's speech and it seemed to Mike the result of a larger mistake—the theory that foreign policy could be neatly and specifically codified like some financial exercise. He did not anticipate, either, that it would be so codified, with a grand flourish, in six glossy booklets in June 1970. They did not satisfy Trudeau (though some of his language was unmistakable in them) or much impress the public.

As Mike viewed foreign policy, it should set broad objectives and pursue them within that context, but it must be kept flexible because circumstances varied from year to year, almost from day to day. He had no quarrel with the government's objectives when, in fact, they had always been his own, but why did Trudeau limit his ground of future negotiation? Why encumber himself with positions fixed in advance and likely to be outdated by events? And why (as Mike said after the booklets were published) had the government declared that Canada must cease to act as a "fixer" in disputes between its foreign friends when the old role, which Mike had often played (and thereby won a Nobel Peace Prize), was respectable, sometimes inescapable?

Mike's point was soon demonstrated. Within a year of issuing his policy papers Trudeau found himself playing that very role at the Singapore meeting of the Commonwealth and, as he had good reason to believe, saved it from disruption. Against all his earlier protests he had necessarily become a "fixer" far more skilful than anyone expected.

While these events were not yet foreseeable, Mike instinctively distrusted not the Trudeau government's aims but its new operating methods; in both foreign and domestic affairs it now relied on flow charts, blueprints, and tidy, long-term schedules. If the government put the right data into the computing machines the right answers would come out, but who could tell whether the data were right when so many accepted facts were so frequently wrong?

The well-meaning experts of Mike's own government, he said, had prepared such diagrams for him, with figures doubtless accurate at the time but transient, since they were subject to sudden change with changes in the nation and the world. He had studied the diagrams, plastered all over the office walls, an impressive sight, and then done what he had to do, seldom what he wanted, in the political art of the possible. Well, Trudeau, a quick student, would learn that art for himself by experience, the only reliable teacher.

Thus Mike rambled on at Vancouver, his spasm of hot anger soon cooling. In this or some previous conversation he recalled his memorable and misunderstood speech as Prime Minister urging the American government to interrupt the bombing of North Vietnam as an exploratory step toward a negotiated peace. Why, I asked, had he chosen to make the speech in the United States where he was, after all, a guest with a guest's obligation to his host? Why had he given no advance notice to his cabinet or officials? And did he realize how gravely he had offended Lyndon Johnson?

Yes, he had seen the President's rage at first hand. It was expected. But the reasons for the speech were simple enough, though Mike could not explain them publicly. He had decided on a constructive intervention, a piece of friendly advice from a good neighbor, knowing, however, that if the External Affairs Department heard about his plan every possible objection would be raised to stop him, the cabinet's discussions leaked, the whole initiative bungled before it could begin. So he had told nobody, not even his closest colleagues.

Besides, he added, with an air of mystery, he had been pressed to intervene by persons highly placed in the United States government who were loyal to Johnson but disagreed with his Vietnam strategy and hoped to moderate it. This suggestion had come in particular from one Democratic statesman still powerful in Washington today.

Mike did not regret his speech. It had been controversial but useful, like that other famous speech, before he became Prime Minister, warning the United States that its future relations with Canada would never be easy or automatic. These things were awkward but, he believed, necessary in candor between friends.

Sometimes he applied his solitary methods in Canada's own

internal affairs, to the confusion of enemies and friends alike. When, for instance, he announced the decision to adopt a new Canadian flag his cabinet, while it agreed on the policy, heard nothing of the announcement before it was made. One of his chief lieutenants, who happened to be in my house that night, was astounded by the news on the radio.

Again, the decisive Scarborough Speech, which Mike wrote and rewrote alone in the middle of the night, to favor nuclear weapons for Canada reversed Liberal policy without warning and finally ensured Diefenbaker's ruin a few weeks later. Yet many Canadians assumed that Mike was naturally timid and knew little of practical politics — this late-blooming politician, who in only four years (with Diefenbaker's invaluable help) destroyed the largest Conservative electoral majority since Confederation.

Mike's outward simplicity was always deceptive. It covered a multitude of contradictions. If he looked soft and easy-going and lacked the butcher's instinct that had served King so well (also the egomania common to most successful leaders), he could be very tough when necessary. But his anger quickly passed. It was difficult for him to hate anyone for long. A more serious flaw in politics was his often poor judgment of men. With all his experience, he chose some thoroughly incompetent colleagues and found it almost impossible to get rid of them, though he did dismiss a few weak sisters, usually by promotion to the Senate.

His worst mistakes were in the field of economics. Even when coached by the great economist John Deutsch he could never put his heart into the dismal science. As part of the job he crammed his memory with statistics for recital in some penetrating speeches now forgotten. But to him economics was territory more foreign than foreign affairs and he ventured into it with reluctance, as seldom as possible. If his economic mistakes, based on the counsel of the best experts, were many and grievous, those of his successor have dwarfed them. As economists both men have proved failures as dismal as the science.

Some months after our meeting in Vancouver I asked Mike whether he had confronted Trudeau to protest the attack on earlier Canadian foreign policy. Rather sheepishly, he admitted that he had dropped the argument. In fact, he had rarely talked with the Prime Minister, who had never consulted him on any government business. Following a long silence, Trudeau had called at Mike's house, near midnight, so worn out by a hard day in Parliament that Mike could not bear to question and badger him. The man had more than enough trouble already. Even to this day, perhaps, Trudeau does not know how deeply he wounded his predecessor by a single foolish speech.

Now, in the autumn of 1972, at a moment of political crisis, Mike was dying. Trudeau had just escaped defeat in the recent election by a narrow, humiliating margin, had been morally defeated after one term of office, and had suffered the first serious failure of his life. He seemed unlikely to survive the new Parliament of minorities. My few confidants in the government doubted that it could last through the winter.

The crisis interested me only as a reporter who had seen many others. I was not thinking of politics as a taxi drove me to the Pearson home. I was thinking of old times with the young Mike in Ottawa, of my marriage there almost half a century ago and its end in the same place, of the friends who had come and gone, of the good days and the bad.

Where, I asked myself, did Mike fit into the historical sequence far longer than any man's life? With all his successes and failures, all the effervescence that screened his haunting doubts, what purpose had he served? As I saw it, he had been a kind of bridge not merely between two governments but between two distinct stages of Canada's evolution. In one half of his nature he was a product of Mackenzie King's stage, conditioned by its innocent political and economic doctrines, assured of human progress. In the other half he was a modern, ahead of his time, a member *ex officio* of the avant garde.

More clearly than most men around him, he knew that society

was not changing only on the surface; it was changing at its deepest roots, changing organically in defiance of all the textbooks and known rules. While no man could measure the time frame of this process, he was convinced that society, if it were to remain free, must steadily reform its institutions, governing methods, and economic arrangements or finally explode from the mounting pressures within it.

He would not live long enough, of course, to see the outcome or perhaps have much influence on it, but he must try at least to relieve the immediate pressures. So, in a stumbling, experimental fashion, with fallible expert advice, he invented safety valves of social legislation. Some experiments worked. Some failed. Some were wise and permanent, others impractical and temporary. Mike's ambivalence — the old-fashioned precepts and the new-fashioned radicalism—produced many curious results, most of them vague, three specific.

First in order of occurrence was his downright internationalism, his view of the world as totally interdependent and his work of persuading Canada to play a bold part in it. He was a Canadian nationalist, too, but his internationalism differed from that of men who tried to isolate Canada from the world as if, like a tender hothouse growth, it needed artificial protection against killing foreign frosts.

Such men, often as sincere as he, and close to him in politics and friendship, were tormented by contrary and irreconcilable impulses. They preached the brotherhood of humanity, defended the ideals of the United Nations, but at home their devotion to Canada sometimes became crude xenophobia, poisoned by visceral antipathy to the United States and colored by a sick inferiority complex.

Mike had more trust in his nation. He believed that Canada must and would survive on the resources of its land, above all, of its character. Lacking the character, no synthetic props could sustain it. With him nationalism and internationalism were not contradictory but complementary principles. He saw Canada as

a piece of John Donne's "maine", but a separate, individual piece, most useful to the whole, and to itself, if it nourished its own native talents in the general interest. Yet this hopeful world view was always overhung by his deepening alarm at mankind's prospects. He knew for whom the last bell might toll.

Second, Mike committed himself and the nation to more and more domestic reform as he grew older, the costs and other consequences sometimes recklessly ignored. The tide was running that way and, apart from political necessity, his instincts ran with it. By the rough definitions of politics, he stood to the left of the Liberal Party's gravity centre. On the foundations already laid by King and St. Laurent he vastly expanded the structure of the welfare state and prepared the ground for what his successor (even more reckless of costs and catchwords also) would call the Just Society.

Third, Mike grasped more clearly than any English-speaking politician of his time the so-called French Fact, which had baffled so many prime ministers. With King it had been a nagging fact of practical politics to be managed at second hand through his surrogates, Lapointe and St. Laurent. With Mike it was a human fact to be understood and treated in human terms.

As an Anglo-Saxon he could not hope to understand it as the people of Quebec understood or, more accurately, felt it. But unlike most of his colleagues he understood by instinct rather than facts that Quebec was nearing a dangerous crossroads; and he believed that if it separated from the nation, Canada, fatally split, could not survive at all. In his considered opinion an English-speaking state with a French wedge between its eastern and western segments was a chimera, an absurdity. All three segments must be sucked, sooner or later, into the larger state on their southern flank. Canada, for all its diversity, was one thing or nothing.

Unlike King, who had his Lapointe and St. Laurent, Mike lacked a working political apparatus to deal with the French-Canadian crisis. He could never find, until Trudeau's late arrival, any adequate Quebec partner, or build that unwritten coalition which alone can successfully govern a dual state. Moreover — a fact often overlooked by his critics — he never controlled a majority in Parliament, and his government lived at the daily risk of defeat.

With all the weakness of his position, he knew that the Quebec explosion must be defused somehow, and his method of defusion was typical, the method learned in foreign affairs. By establishing the commission on Bilingualism and Biculturalism he bought precious time, educated the rest of Canada in the French Fact, and began to change the climate of politics subtly, gropingly, but decisively. Without this breakthrough, more of public attitude than of official policy, a breakthrough possible only for an English-speaking leader, his successor's career would have been impossible, whether Trudeau understood that fact or not.

Trudeau's thoughts and talents still had time to reveal themselves in the first real test of his career, now suddenly facing him. The final thoughts of the dying man would not be revealed. The book that, even in his last days, he was vainly trying to complete, tells something of those thoughts but not much. Despite his apparent candor, they would die with him. And yet I was sure, whatever he thought, that his life, public and private, had always been governed by the faith learned in the parsonage of his boyhood, a faith all the stronger for his silence.

These speculations, prejudiced by friendship, churned in my memory as I knocked on Mike's door and his wife, Maryon, opened it. Though he did not rise from his chair, Mike looked as well as ever, just a little tired, and he greeted me with his familiar grin as if nothing untoward had happened to him. The chubby pink cheeks, the gaudy bow tie, the wrinkled suit, the wry chuckle—everything apparently was the same. But of course we both knew that everything had changed forever. Of that change neither of us spoke. No words were needed.

Instead, Mike talked briskly about the recent election, the slim chance of the government's survival, the breaks of the game that he had managed to survive. In this entirely unforeseen crisis Trudeau had consulted him, over lunch at 24 Sussex Drive, but Mike's advice, he told me, had been of little use, only that a constitutional crisis like that of 1926, and any embarrassment to the Governor General, must be avoided. How Trudeau would meet his test Mike did not know and it occurred to me again that he had never really understood Trudeau, either.

The talk continued for an hour or so, small talk and chit-chat masking the truth known to us both, while Maryon, a brave woman, served tea and helped us maintain an air of cheerful banter. Only once did Mike mention his health and then obliquely. He hoped that his doctors would let him go to Florida and escape Ottawa's cold winter, and for a passing instant, the desperation of the hope was written on his face. I pretended not to notice it, and hastily interjected some light gossip of politics until Jack Pickersgill came to pick me up in his car. When I shook Mike's hand and left his house both of us understood that we would never meet again. Jack understood, too, but said nothing. There was nothing to say.

30

The Cockpit

Even in its physical look the Ottawa of Pierre Elliott Trudeau seemed to proclaim the new time and the new man, both misunderstood. Goldwin Smith's "sub-Arctic lumber village converted by royal mandate into a political cockpit" had become a town when I was young, a typical Canadian small town of quiet homes, friendly neighbors, and a few national politicians, prime ministers among them, who walked to work or rode on the rattling street cars. Now it was a city, would soon be a metropolis, and must always remain a cockpit. Not just governments and their policies but everything else had changed, most of all the mental climate; changed from sleepy isolation, starched respectability, and cautious thrift to a mood of euphoria, financial profligacy, and swaggering display.

The jungle of new buildings to house a teeming bureaucracy, the ghastly and pretentious External Affairs complex named, with peculiar irony, for Lester B. Pearson, the brassy skyscraper hotels, the abstract monuments of twisted steel, debris from some bankrupt boiler factory (the supreme artistic masterpiece evidently the bleeding entrails of a monster from the deep), the glittering cubes of concrete and glass, the spacious parks and leafy driveways no doubt were a triumph over nature—magnificent, worthy of the nation here symbolized, an architect's dream. But to a rude countryman from the hinterland they were not a Canadian dream. They smacked too much of imports from foreign lands. Downtown Ottawa was beginning to look too much like an imitation New York.

Still, it suited its new inhabitants, whatever they thought of the new Prime Minister. Like Washington and other capitals it lived as a splendid parasite, the kept woman of taxpayers who would never enjoy her charms. With a mixture of pride and horror, remote Canadians saw their symbol grow by ceaseless division and sub-division, cell on cell, layer on layer, bureau on bureau, empire on empire, the empire builders of officialdom hungry for money and power, the ravenous appetite of all capitals.

The public service was said to be, and I believe it was, as competent and honest as any in the world. It had recruited some men and women, the anonymous, unappreciated élite, who overworked themselves, forestalled the government's worst mistakes when they could, and served the nation, as I well knew, at great personal sacrifice. But the mighty organism contained many of a different kind who enjoyed an easy life at public expense, and it had grown so top-heavy that no cabinet minister knew what it was doing beyond his own cell. Nothing could arrest its amoeba-like proliferation governed by Professor Parkinson's first law, the work force always increasing faster than the work.

Of the Ottawa I had known as a cub reporter only the tangled towers of Parliament were left intact like a natural, almost a vegetable, growth out of the virgin soil, stern and cleanly against the steel-blue Gatineau sky, Gothic remnants in the age of the political baroque.

If that noble silhouette was unchanged I could recognize few inhabitants of the Hill. They had changed with the changing nation and helped to change it. Their ideas, ambitions, work habits, even their dress and shop-talk idiom, reflected a nation that had suddenly discovered wealth and luxury out of all proportion to its numbers. And yet the nation's happiness was marred by a comical misgiving. It still longed for that identity long established and endangered by none except Canadians themselves.

Canada's unwonted affluence was strong liquor and had gone

to Ottawa's head, inflating its currency and its ego; the inevitable hang-over lurked not far ahead, unforeseen and denied even by the most sober politicians. All this reflected more than a change of generations. It was a change, at least on the surface, in the nation's personality. For some three centuries Canadians had endured poverty, hardship, and grinding toil and they had thriven on it. But as events were soon to show, they had not learned how to manage prosperity or to keep it.

The nation's spirit level, as I saw it, had fallen while its gross national product and all the other misleading indices continued to rise. The oldest Canadian legend—a folk not especially gifted with talent but shrewd, self-disciplined, and plain-living, their feet firmly on the ground — had been questioned for the first time. Had the legend ever been true? Was it now repudiated? Or was the current mood only a brief aberration, Ottawa a false mirror? Whatever the truth might be, the mood, temporary or lasting, was more accurately reflected by Trudeau than by any other Canadian and already he had miscalculated its consequences.

On his arrival in Ottawa, rather like an Unidentified Flying Object from outer space, some of us wrote that the Canada existing until then would not have accepted such an exotic leader, different from any before him. He was acceptable, we solemnly concluded, because that Canada existed no longer. Our glib cliché possessed some truth but, as it turned out, less than we (and Trudeau) supposed. Had we underrated, or overrated, man and nation? Even today that question is unanswered.

All Canadians have seen Trudeau in the flesh or on television, the handsome-homely face, barometer and weather map of an April day, instantly registering sunshine or storm, tenderness or ferocity, hope or dejection. Many Canadians have known part of this strange man. None, so far as I can find, has known the whole. After my infrequent talks with him I cannot claim to know much more than I learned, or surmised, at our first meeting on the verandah of his mother's house when the nation had not yet heard his name. But no one who reads his books and miscellaneous writings can fail to see that they issue from a mind of extraordinary brilliance, perhaps the finest piece of machinery ever applied to Canadian politics.

Of the politicians I had watched, only Meighen could approach Trudeau's intellectual power and, as Prime Minister, Meighen had failed, his talents mired in King's oozing quicksand. So, too, the brilliant Edward Blake had lost his way in Macdonald's murky labyrinth. If Trudeau had a special talent of his own, that was no guarantee of success. Wrongly directed, it could easily become the opposite.

Canadians have always been distrustful of genius in their leaders and, by 1972, were disenchanted with Trudeau after only four years of dwindling Trudeaumania. Already the genius had been misdirected. The philosopher who read and admired Lord Acton had not been corrupted but he had been deceived and dazzled by power and he loved it. His moments of outward arrogance, much clearer to the public than his inward humility and hypnotic charm at close range, his philosophical soliloquies on street corners, his angry outbursts and cheap sneers, sometimes his downright vulgarity, produced political disaster and personal anguish. He blew his second election single-handedly.

Only in trouble, the first he had known, did the full measure of the man appear. He blamed no one but himself, learned from his mistakes, and patiently began to repair them against all the obstacles of politics, his own wounded pride, and the despair of his friends. By 1974 the original public Trudeau, remade with an authentic mien of penitence, had re-won his majority — a single-handed feat of recovery equalled only by Macdonald and King in their times. And quite apart from his own abilities Trudeau's time, a time of trouble everywhere, had necessarily made him a pre-eminent figure in the nation's history. But still a mysterious figure.

After all this victory, failure, and revival Canadians did not understand him. Among the diverse Trudeaus warring in a man lonely and rebellious by nature, a public man by chance, it was never possible, at any given moment, to tell which one was dominant, if he knew himself.

The scholar who asserts his faith in reason and logic but often defies both in childish petulance; the Christian who believes in man's immortality; the athlete and outdoor adventurer whose body looks small and frail but is all muscle and sinew; the amateur of judo who grapples with the best masters in Japan and receives their sacred black belt; the student of Western philosophy and occult Eastern religions; the actor of roles innumerable from comedy to tragedy and slapstick farce; the ungifted orator who reads the speech writer's dull script boring himself and his listeners and then, in a spontaneous aside, whispers some flashing epigram or announces some major policy of state — such a human creature of infinite variety prompts both friends and enemies to speak and write much nonsense about him.

To that nonsense journalists like me have made minor contributions but he has made far more. The short-lived gimmick of "participatory democracy", the mocking gibes at the "work ethic", the promise to "wrestle inflation to the ground" just before it rose into the stratosphere, and the occasional lapses into language unprintable were unworthy of man and office. But they did not conceal the brilliance and sweep of mind given more to solitary adventure than to practical business.

In that spacious horizon there were odd lacunae. If, for example, some researcher of malignant disposition analysed Trudeau's speeches on economic affairs the record would sound like the conversation at the Mad Hatter's tea party or a monologue by the Jabberwock in person. The truth, as I surmise it from his public utterances and some pretty sharp argument with him, is that he rarely turned his highest faculties to bread-and-butter concerns and never really understood them as less brilliant minds often do in the scramble of daily life.

While skilfully interpreting the nation's dual communities to each other, at least in words and constitutional niceties (with political results unknown at this writing but likely to be momentous), he grossly mismanaged the economy, deranged the federal budget, and was late in recognizing his greatest blunder. Then, in sudden fright, he declared that Canada must change course or go "down the drain". He admitted the risk but did not acknowledge his large share of blame in setting the wrong course.

No admission was required. The facts spoke for themselves. Under his government the state of the nation — economic, financial, and mental — gravely deteriorated in spite of all his attempts to improve it. Certainly all this was not his fault. Every Western nation suffered more or less the same decline. But it was over-dramatized in Trudeau's case by the exaggerated hopes of his early days, his mercurial temper, his warmth, charm, and modesty at close range, his outbursts of arrogance in public, his weakness for the cutting phrase, and his habit of making things appear better, or worse, than they were.

Thus in 1974 he rejected with jeering contempt the strategy of price controls advocated by the Conservative Party, defeated it on that issue, and in the next year imposed the same controls himself. After his brazen reversal, carried through with a bland air of consistency, he began to talk of a "new society" and to suggest that free enterprise had ceased to work in its existing form. There was much truth, though nothing original or very alarming, in these ideas when no economic system, free or otherwise, worked according to plan, and society had long been changing fast everywhere until it was already new by any known definition. But with his lean and hungry look Trudeau thought too much aloud and for a party leader such thoughts were dangerous. They terrified the primitives, divided the intellectuals, and confused everybody.

If the leader had advanced far ahead of his followers he knew that more critical dangers must soon face the people if they refused to think. While he was at his best in goading the public's mind and stimulating its imagination, as no previous leader had dared to do, the exercise could destroy him in the end because abstract thought is the least salable commodity in politics, the last extremity in troubled times, to be avoided at almost any cost, even the cost of thoughtless disaster.

Considering the economic and political misjudgments that marred his flashes of insight, it is impossible to guess whether history will regard Trudeau as a success or failure. But why the misjudgments? My own guess is that he was haunted and diverted by larger, non-economic problems which seldom interest the so-called practical politicians.

To him, or to any thoughtful man, the veneer of order and civility, the envelope of civilization itself, must look thin, tattered, and stretched to the breaking point in the world's deepening anarchy. Beside the clear threat to the whole human future the technical cant of his hired economists, which he dutifully mouthed and often garbled, must sound trivial, nearly irrelevant. Yet in all his moods, happy or despondent, he understood better than his colleagues the central fact of his brief passage through the nation's life.

He understood that civilization, even without a final war, was reeling through a revolution different not only in size but in kind from any past experience. He understood, too, that in Canada he presided over the liquidation of one epoch and the birth of another.

At the start of his first campaign, before his first public doubts, he had given an omnibus name to the hopes of the epoch, calling them the Just Society. After the second and third campaigns that fine ideal must have looked like a far-distant possibility, maybe a lost cause in his time. For his enemies the Just Society became an easy target, for him a politcial albatross in a world where the majority of humans knew only the justice of tyrants or mobs. Even in a legally just Canada, social justice, despite all his efforts and their cost, was still a future promise far short of a present reality.

If Trudeau was mistaken in the timing of his hope, he was honest in his reassessment of the world, the nation, and his own mind. If the intellectual machinery stuttered and hesitated now and then it still worked brilliantly. His problem was not to think for himself but to keep the public's thinking abreast of his own, the most important and hardest task of any leader.

One of his most self-revealing speeches described the baffling new difficulties of the task in the new revolutionary epoch. Fumbling for words understandable to the public, he said that modern society had discarded its old values and had yet to find valid substitutes. It confronted a moral void or interregnum like those that afflicted and sometimes destroyed the great societies of the past.

True enough, and obvious, but where could the new values be found and in what form? Trudeau did not say because, as a human being, he did not know. In the necessary oversimplifications of leadership these imponderables could hardly be discussed at all by more than dark hints, eloquent shrugs, calculated indiscretions, and painful murmurings.

They delighted his jeering critics, who had no clear alternative thoughts to offer, provided rich editorial fare in the Opposition press, inspired the cartoonists to dizzy flights of ridicule, and usually bewildered — or bored — most of the people. But the people began to realize that if the man was often wrong in policy he could think in historic terms, and he set them thinking, too.

This symbiotic process, the leader and the led sharing the same doubts, was conducted on a level above practical politics. On a lower level of political management Trudeau succeeded with his own methods different from those of any predecessor. After his recovery from the fiasco of 1972, he totally dominated his cabinet and turned the Liberal Party into a Trudeau Party. In his hands that ancient apparatus and Family Compact, with its secret laws, rewards, and penalties, became efficient, smug, and invulnerable for the time being, its inner frictions well hidden— for the time being.

Certainly Trudeau had marvellous luck, the luck of a Conservative Opposition addicted to regicide and suicide, but luck alone does not explain the Liberal hegemony. Trudeau, of course, had not invented it. He had inherited it from the always lucky King, the sometimes lucky St. Laurent, and the unlucky Pearson. But Trudeau worked sedulously to modernize his hereditary estate. That job had been under way for half a century.

Though most of King's supporters failed to see his purpose when they chose him, the first truly modern Prime Minister was determined, as clearly as he determined anything, to turn the Liberal Party around; since he planned a turn of some 180 degrees, the process required time and patience. King had both and, in addition, the Hidden Hand, the sure guarantor of his manifest destiny. Under this twofold guidance, slow and stumbling, the party sloughed off its historic *laissez-faire* creed, its harsh Darwinian economics, its faith in the unerring competitive market, and its hatred of big government, to embrace (and burlesque) the theories of Maynard Keynes. With Trudeau as its latest architect it went on to build the biggest, most costly, and most powerful government ever known in Canada.

Then, under a Prime Minister who had first attracted general notice by declaring that the state had no business in the bedrooms of the nation, the state invaded all the other rooms from attic to basement. The public protested the invasion but demanded its benefits and hoped that someone else would pay for them.

Something still more remarkable and less understood had happened to the party. In its transfiguration it quietly forgot, or declared in only ritual pieties like the husks of an old religion no longer believed by anyone, the oldest Liberal sacrament of Free Trade. The net result, its irony overlooked, was one of the highest tariff walls in the Western world.

This perfectly suited the great protected industries of central Canada that, for the most part, otherwise distrusted or detested the Trudeau government, but usually bankrolled the Trudeau Party for lack of a better alternative. The Trudeau government drew its winning votes from the industrial heartland, not from the old prairie and Maritime strongholds of Liberalism. But with a vacuum between the Lakes and the Rockies it was no longer a truly national party and Conservatism, barred from Quebec, was even more splintered. Confused politics reflected a confused nation.

All the circular motion of geography and necessity, of honest conviction and mere cunning, had taken a full century to bring Liberalism back to Macdonald's National Policy, which it had so long denounced. In stealing the policies of others the Trudeau Party had proved to be a peerless cracksman. From the Conservatives on the right and the New Democrats on the left it took whatever it thought useful, stuffed the booty into its infinitely expansible Gladstone bag, and, blending the contents, produced, when occasion required, a new ad hoc policy of its own, always described as consistent, lifelong Liberal doctrine.

Despite all the wriggling contradictions, there was a certain logic in the Trudeau Party's outright political pragmatism. The original Liberal charter had been overlaid by countless writings and rewritings but beneath the blurred calligraphy a pattern of sorts remained legible. If Liberalism had reversed many of its immemorial canons, it stood, or tried to stand, for its highest ideal, the collective public welfare against the privileged few, the weak against the strong, the little man against the big.

In modern dress this was still the old philosophy, though Liberalism often botched it in action, to injure no one so much as the little and the weak. And if the Trudeau Party's convolutions were designed primarily to win votes they represented in crude, bungling fashion the historic imperatives of the time. So, at least, the party believed, or hoped.

The imperatives, and Trudeau's reaction to them, could be given any label of respect or contempt. His admirers insisted that he was obeying the compulsions and exploiting the opportunities of the new age. His enemies replied that he was and always had been a scheming socialist as proved by his books, a child born to privilege and guilt-ridden by his wealth, a man dedicated and sinister. On the one hand, he was denounced by the New Democratic provincial governments in the West for his reactionary social attitudes, his apostasy to the cause of his youth. On the other, he was condemned by most businessmen for his radicalism.

In my own opinion, for what it is worth, he was neither a socialist nor a capitalist when both those smear words, like the party labels, had lost all meaning. He was exactly what he claimed to be, a pragmatist who had lost his callow illusions and had yet to find mature certainties.

In any case, the imperatives marched on, self-propelled, and the general direction of their march was becoming plain to everyone. Society, the beneficiary or victim of three contending giants, the state, the business managers, and the labor unions, moved by fits and starts toward that egalitarianism and redistribution of wealth which the rich young Trudeau had foreseen and advocated.

How much of the state's expanding power was inherent in a technological society, brittle, hybrid, and incestuous, each part dependent on all the others? How much was deliberate design? Had Trudeau's presence made any real difference one way or the other? Nice questions but unanswerable in his time.

Meanwhile the march continued under its own momentum, its destination unknown. Often its speed was disconcerting to an essentially bourgeois government and nation, its cost in taxes and debased currency so appalling that Trudeau, the pragmatist, was driven back to the credo of his book—"My political action or my theory, inasmuch as I can be said to have one, can be expressed very simply: create counterweights."

Counterweights to what? To many things, among them the inflation which he had completely misunderstood and foolishly discounted at the beginning. But the counterweights had a purpose far beyond the immediate economic muddle. In the face of the actual world he deplored the impossible expectations of ever-increasing affluence which his government, like all governments, had so long encouraged. In the face of a worldwide materialism, without the means of supporting it, he attacked "the great god G.N.P." (his own words) which, until then, had been universally worshipped. In his new realism, the old Canadian folk wisdom suddenly returning, he saw that a Just Society, or even a viable society, could not be made of physical goods however justly distributed and now definitely limited by the world's rising population and finite resources. And when he blurted out to his assembled party that, without a miracle, millions of humans would starve, it was evident that the man's private cosmogony had suffered a violent soul-shock.

His adventures and misadventures have been recited here, at weary length, not because I have access to his mind—who has?—but because, at this writing, they are largely the chronicle, accurate or inaccurate, of the nation's recent life.

By midsummer, 1976, both man and nation, each reacting to the other, had begun, only begun, to realize that they faced a deepening crisis of politics, economics, finance, and cultural friction which neither had foreseen.

After his miraculous revival of 1974, Trudeau's political fortunes had sunk below their nadir of 1972. The national economy was recovering from a slump but much more slowly than the government had expected, carrying the largest trade deficit in the Western world, piling up foreign debt for future repayment, pricing itself out of markets at home and abroad, inflating its currency on a ruinous scale, and failing to cure unemployment.

Even in the management of the two Canadian communities Trudeau's sure hand had faltered, and though he announced (somewhat prematurely) that separatism was dying in Quebec, the old Anglo-French discord seemed to be rising again in its latest spasm. It would be wrong, of course, to suppose that these historical forces were under the control of any prime minister.

But the man in office is always blamed for their collision, and they destroyed a leader as great as Wilfrid Laurier.

Thus the dismal year of 1976, when this book went to press, had raised three interdependent questions: Was Trudeau, that cool cat with at least nine lives, able to regain anything like his former strength by a second miracle of politics, to reunite his quarrelling party and re-demonstrate his ability to govern the nation? Would any alternative government do better? And was the nation ready, at last, to admit that no government could govern successfully until Canadians themselves had revised those impossible expectations which long preceded Trudeau's first appearance and which, in his early days, he had needlessly magnified and then sought desperately to restrain?

For almost three centuries, in war and peace, Canadians had met every challenge and, by their own curious methods, had mastered half a continent of treasure and built a unique dual state. But they had still to prove that they could stand prosperity. If they replaced Trudeau and installed a new government tomorrow morning its arrival would change nothing of real consequence unless they had also changed their current attitudes. In short, the character of the nation, not the temporary failure or success of Trudeau, is the sovereign question, far more important than any man or government. It has yet to be answered.

I tried to follow this uncharacteristic chronicle but now had only a handful of friends in the ruling Establishment: old-timers like Mitchell Sharp, the skilled technician of the cabinet; Paul Martin, the tireless work horse, strategist, and organ-voiced expositor of true Liberalism; and a few others. They still talked to me with trusting candor, for old times' sake, even when the *Sun* opposed their government in the 1974 election; that infidelity was attributed, I suppose, to my dotage and kindly unmentioned.

Despite the wide generation gap, I also found an improbable young friend in John Turner. Since he had been a college mate of my own son, Robert, I observed his progress with avuncular interest and high anticipation. He seemed to regard me as a frail antique to be treated with care lest I crumble, or, on occasion, as a wailing wall.

For a career in politics John was richly endowed—a movie star's masculine good looks, a mind as tough (though not as subtle or imaginative) as Trudeau's, the memory of a computer bank, a sharp ear for nuance, a way with ordinary people that Trudeau could not match, and a restless energy frightening to behold.

But there was more to John than his drive and romantic persona, more of ability and much more, too, of trouble which he was very late to recognize. The winsome smile and boyish manner were balanced by an eye of Arctic ice and, beneath the alternating persiflage and technical jargon, a quick grasp of essentials. A politician born and thoroughly self-educated.

As Trudeau's coadjutor and prospective heir, the second man in the political partnership of the nation's two cultural communities, John kept its secrets but he never disguised his own ambition. Almost from the cradle he had aimed at the top, impatient for his chance, aware that it might never come.

While the partnership worked well enough for a time, the partners were not real friends and that fact was no secret. They could not truly understand or even like each other because their origins, attitudes, and temperaments made them incompatible. Only the accidents of politics had put them into the same government. Contrary to the normal pattern of age, the younger man stood philosophically far to the right of the older, who stood to the left of the Liberal centre as vaguely defined in the days of King, St. Laurent, and Pearson. For John it was a solitary perch with few comrades of like mind in the cabinet, reinforcing the traditional isolation of finance ministers always under attack by hungry colleagues. I had long believed that he would have been the natural leader for a Conservative Party lacking any man of comparable talent, but politics, seldom logical, had decided otherwise—with curious results.

Though John intended to be thrifty treasurer, his budgets grew like Topsy to astronomical dimensions. The galloping statism of the times may have been irresistible but it ran against the whole grain of his character. The inflationary disorder, the Keynesian system debauched and parodied by its disciples, mocked all his early hopes and later resistance. He was caught in a worldwide debacle, as were all public treasurers. He found himself preaching "restraint" though he could not restrain his own government.

When the end came it surprised no one who had watched his losing struggle. His resignation in 1975 was surprising only in its long delay. He should have resigned at least a year earlier, before he was persuaded out of cabinet loyalty to introduce the last two budgets, which expressed the will of the majority, not his own best judgment. The delay gave his enemies the chance to say that he had remained on board while the ship was safely afloat and leaped ashore once it began to leak. The charge was unfair but helpful to a government gravely weakened by his departure.

Much more surprising was Trudeau's apparent failure to see how the resignation would affect him and the Liberal Party. To regard Turner as expendable, like some ordinary minister, and to bid him farewell with no more than polite regret, as if he could be easily spared, was to disregard the fundamental law of Canadian government. It can succeed only as a tacit coalition between an English-speaking and a French-speaking leader, each in full command of his own constituency. This law had been repeatedly demonstrated since the coalition of Macdonald and Cartier that built the nation in the first place. And the brief, tortured life of governments without a bilingual alliance—those of Meighen, Bennett, and Diefenbaker, for example—confirmed the law.

The Trudeau-Turner coalition was secure, or at any rate credible, so long as the partners stood together; and it might be replaced by another coalition if Trudeau could find Turner's equivalent outside Quebec, but at the moment no such man was in sight. One of the two central pillars of any successful government was allowed to fall by neglect, misunderstanding on both sides, and rival ambition. If Trudeau understood the damage thus done to Liberalism, and the future risk of hiving it in his own safe constituency of Quebec, he showed no alarm. He merely shrugged off the resignation with the pretence that no disagreement of high policy was involved when, of course, it was the climax of a disagreement inevitable from the beginning.

Before this book is printed many things will have happened to outdate the breakdown of the coalition, and perhaps a durable substitute will have appeared. In any case the split between two able men was only one symptom of a political process in wild disarray, clumsily seeking a redivision of party lines on the basis of new issues when the old issues, and their slogans, had become almost irrelevant. The Right and the Left (to use these vague labels) were polarizing in Canada as elsewhere to reflect the real facts of a changing society.

As for Turner, he could look after himself, prosper in law or business, and be quietly forgotten. Or he could return to politics later on, his original target possibly within reach while he was still relatively young and Trudeau had retired. But neither man could see that far ahead at a time of turmoil in all parties, governments, and nations.

Having lived down my flattering reputation as a Liberal propagandist, I observed the turmoil in both national parties without any emotional involvement. Even the Conservative back rooms were open to me without suspicion of espionage or larceny.

After the *Sun*, long a Liberal advocate though not a party organ, had supported Robert Stanfield in his last election—with serious misgivings but of necessity because we supported his anti-inflation policy of wage and price controls while the government offered no policy at all—the Opposition leader evidently concluded that I was at last neutral and harmless. He talked freely to me and I thought him one of the finest men I had ever known in politics. But perhaps, like Turner, he was in the wrong party. Stanfield's views seemed more liberal, in the non-partisan meaning of the word, than those of many men who called themselves Liberals, some inside the cabinet itself. However that may be, I judged that Stanfield, given the chance, could have governed effectively without spectacle but with quiet wisdom. For two reasons, apart from his own mistakes, that chance eluded him.

His Conservative Party was shut out of Quebec by memories as ancient as Louis Riel's execution and as recent as the second conscription crisis in 1944, and above all by a French-Canadian Prime Minister beyond challenge among his own people. In the English-speaking provinces, where Stanfield twice carried more seats than the victorious government, he found Conservatism split between its primitives, who imagined that the world clock could be turned back, and the sophisticates, who were hardly distinguishable in their thinking from Liberals like Trudeau.

Only a Conservative leader as wise and subtle as Macdonald could have filled this double vacuum of history and ideology. Stanfield was no Macdonald but he was much abler than most Canadian voters supposed. His intelligence, not as brilliant as Trudeau's, contained, I believed, more common sense, a deeper human compassion, a superior knowledge of economics, and much less arrogance—indeed none. His scholarship was far-ranging, his private conversation lively, his wit scintillating, often devastating, his honesty unquestioned. In electoral politics his fatal defect was not his character, which everyone admired, but his inability to project it. The real man was suddenly frozen by the television camera. The hot-shot public relations hucksters always tried to remake his homely Maritime image but he always insisted on being himself. He was a thinker, not an actor, when politics had become increasingly an art of the theatre.

Even so he failed by only a hair's-breadth to win the 1972 election, and won it easily outside Quebec. After that combination of bad luck and bad management, repeated with worse results two years later, the public soon forgot—if it ever appreciated—his unique service to Canada. History will remember it, as Trudeau already does.

If Stanfield had been less of a patriot and more of a careerist he could have disrupted Trudeau's major lifework, the reconciliation of the Canadian communities. If he had been an enemy instead of a friend to Quebec, he could have roused all the old ghosts of bigotry elsewhere, inflamed his own primitives, and probably climbed to power in a nation newly sundered. This temptation would be hard for any ambitious leader to resist. Stanfield resisted it without a moment's doubt. If Quebec failed to respond, Trudeau understood and had the grace to applaud his opponent's contribution to their joint enterprise of national unity.

The contrast between the two men, the decisive factor that brought victory to one and defeat to the other, is now of historical interest only. But Stanfield, though he lost the prize, could depart in peace. And nothing so became his political life as his taking leave of it.

When in 1976 the Conservative Party gambled and daringly chose its youngest and least-known leader, Joe Clark must have asked himself what had happened to it before and during his lifetime. Were its misfortunes accidental or had the egalitarian, statist, and neo-socialist age denied to Conservatism any useful place or function? Or, if the Trudeau government won the next election for Clark, which seemed quite probable, how would he interpret a negative mandate? Where, in fact did he and the nation wish to go?

Such questions cannot be answered by one election, one man, or one policy, and honest men will always disagree on the long-term answers. But in my view at least, all societies, whatever their ideology and direction, need a party of the right (whatever name it bears) to curb the excesses of the left. That balance wheel is especially needed when the leftward lunge is out-running its resources, physical and moral, and all the Western nations live wildly beyond their means on promises mathematically absurd.

Even Trudeau, the great reformer, searches desperately for social counterweights and his eclectic Liberalism has its own conservative qualifications, its speed limits and safety brakes.

This may be abstract, iffy stuff but it identifies the practical dilemma before Conservatism as an ancient philosophy lacking contemporary philosophers and interpreters. What values, in short, are Conservatives trying to conserve? Only the conventional, vote-winning, short-run values of gross national product, affluence, and leisure?

If so, Conservatism can never compete with its rivals, who will promise much more of the same. And if history teaches anything it is that the society based on those values will not long enjoy them. It will die slowly of surfeit or quickly at the hands of another society whose values are different and tougher. From imperial Rome to modern Ho Chi Minh City human events have taught that lesson over and over again. If Canadian Conservatism understood these simple verities and interpreted them in politics it might not win immediate popularity, but it would have both the chance and the right to regain its former integrity and strength once the people realized where the current values were leading.

These questions were outside my narrow affairs (though I suspected that the public had begun to think further ahead than most politicians). The ultimate values did not disturb me much when I visited Ottawa since they would be settled by younger men. A new generation must solve the problems inherited from mine, and good luck to it. Anyhow, I had become only a fleeting visitor in the haunts of my youth, but some remnants of the old town and my old friendships survived time and trouble.

Alice, Grant Dexter's widow and a devoted, lifelong friend to Dot and me, was still in the Rockcliffe house where I had last seen my wife on a certain morning. Next door Dr. John and Margaret Wherrett had shown me a very special kindness which only they and I remember. The cosy, old-fashioned house of Louis Audette, a retired mandarin of many high official posts, with his priceless art collection and good talk, was open to me at any hour. So was the hospitable home of Jack and Margaret Pickersgill with its priceless political secrets of days long past. If I needed economic counsel, Graham Towers, until his death, and Louis Rasminsky, the wise ex-governors of the Bank of Canada, and their able successor, Gerald Bouey, gave it freely from worldwide experience. While such friends remained I could be no stranger to the old Ottawa, now buried under the new.

In the current Press Gallery, full of strange faces, I was fortunate to know, as colleague and confidant, a true scholar, Maurice Western, who had long distinguished the commentary of the *Free Press*, and its other correspondent, Victor Mackie, who seemed to have pipelines into Government and Opposition alike. A younger friend, David Ablett, with bright prospects ahead of him, had lately appeared and soon took charge of the *Sun*'s editorial page.

My newspaper circle had shrunk. Grant, the unrivalled analyst of politics and my closest companion, was dead. So was Blair Fraser, the foremost magazine writer, both before their time. Of the original group only Grattan O'Leary was left, his Irish eloquence promoted, alas, to the Senate; and now he, too, is gone.

Shrunken as it was, the circle supplied all my needs for information and companionship. I still felt at home in the capital despite all the changes. But in a distant place, almost a different world, I now began to grasp some other changes of greater moment and they changed my whole outlook on the future.

31

The Grand Postulate

It had taken me a long time, some seventy years, to reach a certain place and ask a certain question of a man who perhaps might understand if he could not answer it. The place was improbable—the sunken garden of Princeton University where its onetime president, Woodrow Wilson, had meditated on the same question, with mixed results. My companion, that day, beside the last blazing flowers of autumn, was the foremost living authority on Thomas Jefferson, who had raised the question in his time and answered it, as he believed, for all time.

But did the answer, given in his immortal Declaration, still hold good? Were the Unalienable Rights of man still guaranteed by the Laws of Nature and Nature's God, or at least by the Constitution of the United States? If so, what had gone wrong with the pursuit of Life, Liberty, and Happiness? Could it be that Jefferson's postulate, man's ability to govern himself in freedom, no longer was true in a nation and a world which he could not imagine? A grand and noble postulate, yes, the wildest of all surmises, but was it a practical proposition for our time?

As to many other distinguished men along the way, I put that old and ever new question to Julian Boyd because he, better than any of my friends, had earned the right to an opinion. Author, historian, philosopher, editor of Jefferson's papers, and a truly big man unimpressed by his reputation, Boyd had spent a life almost as long as mine considering these things, until now, I judged, without any doubt about the answer. But the latest course of human events in Richard Nixon's White House and elsewhere was enough to shake even the devoted Jeffersonian.

Boyd, though shaken like every intelligent American, had not lost faith in the postulate so far as it concerned his own people. The surmise did not appear too wild for him. The Republic, wounded at home and abroad, stood invulnerable. The pursuit, its direction changed, would continue. The road to happiness, its goal revised, would be found again.

Thus spoke Professor Boyd, who was fully entitled to speak. And yet he knew, we both knew, that the question could not be finally answered within the limits of a single state however rich, strong, and free. The postulate must face a far wider and more dubious test in which all faiths now stand on trial for life. The daring experiment of liberty has taken myriad forms but in essence they are all the same thing—the purpose of man in the universe.

Why such trite and commonplace notions should have disturbed me as suddenly critical in the garden of an American university I cannot tell. You never know when a moment of numb perplexity will halt you on the road. From ambush, with no warning, unseen marksmen discharge their arrows of truth or, more frequently, of error. It is then you most need a friend who has already travelled the road and knows its perils.

On my own erratic journey some rough experience, surprise, and disappointment had nullified much of my faith in all political, economic, and social postulates while re-establishing it in others more important. I had learned enough, anyhow, to realize that my question to Boyd and any answer to it, however wise, could touch only one part and not the main part of the whole. And lately I had realized, too, that the parts were more complex, numerous, and dangerous than I had assumed throughout my life.

The first big shock had not come at Princeton where, after all, my speculations were pretty obvious, but two years earlier in a place just as improbable, at Harvard University and the adjoining Massachusetts Institute of Technology. There the shock was delivered by a man very different from Boyd, the two alike only in the range of their minds.

Jay W. Forrester had been represented to me as a genius of mathematics but he looked more like a successful small-town businessman, a family doctor, or a grade-school teacher. He was reserved and tense, his speech formal and precise, the idiom of a textbook. As he answered my clumsy questions he might have been explaining a minor mathematical problem to a group of retarded pupils. In fact, he explained the approaching ruin of human society as disclosed by his computers.

Warming to the subject, he scrawled figures and drew graphs on his blackboard, none of them understandable to me but their purport seemed clear—mankind's population, appetite, and stupidity were gutting a tiny planet and the attempt to devise synthetic substitutes for its dwindling natural resources would pollute its soil, water, and atmosphere until it became unlivable.

This equation is familiar to everyone nowadays, accepted or denied with equal fervor and so generally argued as to be almost a bore. When I talked with Forrester it was a new heresy, derided by its cackling critics as the incubus of sick academic minds. Or else it was the result of erroneous data fed into the computers by a group of amateur mathematicians calling themselves the Club of Rome.

While Forrester scribbled his diagrams and over-simplified his thesis for my benefit, it occurred to me that the Club of Rome had chosen a ridiculous name, like the title of some Italian gangster movie. What had Rome to do with the Institute of Technology in Cambridge, Massachusetts, a few miles from Lexington and Concord where the American Revolution began to repudiate the Old World of Europe, its history, and its evils?

On second thoughts I saw a grim, if unintended, parable in the Club's name. As the Roman Empire had been destroyed by revolutionary forces beyond its control, so the American Revolution, and much else besides, were threatened by forces beyond contemporary man's understanding, or even his imagination.

On third thoughts, I saw that this parallel, though widely believed, contained a basic fallacy. Rome had not collapsed for lack of physical resources for they were abundant in the Old World and still larger supplies had yet to be discovered in the virgin lands of the New. Moreover, Rome had not learned to pollute its environment, except in its metropolis, or to discover the final pollutant of atomic fission. The Roman revolution, whatever its causes, and all succeeding revolutions, whatever their time and place, differed from the current revolution not only in size but in kind.

Yet the parallel, whether strictly valid or not, contained some truth. By historic reckoning, or at least by an imaginary time frame of my own, the modern world seemed to be living again in about A.D. 400 with most of Rome's problems and many others of later invention, its circuses less violent but more expensive and vulgar than the originals, its bread in shorter supply, its gods and moralities just as neglected and decayed. The new enemies outside the walls, no longer barbarians like the old, were just as strong, healthy, and envious, and they now carried the best nuclear weapons.

How could it be assumed, as it generally was, that the weapons would never be used when any nation with sufficient money could possess them without necessarily possessing a sane government? This was doubtless the only tolerable assumption, all others being intolerable, but I could find no basis for it in human experience. The repeated lessons of the past taught the opposite conclusion. There was the question of questions, beyond the reach of man or computer, so terrible that men seldom dared to face it, preferring to ignore the obvious. Perhaps they were wise to do so lest they lose their sanity but the obvious was sometimes true.

In any case, the Club of Rome's computers, though inaccurate, as Forrester agreed, because their data were incomplete, had identified a crisis literally without parallel in the course of human events. Not knowing, then or now, what a computer is or how it works, I could understand its broad verdict and it sounded hopeless to me. But not to Forrester. If the crisis were insoluble, he said, men of his sort would not be wasting their time on futile remedies.

No, he did not regard the prospects with despair. Human intelligence, he thought, could still revise the computed equation before it became unalterable. The genius of mathematics evidently shared Jefferson's postulate of politics, even if the computer didn't.

Nor was this surprising. Forrester and Jefferson, separated by two centuries, were both products of the same history, the same American Revolution and its boundless hopes. Nevertheless Forrester and men like him knew, as Jefferson could not know, that the permitted time and safety margin of civilized life was exceedingly narrow, the test of human intelligence harder and more uncertain than any previous test.

All these measurements are scorned by "the conventional wisdom" and by John Kenneth Galbraith, who invented that phrase. When, after leaving Forrester, I talked to Galbraith he almost overflowed his Harvard office, standing close to seven feet high, with gaunt eagle's face, like some avian prodigy of a vanishing species poised for flight. He was bubbling, as usual, with his own economic heresies, his unconventional wisdom, but the danger of physical shortages did not appear to worry him. Science would devise plenty of substitutes for scarce materials. To the great economist the solutions were all available. What alone worried him was the stupidity of governments that refused to recognize the obvious, to make the unconventional wisdom conventional.

A genius in his own field, whether right or wrong in his conclusions, Galbraith did not suffer fools gladly. He did not suffer them at all. But for all the icy sarcasm of his conversation and books, his genius was not merely negative. He had evolved his positive remedies (which most of his colleagues rejected as unworkable) and, like Forrester, did not despair. The rancorous critic and transplanted Canadian had become a natural American optimist, an old-fashioned Jeffersonian in an economist's disguise.

On the other hand, some Harvard professors were as pessimistic as the computers. One of them, whose name is a household word among scientists, told me that the population problem, the supreme problem, would solve itself, not long hence, by famine, plague, or, quite possibly, nuclear war. I had better get used to the news of mass starvation, or something worse.

It was all very well, and theoretically true, to say that the nations could grow or synthesize enough food for their needs, even to raise the living standards of the poor, but had I considered what this stupendous feat of organization required? It required nothing less than a world government of some kind empowered to redistribute wealth on a ruthless scale at the drastic sacrifice of the rich people's living standard. The real problem, in short, was not scientific and physical. It was political or, more accurately, psychological and moral. Human intelligence and morality, at their present state of evolution, did not appear equal to the sudden demand on them.

Could anyone imagine, he asked, that the necessary solutions, unlike any in the past, would be applied in time to forestall the onrushing calamity? Of course not. Supposing, for the sake of argument, that tomorrow morning the living standards of the poor nations were miraculously raised to the level—or half or a quarter of the level—enjoyed by the rich, what then? Why then the world's total consumption, apart from the resulting deadly pollution, would exhaust its resources by tomorrow night.

But even this great scientist, who spoke the language of despair, could not escape the heritage of the American Revolution and its grand postulate. When I next read his name in the press he was attending some international conference assembled to plan solutions for the insoluble.

A third man at Harvard, I felt, had thought more deeply than the economist or the scientist. The real problem, he said, lay outside science, economics, and even politics. It was philosophical. And while the nation had plenty of scientists, economists, and politicians of high quality, it had failed to produce a single philosopher of any consequence in the present generation—a fatal lack not of machinery and institutions but of common belief, the only cement that ever held a society together. Once it leached out, what was left but a rubble of broken bricks? Yet this philosopher manqué, being an American, did not despair. He hopefully awaited the revival of belief. Always the shade of Jefferson hovered somewhere in the background.

To me the talk at Cambridge was new and shaking, though it is hackneyed now, the bland pablum of debate everywhere. Shaken all the same, I began to see, rather late, that most of my accepted ideas were obsolete. At my age, however, it was useful, if painful, to rethink a lifetime of very conventional wisdom, an accumulated baggage ready for the junk heap.

From Cambridge I went on, that fall, to Washington, where the pre-Watergate weather was still fair, Richard Nixon's White House apparently chaste and stainless, the conventional wisdom hardly questioned by its latest interpreters.

One of them, a high priest close to the inner shrine, undertook to set my mind at rest. The situation might be confusing in detail, he said, but in essence was simple. As the United States, with its unequalled technology, had been the first nation to encounter the problems of Galbraith's Affluent Society, so, inevitably, it would be the first to solve them (though not by Galbraith's impractical methods). The intelligence which had launched the technical revolution would correct its abuses with methods then being shaped by a conscientious, practical government. But even in the presence of this excellent interpreter I detected a clanging *non sequitur*.

Why did it follow that the nation that had led all others in the discovery of affluence must lead them in the discovery of the cure for its diseases? It seemed much more likely that the discovery, if made at all, would be made by some people who had not yet achieved affluence and were warned in advance by the American example to beware its dangers.

With these idle thoughts I left the State Department and strolled to the Lincoln monument and, in the twilight, stood alone before the brooding, haunting, almost living figure of stone, the noblest outward expression of the American Dream. Those two words had been debased in the market place of language, like coins of spurious value, but here the metal ran true, the Dream lived, and Lincoln's own words, carved on the stone walls, could not be counterfeited or silenced.

What did they really mean? For his time they meant that a state born in revolution and reborn in civil war had the wisdom to survive worse perils. But did it have the wisdom to survive the greater revolution of our time? If one dared to paraphrase his speech at Gettysburg, would a modern society conceived in affluence and dedicated to the proposition that all men are created primarily to consume, waste, and defy the natural order of things—would any such society long endure? I had no doubt of the negative answer and dared to think that Lincoln would agree with it. And what about government of the people, by the people, and for the people? Must it perish from the earth when the people, bewildered by too much information, no longer understood the workings of their government and government hardly understood itself? That question might sound preposterous to the residents in Nixon's smug White House but not in the temple of America's boldest dreamer.

Soon I had the chance to continue these vague reflections in two other places where they were first argued by Lincoln's predecessors, and fortunately I found a reliable guide.

Joseph Scott was a Texan by birth, by residence a Virginian, by profession a Foreign Service officer of wide experience. Better than most of his friends, I had come to know this quiet man with his bronzed western look and soft southern speech because identical circumstances of private misfortune, happening at exactly the same time, had brought us together in mutual recognition. There were few men to whom I owed so much, not only for the welcome of his picturesque home in Alexandria but for the contents of a mind rich in learning, common sense, and profound loyalties.

Among other things he was a disciple of Jefferson, from whose University of Virginia he had graduated after catching some of the sage's old magic. All the rough life of diplomacy in queer places around the world could not shake Joe's faith in the Self-Evident Truths or the Dream. But apparently doubting my faith, he and Claretta, his lovely young bride, herself a Foreign Service officer, carried me off to Monticello. There, they hoped, I too might catch a fragment of the magic.

Close at hand it was easily perceived. The house on the Little Mountain, with Jefferson's eccentric gadgets, the jewel-box architecture of his university, and behind them the hazy autumn gossamer of the Blue Ridge, must touch even the most witless foreigner.

Joe said nothing. He let Jefferson speak for himself across two centuries. Perhaps I heard him faintly in dull alien ears but I'm not sure. Still doubtful of my hearing, Joe and Claretta then took me to Williamsburg. Any visitor, native or foreign, would be impressed by the faithfully restored town in which Jefferson and his fellows planted the philosophical seeds of the Revolution.

The usual resort of tourists is a loathsome thing, God wot, but in Williamsburg I saw no tourists acting or feeling like tourists, no holiday mood, no cheap exploitation of history. I saw only a throng of plain Americans who wore a look of reverence seldom seen elsewhere, their voices low, their manner restrained, their homage visible. Then they went home to their brawling cities each with a shard of memory and renewed faith. At least they seemed to revere their heroes as Canadians do not. Here, I thought, was something from the past more important to any nation than all its wealth, power, and technology, something overlooked by computers, something that might outlive the current dementia.

Another thing struck and saddened me. The visitors at Williamsburg, like all free peoples, looked back with nostalgic longing to an earlier time whereas men like Jefferson looked ahead with total confidence in the future. So the people of the Dark Ages must have looked back on Rome, never hoping to renew its lost glories. Time and hope had rounded a long circle which Williamsburg, as an American symbol, clearly defined.

In the following years the zig-zag trail of friendship brought me at last to Princeton when Bill Bundy became editor of *Foreign Affairs* and settled his family in a stone house of venerable age. The surrounding forest, wild flowers, birds, and cheeky deer must excite any wood-chopper like me in the cool conflagration of autumn foliage. There we chopped dead trees, while planting many live ones, to accumulate fuel against hard winters and an oil shortage suddenly imposed by the OPEC cartel.

As in pioneer days, the neighbors, mostly professors from the university near by, joined these working parties and worked with the passionate energy of amateurs who have discovered a new sport. Princeton, that ancient seat of abstract culture, was getting down to essentials, returning, on week-ends anyhow, to the thrifty habits of its founders.

On Monday morning the academics were back at their brain work in the university. Its Gothic towers, ivy-covered walls, and the memories of men like Woodrow Wilson and Albert Einstein intimidated me at first, but under the sponsorship of Julian Boyd I found the inmates friendly and not at all condescending. They knew how little their knowledge meant in comparison with the yet unknown.

Still a small town in population and character, set among the meadows of New Jersey, Princeton provided refuge for a remarkable coterie besides the professors. In this diverse group I was lucky to meet two people famous in my own trade. Beatrice and Bruce Gould, long the joint editors of *The Ladies' Home Journal* when other giant magazines were dying, had been perhaps the most successful American journalists of their time, and the most perceptive.

Bruce was tall and ruddy, his face unlined by age. Given a plumed hat and rapier, I thought he would made an exact model for a portrait of a cavalier by Van Dyck. At such a fancy Bruce would laugh, as he was always laughing at the human comedy. His laughter failed to deceive me. He had seen life's grimy side and much struggle as newspaper reporter, theatre critic, playwright, story writer, and editor. He had known many of the world's great personages, published their works, and judged them for himself, without illusions or disillusionment. A man of warm heart and he warmed mine.

Beatrice, a great editor in her own right, perfectly complemented him. She was gentle of disposition and manner, listening more than she spoke, but now and then her quiet, shattering comment on the nation's business revealed a mind as strong and worldly-wise as her partner's. He considered it superior to his own. While their success in journalism had been ensured by talent and toil, it was incidental, I am sure, to a lifelong love affair. Incidental, too, was the ruined farmhouse amid green fields which they had bought in their young days and rebuilt until it became a treasury of art collected from the earth's far corners.

Trying to keep up with Bruce's rapid pace across the meadows, I would pester him for recollections of the legendary magazine era. He yielded them reluctantly and then, mischievously, encouraged me to fulminate at length upon the madness of our times. Yes, they were pretty mad, he agreed, but he refused to get excited about them and, possibly thinking me a little mad also, seemed to relish my poor tirades as he relished everything.

If all this sounds like the rambling dotage of two old newspapermen there was more to it. Bruce had been not only walking but thinking far ahead of me. So I suddenly discovered when I read his book *Conversations on the Edge of Eternity*. He had transcribed it from the spoken thoughts of his late mother-in-law, Mary K. Blackmar, just before her death at ninety years of age.

That book started me thinking too, or rethinking. For here I found stated in language reminiscent of Jefferson's Declaration some Self-Evident Truths that he had failed to mention and may not have believed. His prose rolled like thunder. Mrs. Blackmar's conversations fell gently like summer rain but penetrated deep into the earth of common things.

What a wise old lady she must have been to record these thoughts on the edge of eternity:

> Americans aren't held together by blood or tradition but by belief. They are united simply by a political philosophy which is unique . . . based on the Christian attitude, the brotherhood of man. There's only one thing in our present state of life here in this country that worries me. That is that we might grow too scientific. There is a tendency when a people is successful in any endeavor to kneel down and worship that accomplishment. We've done wonders in science. And it has minimized our sense of dependence on mysterious forces over which we have no control. Whenever a time comes that a scientist can create a man, or a thinking being, then would be the time to bow down and worship science. But until that time comes we'd better remember that we are all born and brought up to live and die in a great mystery which no man has yet solved.

To Mrs. Blackmar's warning Bruce had added in the margin a self-revealing comment: "It's almost as difficult to be a real American as it is to be a real Christian." Jefferson apparently had not foreseen that difficulty. As I understood him he assumed the inherent rationality and benevolence of men if tyrants did not corrupt them. Left to their natural instincts, they could be real Americans even if they were not real Christians; even if, as honest pagans, they believed in nothing more transcendental than democracy and the United States Constitution. Yet Bruce was right. The grand postulate raised some nice riddles of behavior and conflicts of interest for all who still tried to live by it nowadays.

So, after a journey of several years, many miles, and much back-tracking, I found myself in Woodrow Wilson's garden beside the editor of Jefferson's papers. With the unfair advantage of surprise I put to Julian Boyd my original question—could democracy, technology, and affluence co-exist in freedom? Of course the great Jeffersonian had no sure answer to the unanswerable. He had only hope. But this scholar was too honest to suppress any morsel of evidence against his own conclusions whether he accepted it or not.

As a parting token he gave me a rare exhibit from his files, a photostatic copy of the letter written by John Adams, the second President, to the sixth, his son John Quincy, on August 26, 1816. Despite the gap of 160 years, Adams's fatherly counsel still poses the sovereign test facing his nation, and all free nations today.

> The people of U.S. [he wrote] are the most conceited People that ever existed on this Globe. The most proud, vain, ambitious, suspicious, jealous, umbrageous and envious (and I am as guilty as any of them.) Have a care of them! They remind me of Helvetius. This Philosopher was promenading with a Brother Philosopher on the Bulvards. The People were dancing and skipping, laughing and singing in every direction. "These People are happy," said the Brother. "Oh! No!" said Helvetius. "See how civil they are to you and me, to one another and to every Body. If they were happy they would be insolent."
>
> If ever a People had this Proof of Happiness it is the People of U.S. We cannot bear Prosperity. Calamity alone and extream distrys will ever bring forth the real Character of this Nation. Foreign War can never do it. Nothing short of foreign War, and civil War at once, will ever effect it. And then you may depend upon it they will follow a Bonaparte, or several Bonapartes, rather than Jeffersons, Madisons, John or John Quincy Adam's. Hamiltons and Burrs will be preferred to Hancocks and Washingtons.

After leaving Boyd I happened to read Adams's final verdict on the grand postulate: "Democracy never lasts long. It soon wastes, exhausts and murders itself. There never was a democracy yet that did not commit suicide."

Two of America's greatest thinkers—Jefferson the total democrat and religious sceptic, Adams the natural aristocrat and religious believer—had given opposite answers to the old question and between them personified the grand dilemma of our time. But when I returned to the Pacific wilderness of Canada the non-human inhabitants silently obeyed a postulate and gave answers of their own more convincing than any human document.

32

The Swamp

It wasn't much of a swamp, not really a swamp at all, just a few acres of marshy ground that Dot and I acquired for a song when we were young and the wilderness was cheap. The first loggers had come here almost a hundred years before us but left the largest trees uncut because ox teams could not drag them to the lake, half a mile distant. Wasted, as the loggers thought, the mighty firs and cedars, several centuries old, shaded the brief generations of maple and alder, the shaggy sword ferns, deer leaf, salal, nettles, white trilliums, yellow violets, pale bleeding hearts, pink lady slippers, and all the humbler siblings of the rain forest to make it impenetrable. We cut a trail through our miniature jungle and, for lack of a better name, called it the Swamp.

So, in our private lexicon and certain memories, it will remain for some time yet, until civilization finds more practical uses for it. Then, no doubt, the oozing black soil will be drained, the rank and pungent vegetation cleared away by bulldozers, the useless trees replaced by efficient, symmetrical concrete barracks, the ledges of rock and moss blasted for swimming pools, patios, barbecues—all in the pursuit of a superior happiness that Jefferson would hardly understand.

Untouched by modern improvements, the Swamp will last my time. It should last my grandchildren's time also and even their children's, if they have the wish to preserve it and the money to pay the taxes. Meanwhile its teeming life, mindless but more enduring than man's, is still present in what, I suppose, the naturalist would call a minor ecosystem. That name was too grand and scientific for us. We did not use it but, in cheerful ignorance, watched at all seasons of growth, rest, and decay, the myriad vegetable forms, the insects, frogs, birds, and animals, only man a stranger.

The Swamp was never strange to us in its perpetual summer twilight or lonely on the darkest winter day. Though we knew nothing of botany, zoology, or mineralogy, we knew enough about the woods to see that the ecosystem worked more efficiently than any social egosystem devised by men. Here every member, every molecule and atom, of a complex but coherent society was in its appointed place, from the invisible bacterium under the surface, to the raven quarrelling hoarsely with his wife atop the highest fir.

Competition between the members was ruthless. The struggle for moisture, light, and earth chemicals never ceased for an instant. The strong survived, the weak perished, but weakness and strength were deceptive. Often the strongest-looking trees would die from no apparent cause, falling, like the giants of the human family, while the scrubs beside them inherited their precious space to flourish in turn. There were casualties in this silent warfare, great and small, every day, every hour, but no net loss. The withered leaf, the rotting log, each infinitesimal speck of matter, was jealously repossessed and reconverted into soil, and soil into new life. Unlike man's shrinking planetary estate, the Swamp grew richer, by minute increment, with each passing season.

When man cuts or fire burns the Pacific forest it begins to renew itself overnight, the unravelled fabric knitted up with the first sure stitches of fireweed and creeping blackberry, then the ferns and nettles, and finally the thrust of conifers that, in the end, will dominate a flawless economic system, demand and supply always balanced, the currency of root, sap, and wood always stable, inflation and depression unknown. Here, too, was a political system of sorts, a democratic process functioning smoothly without constitution, revolution, or thought.

Probably we exaggerated the beauty and the mystery of our Swamp. The stranger might find here only some trees and rocks and prickly underbrush, hard on city clothes and skin. The Swamp lived mostly, perhaps, in our imagination which, stretched a little, could even identify a site of Canadian history.

Not far away, on the bare slope of Mount Malahat, Sir John A. Macdonald had driven the last spike of Robert Dunsmuir's Esquimalt and Nanaimo Railway. That day of August 13, 1886, must have been trying for the old man. Mrs. Dunsmuir, a lady of strict temperance principles, would allow no liquor on the special train, and her husband, perforce, took the Prime Minister to the depths of a Nanaimo coal mine, late in the afternoon, for essential restoratives. In my single success as a crusading journalist of high causes I persuaded the national authorities to erect a stone cairn, with a bronze tablet, to mark the spot at Cliffside where two thirsty men completed a project not as important, to be sure, as the CPR and the rites at Craigellachie, a year earlier, but a necessary steel fibre of Confederation.

Often in the summer evenings, Dot and I walked along the E. and N. tracks, as shameless trespassers, and paused to salute the cairn and deplore its public neglect. From our cabin beside the lake we could hear the chuffing, laboring climb of the midnight freight train over the steepest grade in Canada, the locomotive's triumphant whistle at the summit, the echoes bouncing from hill to hill. That authentic Canadian resonance seemed to tell us that Sir John's last spike, or a dependable successor, still held firm. Confederation would survive its strains and follies until morning. Man's railway system was working almost as well as the ecosystem in the Swamp.

By long association the night-time whistle, though uttered by a machine, was a truly natural sound in Canada, like the murmur of the forest and the gurgle of the lake. But the daytime sounds were unnatural and they told a different story of a nation forever changed.

In our youth only rowboats, sailboats, canoes, and half a dozen wheezing launches travelled the lake. The virtues of the internal combustion engine were not then fully appreciated. Human muscle provided the main source of power for navigation, wood supply, and water carried in buckets. Now, as on all Canada's accessible lakes, a navy of speedboats conducted their intricate manoeuvres all day long, in tireless gyration of foam and clamor, perfuming the air with the fragrance of gasoline, squandering the nation's fuel reserves, introducing Galbraith's Affluent Society to the wilderness, and confirming, in local microcosm, the Club of Rome's global macrocosm. Or so a man of a different time and a sour disposition viewed this innocent dance of the mechanized water sprites.

The urban dwellers once came to the lake in search of nature and solitude, as escape from the swarming city. Now they brought the city with them, its machinery, its amusements, and its television, to watch at second hand a counterfeit of the world which they had fled, and sometimes even of the Canadian wilderness around them, a spectacle too savage to be risked at first hand. Only the youngest children seemed to understand the irony of this curious parable. They still sought the woods to build their tree houses and Indian encampments, but by the age of ten at most they preferred to drive the engines of internal combustion, unaware, like their parents, that the engines drove them, and all mankind.

A cranky old observer like me could learn much about the human situation on this minor lake, where not long ago nothing more strident than the loon's cry, the trout's splash, the dip of paddle, or the creak of oarlocks broke the silence.

As always, I put my neighbors' habits to sordid commercial use. What I wrote about them in the newspapers should have been punishable for libel by any court of law, but they did not sue me. They smiled at my dotage and waved a friendly greeting from their boats when they passed the cabin in which I write these words of fraudulent remorse. Canadians are a tolerant breed.

My summer fantasies, printed and unprintable, were shared now with the one man who was trained to understand them. Besides, he shared the unending labor of the camp and actually enjoyed it. Together, in the spring, we unlocked the door of the cabin after its solitary winter when it had been inhabited only by field mice, squirrels, and visiting burglars, but possessed, as we liked to think, a life of its own and silently echoed some voices speaking aloud no more. Together we turned the key again in the autumn and looked back from the bend in the trail for the last time, perhaps the very last—a ritual known to camp men alone, inexplicable and absurd to others.

Dr. Alfred Carlsen, the last friend I was likely to make at my age, had distinguished himself as a professor of economics, but had risen above his affliction and I never held it against him. In all except professional working hours he was a forest denizen, an incorrigible romantic, and a fine artist whose sculptures of wood were boldly carved like his own features, whose sensitive eye and cunning hand produced delicate jewelry of native metal.

This passion for the wilderness came instinctively to a boy born of Norwegian stock in the remote valley of Bella Coola, where, after a few years' schooling, he earned a meagre living as logger and fisherman, rode the rails in the days of the Great Depression, worked his way through college on thirty dollars a month to win his doctorate, and went to the war in Europe. Luckily for Dot and me, Al settled down in Victoria with a young wife, Martha, from Boston, her beauty as delicate as his jewelry and her New England character as rugged as his sculpture. Such a woman would bring serenity and radiance to any home. Such a man redeemed economics. Al could even explain it to his students and to me. But we had more important matters to discuss.

In the spring when the ferns uncoiled their croziers and the Swamp was dappled with blossom, in the summer of drought, crackling twigs, and insect buzz, when the forest seemed to pant and droop with thirst, in the winter of sluicing rain and demented winds, Al and I cut wood and, in a pagan fashion worshipped it like elderly Druids.

We also worshipped fire. Once the woods were sodden and safe, the lake deserted by its worshippers of internal combustion, our blazing brush piles repeated, for our ears at least, the sounds of all the seasons, the bubbling water sound and bird squeak of spring, the dry tick of summer, the first rain drip and sudden pause of autumn, and winter's manic storms. The year's whole record of work, life, and death was audible to us in the flames of our funeral pyre. Doubtless we were both half mad as we toiled long days without wages and rejoiced in our madness without expecting the sane to understand us—wood snobs, élitists, with a fine sense of moral superiority over the amateur holiday makers. But we enjoyed ourselves while the sane appeared to mope in despair and age prematurely, and we cut a lot of fuel, all from dead trees. With comic frenzy we heaped up more than enough cordwood for years ahead. The stoves and roaring fireplaces of two adjoining camps, my own and my son's, never went short.

We were miserly as well as mad, with secret woodpiles on distant trails where no one else could find them and even the misers lost count. My avarice had long been the camp's favorite scandal. Everyone agreed that I always refused to let Dot have wood of better quality because she would only burn it to heat the oven. That was a slight exaggeration, very slight.

Our antisocial behavior generally went unobserved because visitors to the camps, who came in swarms, rarely ventured off the main trail lest they be conscripted and put to work. We roughly fed, bedded, and irrigated them with needful stimulants, and they unwittingly paid their board by furnishing me with libellous newspaper columns, sometimes almost accurate, which they never read.

Many improbable guests arrived over the years, forgotten waifs and strays of all sorts, television crews with cameras and sound apparatus lugged on the trail by wheelbarrow, politicians in search of publicity, journalists in search of copy, or jobs; among others the unforgettable English author and penetrating soul-searcher J. B. Priestley, who had made a fool of me in a transatlantic radio debate and now came to see his victim in the flesh and to explain, with pencil diagrams and an array of salt cellars on the table, his theory of time and human immortality — the mysticism of an earthy man which we could not understand, if he did.

Though I have written so much about it here and, for mercenary purposes, in the newspapers, the camp was open only for the summer months of the children's school holidays, that inflexible time frame of North American life. Most of the year we lived on the fringe of Victoria, land-poor and tax-ridden under the advancing siege of real-estate developers. But we still owned the little house that Dot and I had built and rebuilt in our first years together, and the garden of shrubs, fruit trees, and vegetables around it.

Above all I was fortunate in my children, whom I never fully appreciated in my early parenthood. In my age I rediscovered them when they were suddenly in middle age themselves with children, lives, and problems of their own. That was a shock common, I dare say, to all parents.

When I was left alone my daughter, Joan, her marriage ended, took charge of my home and me, bringing with her two sons, Bruce and Ross, the third generation in the same house. To Joan, after her mother's departure, and to my son, Robert, I owe more than to anyone now living.

With Joan as housekeeper, financial comptroller, trained nurse, and broker between youth and age I was comfortable, the house pleasantly disordered by the mysterious affairs of small boys who soon overtopped their grandfather. Bruce, the elder, was an inspired mechanic of bicycles, automobiles, and thundering electronic sound waves known as music. Ross preferred violent athletic games, wilderness camps, and trout streams.

Our son's career had amazed Dot and me. The boy in his sailboat and tree fort, our companion on fishing and riding trips, then the college athlete and Olympic track runner, succeeded in his profession of the law far beyond our hopes. But tempting offers could not lure him from Victoria. Robert's life was centred in a legal firm nearly as old as the town, in the woods, and in his home.

He had the wisdom and luck to marry Corinne, the daughter of Stanley and Peggy Moore, a pioneer lumbering family. She was gifted not only with beauty but a character of quiet strength that ruled her household and three fine children. Richard, the eldest, was an all-round sportsman and zealous university student. Jane, our golden darling, also became an earnest scholar, unspoiled by her troops of admirers. James, the youngest, showed a vivid imagination in his paintings, collections of tropical fish, and botanical experiments, these hobbies presaging, as we thought, a bright future.

Such was the lively establishment of my son, a better parent, an abler, kinder man than I had ever been and—no common thing between the generations—my friend, almost my guardian. He managed my affairs, encouraged my work, even read my books, and, like his jolly sister, put up with my crotchets. Both gave me more unspoken fidelity than any man deserved.

When I needed them, as I often did, the McDiarmids, Dot's side of the family, were always on hand—Lucy, Neil's widow, now the beloved matriarch, her son, another Neil and a successful lawyer, and her daughter, Barbara. The clan, its Scottish instincts surviving time and distance, continued to increase with grandchildren, and even great-grandchildren, scattered over North America.

Through all these years I was especially blessed by my neighbor, an ever-present help in all times of trouble. George Rogers, a man close to my age, still held a diminished acreage of his father's historic farm across the road from us, land broken and cultivated by the Hudson's Bay Company in the days of Fort Victoria. His tall, rugged figure, plowing in the spring and harvesting in the fall, pampering his little herd of beef cattle and jealously preserving the wild flowers and gnarled oaks of Christmas Hill, confirmed my faith in the old Canadian breed.

George loved his ancestral land as only that breed can love it, nourished it with organic stuff from his huge barn, and, every Christmas, presented me with a heaping truckload of fertility more precious nowadays than gold, frankincense, and myrrh. Thus enriched, our vegetable garden produced as much in its fiftieth year as in its first.

It also produced a second crop of newspaper columns, inedible but profitable, nearly sufficient to pay the running costs if my time, labor, and waning energies were not included. At legal minimum wages every onion or apple would have cost at least a dollar but I kept no reckoning lest it discourage me. In life generally, and gardening particularly, it is never wise to look at the facts. In both what alone matters is the next crop. The Government of Canada, ignoring an obvious tax loophole, required no account of my most valuable income and capital gains. Luckily the experts at Ottawa know nothing about life's essentials or they would have closed the loophole long ago and doubtless will, once they discover it.

With regrettable lack of aesthetic taste I always enjoyed growing vegetables more than flowers and there may have been an obsure logic in my preference. It had taken most of my lifetime to grow a thicket of blossoming shrubs. Many human lifetimes had passed before the trees of Christmas Hill and the Swamp reached their middle age. But one season completes the whole growth process of nature's humble species and even the short-lived grower has time to learn something from them.

In the spring he plants his seed and, if he is worthy of it, can feel in his fingers, like a faint electric shock, a new life yet to quicken touching an old life soon to end. Then, of a sudden, come the first green wisps, minute but of strength immeasurable, breaking the earth's hard rind and pushing by sure direction toward the sky. As I knelt down to sprinkle the seed, in the gardener's non-denominational posture of reverence, and watched that tiny miracle year after year it seemed to tell more about the universe than all men's books and philosophies.

Unfortunately, however, most of my work was done indoors. It looked easy and so it had been in earlier times. Without the artificial stimulus and momentum of an office it became unbelievably harder and slower. But my luck held. Dick Malone, presiding in Toronto over his far-flung newspaper chain, Stu Keate publishing the *Sun* in Vancouver, and Peter McLintock editing the *Free Press* in Winnipeg—friends of great heart and inexhaustible patience—and kept me going long past the normal retirement age.

Almost sixty years of politics from the outside had left only a professional, bread-and-butter interest in the game. I responded automatically, like an old fire horse, to every alarm bell but it no longer surprised or excited me. For I knew by now that the improbable was sure to happen, the impossible repeating itself, the actors and scenery alone changed. In a harmless exercise of the absurd I had even formulated and thought of copyrighting the laws of politics throughout the ages, as valid today as Hammurabi's Code.

By the Law of Inevitable Contradication any government elected on a specific policy will do the precise opposite on reaching office—as Woodrow Wilson was elected to keep the United States out of war and promptly took it in; as Franklin Roosevelt promised to balance the budget and, out-Hoovering Hoover, inaugurated the New Deal of deficit finance; as Richard Nixon ushered in the new era of law and order and was ushered out with his successor's criminal pardon; as Pierre Trudeau contemptuously rejected price controls to win the election of 1974 and the next year imposed them.

Then the Law of Chronic Irrelevance, which fastens the public mind on the temporary and unimportant, a sensation of the moment, the vital news often buried in the back pages for later exploitation, the reader straining eyes and neck as he tries to watch events like a spectator at a tennis game, the ball bouncing from one court to the other and back again.

The Law of Generational Void by which the young are too inexperienced to grasp what is really happening and the old too jaded to prevent it.

The Law of Cyclical Time Lag ensuring that the view held among the current majority is out of date, the government's latest policies designed for a situation already ended, as generals plan their strategy for the last war.

Above all, the Law of Ultimate Necessity, the one hopeful law which, with luck, can revoke all the others if someone, somewhere, conceives a workable idea just in time to forestall imminent disaster.

Since I was regarded as a political reporter, and never denied this quaint label when it provided a good livelihood, I was often invited to make speeches, though all my ideas had been printed and reprinted like thin soup constantly reboiled from the same old bone. Therein lies a Canadian mystery or conspiracy, diabolical but little understood.

Once a man's name has appeared in the press for a week or two, a secret apparatus is instantly mobilized by telephone or smoke signal. Every chamber of commerce, women's club, philatelist society, sewing circle, and flat-earth congregation across the land sees him not as an interpreter of truth, perhaps with some idea to communicate, but as a provider of free entertainment, a recipient of undeserved charity, and if he has vocal cords no other equipment is needed.

My own method of avoiding cruel and unnatural punishment, a Canadian rite as sacred as the Stanley and Grey Cup finals, was not brave or subtle but it usually succeeded. The well-trained secretaries at the *Sun* office declined all invitations with thanks and cynical regret. I was travelling, they explained, in some nameless foreign country, or had an unbreakable engagement on the appointed night, or was sick of a communicable disease, leprosy by preference.

Occasionally, however, these precautions failed. There were speeches that even the artful dodger could not escape. There were friends to whom I owed the last full measure of devotion, the preliminary cocktail warm-up, the ritual dinner of plastic chicken and melted ice cream, the chairman's unctuous introductory remarks, usually longer and better than mine, the glazed dead-fish eyes around me, the attempted joke and faint responsive titter, the polite applause at the end, the subsequent nervous breakdown and slow recovery. Oh, the pity of it. Yet any nation that can endure such ordeal by oratory, and pay money to suffer these nights of masochism, is surely indestructible.

My public ventures had become infrequent, my circle narrow. Those friends still left from earlier times I grappled to my soul with hoops of steel, rusty now and brittle, but strong enough to last the course.

Every autumn I visited Mary and Bill Bundy at Princeton, never quite understanding why, in our disparate age and circumstances, almost our separate worlds, that friendship was so deep and durable. With the Scotts in Alexandria, too, I was equally at home. Al Carlsen, the peerless axeman, toiled beside me in the Swamp and his capable Martha sustained us on tangy New England fare. Jack Wilson, retired from the Chief Justice's bench in Vancouver, often visited the camp where bed, board, and his own hand-made trails awaited him. When he could spare time from his forest empire, our mutual companion, Jack Clyne, would swoop down on the lake in his plane to the rapture of the young and the alarm of the old.

After a many-sided career as magazine editor, film-maker, ambassador to three foreign capitals, and publisher of my hometown paper, the *Times*, Arthur Irwin had settled in Victoria, wise and unruffled, a trusted counsellor since our days as cub reporters in Ottawa. His wife, Pat (better known to the public by her maiden name of P. K. Page), was my only friend who could be properly called a genius. She will cringe from that word in print, but it is fully warranted by her paintings of delicate arabesque or haunting creatures from the stuff of dreams, her poems of surgical precision, her imagination roving latitudes far past my reach.

Victoria seemed to attract talent, usually without recognizing it. Agnes Newton Keith, the American writer whose books of travel and whose epic story of her wartime Japanese imprisonment in Borneo were known throughout the world, lived here quietly, the books read, the author overlooked. But she and her Harry, once the reckless adventurer of jungle and desert, thought the world well lost.

In this circle Halcyon Carson always seemed to be the centre, her home the unfailing resort of the friendless, with charities beyond count and that earth-wisdom, a genius of sorts, that came from her years on the lonely mountain ranch. Near by lived my other comrades of the old time, Dr. Bobby and Cynthia Hunter, who had made horticulture a fine art, seldom left their matchless garden, and in their autumn still wore the look of spring. So did Alice Ullock, Dot's girlhood friend and mine since boyhood.

T. A. Crerar, Canada's oldest Privy Councillor, the only minister of two wartime governments, leader of the Progressive Party, and then a Senator, found that Victoria's climate suited him in his declining years after a lifetime of politics on the cold Prairies. In his big house filled with mementoes of that long service I was one of the few Victorians who knew and frequently visited the patriarch to hear his memories and certain political secrets yet unheard by the nation. Victoria ignored its most distinguished citizen until death came to him, unfeared, as a happy release.

All these friends had overestimated me. None is likely to understand what I have been trying to say between the lines of this book when I am unsure myself. But the changes of mind and the outright contradictions are plain enough, not to be reconciled. Standing in the Swamp today, the last day of summer, autumn's cool breath already in the air, I regretted nothing and everything, in that final contradication that must come to all men at the end.

The work I might have done, the chances missed, the failed

ambitions of my young days—these disappointments and mistakes don't seem to matter now. The real regrets are larger because they concern the little things known to me only, the simple acts of kindness undone, the friends neglected, their needs too often overlooked, my own coming first in the skimble-skamble of life. The little things—so big.

When a man grows old he is supposed to become toughened, building around himself, layer by layer, a protective carapace, but I have not found it so. On the contrary, as the shell of youth crumbled and the defences collapsed, age brought a deepening sense of vulnerability and nakedness. In self-pity mixed with pity for others every hurt went deeper, every mistake seemed worse, every loss harder to bear.

Inspecting the ledger, too late, I found it grossly unbalanced. A long life had given me far more than I had put into it, all I wanted in material terms, far less than I hoped for in terms of greater moment. My harvest of wisdom, satisfaction, and gratitude can be held in one hand without a grain spilled.

What, in fact, had I learned? Not nearly as much as my ocean of written words seemed to contain. I knew, for example, or was thought to know, a good deal about Canada and had brashly interpreted it in countless newspaper and magazine pieces, but I also knew that the nation had changed so fast in my time that it hardly knew itself. My own knowledge of it looks obsolete now, perhaps irrelevant, when I am no longer sure that the nation, the Western democratic culture in which it lives, and the civilization built through five millennia of toil and torment can survive human folly and nuclear death-wish.

I knew something, too, about political and economic systems, thanks to men who knew much more. But these fragments of information, bits of broken glass and rat-pack treasure, useful in my trade, no longer supported and usually denied my personal judgments, my autumn fantasies in the Swamp. For what were systems? Just names, theories, and wilder fantasies given in retrospect to men's rough trial-and-error methods of solving problems as they occurred or, more likely, failing to solve them. Each system, whatever its name, merely rationalized and sanctioned a current way of life, the working habits of a people in a tribe called a nation among many other tribes whose ceaseless quarrels threatened the destruction of all.

Thus the changed, almost unrecognizable system still known as Private Enterprise, even though government has invaded much of it and dominated the rest, can claim unique success in economic affairs but that success cannot satisfy its better rationalists and myth-makers. They rationalize the individual acquisition of wealth not merely as the best means of increasing it for everybody but as an ethical doctrine, Christianity in business, Jesus the first capitalist. Socialism rationalizes the benign, all-wise state not merely as the rightful owner of productive property and guarantor of social justice but as the worker of miracles economically and physically impossible, Jesus the first socialist. Communism rationalizes iron dictatorship at home and brutal adventure abroad not merely as the most efficient method of production and distribution but as rule by the workers, peace enforced by violence, democracy perfected by tyranny, Jesus if He ever lived, the first communist even if He was not the son of God because there is no God.

All the systems have their good points and bad, all the rationales their prophets, but no system is pure except in its textbooks, which the men of real power always disregard in action. Every system is eclectic and takes what it wants from its rivals while always denouncing them. Hegel's familiar thesis, antithesis, and synthesis revolve in a harmony too subtle and silent for any man to detect it in his own lifetime. Every system manages to disguise or defer problems by their nature insoluble until unforeseen events solve them to create new disguises of the latest style.

Since they are based primarily on economic determinism, all systems have one goal in common and one grinning spectre in the background. Karl Marx is worshipped by some, repudiated by others, yet stands regnant on his grimy central dogma, despite his wildly mistaken prophecies of detail.

All systems accept the same assumption of natural human greed which, as they now begin to see dimly, perhaps too late, cannot be satisfied by an earth-speck of finite resources and multiplying inhabitants when demand outruns supply and pollution of the vital life-stuff mocks the whole planetary rationale.

All systems (except in their rhetoric) assume that man's ordained purpose in this world is to grasp as much of its goods as possible. The other world, if there is one, can be safely disregarded and left to its credulous believers like an old wives' tale to keep the groundlings in order, the animals quiet for their own good.

When the system begins to leak at the seams, as all systems are leaking now, a new institution is devised to plug the leak. If man has lost faith in his gods, his tribal cultures, and himself—the supreme inner event of the twentieth century—he never doubts, or is allowed to doubt, that expanding institutions, governing mechanisms, and wise laws will fix everything, if there are enough of them managed by the right managers. The bigger the apparatus, surely the more efficient it must be. If more power is transferred from the individuals who work and produce to the bureaucracies, governmental and corporate, that only manage without producing, then the individual will have more wealth, more freedom, and more happiness, whether he appeciates them or not—an assumption almost universal and denied by nature everywhere.

So ruminating in the Swamp today, and realizing that I had been as greedy as the next fellow, I sat on an old fir log and observed an efficient society of ants burrowing their intricate labyrinth through the rotten wood. If maximum size, wealth, and power ensured maximum contentment then some imaginary ant, grown to a length of six feet, should be stronger, more efficient, and happier, too, than any man, But as any first-year student of physics is aware, such an ant would be unable to work, move, or eat.

Here, by humble analogy, the rationale of size achieves its ultimate *reductio ad absurdum*, Euclid's theorem confirmed. The ant in his society, and all the inhabitants of the Swamp in theirs, are of optimum size, and man's faith in ever-proliferating institutions is unknown. What a charming irony was presented by that rotten log when men's societies, always growing bigger, more complex, and less governable in the search for the perfect free government, were becoming more ant-like and unfree all the time while the log of human affairs continued to rot!

No matter, the institutional faith continued to grow even if few men understood how any institution or system actually worked, though almost any man, however ignorant of the workings, had categorical opinions on them, like some illiterate savage diagnosing a diseased organ and undertaking to remove it by surgery. Again a queer irony. For the ignorant were often wiser in their blind judgments than the educated, the commonality of mankind more trustworthy than the experts.

All this, as I well knew, was obvious but so ugly and repugnant that man has built his machinery of institutions and bustling lifeways to exclude, blur, or evade the plain, intolerable facts.

It was obvious also that the old, innocent cabal of self-deception was breaking down, the new creed of automatic progress already dying, after brief life. The things called reason, rationalism, and scientific humanism failed to work according to the known rules in the fragile organism called society. But what else could be expected when, as it seemed to me, no truly great thing ever came out of the reasoning process, even among scientists, only from those unreasoning depths that we call the subconscious, though it is the true consciousness if we could tap it.

There, as in the Swamp of sub-human residents, the accepted theories are disputed or nullified by non-facts, principles and patterns rearranged in mute symmetry, opposites continually merged, the theoretician derided, the philosopher baffled. To suppose that any mind reasons its way to truth is like supposing that Shakespeare created *Hamlet* by studying the classic laws of the drama, that Michelangelo carved his *David* because he had measured the male anatomy, that man could conceive the universe if he fully understood the laws of physics.

As I had come to believe, toward the end, man *conceives* nothing but if he is wise enough, or rather if he frees himself from the elegant prison of intellect, he may *recognize* something now and then, and it will never be what he was taught to expect or desire. Such, I take it, was the intent of Plato's famous parable—mankind chained in a dark cave, seeing no more than the shadows of reality as it moved in the sunlight outside. Such, too, was the inward meaning of all the great religions before they had been reasoned, organized, and secularized into mere ethical doctrines, codes of good behavior, or superstitions, their juices drained, their essence lost.

My own recognition, despite all these bold words and Swamp fantasies, was late and dim, the shadows dark and inscrutable, but after a life of scepticism I cannot doubt that the sun shines and a different life moves outside the cave. I understand and respect the man who believes nothing unknown to the senses of his body, but I cannot understand why he should boast of that limitation as if it were a laborious achievement. Anyone can do it, and it simplifies everything since there is no further need to think. Nor can I understand why the agnostic should boast that, after profound thought, he has no opinion at all, as a judge in court might claim superior wisdom because he could reach no verdict. Above all, I cannot understand why a man who believes in things beyond the senses should be afraid to say so, as if belief were somehow shameful and neutrality more respectable than commitment.

Yet so belief is widely judged, in Western society at least, and its terminal disease comes not from the failure of its institutions, laws, and leaders but from a sudden loss of trust in itself, in the rationale of life which, lacking trust, must be irrational.

While I had lived through five distinct periods of modern history—the genial, illusory Edwardian age, the First World War, the postwar breathing space of boom and depression, the second war, and again the postwar world of unfilled hopes—all these twists and turns on the street of the twentieth century were marked by a single division as clear as any watershed. Man had climbed to the summit of reason, of trust only in big things and sure upward advance, and he had found the summit bare, the street running downhill, the end unseen and best not asked.

But after the descent, the young, I was persuaded, would climb the next long summit in their vehicles of new design or, if necessary, on foot, wisely disregarding the failures of the old, all the stronger for youth's short memories. The prophets of despair would be left behind, sputtering and forgotten.

This century's stark division had its rough equivalent in my own watershed, the years with Dot and the years when she was gone and the music stopped. And yet if I have sputtered here and elsewhere I do not despair. With age came unexpected tranquillity, even a kind of happiness.

The private music had stopped for me alone. A livelier public music still played on the busy side of the street. The mixed, unmistakable Canadian band was marching there and so it had marched across the centuries and the continent with English bugles, French horns, Irish drums, and Scottish pipes from the lone shieling and the misty island beyond the sea. Nothing could halt that march wherever it might go. Brave music, lucky breed. And as spectator on the safe, empty side I saw in the van my father's flaming umbrella, held aloft like a torch to defy the weather and light the way.

Index